METROPOLITAN UNIVERSITIES:
AN EMERGING MODEL IN AMERICAN HIGHER EDUCATION

COMPILED AND EDITED BY

DANIEL M. JOHNSON AND DAVID A. BELL

FOREWORD BY ERNEST A. LYNTON

UNIVERSITY OF NORTH TEXAS PRESS
DENTON, TEXAS

First printed in 1995 in the United States of America

10 9 8 7 6 5 4 3 2 1

The paper in this book meets the minimum requirements of the
American National Standard for Permanence of paper for Printed
Library Materials, Z39.48.1984.

Library of Congress Cataloging-in-Publication Data

Metropolitan universities : an emerging model in American higher edu-
cation / compiled and edited by Daniel M. Johnson and David Bell ; foreword
by Ernest Lynton.
        p.   cm.
Includes bibliographical references and index.
ISBN 0-929398-93-9 :
        1. Urban universities and colleges—United States. I. Johnson, Daniel
M. (Daniel Milo), 1940– . II. Bell, David (David Arnold), 1945–   .
LB2328.42.U6M48 1995
370'.9173'2—dc20   94-47375
                                                      CIP

All of these articles first appeared in various issues of
Metropolitan Universities, Executive Editor Ernest A. Lynton
The Foreword was originally published as
"Metropolitan Universities: Partners with Community and Commerce,"
in *The Maine Scholar* 6 (Autumn 1993): 93–103.

CONTENTS

ACKNOWLEDGMENTS

We wish to thank the following persons who encouraged and assisted us with this project: Ernest Lynton of the University of Massachusetts and John Brain of Towson State University, the editor and publisher, respectively, of the journal *Metropolitan Universities: An International Forum* for their sage advice regarding the selection of articles and the intricacies of publishing an anthology of this type; Alfred F. Hurley, our Chancellor at the University of North Texas, for the dedication he has shown as co-chair of the Coalition of Urban and Metropolitan Universities along with Hoke Smith, the President of Towson State University; and the Steering Committee of the Coalition of Urban and Metropolitan Universities for urging us to proceed with this volume.

We also wish to thank the Editorial Board of the University of North Texas Press for its endorsement and support of the project, with special gratitude to Fran Vick, Director of the UNT Press, and the press staff who have encouraged and advised us at every step of this project.

Finally, we wish to express our appreciation to the authors of the many fine articles found in this collection.

DECLARATION OF METROPOLITAN UNIVERSITIES

A number of presidents of metropolitan universities have signed the following declaration.

We, the leaders of metropolitan universities and colleges, embracing the historical values and principles which define all universities and colleges, and which make our institutions major intellectual resources for their metropolitan regions,

- reaffirm that the creation, interpretation, dissemination, and application of knowledge are the fundamental functions of our universities;
- assert and accept a broadened responsibility to bring these functions to bear on the needs of our metropolitan regions;
- commit our institutions to be responsive to the needs of our metropolitan areas by seeking new ways of using our human and physical resources to provide leadership in addressing metropolitan problems, through teaching, research, and professional service.

Our teaching must:
- educate individuals to be informed and effective citizens, as well as capable practitioners of professions and occupations;
- be adapted to the particular needs of metropolitan students, including minorities and other underserved groups, adults of all ages, and the place-bound;
- combine research-based knowledge with practical application and experience, using the best current technology and pedagogical techniques.

Our research must:
- seek and exploit opportunities for linking basic investigation with practical application, and for creating synergistic interdisciplinary and multidisciplinary scholarly partnerships for attacking complex metropolitan problems, while meeting the highest scholarly standards of the academic community.

Our professional service must include:
- development of creative partnerships with public and private enterprises that ensure that the intellectual resources of our institutions are fully engaged with such enterprises in mutually beneficial ways;
- close working relationships with the elementary and secondary schools of our metropolitan regions, aimed at maximizing the effectiveness of the entire metropolitan education system, from preschool through post-doctoral levels;
- the fullest possible contributions to the cultural life and general quality of life of our metropolitan regions.

PREFACE

Over the past four years, the journal, *Metropolitan Universities: An International Forum*, has done an excellent job of shaping the metropolitan university model, articulating issues with which these universities are concerned, increasing their visibility, and helping set the agenda for a major component of higher education in the United States. Although the journal has made significant progress in developing and refining the metropolitan university model, there remains little literature outside this source to inform the higher education community of the importance and characteristics of this "movement."

An important task for metropolitan universities in the next few years is to help broaden the understanding of this emerging model in the higher education community and among state legislatures. No less important is the responsibility metropolitan university administrators and faculty members have for clarifying the implications and significance of the metropolitan model for their own campuses. Those who read the journal will have developed a general understanding of some of the issues and challenges facing metropolitan universities; those outside this growing circle of readers, however, have few sources to which they can turn for help in broadening their understanding.

Although urban universities have been a major part of the higher education landscape for a century or more, the concept of "metropolitan university" is relatively new and novel. It is important, then, that university board members, administrators, faculty, students, legislators, education policy makers and citizen groups associated with these universities know how their institutions are different and the special challenges they face as they strive to play more responsive, constructive roles in addressing the nation's major urban issues. The purpose of this collection of readings from the journal is to help address this need for a convenient source of information on metropolitan universities, their unique mission and characteristics.

In selecting the articles for this anthology, we asked ourselves, What would I like to know about metropolitan universities if I were:

1. a regent or board member responsible for making major decisions about the life and future of this institution?

2. accepting a faculty or administrative position at such an institution?

3. an education policy maker of a state higher education coordinating council?

4. a student attending or selecting such a university?

5. a faculty member at an institution that has begun referring to itself by this name?

6. a mayor, city manager, local government official of a major city with such a university?

7. a CEO or staff member of a non-profit organization in a major metropolitan area with such a university?

8. a program officer of a foundation that makes grants to institutions of higher education?

9. a president or provost exploring the possibility of leading my institution in the direction of this model?

10. a student of higher education?

We quickly realized that there are numerous needs for a general overview of the philosophy, history, and mission of metropolitan universities and their implications for all aspects of the university and the communities they seek to serve. Our hope is that this compilation of articles on the key concepts related to metropolitan universities and their implications will speed up the process of educating faculty members, administrators, community leaders, and education policy makers to the nature and importance of the metropolitan university mission. We are increasingly convinced that metropolitan universities represent a major resource for assisting in the development of solutions to the major problems and challenges of our nation's metropolitan communities.

FOREWORD

WHAT IS A METROPOLITAN UNIVERSITY?

Ernest A. Lynton

Anew breed of American universities, the metropolitan university is an institutional model committed to be responsive to the knowledge needs of its surrounding region, and dedicated to create active links between campus, community, and commerce. "Metropolitan universities are best recognized by an active philosophy by which these institutions establish symbiotic relationships with their metropolitan areas" (Hathaway 13).

A metropolitan university addresses the broad spectrum of instructional needs of the regional population. It offers undergraduate as well as graduate programs not only at traditional times and places, but also in ways which make higher education accessible to older students and working professionals. The make-up of its student body reflects the broad diversity of the surrounding metropolis. It includes students of many ethnic and racial groups, residential students as well as commuters, full time and part time matriculants, and students spanning a broad age range. Many of its students attend more than one institution as they move toward a baccalaureate degree, and most of them take more than four years to complete this process.

A metropolitan university contains a number of professional schools which provide both preparatory and continuing education for practitioners. That task is quite different from the preparation of future scholars and researchers which is the focus of graduate and professional education in the traditional research universities. Preparing for practice does not mean being narrowly vocational. Rather, such preparation is based on a systematic and reciprocal linkage of theory and practice, with early and repeated use of clinical experience in the curriculum. Metropolitan university programs in professional areas, and often in the arts and sciences as well, emphasize field work and internships which make full use of the private and public sector opportunities in the metropolitan region.

Furthermore, metropolitan universities engage in applied research and in professional outreach which address the complex issues of its surrounding communities. Metropolitan universities often work with local schools, provide technical assistance and instructional programs for local and state government, and collaborate with regional business and industry. For example, the metropolitan University of Southern Maine (USM) is gaining a national reputation for its innovative collaboration with primary and secondary education; USM's Muskie Center also provides assistance for regional government. The opposite of ivory towers, metropolitan universities are highly interactive with their surroundings; they are of their region and not just in it. They maintain close relationships with their communities, for which they constitute a major intellectual resource.

Those relationships consist of a two-way flow of ideas, experience, and information. If it is to fulfill its external mission with optimal effectiveness, a metropolitan university must work with its constituencies and clients in defining problems and issues, identifying pertinent factors, and developing appropriate approaches. Scholars in metropolitan universities increasingly recognize that a great deal of applied and problem-oriented research can only be carried out in a practice context, and that the flow of information from the outside in is as important as any transfer of knowledge to the inside out (Lerner 27–32). Increasingly, as well, academically trained faculty members in metropolitan universities recognize the pertinence of what might be called the "wisdom of practice" of the practitioner (Shulman 12). Thus outreach for metropolitan universities becomes a joint undertaking, a reciprocal relationship between internal expert and external client.

This kind of collaboration requires a substantial change in the prevalent culture of academic institutions. There is emerging an interesting parallel between the teaching and learning process in the classroom, and outreach activities to external constituencies. Teaching, in too many classrooms and lecture halls, is *ex cathedra*, with the professor dispensing knowledge to the passive student. Similarly, outreach is still viewed too frequently as the expert in the white coat dispensing knowledge to the passive client. Just as academics are beginning to realize that good teaching must be an interactive process requiring active involvement by the student, they are also recognizing that collaborative projects with schools, with government agencies, with business and industry, must involve a true partnership, based on both sides bringing their own experience and expertise to the project (Barnes and Miller 51–60).

A metropolitan university's regional orientation and strong commitment to serve the intellectual needs of its surrounding communities and constituencies, the resulting diversity of the student body, the focus on the education of practitioners, and the emphasis on outreach through applied research and technical assistance add up to an institutional model very different from that of the traditional research university. It is a model based on the recognition that the American university in the post-industrial, knowledge-based society must take seriously and translate into tangible reality all three elements of the traditional triad of institutional responsibilities that are stated, but not respected, in every mission statement of every academic institution: research, teaching, and service. Society needs all three in equal measure, and all three must interact and reinforce each other. Metropolitan universities accept this challenge, and are, therefore, of great importance to the societal well-being of this country.

The emergence of the metropolitan university model is much overdue. Until recently, all academic institutions other than community colleges were forced to fit into one of only two widely recognized categories: either that of an undergraduate teaching institution, or that of a research university. Yet during the rapid and substantial expansion of higher education during the fifties and sixties, many universities came into being which have never fit into either category. There are between 150 and 200 such institutions in this country, enrolling well over 2 million students. Some began as new institutions, others were created by the merger and transformation of older colleges. Most of these universities are located in metropolitan areas. They typically have enrollments of ten- to twenty-thousand students—in some cases, more—and offer a broad range of graduate and professional programs, often including doctoral ones. They differ markedly in their comprehensiveness and size from the traditional undergraduate college that concentrates solely or primarily on the arts and sciences; in many cases they also differ in the nature and interests of their faculty, a large proportion of which is engaged in first rate scholarship. They are true multi-faceted universities; however, for a long time they aspired to the more notable of the two available categories: to be a research university. That was the category with prestige and visibility, that's what everyone wanted to be, because "lay persons and academics alike are inclined to equate prestige with quality" (Astin 5). As a result, universities throughout the country tried to foster that for which they had neither the resources nor the working conditions, and did not pay enough attention to that which society really needed and which they could—and in some cases did—provide with great quality. In our book, *New Priorities for the University*, Sandra Elman and I said, "By believing themselves to be what they are not, these institutions fall short of being what they could be" (Lynton and Elman, 13).

Since these words were written, the emerging model of the metropolitan university has begun to remove many of our academic institutions from the horns of the dilemma created by the inadequate variety of available alternatives to the definition of institutional mission and priorities. By accepting the challenge of becoming metropolitan universities, these institutions can dedicate themselves to respond to the wide range of knowledge needs of their region through a multidimensional and mutually reinforcing combination of instruction, applied research, and professional outreach.

The movement toward broad recognition of the metropolitan university model is gaining strength. Two national conferences on the topic have been held, one in Dayton, Ohio, in 1990, and one in Denton, Texas in 1993. A quarterly journal, *Metropolitan Universities*, published jointly by Towson State University and the University of Massachusetts at Boston, has begun its fifth year of publication. As this is written, the informal association of a number of metropolitan universities is being transformed into a more structured Coalition of Urban and Metropolitan Universities which will sponsor future national as well as other meetings, support the journal, and engage in other pertinent activities. It will operate under the joint sponsorship of the National Association of State Universities and Land grant Colleges (NASULGC) and the American Association of State Colleges and Universities (AASCU).

The Challenge of Being a Metropolitan University

The multidimensional task undertaken by metropolitan universities is not only of great societal importance, it also constitutes a challenge which may be greater than that faced by any other category of academic institutions. To be successful, metropolitan universities must achieve and maintain excellence in a widely different set of activities. They must become outstanding teaching institutions because of the enormous importance of effective education in contemporary society. They must engage in a substantial amount of excellent research, especially in applied areas, because this provides the intellectual base for both their teaching and their outreach. This outreach must be of the highest quality if it is to be of any use to the metropolitan university's constituencies. To strive for excellence along these several dimensions is a daunting task. Teaching, research, and outreach have all become substantially more difficult than in earlier days.

To appreciate the importance of the multi-dimensional mission of metropolitan universities in the context of contemporary society, and to understand the challenge of that task, it is useful to look back on the conditions under which higher education has been operating during the half century since World War II. During that time, the societal context for our colleges and universities has changed significantly.

Probably most striking is the enormous expansion of higher education during the past forty-five years, with substantial growth not only in absolute numbers but, perhaps more significantly, also in the participation rate of the post-high-school-age cohort. The impact of this has been felt most especially by metropolitan universities. They have a substantially diverse student body: diverse in ethnic and socioeconomic background, in career aspirations, in pattern and timing of attendance. In addition, they cater to a growing number of older adults who are either returning to higher education or getting a late start, increasing the average student age and bringing into our classrooms large numbers of working individuals with family obligations and a very different set of experiences and expectations from those of the more traditional student. All these changes have created a substantial pedagogic challenge. Particularly in metropolitan universities, teaching today's students is much more demanding than teaching the more homogeneous, better prepared student body of an earlier age.

Further changes have occurred in the societal context of higher education which have intensified the importance as well as the difficulty of both teaching and outreach. We have witnessed the shift toward what has been called a post-industrial, knowledge-based society. The usual descriptions of this concept are full of clichés and oversimplifications, but everyone agrees on some basic elements.

First, there is much greater need, both quantitatively and qualitatively, for a highly skilled work force, with a steady increase in the required educational level. There was a time when higher education had more of a screening than a developmental function, but that is no longer the case. The content and impact of what our students learn has really become important. The need to educate, rather than to train, by balancing immediately applicable skills with longer range attributes has intensified the pedagogic challenge created by diversification of the student body.

Second, a knowledge-driven economy requires effective dissemination and rapid application of new ideas, discoveries, and knowledge, especially in view of the accelerating rate of technological and also political and social change. We must take a very different view of the role of universities: they must become actively involved in the flow of knowledge to the places and the individuals where knowledge is applied. They cannot limit their task to the creation of knowledge and its dissemination within the profession. Nor is the need for outreach met by a passive delivery of pre-packaged knowledge. The societal issues requiring attention are complex and often ambiguous. Each situation has its unique elements, and is likely to demand much creativity based on professional expertise so as to formulate and address complex problems.

Third, the acceleration of change also creates need for ongoing renewal of knowledge and a shift of emphasis from preparatory to continuing, lifelong education. More than a decade ago, members of the Department of Electrical Engineering and Computer Science at MIT called for an ongoing pattern of learning which they called Lifelong Cooperative Engineering, pointing out that "engineers are faced with the problem of learning, during their professional lives, what new generations of engineering students are currently learning in school" (Bruce 11).

Fourth, there is a shift and a broadening as well in the nature of research, with more of a continuum linking theory and practice, basic and applied research and applications. Indeed, the creation of new knowledge has increasingly become a highly nonlinear, cyclical process, requiring a two-way flow of communication between theory and application. In most of the social sciences and even in technical fields such as materials science and environmental studies, research requires considerable involvement in practice and application.

Graduate Work at Metropolitan Universities

Due to the burgeoning need for advanced skills, it is very important for metropolitan universities to provide graduate instruction. In a growing number of fields, the master's degree is becoming the first professional degree needed for entry; thus, programs leading to the master's are in great demand both by those who are still preparing for their career, as well as those already working but lacking the currently expected degree. Students in the first group as much as the second are likely to hold jobs while pursuing their studies. Hence metropolitan universities face the challenge of being accessible to place-bound, working individuals by organizing graduate programs on a part-time basis, at nontraditional times and places, and, in a growing number of cases, using nontraditional modes of delivery. At same time, it is important for all graduate programs to have coherence and continuity, and to develop among students a sense of being part of a mutually supportive cohort. In order to achieve these goals, many metropolitan universities are using program formats containing intermittent short periods of intensive full-time work (students may attend on a full-time basis for one or two weeks a year.) Frequent use is also made of intensive weekend sessions, or of scheduling all course work during one full day each week.

Graduate programs for working individuals also face the question of expectation with regard to student work. Such programs must insist on high quality of performance, but guard against confusing that with quantity of effort. Yet the maintenance of quality often requires substantial background reading, generating time demands that at times exceed what working professional can do.

Metropolitan universities are also responding to an increasing need for practice-oriented doctoral programs in fields such as education, policy studies, clinical psychology and other human service fields. To the extent that master's degrees are becoming entry-level requirements, doctoral degrees assume importance as qualification for more advanced levels of employment. For such programs, the importance of maintaining both coherence and a sense of community in a part-time program for working individuals is even greater than is the case for master's programs: the question of expected student work is also intensified.

In addition, doctoral programs for practitioners also face questions about the nature of final "performance": the dissertation or its equivalent. These doctorates are not intended to be research degrees, and hence it is not appropriate to demand a traditional research dissertation. It is important to confront the nature of expected outcomes. What should graduates be able to do, and how can they best demonstrate that they are able to do it ? What kind of project is needed to demonstrate the ability to analyze a complex, practice-based situation, to formulate a central question, to determine the information needed and the methodology to be used, and to carry the process through to a point at which it can be assessed even though there may not have been enough time to obtain concrete, measurable results?

The attention in a practice-oriented dissertation is likely to focus much more on process than on outcomes—a very different approach than one appropriate to research dissertations. In addition, there is a further basic conceptual difference. A traditional research dissertation is, or should be, the ultimate word in expertise on a specific, usually narrowly defined topic, with primary emphasis on depth of expertise. It is sometimes said that an individual completing a dissertation is at that moment the world's leading expert on that specific subject. By contrast, a practice-oriented dissertation needs to emphasize breadth. Obviously there needs to be a reasonable degree of depth: a knowledge base in pertinent subjects adequate to identify and carry out the necessary observations and analyses. But an individual needs above all to show her or his ability to deal with a complex, reality-based situation: the formulation of the problem is often more difficult than its treatment. That requires much breadth of knowledge, and a sense of how different pieces, different bodies of knowledge, and different methodologies relate to one another and can supplement one another.

Scholarship Reconsidered

If metropolitan universities are to develop excellence in all three elements of the traditional triad—teaching, research, and professional service—they must bring about not only a *quantitative* change in the attention they pay to the teaching and professional service dimensions of their missions, but a profound *qualitative* change as well in the way in which these activities are viewed. Both teaching and professional service—defined here as an application of a faculty member's professional expertise to problems and tasks outside the campus in the public and the private sectors—have become not only more important but, as indicated above, also considerably more difficult, more intellectually challenging. To do them well requires the very habits of the mind which we identify with scholarship. That means that the concept of scholarship must become more inclusive, and that the system of incentives and rewards which sets priorities for faculty work must give due recognition to scholarly work in teaching and professional service. Achieving these changes must be a major objective for metropolitan universities.

The dominant view in academic circles, even in metropolitan universities, continues to be that only research—and in many people's opinion only basic research—constitutes scholarship. This attitude is also a direct consequence of developments in the period following World War II and Sputnik. The enrollment growth and its concomitant pedagogic challenges described earlier were accompanied by major growth in federal research support—a development which came to dominate the nature, aspirations, and value systems of universities and even of many colleges far more than the growth and change in enrollment. Research dollars and research productivity became principal indices of academic quality at both individual and institutional levels, not only for those relatively few universities which received the lion's share of federal research funds and carried out most of the research. To be recognized as a "research university" became the ambition of other universities as well, especially in the absence of an accepted alternate model, and even liberal arts colleges were affected. Of course, federal research support has leveled off in recent years, but academic priorities have remained the same. Former President Derek Bok of Harvard stated in 1991 that "research has come to dominate over all other factors in choosing, recognizing, and rewarding faculty" (Bok 12). A recent study by Penn State Professor James Fairweather shows not only that contributions to teaching are not adequately rewarded, but that, on the whole, teaching is a "negative factor in compensation, especially the percent of time spent on teaching and instruction" (Fairweather). Clearly the simultaneous growth in student enrollment and rate of participation in higher education, on the one hand, and the intensification of the status of research, on the other, were, to a considerable extent, at cross purposes, a situation which contributed substantially to the student dissatisfaction of the late sixties.

Fortunately, a change is beginning to take place. The title of this section reflects the conviction of a growing number of individuals throughout higher education—joined by many outside the academy—that there is great need to reconsider the nature of the academic, scholarly profession. Some of us have been writing about this for a number of years (see Lynton and Elman). Ernest Boyer's report *Scholarship Reconsidered* has triggered national attention to the topic, becoming the best-selling volume in the Carnegie Foundation's history. Metropolitan universities are deeply involved in this reconsideration because they recognize that, in order to meet their multi-dimensional challenge, they must move rapidly and decisively to improve the balance of esteem and reward among the traditional triad of teaching, research, and professional service. On campuses throughout this country, in a number of professional associations, and through the newly established Forum on Faculty Roles and Responsibilities of the American Association for Higher Education (AAHE), the basic issue of the nature of faculty work is being raised in a much more sophisticated and profound way than ever before.

There is growing recognition that effective teaching and professional outreach require the high degree of creativity and intellectual effort appropriately associated with scholarship, and that they should be carried out and rewarded accordingly. In the area of teaching, the mission of metropolitan universities requires not that faculty members should spend more time in the classroom but rather that their pedagogic responsibilities be elevated to as prominent and as intellectually challenging a component of their professional activities as their research. And the same is true of professional service and outreach. The challenge is not to have faculty members volunteering some additional hours in community-oriented activities, or in some similar ways exercise their civic responsibilities. Rather, there is need for more faculty to apply their professional expertise and experience to issues and problems in the public as well as the private sector, an activity which can and should be as rigorous and as demanding as most traditional research.

In short, both teaching and professional service should be recognized as legitimate dimensions of scholarship, not just responses to societal demands. And as a corollary we must of course also insist that teaching and professional service, as well as research, be carried out at an appropriately scholarly level of intellectual excellence, and measured by their quality and not their quantity. Such a more inclusive conception of scholarship is both possible and legitimate because the process of scholarship is very similar in teaching, in professional service, and in research. Whether engaged in research, teaching, or professional service, the scholar is not content to take a standard package from shelf, to repeat a previous project, or to use a prescribed model or a standard protocol. What most clearly distinguishes the scholar from the mechanic or technician is the ability as well as the propensity of the former to analyze each situation *de novo*, to recognize both the elements which are repetitive but also those in every situation which are unique. The scholar defines the problem within its particular context, and chooses desired outcomes, pertinent variables, and appropriate methodology accordingly, staying intellectually "on line" so as to adapt in an ongoing fashion. From this, the scholar learns something which in turn can be generalized and applied to future situations; and shares this new insight with others.

The shared scholarly nature of research, teaching, and professional outreach is reinforced by the considerable overlap and reciprocal reinforcement among all three. The growing need for research in a practice context has already been mentioned, together with the extent to which new information and new questions flow from interaction with external constituencies and the application of knowledge. Equally evident is the extent to which almost all professional outreach has a teaching dimension. The instruction may not take place in a formal setting (although even that can be part of a technical assistance project) but it is nevertheless integral to the activity. And of course faculty involvement in applied research and professional outreach is of great importance to their ability to teach future practitioners, and even more to provide continuing education for experienced students. Furthermore, such involvement provides opportunities for student participation.

Conclusion

Because it is committed to being responsive to regional knowledge needs, the metropolitan university is becoming a major factor in the relationships and reciprocal flow of information and ideas between higher education and the community. By means of its instructional activities as well as its applied research and professional outreach, metropolitan universities interact both with the public as well as the private sector of their metropolitan area, to the mutual benefit of all. The model of the metropolitan university is new and still being shaped and clarified. It constitutes a philosophy and a commitment rather than a specific institutional blue print: metropolitan universities will vary widely in size, emphasis, and the mix of instructional and other services they can provide. But their priorities are similar, as are some of the issues they face, such as those with regard to faculty roles and rewards. Progress is being made, and there is every reason to anticipate that metropolitan universities will emerge as major actors driving the social and economic development of their regions.

SUGGESTED READINGS

Astin, Alexander W. *Achieving Educational Excellence: A Critical Assessment of Priorities and Practices in Higher Education.* San Francisco: Jossey-Bass, 1985.

Barnes, Richard and Lynne Miller. "Universities and Schools: The Two Sides of the Street and in Between." *Metropolitan Universities* 2, no. 1 (1991): 51–60.

Bok, Derek. "The Improvement of Teaching." ACLS Occasional Paper, New York, American Council of Learned Societies, 1991.

Boyer, Ernest L. *Scholarship Reconsidered.* Princeton, N.J.: The Carnegie Foundation for the Advancement of Teaching, 1990. This report has become the second best-selling volume in the Carnegie Foundation's history.

Bruce, James D., et al. *Lifelong Cooperative Education.* Cambridge, MA: MIT Press, 1982.

Fairweather, James S. "Teaching and the Faculty Reward Structure." Unpublished Report, National Center on Postsecondary Teaching, Learning, and Assessment, Pennsylvania State University, June 1992. This report was later published in *Metropolitan Universities* 4, no. 4 (Summer 1994).

Hathaway, Charles E., Paige E. Mulhollan, and Karen E. White. "Metropolitan Universities: Models for the Twenty-First Century." *Metropolitan Universities* 1, no. 1 (1990): 13.

Lerner, Richard M. "Changing Organism-Context Relations as the Basic Process of Development: A Developmental Contextual Perspective." *Developmental Psychology* 27, no. 1 (1991): 27–32.

Lynton, Ernest A., and Sandra E. Elman. *New Priorities for the University.* San Francisco: Jossey-Bass, 1987, 13.

Shulman, Lee S. "Knowledge and Teaching: Foundations of the New Reform." *Harvard Educational Review* 57, no. 1 (1987): 12.

PART I

PHILOSOPHY, HISTORY AND MISSION

INTRODUCTION

Destined to become land-grant institutions of the twenty-first century, serving urban and metropolitan regions in which eighty percent of the American population will be living, metropolitan universities are responding to the needs of their communities and the expectations of the public. While the particular characteristics metropolitan universities share may vary from institution to institution, a single philosophy is the distinguishing feature of this evolving model for higher education. It is the commitment to interaction with the metropolitan area and the willingness to adopt a leadership role in responding to community needs through, among other things, increased emphasis on courses of study that are flexible and adaptive to changes in student demography, and research that is relevant to the well-being of the region, state, and country.

In their article "Metropolitan Universities: Models for the Twenty-First Century," Charles E. Hathaway, Paige E. Mulhollan, and Karen A. White begin with an overview and brief history of the metropolitan university concept and move to a discussion of the potential prestige and eminence for institutions willing to adopt this model.

In view of the changing patterns affecting urban life, the complex challenges facing metropolitan institutions should not be underestimated. In addition, institutions of higher learning are also undergoing change. In his article, "Metropolitan Universities: Past, Present, and Future," Blaine A. Brownell describes this context and the forces at work in shaping metropolitan universities. Pressures to serve an immensely broad constituency in multitudinous ways impel metropolitan universities forward, but fiscal constraints, increased external supervision, and other internal issues hamper the capacity to respond. In spite of pressures to narrow its focus to either the city or the suburbs, a metropolitan university, Brownell insists, must be many things to many people. Its most important role, he argues, is to stimulate the dialogue necessary to bridge the

gap between urban and suburban areas, to identify areas of mutual
interest and create opportunities to work together.

Metropolitan universities accept responsibilities to meet
community needs in a way that is well beyond the mission of
traditional institutions. In "Aligning Missions with Public
Expectations," Mulhollan argues that the time has come to make
the case for appropriate support and recognition for metropolitan
universities. To do so, a set of guidelines and measures of excellence
for such institutions must be developed that reflect their unique
mission. "We should not be measured against inappropriate
standards. We must agree among ourselves and promulgate to our
constituencies the standards that are appropriate to our mission."
Mulhollan concludes that the metropolitan model responds to public
expectations for higher education and that a greater recognition of
this important work will require clarifying institutional purpose and
mission statements. He sees the metropolitan university model as a
transforming vision for both the university and its environment.

METROPOLITAN UNIVERSITIES: MODELS FOR THE TWENTY-FIRST CENTURY

Charles E. Hathaway, Paige E. Mulhollan, and Karen A. White

Our society increasingly expects public universities to address relevant contemporary problems: economic competitiveness, improved public education, and governmental leadership and efficiency. As a result, many universities, particularly those located in metropolitan areas where the problems are most severe, are responding with increased emphasis on career-oriented education, collaboration with industries and public education, and research that contributes to the well-being of the city, state, and country.

It is true that the university is and must remain an independent institution within the society of which it is a part. The responsibility of the university in the sharing, pursuit, and application of knowledge ensures that our basic culture and heritage will be preserved. The university must guard its existence as an independent institution in order to achieve these primary functions. However, the university must not stand apart from its society and its immediate environment but must be an integral part of that society. The university best serves itself and society by assuming an active leadership role, as opposed to its traditional stance of somewhat passive responsiveness.

In his insightful book *Academic Strategy*, George Keller writes: "For decades, most colleges and universities have been inner-directed, formulating their aims on the bedrock of their own religious commitments, tradition, faculty desires, and ambitions for growth, largely ignoring the world outside. . . . Colleges are switching from a self-assertion model of their existence to a biological mode of continuous adaptation to their powerful changing social environment" (Baltimore: Johns Hopkins University Press, 1983, p.

3). The tension between the traditional view held by academics and the expectations of society for its universities can be either a creative or a counter-productive force for the continued evolution of the university, depending on how the academy responds.

It is a myth, sometimes promulgated by the academy, that universities are cloistered halls of reflection and learning, apart and immune from society. Our origins are embedded primarily in the twelfth and thirteenth centuries, when the first universities, located primarily in the great cities of Europe, came into being. These early universities were formed to train students in the professions of law, theology, and medicine, as well as to study the rediscovered works of the Greek and Arabic scholars. These institutions, from Salerno in the ninth century to Paris in the twelfth century, were thus highly specialized and responsive to societal needs.

It was in the United States in relatively modern times that the liberal arts college first appeared extensively as a separate institution apart from other professional elements traditionally associated with universities. The origins of many of our most prestigious institutions known today for their commitment to the liberal arts were related primarily to professional training.

Probably the most widely known American contribution to the evolution of universities occurred with passage of the Morrill Act of 1862, when the federal government extended its financial support to stimulate the creation of our land-grant institutions. The new public universities were specifically charged to help solve the new nation's economic problems through emphasis on agricultural and engineering teaching and research. Subsequent extensions of federal policy, particularly the Hatch Act of 1887, from which came our agricultural experiment stations, made the "practical" relationship of land-grant institutions to contemporary society even more explicit.

However, the greatest contribution of this nation to the evolution of higher education is its concept that all citizens have the right to access—an idea initiated boldly in the Northwest Ordinance of 1787. The evolution of this concept has produced an open-door policy for essentially all high school graduates and created new institutions and branches located in major metropolitan areas to serve place-bound populations. The placement of universities in population centers to ensure access to higher education for all citizens represents a major commitment unique to our country.

After World War II, the evolutionary forces born of this concept accelerated as veterans, carrying with them federal educational benefits, flocked to universities to ensure their economic future. Thus began a period of rapid growth in the number and size of higher education institutions, that escalated during the sixties when we added a commitment to educate previously underserved student populations. The new students, representing a broader cross section of our society, were agents of transformation for our campuses. From increased numbers of different kinds of students and significant federal support of research initiated during World War II, the current multiversity was born.

Throughout the postwar period, or at least through the 1960s, states sought to meet the demand for access to higher education by creating new types of institutions to serve major population centers. During the twenty-year period from 1955 to 1975, they created 573 community colleges. At the same time, states built new or absorbed existing four-year institutions into complex state systems. Whereas states had traditionally built colleges as residential entities away from major population centers, states now sought to create universities to serve a nonresidential, place-bound student. This movement peaked in the sixties. A cursory examination of the 1988 *Higher Education Directory* indicates that at least four dozen new institutions offering four-year baccalaureate programs were established in population centers in that decade. These institutions, along with others formerly private or municipal, have become a significant but not fully recognized force in higher education.

Four different types of universities serve our population centers today:

1. Institutions born as a part of a central city prior to World War II (e.g., the University of Cincinnati and the University of California, Los Angeles).

2. Institutions created as wholly independent universities after World War II for the specific purpose of serving the needs of a population center (e.g., George Mason University and Wright State University).

3. Institutions established as branches of major university systems in order to serve metropolitan populations (e.g., the University of Illinois at Chicago, the University of New Orleans, and the University of Missouri at Saint Louis).

4. Institutions originally created for a more specialized purpose, frequently as normal schools, today have an expanded mission in serving a population center (e.g., the University of Tennessee at Chattanooga, Towson State University, and Southwest Missouri State University).

Universities located in the population centers of our country now have a privileged role to play as we approach and move into the twenty-first century. To comprehend the significance of these institutions in the future, we must understand their immediate surroundings and the symbiotic relationship between these universities and their environment.

The concentration of our population into major centers has continued unabated and will not be reversed. The 1990 census will likely describe the following situation:

1. The nation's metropolitan populations exceed 200 million, with approximately 80 percent of all Americans living in the metropolitan areas.

2. The most rapid growth in the metropolitan areas is in peripheral areas and in the beltways connecting our cities.

3. The greatest challenges faced by the nation occur in the metropolitan setting.

Thus, as we approach the twenty-first century, metropolitan areas have become our greatest resource and our greatest challenge. For those institutions located in this environment, the opportunities and expectations will be formidable.

Andrew Young, mayor of Atlanta, has spoken for leaders in every state and city:

> At the local level, there's a crying out in urban America for people to do for urban America what state universities did in the last century for rural America. We have the most productive agricultural system in the history of the world. It did not come about by accident. It came about through land-grant colleges. It came about through state farm programs. It came about as a result of the integration of the university system with the agricultural community. The benefits that accrued from that relationship fed not only America but the entire world.
>
> A similar kind of relationship between universities and the cities is necessary. ("Public Expectations of Higher Education Beyond 1984," *American Association of State Colleges and Universities Studies,* 2:3-11)

We believe that those universities best suited to respond to this need, universities we classify as metropolitan universities, will emerge as very significant institutions in the twenty-first century.

A metropolitan university is defined first and foremost by its

philosophy. It accepts its relationship to the surrounding metropolitan region as its essential rationale, its reason for being. A
metropolitan university is not defined solely by its location, its
student population, or any other characteristic. A university may be
located within the metropolitan area, even in the central city, and
yet not be of that city. A university may even draw an appreciable
enrollment of students from its metropolitan area and yet not be
philosophically a part of that city.

Although metropolitan universities are likely to share certain
characteristics, such as a high enrollment of commuter and minority
students, metropolitan universities are best recognized by an
interactive philosophy by which these institutions establish symbiotic
relationships with their metropolitan areas. In some institutions,
such interaction is focused primarily in a few well-defined units,
such as a college of education or a center for urban studies; however,
we envision a metropolitan university as an institution where the
commitment to interaction with the metropolitan area permeates
the entire institution. At such universities, applying resources to
improve the metropolitan quality of life must be an institution-wide
commitment.

The phrase or descriptor used to identify a model of a university
is much less important than its operational mission statement and
philosophy. At Wright State University, we have chosen the descriptor
"metropolitan university" for a multitude of reasons, not the least of
which is to use a term that is broadly inclusive of many institutions
located in or near population centers. The term urban, not used much
until the nineteenth century to describe population centers, refers
in the minds of many of our constituents only to the core or central
city. For too many, the term "urban university" refers only to a set of
shared *characteristics*. The metropolitan university must address
the challenges presented by the inner city as one facet of its overall
responsibility, but those challenges do not exist in isolation from
those of the whole metropolitan area, nor can they be addressed
successfully in isolation. The important element that distinguishes
a metropolitan university is its philosophy, not characteristics such
as size, student profile, and program mix.

Recent metropolitan growth is far different from the classic
urban development that characterized the earlier part of this century.
Where once urbanization began with a highly centralized core and
spread outward in a concentric circle, the emergence of our system
of transportation has given rise to the rapid development of highly
localized nodes of industrial and commercial activity, related to and
dependent on the whole of the metropolitan area. Rapid development

now occurs in villages and towns peripheral to the core area and along the major arteries connecting them. Ironically, the construction of interstate bypass highways, originally intended to allow traffic to flow around major urban concentrations, has given rise in many instances to substantial commercial and industrial development away from the core city. In addition, the interstate highway system has promoted intracity growth, causing the rapid coalescing of two or more substantial population centers into a metroplex, such as Dallas-Fort Worth. Regional planners sectors forecast a similar megalopolis in Ohio stretching from Cincinnati on the south through Dayton to Springfield and east to Columbus. Similar "metropolitan strips" are developing elsewhere. Within this environment, many states have located major educational facilities near the core city, e.g., Cleveland State University. However, those institutions created in more recent years are more likely to be placed on the periphery of the metropolitan area, such as the University of Texas at San Antonio. Only by addressing the manifold needs of the extended metropolitan area can UT-SA and similar institutions truly serve the needs of their inner city. Quite frequently, the new institutions themselves stimulate yet another center of commercial and industrial development. It is to this environment, a complex governmental and cultural environment, that the metropolitan university, be it in the core city or on the periphery, must seek to relate. George Mason University is an outstanding example of an institution that understands the necessity and the wisdom of addressing the needs of the multitude of population centers that are occurring in the complex metropolitan area in northern Virginia around Washington, D.C.

Frank Newman, in *Choosing Quality,* identifies the establishment of an appropriate niche as a prerequisite to achieving institutional excellence. One's niche depends on many factors, including the rationale for founding the university, the university's location, and its response to changes in society and the development of knowledge. Metropolitan universities should seek to develop an identity that recognizes not only the academic and scholarly values common to all universities, but also the empowering concept of a strongly interactive relationship with the metropolitan area around it. The metropolitan university shares the same commitment to the discovery, transmittal, and application of knowledge as do the institutions that represent the older land-grant and liberal arts institutions. Ultimately, the success of a metropolitan university will depend on its response to both the historical values that define a university and its interactive relationship to its metropolitan area.

One does not preclude the other; in striving toward one, we naturally achieve the other. The vision of becoming an eminent metropolitan university is an enabling one. By choosing to fit into the metropolitan university model, a university accepts the added obligation to extend its resources to the surrounding region, to provide leadership in addressing regional needs, and to work cooperatively with the region's schools, municipalities, businesses, industries, and the many other institutions and organizations in the public and private sectors. By accepting this mission, a university affirms that it not only accepts the academic and scholarly obligations and responsibilities incumbent upon all excellent universities but that it intends to extend the expertise and energies of the university to the metropolitan region in somewhat the same way that land-grant institutions served the agricultural society during the nineteenth century.

While it is useful to draw an analogy to the land-grant university, we must take care not to extend the analogy too far in speaking of metropolitan universities. The mission of the land-grant institution was narrowly focused compared to the mission that metropolitan universities seek to address. In establishing interactions with the metropolitan environment, we must think creatively of how we might utilize the entire body of the university as an urban-based experiment station. The challenge for the metropolitan university is to transform itself by empowering the entire campus to utilize the metropolitan area as a living laboratory. As the metropolitan university concept evolves, we will see many variations in the model emerge. There can be no single interpretation of the model for a metropolitan university.

The time has come to advance the metropolitan model among a national constituency to create a defined peer group of metropolitan universities, among which program excellence can be measured and by which external evaluators, federal funding agencies included, can appropriately judge the institutions. In the process, we may arrive at definitions of excellence that will shape new priorities and directions for higher education in America.

Ernest Lynton and Sandra Elman have written:

> The existing, narrowly defined mold into which almost all universities have tried to cast themselves is not adequate to the expanding needs of our contemporary, knowledge-based society. A large number of institutions are failing to realize their full potential because their internal system of values, priorities, and aspirations primarily emphasizes and rewards traditional modes of teaching for which the clientele is shrinking and basic research for which most of

these institutions cannot receive adequate support. This has resulted in a real crises of purpose. By believing themselves to be what they are not, these institutions fall short of what they could be. This . . . deprives society of the substantial intellectual services that these universities could provide. *(New Priorities for the University,* San Francisco: Jossey Bass, 1987, pp. 12-13).

Acceptance of a new model in higher education will not be easily or quickly achieved. Too many people recognize as worthy only the traditional higher education models that were part of their own educational development. This attitude characterizes both faculty—mostly educated at comprehensive research institutions—and citizens in the community itself, few of whom attended metropolitan universities and many of whom view regional and commuter emphasis as trivial. As a result, a primary task in establishing a new model is educating the university community. Endorsement of the model and commitment to the philosophy within the institution enhances the success of acceptance in the broader society, and performance—success in useful institutional interaction with the community—will gradually produce public recognition and appreciation. And we have the advantage that more and more recent graduates, who are taking their places in metropolitan power structures, attended our institutions.

New definitions of academic prestige and eminence must be formed to accommodate the new model. The Carnegie Foundation taxonomy of higher education institutions provides no adequate niche for this large group of institutions. Other popular classifications, such as the annual ranking of institutions by *U.S. News and World Report,* categorize rankings on bases that do not serve the academy well.

The journal *Metropolitan Universities* seeks to provide an opportunity for dialogue on the metropolitan university model in order to clarify better the philosophical variations on the model, to discuss the challenges we face both internally and externally, and to share successful and not so successful interactive strategies between the university and its environment. The dialogue will of necessity encompass all of the issues that our society faces, plus those that are unique to the academy.

This article is not intended to speak at length to the various implications that flow from accepting the metropolitan model, but more simply to bring to the attention of the many potential metropolitan universities the significance of the role they can assume as we approach the twenty-first century. All institutions cannot fit easily within the model. All that might do so will not choose the model. But the vision of the metropolitan model is one in which many institutions may seek recognition and prestige. The vision can be a liberating one, allowing us to be evaluated on the basis of what we choose rather than against criteria established for other institutions at other times. It can free us to cooperate enthusiastically with other institutions (public and private) whose mission differs from ours but with whom a combination of resources can bring mutual rewards. It can free us from destructive competition with dissimilar institutions within our state systems and thus enable us to respond to appropriate public concerns regarding unnecessary duplication. Finally, the vision can be a satisfying one by allowing us to achieve eminence based not on being a second- or third-tier copy of someone else's vision, but excelling within our own.

Metropolitan universities are agents of change. These institutions must play a role in the transformation of society, but the transformation is not unilateral. Just as the university is a transformer of the society of which it is a part, so it will be transformed by that society.

It is important for the metropolitan university to define clearly and to control the interactions that occur within the metropolitan environment. Only if the university is willing to assume leadership in defining such interactions can the institution guard and maintain the independence that is essential and necessary for all universities. This independence cannot be yielded. The university must develop a clear understanding of when it should turn down what may appear to be a window of opportunity. The metropolitan university must be able to say "no" in its own best interest. However, the metropolitan university must also remain constantly in contact with its environment and be alert to opportunities to say "yes" by creating interactive initiatives that serve the interests of both the university and the metropolitan area.

Protecting traditional values must not be defined as maintaining the status quo. The transformation of metropolitan universities is likely to involve a basic reconsideration of our traditional discipline-centered mentality. Solutions to current metropolitan problems will not come via a breakthrough in an isolated laboratory but through the patient application of skills by scholars working together in a variety of disciplines.

In the course of our transformation, our metropolitan

universities will have to reconsider internal priorities and reward systems. Our institutions owe their existence to the need for access, and teaching must therefore be our first priority.

More than any other institutions, universities located in the metropolitan areas have a special role to assume in preparing our students to live in our pluralistic society. Historically, minority and disadvantaged groups have migrated to our cities, and the metropolitan universities will always have a large population of diverse students. We will face the challenge of helping students, not always well prepared, to succeed in university studies. As these new populations enter metropolitan universities, we must develop the necessary support structures to ensure their success. And we must broaden the understanding by our majority students in order that they may accept and appreciate the diversity of a more pluralistic society.

Our reward system will have an important impact on determining faculty activity. The current policies on promotion, tenure, and merit salary increases served our institutions well in the past but now require serious reconsideration. All research has always been for some purpose, some ultimate application. But the time lapse between inquiry and application has so shortened as to make the distinction between pure and applied research meaningless. The importance of the problem tackled and the quality of the work performed must become more significant factors in evaluations than is the artificial, traditional distinction between pure and applied scholarship. Similarly, professional service—the application of one's disciplinary skills to real problems in the real world—must receive more than the lip service it has traditionally been accorded.

In *New Priorities for the University,* Lynton and Elman make the case clearly and convincingly:

> The institutionalization of a reward structure for faculty engaged in such activity does not imply a reduction in the importance of traditional scholarship. Rather it elevates to a comparable level of esteem—and subjects to a comparable level of quality control—a broad continuum of knowledge-related scholarly activities. We believe that the quality of the academic environment will be enhanced through close reciprocal relationships between strong teaching, traditional scholarship, and externally oriented professional activities, with the whole being greater than the sum of the parts. (ibid, pp. 148-149)

Surely the time has come to cease talking about a more appropriate reward system and to begin demonstrating to faculty by performance that we are serious about a change.

Though it is not likely that all disciplines within the academy will share equally in interaction with the metropolitan area, we must hold out the vision for all. One might anticipate that colleges and schools that offer professional programs will most easily establish symbiotic relationships with the region. However, all disciplines should be challenged to consider the possibility of such interactions, must be encouraged to shape the nature of their interactions, and must be nurtured and rewarded for their effort.

The disciplines that resonate to a more conservative and traditional form of scholarship and service must not be punished or restricted but can and should be challenged to reexamine their current assumptions. They must be challenged not to withdraw toward a more conservative (or defensive) stance but instead to play an active role in defining the measures by which we will judge contributions to scholarship and professional service on this broader basis. Elman and Lynton point out that this asks a great deal of the academy:

> If universities are to respond more systematically to external knowledge needs they must raise, rather than diminish, the intellectual standards and challenges for both their institutions as a whole and for participating members. . . . For universities to carry out their expanded scholarly function and to provide competence-oriented teaching, faculty must be more than scholars in a discipline, not less; they must be scholars with a broad perspective on the interrelationship of disciplines and their practical applications. (ibid, p. 134)

Metropolitan universities will not come into full being without the leadership of the president, chief academic officer, deans, and key faculty. The president and chief academic officer must assume the responsibility of educating the faculty on the wisdom of embracing the metropolitan model, helping to shape a mission statement clearly stating the purpose of the institution with respect to the metropolitan environment and devising a strategic plan to achieve the mission. Both leaders must join together to assure that budgetary allocations are directed toward the strategic plan. George Keller has put it well:

An academic strategy asserts that neither willfulness nor acquiescence to the fashions and temporary external conditions is an appropriate course. Rather a university's own directions and objectives need to be shaped in light of an emerging national situation and new external factors as well as the perennial needs of youth, truth, and intelligence. And because the external environment is in constant flux, strategic planning must be continuous, pervasive and indigenous. (*Academic Strategy*, p. 145)

The concept of the metropolitan university can provide a worthy vision for many institutions that seek a niche within which they can provide opportunities for faculty and students, while at the same time providing the prospect of institutional pride and success. Committing an institution to the model does not require vast new resources. Although Title XI may hold some promise of funds for universities to provide for the needs of our population centers, metropolitan universities cannot afford to wait for federal funding to begin those interactions with metropolitan areas that are needed now. The tenor of our times is such that significant funding of Title XI is not likely to occur, and metropolitan universities must selectively focus toward building symbiotic partnerships.

A frequently misattributed Old Testament Proverb (29:18) advises us, "Where there is no vision, the people perish." We in higher education can continue doing business in the same old ways, and we are not likely to perish. But the metropolitan vision can afford us the opportunity to help our students and faculty achieve their highest potential while at the same time improving the quality of life for most Americans—and can bring institutional success and satisfaction, as well.

SUGGESTED READINGS

Grobman, Arnold. *Urban State Universities: An Unfinished Agenda*. New York: Praeger, 1988.

Keller, George C. *Academic Strategy: The Management Revolution in American Higher Education*. Baltimore: Johns Hopkins University Press, 1983.

Lynton, Ernest A., and Sandra Elman. *New Priorities for the University*. San Francisco: Jossey Bass, 1987.

Newman, Frank. *Choosing Quality: Reducing Conflict Between the State and the University*. Denver: Education Commission of the States, 1987.

METROPOLITAN UNIVERSITIES: PAST, PRESENT, AND FUTURE

Blaine A. Brownell

The metropolitan university in the United States is indeed defined by its name. It means to be a university in every sense of the word—an open intellectual community in which faculty and students share knowledge, pursue truth, hone analytical skills, and provide training in the professions. It is also an integral part of the modern American urban region, with all its complexity, opportunity, conflict, and confusion. This dynamic tension, between institutional purpose and an environment that both impels and hampers it, has produced the metropolitan university and also shaped its options and its future.

I hope to tie metropolitan universities to the national and urban history which produced and continues to shape them. I will briefly touch on definitions of the metropolitan university, problems of institutional mission, the dilemma we currently face, and the response we should make to it. I will also suggest that—just as the urban region is *the* critical arena within which we will either resolve our gravest national dilemmas or succumb to the weight of our accumulated difficulties in increasingly competitive global economy—the metropolitan university may be key to the future of the metropolis and the country as a whole.

Patterns of Urbanization

The settlement of North America, from the earliest days through the nineteenth century, was presaged and fulfilled by towns and cities. Seaports provided links with Europe and other colonies, while frontier towns secured new territories and sustained the farms and smaller villages that grew up around them. Commerce on the great

17

rivers—the Ohio and the Mississippi—was nurtured by towns that provided the vessels, products, services, and populations that made commerce profitable. By the early twentieth century, the United States, which took such pride in its frontier and rural traditions, was in one basic sense already an urban nation.

The census of 1920 revealed for the first time that more than half of all Americans lived in towns and cities, and that some of these places were rather large: a dozen had more than 600,000 people, three had more than one million, and New York City, with its five million inhabitants, was a metropolis by any definition. The main point is that the country ceased to be defined and driven by producers on the land, all of whom were remarkably alike in ethnicity and background; the new force in national life was the city, with its polyglot populations and assorted problems. Some saw in this the ruination of the American experiment; but most Americans escaped to urban attractions and amenities at the first opportunity.

The same city-building dynamic exists today. New communities are created on new land or within already settled areas. Some older neighborhoods are transformed by new patterns of access or technology, while others are abandoned like fallow fields no longer capable of sustaining life. Tyson's Corner, Virginia is, in its way, as much an expression of economic imperatives, mobility, and entrepreneurial enthusiasm as the smallest Missouri settlement in 1810. And it is, regrettably, no better planned.

Urbanization in the United States was a vigorous and varied process, but with certain recurring patterns and consequences. Whenever technology permitted, cities grew outward. As long as distances were traversed only on foot or by horse, urban settlements were tightly-knit and different uses and functions were close together. The steam railroad in the antebellum era allowed some of the very wealthy to live rustic lives in new outlying estates. But the streetcar in the 1890s began the genuinely radical transformation of the American city, encouraging urban growth over a much larger territory, though according to the regular patterns etched by rails and roadbeds.

The technological completion of this transformation was underway in the 1920s with the arrival of the motor vehicle, without which the metropolis as we know it simply would not exist. This highly individualistic and compelling appliance vanquished space and distance and opened vast new territories to urban settlement, a bonanza of land development only dreamt of by the western pioneers. Thus did the predominant urban form in America change from the cluster to the marketplace, to the radial center, to the vital fringe, and within the last decade—to the multi-centered metropolis.

Throughout these changes, American cities grew larger and more dominant in the national life. As they covered more and more territory, their uses, functions, and people became increasingly separated. Working and living arrangements, once close together in the center, were later divided between center and suburb, linked by rails and roads. The modern city was one of clearly distinct functional areas—manufacturing, commercial, residential, and variants thereof—engraved in new zoning codes enacted in the early twentieth century. Perhaps most importantly, people once separated by social class, race, and occupation were now also much more separated in space. The Chicago sociologists in the 1920s described these patterns as if they were the products of universal laws of human settlement— with downtown manufacturing areas and commercial districts giving way to close-in slums and eventually to high-class suburbs. While this pattern was, to some extent, replicated in other countries and cultures influenced by the automobile, it was primarily North American.

The shaping and reshaping of urban America gained momentum after World War II, at precisely the same time that American higher education was also transformed. A wave of returning veterans, impelled by government benefits, flooded the housing market, stimulating the construction of millions of new homes, most of them on the fringe of the established cities. They also flooded the nation's college classrooms and brought a booming business to maternity wards. The greatest democratization of higher education in American history, a massive expansion of the urban region brought on by new migrations, and a large, sustained flow of federal support were the primordial ingredients for the gestation of the modern metropolitan university.

Government policy indirectly financed the suburban boom through mortgage subsidies and new highways that penetrated outlying areas and tore through inner-city communities. At the same time, the decline of inner cities and many older neighborhoods accelerated. By the 1950s, efforts to "renew" deteriorating downtowns—also encouraged by government policy—focused on clearing out slums to make way for sparkling new civic centers, and even a few universities. As the suburbs grew, new colleges were built, and established private colleges in near-by communities became public. These "urban" universities were thus expanding at the same time that some parts of their local regions were in headlong decline.

Urban Crisis

The American metropolis was clearly in trouble. This was partly due to patterns of urban settlement but it was mostly because of incongruities and pathologies imbedded in American life. Whatever their causes, these problems led to the crisis of the cities in the 1960s—tragically illuminated by firestorms of racial discontent and to the first widespread attempt of the federal government to deal with specifically urban problems. Urban universities were among the recommended solutions, and many of them eagerly accepted the challenge.

The urban crisis had many dimensions, but the array of problems was daunting: racism, poverty, crime, deteriorating infrastructure, inadequate and inequitable transportation, and a declining civic mentality. The new suburbs—containing millions of relatively well-to-do, and largely white, urbanites—were regarded by many policy makers and academics as a major part of the problem, since they siphoned off economic resources and human talents from the communities and populations that sorely needed them. Some universities were found in the inner cities while others inhabited the remote suburbs. It should be noted that while the suburbs eventually accounted for over two-thirds of business establishments and the majority of populations and jobs in metropolitan areas, they are not—despite images in movies and on TV—all alike: some, especially close to older cities, were also quite established and suffered the same economic decline and chronic problems as many downtowns.

Problems of Definition

As America became more urban, it became more difficult to precisely define the American city. As the line separating urban from rural, and even downtown from suburb, became blurred, a basic dynamic in American cultural life was gone—namely, the divide between country and city that underlay so much of our literature, art, and popular culture. It also became more difficult to define ways of living that were peculiarly "urban."

The same dilemma confronts us with respect to the university. For just as we cannot readily define a metropolis (other than a large, dispersed urban area), we cannot precisely define a metropolitan university. Since the nation is metropolitan, few colleges or universities except the most isolated do not have at least some metropolitan connections or relevance. Major state universities, regardless of location, have responded to the rising demands to address social and economic problems. Even land-grant institutions typically have academic programs in critical areas like social work, health care, architecture, and planning which may focus economic development and urban problems.

At the same time, universities identified as urban or metropolitan have placed great emphasis on providing solid academic programs in the basic arts and sciences and advanced graduate programs that cannot be distinguished in quality and focus from those in more traditional institutions. The term "urban university" no longer describes, as it once did, an open admission institution with mostly undergraduate and applied academic programs staffed by mostly part-time faculty.

Clearly, though, a reasonable definition lies somewhere in the combination of location and orientation (as expressed in institutional goals and actions), both of which are essential. A location somewhere within an urban region must exist alongside a declared commitment to serve the broad educational needs of that region. And the term "metropolitan" is preferable because it emphasizes a larger, rather than smaller, area of concern and responsibility.

Problems of Mission

Service to the local area is usually expressed by giving priority to local partnerships (public and private), educating diverse populations, and responding to a variety of civic needs. We are already familiar with roles that metropolitan universities have played in facilitating regional assessment and planning, providing skilled expertise for addressing local problems and educated professionals for important local institutions (e.g., government and public schools), developing and applying new technology, attracting higher-wage jobs and industries, and, of course, serving diverse and sometimes place-bound populations previously denied a fair share of educational opportunity.

In many respects, these efforts have been highly successful even when they were not dramatic. But the problems and patterns of American urban development also pose serious difficulties for many major institutions, including the metropolitan university. For one thing, many campuses are located in neglected, blighted areas or at the far urban fringe—impeding access for many people in either case. Shifting patterns of urban migration, investment and disinvestment, and serious ills like poverty and crime can quickly redefine—and undermine—a university's physical environment and its opportunities. For another, the obvious application of faculty expertise to the solution of local problems is deceptively difficult. As we have often painfully learned, the interests and expectations of faculty members, bureaucrats, and neighborhood leaders or special interest groups are often quite different.

In this respect, metropolitan universities may have oversold their capacity to actually solve problems and improve local government and conditions, while neglecting their central role to educate.

The Dilemma

Metropolitan universities confront a dilemma created by their history and environment. They were charged with responding to rising local needs at precisely the same time that local urban areas were undergoing unprecedented, and often perilous, transformations. Impelled by educational demands and local community needs following World War II, metropolitan universities now find themselves hard pressed to meet public expectations that are both rising and conflicting, and to fulfill missions that are threatened by looming budget cuts.

Part of the explanation simply lies in the fact that metropolitan universities are, alas, metropolitan: they are shaped and delimited by the problems and opportunities of their metropolitan environment. At the root of their dilemma, in fact, is a modern American metropolis that is fragmented by race, social class, and economic function and spread over a huge territory, further divided into at least several counties and perhaps dozens of independent political subdivisions. Rather than held together by common interests, large metropolitan areas are rather more often microcosms of conflict across the political spectrum. This internecine warfare is alarmingly sometimes conducted on the floor of the state legislature, often to the detriment of metropolitan universities.

By their very nature and purpose, true metropolitan universities have no single constituency, but rather multiple interests demanding very different things: large and small businesses and various minority groups, neighborhoods, and municipal governments. Rather than one chamber of commerce, there are several or many—some promoting the central city and others marketing the suburbs. City halls may dot the metropolitan landscape, reflecting varied jurisdictional interests. Neither the state nor federal governments are much help, with their ambivalent and shifting attitudes and policies about access and higher academic standards, graduate and undergraduate programs, research and teaching, and financial aid.

The Response

A rational solution to this dilemma, of course—especially considering our funding problems—is to take the modern management approach: to assess, "rightsize," and focus. In such a diverse environment, no institution or group of institutions can be all things to all people. We have heard the advice at innumerable national meetings and workshops: use strategic planning to reveal the greatest needs and opportunities, and pursue these intensively with a new organizational structure configured to new priorities and specific goals. Build on selected, existing strengths, and pick carefully the projects or community groups you intend to work with. Reevaluate the mission statement, refine your publicity and admissions information, and maximize your competitive advantages in more clearly delimited service areas. In short, find yourself a "niche" and fill it.

All this seems to make sense, and it certainly makes regents and legislators happy. But it may also mean the demise of the metropolitan university as we have known it, and an end to the unique role that such institutions can and should play in our nation's development into the next century. For better or worse, the metropolitan university must address the problems of the metropolis rather than selected, limited parts of it. The shareholders of the metropolis are all its citizens. When a major metropolitan problem is the fragmentation of interest and purpose, becoming yet another specialized institution dealing with only several fragments does not present a solution.

The opportunity and burden of the metropolitan university—if it is to be a metropolitan university—is to serve the entire urban region and all its diverse populations, interests, and elements. It cannot deal only with the inner-city underprepared or the suburban professionals; it must be concerned with the needs of both. It cannot identify its interests solely with the largest city in its region or with its suburbs, but rather help them to recognize mutual interests and work together. The most important role of the metropolitan university is to be a facilitator, communicator, convener, and bridge. What other institution, except perhaps the government itself, has the capacity to interpret one group to another, serve as a neutral site and forum where problems can be discussed and resolved, bring the latest knowledge and technologies to bear on the problems of the dispossessed, join the vigor and capacity of business with the compelling needs of the public at large, and, perhaps most importantly, help restore a sense of *civitas,* of belonging to one polity and community?

The metropolitan university must therefore define itself in terms of its environment, with all the potential confusion and uncertainty that entails. It *must* be many things to many people, and it must attempt to do this during the most troubling financial period for higher education since World War II. This is certainly the most ambitious educational agenda since the Morrill Act.

The metropolitan university must of course be selective in the

specific activities it undertakes. But this cannot be at the expense of
any major metropolitan interest or constituency. No institution can
meet every need for local development, but the metropolitan university must be involved in every significant political, economic, and social
dimension of its complex, extensive community. No higher education
institution can solve the problems of the public schools or eliminate
violent crime, but if these are major problems they must in some way
be part of the university's academic and service agenda—whether or
not they have formal programs in teacher education or law enforce-
ment. For the deepest problems of our country are urban problems,
and all segments of our metropolitan areas reflect them.

The metropolitan university cannot even afford to focus precisely
on the local area. For one thing, excellent academic programs cannot
be judged in local or regional terms. For another, in a truly interdependent world, local problems are also global problems. In fact, metropolitan
universities need to be our most internationally minded and oriented,
since most multi-national companies are located in or near our major
cities and the keys to national success in global competition—whether
in manufacturing, technology, communications, services, or education—
are with few exceptions to be found overwhelmingly in metropolitan
areas, and demand up-to-date knowledge, language training, and cultural awareness.

This argues for a very broad-based, long-term approach that recognizes the problem of metropolitan fragmentation (socially,
economically, and geographically) and attempts to work within it and
ultimately to meliorate it. In fact, the method may be as important as
the content, the process as important as the specific goal. As the university is involved, others become involved and engaged. The
metropolitan university may not unilaterally solve any problems, but
it may nevertheless be a critical factor in their solution.

The dilemma gives way to a challenge that will require enormous
knowledge and leadership. It will also require new tools. Even universities with multiple campuses in the metropolitan region cannot
overcome the barriers of poverty, sickness, inadequate transportation
and all the other factors that restrict physical mobility. If the university is to be everywhere at the same time, it can only do so through
technology—the same technology that has the power both to further
fragment and to join metropolitan society. Given its mission, the metropolitan university should almost by definition be a leader in the
development and application of communications technology. In this
sense, "distance" learning is a more pressing need within urban regional boundaries than it is across state or national lines.

In carrying out this ambitious agenda in a time of public skepticism, metropolitan universities must be fully accountable for what they do, and meticulous in explaining themselves and their programs to the public. The more extensively involved they are in diverse metropolitan projects, the more carefully they will need to consider and develop appropriate faculty workload and reward policies, tend to basic expectations such as solid undergraduate instruction, and find better ways of reporting the value of partnerships and public service initiatives. The public will want to know if there is substance behind the rhetoric and whether they are getting their money's worth. More difficult—certainly in terms of the traditional higher education model— is the necessity to prioritize research programs, at least in terms of university support, to determine the degree to which they fit into the metropolitan agenda. Inevitably, this will encourage applied research in general, and basic research, which has particular relevance for local interests.

All higher education institutions must be innovative to make any headway at all in this climate, and metropolitan universities—which often lack extensive alumni bases and established foundations—must be more innovative than most. New necessities include collaboration and resource-sharing with other universities, including so-called "flagship" institutions, to address metropolitan needs; fashioning new and more ambitious partnerships with business and industry; initiating local coalitions to pressure state legislatures or coordinating boards to ease the often heavy-handed restrictions on the use of educational technology, and thus reach many otherwise inaccessible pockets of the urban region and pressing the application of new technologies to the greatest possible extent that resources will permit.

The metropolitan university must be a model and exemplar of its mission, and therein perhaps lies its greatest initial challenge. The most important bridge it builds must be across its own campus. Students from the suburbs come together—often haltingly and suspiciously—with students from other economic and ethnic backgrounds. The university is one of the few places in the metropolitan area where such diverse elements are to be found engaged in common pursuits in such a small space. Hispanics, African Americans, and Asians seek their place along with more established groups in the national future through education. Women lay claim to equal roles with men in the professions and in all intellectual endeavors. A university without diversity, fraught with ethnic turmoil, and failing to address the critical issues associated with social conflict and the need to forge a new community from many diverse cultural perspectives is not in a very good position to provide leadership for others. The metropolitan university must be a microcosm of its region, but one that not only reflects regional problems but also harbors hope for the future through a positive redress of grievances and a sense of new possibility. Only then can it reach out and bridge the metropolitan community. To truly minister unto its region, the metropolitan university must heal itself.

Metropolitan universities must be prepared to carry their case to legislatures and the general public, to request greater support and recognition for an even broader mission. The timing could hardly be less fortunate; obviously, such talk runs against powerful currents of specialization, compression, and reduction. But the future of our urban regions will not wait, and many parts of those regions are clearly in crisis. Though it may seem ephemeral to many, education is the most powerful tool we have to achieve fundamental, persistent change—to raise standards of living, to meliorate barriers of race and class, and to fashion a new civic consciousness that reaches beyond ethnic group or neighborhood and embraces the larger society as expressed by the metropolis. It is by no means certain that we can do this, or that the nation can rise to all the challenges that now confront it; but it is probably impossible without strong, vital institutions of higher education that are dedicated to serving their entire regions by providing good teaching, quality research, a global perspective, and—by example as well as by precept—a new sense of metropolitan community.

NOTE: I am indebted to my friend and co-author, Dr. David R. Goldfield of the University of North Carolina at Charlotte, for his comments on this essay. I have drawn rather liberally from ideas expressed in several earlier publications, especially D. R. Goldfield and B. A. Brownell, *Urban America: A History* (2nd ed., 1990) and G. R. Mowry and B. A. Brownell, *The Urban Nation, 1920-1980* (Rev. ed., 1981).

SUGGESTED READINGS

Abbott, Carl. *The New Urban America: Growth and Politics in Sunbelt Cities.* Chapel Hill: University of North Carolina Press, 1981.

Garreau, Joel. *Edge City: Life on the New Urban Frontier.* New York: Doubleday, 1991.

Goldfield, David R. and Blaine A. Brownell. *Urban America: A History.* 2nd ed. Boston: Houghton Mifflin Company, 1990.

Jackson, Kenneth T. *Crabgrass Frontier: The Suburbanization of the United States.* New York: Oxford University Press, 1985.

Muller, Peter O. *The Outer City: Geographical Consequences of the Urbanization of the Suburbs.* Washington, D. C.: Association of American Geographers, 1976.

Norris, D., E. Delaney, and K. Billingsley. "America's New Cities and the Universities." *Planning for Higher Education* (Fall, 1990): 1–8.

Aligning Missions with Public Expectations: The Case of the Metropolitan Universities

Paige E. Mulhollan

The most important words in the title of this piece are probably "public expectations." During the past several years of troubled economic times in our country, higher education has unquestionably lost credibility with our various publics and come under critical scrutiny from parents, legislators, and state policy makers who believe that our costs are out of control and increasingly question the effectiveness and quality of what we do. In addition, higher education is of course very much affected by the current economic downturn. The most popular form of one-upmanship now practiced when university presidents gather is "I have suffered deeper cuts than you."

Of course, higher education has experienced financial reverses in the past. But the current situation differs in that our difficulties result as much from lost public confidence as from the current recession. Unlike other tough times, we cannot now expect an early return to "business as usual," regardless of when economic recovery occurs.

What then can we do? I recently heard the chancellor of a leading state university system characterize the present circumstances as "the first instance of financial crisis which is beyond the influence of higher education leaders." For the short term, the chancellor is probably correct. Our problems have been a long time developing. They mirror those in the private sector, and will not go away through the application of a term policy Band-Aid. But for the longer term, higher education leaders must fashion a response to the circumstances in which we find ourselves. Our work is simply too important to cop out by concluding that our enterprise is the victim of forces beyond our control.

Institutional leadership can ensure the long-term future of higher education by promoting three principal responses. First, we must overcome the widespread confusion regarding what we are trying to do. In short, we must respond to thoughtful higher education leaders who have for a generation told us that we must develop clear missions and identify institutional niches. Second, we must cease our resistance to defining productivity and relating it to quality and instead insist that our faculty define these concepts in ways that the public finds convincing. And finally, we must embrace assessment as it is understood outside the academy, namely, by demonstrating measurable value added.

To date, we have focused most of our attention on the second and third of these issues, largely because of state-mandated assessment and wide interest in total quality management, which works only with a qualitative baseline and outcomes measurement. But unless we do something about mission uncertainty as a first step, we risk letting others define our goals. They will do so simplistically and narrowly. For example, they might define our task exclusively in terms of undergraduate teaching. If we allow this to happen, we risk the destruction of much of what is valuable in American universities.

Yet up to now we in higher education have done a terrible job of describing our purposes. We pay much lip service to the importance of clear-cut missions, but we fail to articulate them. Most of us have read dozens, if not hundreds, of institutional mission statements. Yet few of them are specific enough to tell an outside observer very much about the priorities or specific objectives of institutional performance. Instead, such documents are pious statements of principles, which are valid but so broad as to be interchangeable among institutions.

Traditional Models of Higher Education

The absence of useful mission statements stems from a larger problem, namely, the absence of acceptable success models. Despite the proliferation of institutions, American higher education recognizes only two models within which baccalaureate and post-baccalaureate institutions want to compete: one of these is the comprehensive research university; the other, the liberal arts college. Prestige can be accomplished only by excelling in one of these models. To choose another model risks institutional isolation and the conclusion, both on and off campus, that one's mission lacks legitimacy and value.

Yet neither of these models provides a satisfactory response to current public expectations. Our comprehensive research universities maintain a global or national focus, usually with little concern for their immediate environment. Their reward system places primary value on research, which furthermore is defined in a narrow fashion as basic research. Teaching, particularly undergraduate teaching, is always highly valued in such institutions, and professional service, except in certain professional fields, remains unappreciated and unevaluated. Liberal arts colleges, on the other hand, give commendable emphasis to undergraduate teaching, but virtually exclude research and professional service, which are the distinguishing characteristics of a university.

One reason so few alternative success models exist is the widespread and unfortunate reliance on the Carnegie Classification, developed originally in order to make statistical comparisons more meaningful. The Carnegie Classification aggregates institutions only on the basis of level of highest degree, size, amount of sponsored research, and numbers of Ph.D.'s awarded. It steadfastly refuses to recognize the existence of other doctorates. Imbedded in the Carnegie scheme is a perhaps unintentional pecking order that defines as prestigious only the models designated Research Universities I or Liberal Arts Colleges I. Everything else is a second- or third-tier facsimile or an ill-defined mishmash called "doctoral-granting" or "comprehensive." The Carnegie Classification fails because it emphasizes a limited number of narrowly defined institutional *characteristics* instead of institutional *philosophy* or *mission*. The Classification counts things while missing the essence of institutional purpose.

Metropolitan Universities Model for Higher Education

In 1990, forty-nine university presidents subscribed to a "Declaration of Metropolitan Universities," (See p. viii.) They proclaimed allegiance to a new success model, which gives their institutions an opportunity to define meaningful missions that respond to public expectations. The model is called the "Metropolitan University," defined in its simplest terms as an institution that accepts all of higher education's traditional values in teaching, research, and professional service, but takes upon itself the additional responsibility of providing leadership to its metropolitan region by using its human and financial resources to improve the region's quality of life. Metropolitan universities consider it their mission to address the problems of metropolitan America; problems that, now more than ever, should be at the heart of the national agenda for the new century. My colleagues Charles Hathaway and Karen White and I described this model in greater detail in the first issue of the *Metropolitan Universities* journal, in the pages of which the model has since been elaborated and given further definition.

The purpose of this article is not to provide further details about the model, but rather to urge all metropolitan universities to promulgate and to use this model explicitly both internally and externally as providing guidelines and measures of excellence for our institutions. Any new institutional model must possess all the necessary characteristics of a success model:

1. The model must be understandable;
2. The model must be valid and legitimate;
3. The model must be inclusive, with room for institutional differences, in order that a sufficient critical mass of institutions can and will choose to adopt it;
4. The model must constitute a vision that can excite faculty, students, community; and, finally,
5. The model must allow an institution to measure its progress and be seen by its constituencies as excelling.

How then does the metropolitan university concept stack up against the criteria that are necessary for a viable success model?

1. Is the metropolitan university mission understandable?
The answer is clearly yes. In the first place, it is easy to grasp the basic idea of a university that interacts strongly with its region in a variety of different ways. Secondly, our metropolitan focus is equally understandable. The nation is no longer composed of cities surrounded by pastoral countryside. Instead, our metropolitan areas now consist of heavily populated strips or metroplexes that include numerous satellite communities as well as a central core, all highly interdependent. The 1990 census places nearly eighty-five percent of the American population within metropolitan statistical areas, most of them living outside center cities. Everywhere, planning is becoming regional. One might choose the designator "urban" to describe this model, and metropolitan universities must accept the urban mission. But they must be more than urban institutions. Our publics understand the distinction between the terms urban and

metropolitan and see metropolitan as more inclusive and more descriptive of our current society.

2. Is the metropolitan university mission valid and legitimate? One may consider this criterion from two completely different perspectives. First, is it legitimate in an organizational sense? Second, is it valid in terms of relevance to the current historical context? In both cases, the answer is again clearly yes. Many of our institutions came into existence in response to community needs. Their missions within their state systems frequently reflect a relationship to community, both by tradition as well as by specific assignment. And increasingly, public expectations reinforce a commitment to community. In that sense, the metropolitan university mission is legitimate. It is also valid in the larger context. The problems of our society are mainly metropolitan problems: promoting regional economic vitality, bringing our minority populations into the mainstream of society, developing political leadership, improving public education, delivering affordable health care, providing for the homeless and the elderly, and addressing environmental concerns. A mission that accepts leadership in solving metropolitan problems— as opposed to simply responding when called upon—is an important mission, and certainly a valid one for the coming decades.

3. Is the metropolitan university mission inclusive, that is, is it one which sufficient numbers of institutions can choose in order for the model to gain national understanding and acceptance? Again the answer is yes, if one keeps the focus on mission or philosophy rather than upon detailed institutional characteristics. The metropolitan mission need not be restricted by geography. Some institutions located in cities will choose other missions. Many institutions located in the suburbs, or even beyond, may choose to accept the metropolitan philosophy. They may be large or small, graduate or undergraduate, doctoral-granting or not, public or private. Service to place-bound students, continuing education, applied research, professional service, and local economic partnerships are all activities commonly found in metropolitan universities, and may prove to be critical functions in solving metropolitan problems, but no one institution needs to emphasize all of them. Between 150 and 200 institutions in our country can comfortably accept the designation metropolitan university. With such a critical mass, and with the mission's inherent responsiveness to public expectations, the metropolitan university could promptly become a nationally acceptable success model.

4. Does the metropolitan university mission constitute a vision

that can unite and excite our faculty, students, and community?
Here the answer is problematic because the vision can only succeed
through active promotion by institutional leadership. We start with
certain handicaps. Most members of our faculties were trained at
comprehensive research universities and tend to define institutional
success in terms of their alma mater. Many of our students define
success in terms of traditional residential universities or liberal arts
colleges, with all of their presumed virtues. Many of our community
leaders define institutional prestige in terms of the models with which
they are familiar. Therefore, leadership will be required to communicate the advantages of creating our own identity rather than
emulating missions defined for others. If they think about it hon-
estly, the faculty, students, and community will recognize that most
institutions will not succeed in duplicating comprehensive research
universities. If nothing else our states will not allow it. Must we
therefore settle for seeking to be among the "best" of second- or third-
tier research universities? I think not.

But the fundamental reason for not emulating the
comprehensive research institution model is that it is the wrong
model for our times. Derek Bok spent much of his final year as
president of Harvard University speaking eloquently about the need
for universities to address our society's most pressing problems:
improving public education; delivering efficient health care; and,
building economic competitiveness. He again expressed this need
most eloquently in his keynote address on "Regaining the Public
Trust," which opened the 1992 AAHE National Meeting. Derek Bok
is absolutely correct, but Harvard is not likely to accept this challenge
as a central part of its mission, and neither is Michigan, Wisconsin,
UC Berkeley, or any other comprehensive research university. And
they need not change. The institutions most likely to transform
themselves and thus to address the real problems of society are in
fact the metropolitan universities. For our faculties, students, and
communities, the metropolitan university model can be a
transforming vision because it speaks to what universities should
be and not to what they too frequently are or have been.

5. Does the metropolitan university mission provide a context
in which our publics can accurately gauge our success? Against whom
do we measure ourselves now? Is there a common understanding of
our successes? Are we credited appropriately for the accomplishments
of our faculty and students? Unfortunately, for many institutions,
the answer is no. Instead, we are compared to institutions with
remarkably different traditions and missions. How much more
satisfying it would be if we were evaluated on the basis of how well

we do what we say we intend to do rather than how we compare to a model or set of characteristics irrelevant to our own purposes.

Substantial progress must be made on two fronts in order to bring this about. In the first place, the defining mission of metropolitan universities must become more widely understood and accepted both inside and outside our institutions, by our own faculty, students, and administrators as well as by parents, business people, legislators, and community leaders. We must continue to strive toward greater recognition of the legitimacy, importance, and challenge of our task. Secondly, we must concentrate on defining and applying appropriate measures of excellence applicable to metropolitan universities. It is not enough to say that we should not be measured against inappropriate standards. We must agree among ourselves and then promulgate to our constituencies the standards that are appropriate to our mission. We need to clarify questions such as:

1. What are measures of educational success applicable to a student body diverse in background, preparation, and mode of attendance?

2. Can institutional standing be defined in terms of value added and outcomes rather than selectivity in admissions?

3. What are the criteria of quality of student life for a commuter campus with many part-time students of all ages?

4. What are definitions of scholarship and standards of excellence for the broad range of faculty activities needed to carry out the metropolitan university mission?

The model of the metropolitan university will not be successful until we develop valid answers to these and similar questions, and gain their acceptance within and outside the academic world.

Conclusion

Competition among institutions with similar missions can be positive and constructive and can ultimately produce "prestige" in the best sense. Prestige is neither irrelevant nor trivial. Prestige will build pride among our students, faculty, and ultimately, our community at large. With sufficient prestige, we can become the institution of choice for students from our community and for our local employers. And community pride ultimately translates into increased private investment in our institutions, as well as strong support within our state systems and legislatures. We will never be prestigious measured against somebody else's model. When a metropolitan university succeeds, satisfaction will come from achieving eminence based not on being a second- or third-tier copy of someone else's vision, but through excelling in one's own.

The metropolitan university model is by no means the only conceivable alternative to the comprehensive research university and liberal arts college. Institutions such as Miami University of Ohio have worked creatively on a "public ivy" image, which emphasizes undergraduate teaching within a university context. Ball State University, located far from any metropolitan area, has worked diligently to define and popularize the model of a comprehensive regional university reaching out to serve a widely dispersed population. But the metropolitan university movement is one that is well underway and is commanding the support of increasing numbers of institutions. A metropolitan university conference held in April 1990 led to the Declaration I mentioned at the beginning of this article. The *Metropolitan Universities* journal, now in its third year of publication, provides a medium through which those of us at similar institutions can share experiences and shape our definition. In April 1993, the University of North Texas hosted the second Metropolitan University Conference, at which we expanded our circle and enhanced the understanding of our model.

The metropolitan university model responds to public expectations for our institutions. By clarifying our purpose, we take an important first step toward defining productivity and quality and assessing our outcomes realistically and meaningfully in ways that ultimately restore the public trust in what we do. The metropolitan university can become the dominant success model of the twenty-first century for higher education.

NOTE: This article is based on a presentation at the National Meeting of the American Association of Higher Education in Chicago on April 6, 1992. The session was entitled "Aligning Missions with Public Expectations: The Case of Metropolitan Universities."

PART II

STUDENT AFFAIRS

INTRODUCTION

Metropolitan university students tend to be older, more diverse in terms of their socioeconomic backgrounds, more likely to be employed and to be commuters rather than campus residents. These characteristics exert unique pressures on the institutions. Unfortunately, these differences are not often understood by campus leaders, education policymakers, and legislators who are working on behalf of the higher education community.

The following articles provide an excellent overview of some of the major issues and challenges associated with student populations of metropolitan universities. Marguerite R. Barnett and Donald Phares discuss the environmental context within which planning for student needs takes place. Using the St. Louis region as a case study, the authors describe a general planning model for addressing student needs that provides a mechanism for institutional learning.

Patricia H. Murrell and Todd M. Davis, summarizing a substantial body of research and theory, describe the unique opportunities metropolitan universities have for contributing to the growth and development of adult learners. Taking advantage of these opportunities, however, requires appropriate missions, policies, and processes.

Commuter students make up a major portion of the student bodies on many metropolitan university campuses. All too often, however, their needs are overlooked or not well understood by administrators and faculty working to improve the quality of student life and learning. Barbara Jacoby summarizes some of the research on commuting students and argues that substantial institutional change is required to address the unmet needs of this large and growing student population.

Similarly, Ann S. Cole's article on "Student Services at Metropolitan Universities" cites a body of research that suggests that many student services are substantially underutilized. This underutilization is, in large measure, the result of ineffective organizational structures and delivery methodologies. Coles concludes, as does Jacoby, that strategic changes are needed in student service structures and processes.

Each of the articles in this section reinforces the view that appropriate planning and the capacity for institutional change are essential ingredients for meeting the service needs of contemporary metropolitan university students. The value of having empirical data on these issues also does not go unnoticed. More research, demonstration projects, and new models are needed as we seek better ways to make the educational opportunities on our campuses more accessible to the residents of our nation's metropolitan regions.

THE METROPOLITAN STUDENTS

Marguerite Ross Barnett and Donald Phares

Metropolitan universities of the twenty-first century face issues and challenges that distinguish it from its predecessor of the twentieth century. Unlike the more traditional role of the rural, public, or private university located in a city, the modern, public, metropolitan university must respond to vastly different challenges due to its diverse setting and rapidly evolving economic and demographic circumstances. It also must meet the different educational needs of urban students. The term "nontraditional," which has come into use to describe many urban, public university students, has taken on a very responsive ring.

We have witnessed during the past quarter century the emergence of a new breed of higher education institutions. Set in our nation's cities and serving the needs of an older, less affluent, largely minority, commuter student body, these institutions fill what previously was an educational void. They share several characteristics that integrate them into their community differently than the private and rural institutions that dominated American higher education well into the twentieth century.

First, as a nation of cities the majority of our population, business and economic activity is concentrated in the relatively small land area of urban America. The emergence and development of urban and more recently suburban areas provide a different milieu for higher education. Public institutions play a pivotal role in promoting and enhancing the economic development of our nation's cities and their residents. This role will become even more pronounced as we approach the year 2000 and the location, composition, and structure of our population and workforce evolve even further.

Second, due to the inherent diversity of urban areas, the metropolitan university must face the challenge of educating a much less traditional and vastly more diverse student population. No longer drawn primarily from the usual 18–21 age cohort, higher education is sought increasingly by older students. Many are the first generation in their families to go to college and enter the world of higher education with some trepidation and little family-based exposure. Others are seeking to upgrade their expertise and talents to remain competitive in a fast-changing labor force. Many seek education intermittently, transfer among institutions, and may take five or more years to complete their studies.

Third, a substantial proportion of urban residents are place-bound. They are geographically limited in the sense that existing family, work, and personal commitments keep them from seeking further education beyond a reasonable commuting distance from where they live or work. The provision of an appropriate program mix, locational proximity, and an accommodating atmosphere—thus allowing the place-bound student educational advancement—becomes a major challenge for the metropolitan university. Without accessibility within a reasonable distance and for a reasonable cost many, perhaps most, would not be able to avail themselves of the personal and economic benefits derived from higher education.

Access becomes a key operative word in the context of the metropolitan university; it assumes several forms. First, the geographical proximity that allows meaningful educational involvement for students who are not able to relocate to obtain either first-time or additional schooling. Second, financial access for potential students whose economic status precludes the high-cost education of a private school even though it may be located close by. Third, and crucial in many respects to individual student advancement and the overall economic development of a region, access to a diverse and responsive program mix that can accommodate a changing economy.

Metropolitan universities also have a role in providing opportunity for minority and disadvantaged students seeking to break the bondage of the unequal opportunities of the past. In this context, it must strive to move beyond passively providing courses and degrees; it must actively promote greater awareness of and involvement with diverse higher education offerings for these clientele groups. At the very least one can consider this duty as exercising good citizenship in the community; more fundamentally, it is crucial to the economic renewal and vitality of both our cities and nation. The promotion of educational opportunities for the disadvantaged can be an effective medium through which the fruits of our economic system may be more equitably distributed.

Fourth, because many of its students are already in the work force, the metropolitan university must seek to integrate more fully the classroom experience with the needs of the workplace. No longer is it possible, nor indeed does it make good sense, to view education as occurring distinctly in one arena and employment in another, with no meaningful connection or association between them. This is not to say that economics alone should dominate the educational experience; there is far more to an education than money. It does, however, recognize that most students at metropolitan universities are there to obtain the education and experience that will allow them to fit into a very competitive labor market.

Of course not every program offered by a metropolitan university should be workplace driven. Traditional degrees and programs will always constitute a curriculum core at any university. However, linking the knowledge derived from higher education directly to on-the-job experience by building on this core curriculum in conjunction with innovative and adaptive new programs, is far too valuable an opportunity to forego. The range of already existing examples is vast, the future holds even greater potential. Some general cases help to illustrate this point.

Students may use their classroom experience at work the very next morning, for example with computer technology or business applications such as accounting and management information systems. Student internship opportunities offered in cooperation with public and not-for-profit agencies provide invaluable on-the-job experience combined with weekly (or more frequent) classroom feedback and faculty guidance. Scientific businesses often work with faculty members and students in a laboratory setting. This may occur on campus or at the business. In the latter instance, students may have access to state-of-the-art equipment and technology not available elsewhere. Clearly all participants benefit. It should be noted that only in an urban area would the possibility of such a diversity of experience and opportunity be possible. Only at a public institution might it be affordable for so many.

Accommodating a Rapidly Changing Environment

The students, actual or potential, and the environment provide a context of diversity and change that challenges metropolitan universities. Social change; demographic shifts in population; an ever evolving economic environment locally, nationally, and globally—all provide the setting within which these universities must function and to which they must respond. The question is how to accommodate such change in a constructive manner.

There are two approaches: one is passive and reactive, the other is proactive. If a university adopts the former, it essentially avoids being a positive, directive influence for the community and simply responds. This option more closely models a traditional university and education. If the latter option is chosen, a university can become a new and directive force in the community and help to align the changing needs of metropolitan residents with a rapidly evolving environment. To fit in the latter, proactive mode, an institution must have a clearly articulated notion of where it has been, where it is now, and where it wants to be in the future.

Students are the focus of a university. Programs are the medium for meeting their educational needs. The faculty, research and support facilities, and staff are the linkage between the two. A careful meshing of these components leads to the accomplishment of a metropolitan university's educational objectives. They do not, however, mesh easily and automatically. This requires careful thought, consideration, and analysis; in a word, it mandates planning.

Planning for the metropolitan university must recognize the non-traditional nature of the student body and the diversity of the urban setting. The considerations and trade-offs are many and might manifest themselves in a large variety of specific programs. The key is that these programs, whatever is determined through the planning process, anticipate and accommodate educational needs by accounting for an area's student demographic profile; the local economic environment and its opportunities; and a balance across the spectrum of full- versus part-time, day versus evening, and on- versus off-campus offerings.

The following outlines a general set of planning steps for promoting greater success in using all facets of a university to promote improved educational outcomes. The critical elements throughout are awareness, clear articulation, involvement, direction, and institutional learning. A specific application of this general framework for a metropolitan university will follow.

The general framework is intended as an analytical guide to the formulation of clearly articulated plans for a university in the context of its mission. Naturally, any plan for an institution as complex as a metropolitan university will contain myriad, interrelated programs and activities. Each, however, needs to relate to an overall mission for the university and can be subject to the specific application of the general planning model described below.

What do you hope to accomplish? The first component of planning strategy is to state with precision those goals and objectives that are reasonable within a certain time frame and given expectations about resource constraints. Care must be exercised here to define goals and objectives that are within the realm of reason, that fit with institutional mission, and that are clearly stated. Being too grandiose can doom one to failure and waste resources that could have been put to better use elsewhere. The intent here is to alter the status quo, to improve, to move from the present status to some future state based on the knowledge necessary to induce the type of change desired. Conscious decisions must be made.

Who is the clientele to be served? The second step entails a clear identification of the group to be educated. Obviously, not every student at a university has the same needs. A strategy devoid of "for whom" at best lacks accuracy and direction and at worst is wasteful. A clear and precise definition of the clientele group allows a program to be more targeted, the outcomes to be more effective, and scarce resources to be most efficiently allocated. For example, the educational requirements of part-time, working students differ from those who attend school full time. Week-end and evening classes better serve the needs of the former group.

Choosing the best approach. Having specified goals and objectives and identified the clientele group, the next step is to determine how best to accomplish what has been proposed. The most serious mistake that can be made in any planning endeavor is to fail to weigh carefully all reasonable options. The educational landscape is rife with alternatives and is being enriched by rapid advances in communication and computer technology. For example, the instructional format can range from the large lecture class of 300 to individualized attention to self-learning. The instructional medium can vary from use of teaching assistants to junior and senior faculty, from hands-on experience to the video classroom, from simple verbal exchange to complex interactive computer learning systems. No one option is a panacea; each has strengths and weaknesses vis-a-vis an educational objective.

Careful expression of alternatives simply reflects the need to make quality choices. Each action has a cost associated with it in dollars, time, and energy. Each action also has associated benefits. Borrowing for a moment the economist's jargon, universities can, conceptually at least, do a cost/benefit analysis of available alternatives to decide which is most suitable. This does not mean always performing a complete technical analysis but at least engaging consciously in the analytical exercise of specifying ways in which something might be accomplished.

The choice of any one alternative has a built-in cost that is related to what might have been accomplished by doing something else (i.e., an opportunity cost). Being aware of this trade-off and choosing an

option based on quality information enhances the educational effectiveness for students and the efficiency of an institution.

Evaluating the outcomes of action. If planning were to stop at
this point, certainly more rationality would be built into the process,
but the ability to learn would have been foregone. Learning in this
context is derived from specifying an objective and identifying for whom
it is intended, reviewing and selecting an appropriate action after
careful consideration, and then observing what has happened as a
result. While the time frame for the assessment of outcomes will vary
with the type of program, universities must consciously inaugurate
the process with assessment as a stated objective. Feedback is important
and the key to truly creative planning and achieving an improved
student experience.

Each educational action taken will have an outcome. Awareness
of the outcome and the ability to examine it qualitatively and/or
quantitatively provide the necessary feedback for appropriate
evaluation. First, goals and objectives must be stated in a manner that
allows for evaluation. Unless this is done, determination of success or
failure becomes a predominantly subjective interpretation that may
or may not relate to any impact on students. Vagueness and broadly
sweeping statements can seriously muddy the planning waters and
undermine the wise use of limited funds. Second, be certain that the
outcome of the alternative selected to accomplish some objective can
be observed and measured. If not, then you have no way of knowing
what has been done or how well.

Admittedly, measurement of educational outcomes is an area rife
with conceptual and empirical pitfalls. However, to fail to monitor and
take outcomes into account, both intended and unintended, at best
relies on good fortune and at worst may allow for actions that might be
counterproductive to the stated educational objective. Do the outcomes
fit the goals and objectives? How much progress has been made? How
long will it take to get there? All are difficult but necessary questions
worthy of careful attention.

Developing institutional learning through feedback. The learning
process commences at this stage. The essence of good policy, educational or otherwise, is to be able to benefit from both success and failure.
We do this as individuals, albeit perhaps unconsciously; educational
institutions can likewise benefit. This is analogous to the marketplace
where the entrepreneur examines a balance sheet in terms of profit
and loss.

A loss signals that some action is necessary to correct for the failure
of past decisions, a failure to use scarce resources at your command

effectively. A profit, on the other hand, indicates a success and the need to examine whether or not to commit additional resources to existing activities that have proven to be successful. Both profit and loss are thus valuable signals calling for appropriate action.

In the planning arena, the terminology may change to success (i.e., profit) and failure (i.e., loss), but concern over outcomes, choices, effectiveness, and judicious use of scarce resources remains. Many questions surface. What is the link between specified goals and objectives and outcomes? Are the goals and objectives stated in a way that allows for meaningful evaluation? Are the goals reasonable? Is further pursuance a waste? Is the clientele group receiving what was intended? Is adequate progress in a timely manner being accomplished? Will some refinement of alternatives produce a better outcome?

The answer to each of these questions forms the essence of the learning process for a planning activity. Feedback from each provides the iterative context for developing, refining, and improving educational programs and experiences for students. It also provides the setting for institutional responsiveness to community and student needs and efficiency in use of limited funds for support of higher education.

An Application of the Planning Model

The University of Missouri–St. Louis typifies a metropolitan university. It is young, founded twenty-five years ago, and is the only public university in the heavily urbanized, Missouri portion of the St. Louis metropolitan area. It provides a full range of educational opportunities, from certificates to the Ph.D., for a large nontraditional student body. All students commute and many are place-bound to the St. Louis area for work or family reasons. The average student age is twenty seven. It enrolls the largest number of minority students of any higher education institution in the state of Missouri. About eighty-five percent of its current 33,000 graduates remain in the St. Louis area. Finally, many students are transfers from a community college or other university and may attend only intermittently, thus perhaps taking six years or more to complete a degree.

The St. Louis area provides an excellent model for developing programs that link the university with the students and their needs on the one hand and with the community on the other. This link creates an educational laboratory in which the social and economic richness of the city provides an opportunity for adaptive, creative, and educational endeavors. This can be viewed as the core of a metropolitan university's challenge.

To help refine and accomplish its educational mission, UM-St. Louis has developed a detailed planning process. From it has emerged a new focus and an associated array of new programmatic and degree offerings that respond to the educational needs of St. Louis area residents.

The key to the success of this process during its three-year history has three facets. First, it builds from the bottom up. Each year changes to existing programs are reviewed and new options proposed. This starts at the level of individual faculty or with staff involved directly with students and then moves to departmental or unit deliberations through a school or college and ultimately into the overall campus plan. At every stage proposals are carefully reviewed by department, school, or college, and campus committees and priorities are established prior to advancement to the next stage. Financial requirements are specified for a proposal and considered at each step in light of available resources.

Second, a formal planning document called *Vision for the 21st Century* is distributed. It describes on an annual basis the programs and activities that have emerged from the faculty and unit level, how available funds have been distributed, and to which components they have gone. Ownership by the campus community is thus enhanced since the actual use of funds is reported annually. Rather than just another report to gather dust on a shelf, this document explains to the members of the campus community where new resources have been applied and how this expenditure affects them.

This ties directly into the third facet. Planning and budgeting for the campus are formally linked and located in a separate unit that reports directly to the chancellor. Rather than planning occurring in one arena, or being widely dispersed without any coordination or connection to resource allocation, *Vision* shows the connection. As new funds become available, they are directed toward those areas providing the greatest promise, that build on existing strengths of the university and its community, and that fulfill student needs.

This formal link of budgeting with planning has a clear importance for rational campus ventures. It also allows for much more effective coordination of campus activities with budgetary mandates occurring elsewhere. *Vision* becomes the foundation from which the annual campus budget request is developed for submission to the University of Missouri system and then for the state Coordinating Board for Higher Education and the Missouri legislature. Unless an item is contained in the planning document, which means it has been through careful scrutiny at all campus levels, it cannot be included in a formal budget request for new funding in the next fiscal year. This adds another layer of both importance and credibility. Being included in *Vision* is not a pointless planning exercise, but a necessity for budgetary consideration.

This type of planning also has improved credibility on campus with faculty and students, within the university system, in the St. Louis business community, and with the legislature. It demonstrates that careful thought, analysis, and involvement provide the basis for all new programmatic development and budget requests.

Adaptive Planning and Innovative New Programs

The outcome of this comprehensive planning process has been an entirely new, programmatic focus for the campus, one concerned with articulating student requirements and with new efforts to address them. The overall plan has been placed under the rubric Partnerships for Progress, which is organized around three major project areas or programmatic groupings. While these project areas are identified separately, they are not independent; their content emerged from the overall planning process. They are clustered not to reflect how they deal with different facets of the campus educational mission, but according to how they interrelate with the overall campus mission.

The Partnerships for Progress rubric reflects the mission of the university and recognizes explicitly the needs of an urban area and its residents. Each priority in the plan (of which there are sixty-eight) relates to a broader theme, called a project. Each project, in turn, relates to the overall mission of the university.

Thus, the individual priority items identified by the planning process, the major project areas, and the overall partnerships theme all relate to each other and provide the programmatic structure through which the university serves the community. Full application of the general planning model must occur at the individual component level since any overall statement of a university's mission is necessarily too broad to be precisely evaluated.

The following paragraphs discuss the major project areas and provide examples of specific priority components within each area that has been identified through the planning process.

Project Compete identifies thirteen program areas that focus on different facets of promoting the talent and potential of St. Louis area young people at the elementary and secondary level. These program areas are designed to help prepare economically disadvantaged students for higher education, to offer in-service training to teachers through the School of Education, and to improve the training of teachers in mathematics and the sciences at the elementary and secondary level. Each of the thirteen areas represents another dimension to improving the training of elementary and secondary teachers and to promoting the active involvement of pre-college students with higher education.

One component, the Bridge Program, is a cooperative venture with local schools in the St. Louis area. It seeks to increase the number of students who complete high school and take college courses in math, science, and technology. It works both with students and teachers in area high schools to promote this objective. Thus, it offers a bridge between secondary and higher education. The program has been acclaimed nationally and receives financial support from major national corporations located in the St. Louis area, such as Monsanto, General Dynamics, Emerson Electric, and Anheuser-Busch.

The focus of Project Advance is different. It builds on existing strengths at UM-St. Louis and in the St. Louis community by identifying new programs to enhance science, technology, and management skills. Thirty-six such areas were specified in the most recent plan. An excellent example of planning responding to local needs is a proposed new undergraduate engineering program. This builds on the fact that seventy percent of all engineers in Missouri live or work in the St. Louis area. It will make available affordable public education in engineering (not now available) to meet future needs, as well as offering further educational opportunities for those already in the profession.

Other notable facets of this project are: a Ph.D. degree in biology offered cooperatively with a world-class research facility, the Missouri Botanical Gardens; a wider range of offerings in the health professions—which builds on St. Louis's status as a major medical center; a cooperative physics partnership with the St. Louis Science Center; and a cooperative physics Ph.D. degree offered with another University of Missouri campus located at Rolla.

This segment of the *Vision* plan responds programmatically to the fact that UM-St. Louis is the largest supplier of professionally trained personnel for the St. Louis metropolitan area. It looks to broaden the scope and depth of the university's response to filling this demand.

The third area, Project Succeed, works to promote greater collaboration among education, industry, and business in advancing the economic well-being of the St. Louis region and its residents. The eight program areas identified in this portion of the plan promote access to education for nontraditional students and establish research centers to better link the university, including its faculty and students, with the community. They include a Center for Science and Technology to work with the almost 40,000 scientists and engineers in the St. Louis area and enhancement of the Evening College to better accommodate the schedules and locational needs of nontraditional, working students. Also, the university's Continuing Education Extension division serves 52,000 students each year by providing credit and noncredit courses throughout the metropolitan area. It is one of the largest such programs in the nation.

Planning and the Metropolitan University's Mission

Fulfilling the role of the modern metropolitan university requires the ability to adapt and respond to an ever changing environment and diverse student needs. A comprehensive planning process formally linked with budget allocation decisions has served to promote efficiency in accomplishing carefully articulated educational objectives. The components of a general planning model and an application of it at UM-St. Louis have already been described.

While the plan will continue to evolve in form, coverage, and substance, a great deal of progress has been made. New degrees, programs, and activities already in place enhance the nontraditional student's access to quality, affordable higher education. Other endeavors identified in *Vision* will be implemented or expanded as new funding becomes available. Faculty involvement and commitment has grown through the clear articulation of needs combined with visible funding outcomes. The community views the university's role more clearly as a result of seeing the yearly *Visions* plan and recognizing the work that goes into preparing it. As a result, far greater support has been forthcoming from corporate St. Louis, private donors, and alumni of UM-St. Louis. While the time and effort expended in developing and implementing the planning process have been substantial, the returns to the university and its students and faculty have also been impressive.

SUGGESTED READINGS

Grobman, Arnold. *Urban State Universities: An Unfinished Agenda*. New York: Praeger, 1988.

Lisensky, Robert and Dennis Jones. *Linking Planning with Budgeting*. Boulder: NCHEMS Management Services, Inc.

Lynton, Ernest A. and Sandra E. Elman. *New Priorities for the University*. San Francisco: Jossey-Bass, 1987.

Shirley, Robert. *Strategic Planning in the Higher Education Setting*. Boulder: NCHEMS Management Services, Inc.

University of Missouri-St. Louis. *Vision for the 21st Century: Five-Year Plan*. St. Louis: University of Missouri, 1987 & 1988.

ADAPTING THE INSTITUTION TO MEET THE NEEDS OF COMMUTER STUDENTS

Barbara Jacoby

Commuter students—defined as those who do not live in institution-owned housing—comprise over eighty percent of the students in American colleges and universities today. Nevertheless, the residential tradition of higher education continues to impede effective institutional response to their presence. Educators have assumed that commuters are like resident students except that they live off campus and that similar curricular and cocurricular offerings are equally appropriate for all students. This assumption has not served commuter students well. Major studies have identified commuters as being at greater risk of attrition, and recent higher education reform reports have expressed the need to improve the quality of the educational experience for commuter students at all types of institutions.

Commuter students attend virtually every institution of higher education. Their numbers include full-time students who live at home with their parents, as well as fully employed adults who live with their spouses and/or children and attend college part time. Commuters may reside near the campus or far away; they commute by private vehicle, public transportation, walking, and bicycle. They may represent a small minority of students at a private, residential liberal arts college or the entire population of a community college or metropolitan university.

In the last decade or so, the definition of commuter students as all students who do not live in institution-owned housing has been adopted as the preferred one by the National Clearinghouse for Commuter Programs, a number of key professional associations within higher education, and the authors of recent higher education reform reports. Despite the diverse nature of the population, the use of the broad definition of commuter student promotes recognition of the substantial

51

core of needs and concerns shared by all commuter students. It also encourages institutions to regard their commuter student population as an aggregate for the purpose of assuring that they receive their fair share of attention and resources.

American higher education is characterized by the diversity of its institutions and students. Predicted enrollment declines in the late 1970s and 1980s have not occurred because of the attendance of an increasingly diverse body of students. As a result, the average student today is much different from the stereotype of a full-time student, eighteen to twenty-two years old, financially supported by parents, and living away from home: this description now applies to less than a fifth of those enrolled in colleges and universities.

Fifty-four percent of all college students live off campus, not with a parent(s), while twenty-seven percent live with a parent(s). The percentage of traditional age, full-time residential students will continue to decline during the coming years. The number of high school graduates is expected to decrease twenty-five percent by 1994, and higher education enrollment of suburban, eighteen to twenty-four-year-old, full-time, white, middle-class students will decline dramatically.

At the same time, enrollments of adults and part-time students have increased dramatically. Over forty percent of college students are twenty-five years of age or older. By 1992, more than one-half of the total college population will be over twenty-five, and twenty percent will be over thirty-five. Related to the age trend, as well as to the escalating costs of higher education, two-fifths of the more than twelve million individuals enrolled in colleges and universities in 1985 attended part time. By 1990, over half of all students were enrolled on a part-time basis.

The composition of students in higher education will continue to change in other ways. Over fifty percent of all college students are women. Enrollments of American Indian, Asian, black, and Hispanic students have risen substantially in the last twenty years, although not at a rapid enough rate to reflect their proportion of the American population. Projections indicate that by the year 2000 more than forty percent of public school students in the United States will be minority children and that the college-age population will be one-third minority.

The vast majority of the students in these increasing populations are and will continue to be commuters, for reasons of age, lifestyle, family circumstances, and financial necessity. Students with spouses, children, and/or full-time jobs are not likely to live in residence halls. This also applies to many students from ethnic cultures which place the highest value on the maintenance of the family unit. And, given that high proportions of minority and low-income students attend community colleges and metropolitan universities which generally do not have residence facilities, it is clear that the opportunity to live in a residence hall is not equally allocated among American college students by ethnicity and income level.

The Student-as-Commuter: Common Needs and Concerns

No matter what commuter students' educational goals are, where they live, or what type of institution they attend, the fact that they commute to college has a profound influence on the nature of their educational experience. For residential students, home and campus are synonymous; for commuter students, the campus is a place to visit, sometimes for very short periods.

To denote the essential character of the relationship of the commuter student with the institution of higher education, the use of the term student-as-commuter is preferred. Although the students themselves are extraordinarily diverse, a common core of needs and concerns of the student-as-commuter can be identified:

Transportation issues. The most obvious concerns commuter students share are those related to transportation to campus: parking, traffic, fixed travel schedules, inclement weather, car maintenance, fares, and finding alternative means of transportation. No matter the mode, commuting is demanding in terms of time and energy. Frequently, commuter students concentrate their classes into blocks and have little free time to spend on campus. Convenience of curricular offerings, services, and programs is of paramount importance.

Multiple life roles. For commuters of all ages, being a student is only one of several important and demanding roles. Most commuter students work; many have responsibilities for managing households and for caring for children, siblings, or older relatives. By necessity, commuters select their campus involvements carefully. It is critical that complete information about campus options and opportunities reaches them in a timely manner. The *relative value* of an activity is a major factor in their decision to participate.

Integrating support systems. The support networks for commuter students generally exist away from campus: parents, siblings, spouses, children, employers, coworkers, and friends in the community. Each semester, students must negotiate with family, employers, and friends to establish priorities, responsibilities, and time allotments. These negotiations are more difficult if significant others are not knowledgeable about the challenges and opportunities of higher education. It is important for institutions to provide opportunities for these individuals to learn about and to participate appropriately in the life of the campus.

Developing a sense of belonging. Commuter students often lack a sense of belonging, of "feeling wanted" by the institution. Some institutions fail to provide basic facilities such as lockers and lounge areas which enable students to put down "roots." In many cases, institutions do not provide adequate opportunities for commuter students to develop relationships with faculty, staff, and fellow students. Individuals rarely feel connected to a place where they do not have significant relationships. Students who do not have a sense of belonging complain about the "supermarket" or "filling station" nature of their collegiate experience.

Effects of the Residential Tradition of Higher Education

Residence halls have been an essential aspect of American higher education since its earliest days. The residential tradition has continued to shape the development of attitudes, policies, and practices, even at predominantly commuter institutions.

In the twenty years between 1955 and 1974, the number of college students more than tripled, expanding from 2.5 million to 8.8 million. To handle this explosion of students, the United States doubled its college and university facilities. Hundreds of new two-year community colleges and metropolitan universities were created, and many existing ones experienced substantial growth. Only 2.3 million students were placed in institution-controlled housing in 1980 when the number of college students was over 12 million. The greatest portion of the growth in the student population was due to commuter students.

However, throughout the 1960s and 1970s, the response to this dramatic increase in the numbers of commuter students was construction of new colleges and universities and expansion of others, based heavily on models of the past. "Staffing patterns, scheduling arrangements, annual cycles of activity, and areas of expertise for student personnel professionals continued to be established for traditional age, full-time, mostly on-campus" students (Schlossberg et al. 1989, 228). Ironically, this was true even in community colleges and 100 percent commuter four-year institutions.

While some predominantly commuter institutions have provided courses during evening and weekend hours, large parking lots and access to public transportation, and lounges and eating facilities, there are no significant responses to the special backgrounds of many commuting students, no attempts to deal with the difficulties they have in discovering and connecting with academic programs and extracurricular activities suitable to them, and no solutions to the difficulties they face in building new relationships with students and faculty members and with the institution itself.

Administrators have accepted "the simplistic solution of eliminating the residential facilities and maintaining essentially the same educational programs and processes" (Chickering 1974, 3). Surprisingly few differences have been found between student services at commuter institutions and those at traditional residential institutions. Metropolitan universities suffer from what has been described by Richardson and Bender as "an overvaluing of traditional ways at the expense of local community needs." Community colleges have adopted "the same procedures, facilities, and approaches to teaching and learning that had characterized four-year colleges and universities since the turn of the century" (Chickering 1974, 1).

The majority of today's faculty members earned their undergraduate and graduate degrees at traditional residential institutions. The time-honored system of instruction with 120 credit hours of coursework earned between the ages of eighteen and twenty-two is a formula that is ingrained in faculty well before they take charge of a classroom. Most faculty members seem to expect the institutions at which they teach to be similar to those they attended and, therefore, impose the values and goals of those institutions (e.g., total immersion in the intellectual community) on their new environments. The image of a residential institution is often "perpetuated by the memories and experiences of faculty, staff, alumni, and others long after a shift to a predominantly commuter student population has taken place" (Stewart 1988).

Many administrators and faculty still have not adjusted to the fact that students frequently attend part time and have job and family responsibilities. It may be difficult for some professors and administrators to accept what may seem to them to be a lesser academic commitment. Many of them have acquired from their own experience as students deeply rooted ideas about higher learning that may hinder their ability to respond to new circumstances. For that reason faculty sometimes shun assignments to an urban campus. And commuters, both of traditional-age and older, continue to be thought of as apathetic or uninterested in campus life.

Institutional Self-Assessment

A fundamental responsibility of institutions of higher education is to conduct research and evaluation to determine to what extent the educational goals and needs of students are being met. Whether an institution has a small number of commuters or serves a 100 percent commuter population, there are basic questions that must be answered if the institution is to understand who its commuter students really are. It has already been established that commuter students are extraordinarily diverse and that the nature of the commuter population is unique to each institution. In addition, the complexity of commuter students' lifestyles and the multiple demands upon their time and energies requires that a wide range of information be gathered if the nature of their relationship to higher education is to be understood. Knowing the answers to the following basic questions will enable institutions to take the first step in dealing with the key issues related to the educational experience of the student-as-commuter.

Questions to Ask About the Student-as-Commuter

1. What percentage of the student population are commuters?

2. How many students fall in the traditional college age range of eighteen to twenty-two years old? How many are between twenty-two and twenty-five? Between twenty-five and thirty-five? Between thirty-five and forty-five? Between forty-five and fifty-five? Over fifty-five?

3. What are the percentages of students by sex? By ethnic background?

4. How many students attend full time versus part time? When are they on campus: How many days? Day or evening? All day or an hour daily? Weekends only?

5. What is the socioeconomic status of students and their families?

6. What is the level of education of their parents? Other family members and peers?

7. How do students finance their education? Are they dependent on their parents or spouses? Are they financially independent? Do they receive financial aid?

8. What is their employment status? Do they work full time or part time? How many hours per week? On or off campus?

9. What about family status? Do students live with their parents? What is their marital status? Do they have children? Other family responsibilities?

10. Where do students live? With relatives, roommates, or alone? In what type of housing? Are they responsible for rent or mortgage payments?

11. How far do students live from campus?

12. What are their modes of transportation?

13. Do students come from the local area? From other parts of the state? From out of state? From foreign countries?

14. Why do students choose to attend this institution?

15. What are their educational goals?

16. What are the relative academic abilities of commuter students? Do they have significant remedial needs?

Frequently, much of the data required to answer these questions already exist at the institution and are available through admissions, financial aid, registration, and institutional research offices. Standardized reports provided to the institution from such sources as the College Board, the American College Testing Program, and the Cooperative Institutional Research Program can supplement data collected by the institution. Where data do not exist, the addition of key variables to various data collection methods that are already in place can often provide what is needed. More and more institutions are conducting separate demographic and descriptive studies of their commuter, part-time, and/or adult students. The National Clearinghouse for Commuter Programs maintains an active file of instruments and reports from these studies.

The institution's climate and self-image; the environment inside and outside the classroom; and the facilities, services, and programs should be thoroughly examined from the perspective of all groups in the student body profile. For example, a residential college with a relatively small percentage of commuter students will want to ask itself the question posed by Ernest Boyer in his report *College: The Undergraduate Experience in America:* "Are commuters simply tolerated because they help pay the bills or are they full partners on the campus?" A large university with a high proportion of full-time, eighteen- to twenty-two-year-old commuters will want to determine whether the quality of the educational experience they receive is comparable to that of residential students. And a 100 percent commuter institution should assess whether all students—be they full- or part-time, adult or traditional age, day or evening—are served equally well by all aspects of the institutions.

The following is a proposed list of questions institutions should ask themselves in assessing whether all their students benefit equitably from the institution's offerings. Each institution should adapt the questions to reflect the profile of its student body.

Questions to Ask About the Institutional Environment

1. Does the institution present itself accurately in its mission statement and its publications? For example, do publications include photographs representative of all types of students and student lifestyles?

2. Do recruiters make outreach efforts in the local area beyond high schools (e.g., community centers, primary employment sites)? Are pre-admissions publications available at these sites and others, such as public libraries?

3. Does the admissions office utilize a system of evaluation (other than high school grades and SAT scores) that reflects the life status of a wide variety of prospective students (e.g., noncognitive measures, interviews, learning, and experience acquired through work and volunteer service)?

4. Do articulation policies exist between the institution and its "feeder" colleges which enable a smooth transition for transfer students?

5. Are orientation activities appropriate for all students? Are various orientation options available (e.g., weekday, evening, and weekend programs; individualized formats; extended orientation courses; video cassettes for home use)?

6. Do scheduling policies accommodate all students, including those who need "twilight" (4 to 6 P.M.), evening, or weekend classes as well as classes that meet once or twice a week (rather than four times)? Are all types of classes (e.g., upper-level, laboratory, and language) offered in alternative formats?

7. Do faculty consider commuter students' lifestyles when structuring assignments (e.g., offering alternatives to group projects or projects that require extensive time in campus libraries and computer facilities)? Do they integrate out-of-class learning and experiences into the curriculum?

8. Does the institution have a program to identify students having difficulty and offer them assistance? Are different kinds of remedial programs readily available (e.g., evening and weekend learning center hours, computer-assisted programs, peer tutoring, materials for home use)?

9. Are academic advising and career counseling services appropriate for students at various points in their lives rather than for traditional-age students only?

10. Does the composition of the faculty and staff represent a wide variety of backgrounds, age groups, cultural experiences, educational institutions, and geographic origins?

11. Do faculty and staff selection processes seek individuals with knowledge of and experience in working with diverse student populations? Are development programs regarding the demographics of the student body and their implications offered to all levels of faculty and staff?

12. Are support groups available for students who may need them (e.g., women, single parents, veterans, individuals experiencing major

life transitions)?

13. Is financial aid distributed equitably to all students (e.g., adults, part-time students, students living with parents, students living independently)?

14. Are there plentiful work-study and other on-campus, part-time jobs that enable students to develop meaningful connections with the institution and with their academic programs?

15. If "traditional" services and activities are provided at no cost to users, are other services and activities (e.g., child care, family-oriented activities) offered on the same basis? Are mandatory student fees used equitably to respond to the interests and needs of all students?

16. Are social, cultural, educational, and intramural sports programs and activities appropriate for all students? Are they scheduled at a variety of times to accommodate students' varied schedules (e.g., lunchtime, early afternoon, evenings, weekends, between classes)?

17. Do institutional administrators and planners keep abreast of and participate appropriately in community decision-making on behalf of commuter students regarding zoning, parking, housing, public transportation, employment? Does the institution provide assistance with students' transportation and housing needs?

18. Is child care offered during day, evening, and weekend classes as well as during cocurricular programs and events? On a drop-in basis? Are referrals made to child care providers in the community?

19. Are balanced meals and snacks available at times and locations convenient for all students?

20. Is parking adequate? Are parking lots for evening students well-lighted and located near classroom buildings?

21. Are adequate study areas, lounges, and lockers provided at convenient locations throughout the campus, particularly in classroom buildings?

22. Are recreational facilities (including lockers and showers) accessible to students at times convenient for them?

23. Are advisers, counselors, and other administrators on "flex-time" schedules so that they are available whenever students are on campus?

24. If the institution has off-campus centers, are student services available there?

25. Can students transact business with the institution (e.g., registration, bill payment) via telephone, computer, and/or mail?

26. Is there a single place where students can go to get accurate information about the institution's policies and procedures, academic and other programs and resources, as well as referrals to appropriate offices or departments?

27. Is there a telephone number that students can call for information about the hours of facilities and services (i.e., libraries, laboratories, tutoring)?

28. Are commuter institutions, which emphasize flexible scheduling of classes and services to meet the needs of part-time students, at a disadvantage under state funding formulas that are based on full-time enrollment?

The process of institutional self-appraisal is nearly as important as the product in confronting negative stereotypes about students and faulty assumptions and about the quality and appropriateness of the institution's programs and services. In order for the process to be most effective, a broad representation of members of the campus community should participate by collecting student data, evaluating their own efforts on behalf of students, and assessing the institution as a whole.

Recommendations for Adapting the Institution

Considerable change would be necessary in most institutions to create an optimal educational environment for their commuter students. Institutional responses to the student-as-commuter generally have been fragmented attempts to deal with immediate, specific problems rather than long-range and comprehensive.

Because each institution is a unique combination of students, faculty, staff, mission, history, curriculum, and environment, it is impossible to provide a blueprint for change. It is the responsibility of each institution to determine its own plan of action using the self-assessment framework provided. Nevertheless, it is possible to identify some key elements of a comprehensive institutional response to the student-as commuter:

1. The institution should modify its mission statement, if necessary, to express a clear commitment to the quality of the educational experience of all its students, and should have this change endorsed by its governing board.

2. The president, vice-presidents, deans, and all other top administrators should frequently and consistently articulate the institution's commitment to the student-as-commuter when dealing with faculty, staff, students, the governing board, alumni, community members, and others.

3. The institution should engage in regular, comprehensive data

collection about its students and their experiences with the institution.

4. Regular evaluation processes should be put in place to assess whether the institution's programs, services, facilities, and resources equitably address the needs of all students.

5. Steps should be taken to identify and rectify stereotypes or inaccurate assumptions held by members of the campus community about commuter students, and to assure that commuter students are treated as full members of the campus community.

6. Long- and short-range administrative decisions regarding resources, policies, and practices should consistently include the perspective of the student-as-commuter.

7. Quality practices should be consistent throughout the institution as students' experiences in one segment have a profound impact upon their experiences in other segments and upon their perception of their educational experience as a whole.

8. Faculty should recognize that their classroom experience and interactions play the major role in determining the overall quality of commuter students' education.

9. Curricular and cocurricular offerings should complement one another, and steps should be taken to ensure that students understand the interrelationship of the curriculum and the cocurriculum.

10. Top-level administrators should actively encourage the various campus units to work together to implement change on behalf of the student-as-commuter.

11. Technology should be used to the fullest extent possible to improve the institution's ability to communicate with its students and to streamline its administrative processes.

12. Executive officers and governing board members should actively work towards assuring that commuter students and commuter institutions are treated fairly in federal, state, and local decision-making (e.g., student financial aid, institutional funding formulas).

As the students pursuing higher education continue to become more diverse, and as students from diverse backgrounds attend a wider range of institutions, an understanding of the student-as-commuter and of the nature of commuter students' relationships to higher education is required to bring about necessary changes. In the current climate, institutions of higher education are seeking "excellence" and are being held accountable for translating excellence into educational outcomes for all students. Institutional change requires substantial effort and commitment; however, failure to respond effectively and comprehensively to the needs and educational goals of the student-as-commuter will make excellence impossible to achieve.

SUGGESTED READINGS

Chickering, Arthur W. *Commuting Versus Resident Students.* San Francisco: Jossey-Bass, 1974.

_____. *The Modern American College.* San Francisco: Jossey-Bass, 1981.

Cross, K. Patricia. *Adults as Learners.* San Francisco: Jossey-Bass, 1981.

Jacoby, Barbara. *The Student As Commuter: Developing a Comprehensive Institutional Response.* ASHE-ERIC Higher Education, Report No. 7. Washington, D.C.: Association for the Study of Higher Education, 1989.

Jacoby, Barbara, and Dana Burneft, eds. *NASPA Journal,* special issue on commuter students (Summer 1986).

Jones, John D., and Jeffrey Damron. *Student Affairs Programs at Universities in Urban Settings.* Washington, D.C.: National Association of State Universities and Land Grant Colleges, 1987.

National Clearinghouse for Commuter Programs. *Commuter Students: References and Resources.* College Park, MD: NCCP, 1987.

_____. *Serving Commuter Students: Examples of Good Practice.* College Park, MD: NCCP, 1989.

Richardson, Richard C., Jr., and Louis W. Bender. *Students in Urban Settings.* ASHE-ERIC Higher Education Report No. 6. Washington, D.C.: Association for the Study of Higher Education, 1985.

Schlossberg, Nancy K., Ann Q. Lynch, and Arthur W. Chickering. *Improving Higher Education Environments for Adults.* San Francisco: Jossey-Bass, 1989.

Stewart, Sylvia S., and Penny Rue. "Commuter Students: Definition and Distribution." In *Commuter Students: Enhancing Their Educational Experiences,* edited by Sylvia S. Stewart. New Directions for Student Services, No. 24. San Francisco: Jossey-Bass, 1983.

PLACES OF COMMUNITY FOR ADULTS

Patricia H. Murrell and Todd M. Davis

Adults who enroll in a metropolitan university are simultaneously engaged in many ways with their city. Hence an institution fully committed to working with adult learners will not only provide a better education for these students but will also have an immediate impact on the community in which they live. However, the settings and methods conducive to adult learning differ from those appropriate to traditional younger students. A metropolitan university must adapt in several ways if it is to serve the educational needs of adults.

Most higher education institutions had their first encounter with adult students with the return of veterans in the 1940s. Few, however, made any special concessions or arrangements beyond setting up veterans' affairs offices and, in some instances, providing housing for married students. More recently, as enrollment of students in the traditional age bracket declined, colleges and universities took steps to attract adults as a stop-gap to fill emptying classrooms. However, most efforts were either aimed at helping older individuals to adapt to the ways of the institution, rather than changing the institution's ways of dealing with them, or consisted of adding on separate adult degree programs outside the institutional mainstream. Neither of these approaches is sufficient to serve the needs of adult learners.

Adult students enter the university with their own life histories and with interests and attitudes shaped by their experiences. The extent to which the academic program can tap this rich lode of experience and enable adults to make meaning of it through new learning determines the success of metropolitan universities in serving these students, and, thereby, their community.

A substantial body of research and theory exists which can assist in that task. Life cycle theories indicate successive phases in the ways in which individuals think of themselves and are motivated to pursue further education. Developmental stage theories describe intellectual growth and changes in the manner of learning. Experiential learning theories explore the learning process itself. These theories not only give faculty and administrators a framework for the design of a learning environment responsive to the nature of adult learners, but also help to define the very purpose and desired outcomes of the educational experience. New information about teaching and learning enables faculty members to present material in ways that dramatically affect learning outcomes. While each of these perspectives is valuable in and of itself, it is when they are used in concert that the most potent learning experiences can be provided for adult students and the impact of their university experience can be maximized.

Life Cycle Theory

Life cycle theory uses chronological age as a basis for describing and explaining predictable individual changes and responses to events and external relationships. Patricia Cross, in her seminal book, *Adults as Learners,* has utilized the work of a number of theorists to provide a synthesis of age-related marker events, psychic tasks, and attitudes that are helpful in observing periods of stability and transitions in the life cycle.

1. From eighteen to twenty-two years of age, individuals begin to separate from their families and become self-governing.

2. From twenty-three to twenty-eight, they fashion an initial life structure, begin to think of themselves as grown up, and construct a dream or vision.

3. From twenty-nine to thirty-four, they reevaluate their life structure, struggle to succeed, and project long-range goals.

4. From thirty-seven to forty-two, they face mortality, reappraise marriage and life work and discard dependent connections to spouse and mentor.

5. From forty-five to fifty-five, they have increased feelings of adequacy and self-awareness, reestablish family ties, and enjoy their choices and life styles.

6. From fifty-seven to sixty-four, they accept and adjust to the aging process and become clearer about the dreams they still wish to attain.

7. From sixty-five on, they experience increased acceptance of self, and disengage from many external relationships and ties.

Clearly, these descriptions are global and do not account for all of the variations in lifestyles and attitudes. However, an understanding of the modal developmental characteristics associated with age can be valuable in determining not only adult students' motivation for pursuing higher education, but also how the institution can best assist the adult student.

Developmental Stage Theory

Stage theories attempt to plot the progressions or changes in how people think as they experience and try to cope with the challenges of their lives. Each stage has particular intellectual tasks and ways of thinking to be mastered before a person can move to the next stage; however, and in life cycle theory, issues are not resolved "once and for all" and must be revisited as crises occur.

William Perry's theory of intellectual and ethical development offers one description of the stages through which people move as their ways of thinking become more inner-directed and complete, and how the decision-making process is affected. It represents the way individuals process information and interpret the world outside of themselves. Each stage represents a qualitatively different way of thinking and a restructuring in the direction of increasing complexity.

As persons mature, they find their way of thinking increasingly inappropriate and at odds with their experience and the learning derived from it. The resulting disequilibrium and dissonance require a transition to the next stage. These transitions are important to the understanding of the developmental process. Writing in *The Modern American College,* Perry suggests that stages may be only resting points along the way and that development is all transition. The stages Perry proposes are: dualism, multiplicity, relativism, and commitment.

In the first stage, *dualism,* truth and authority are so integrally linked that people assume that what is said is true simply because the source is authoritative. In their systematic search for authority, dualistic thinkers place little value on the opinions of their peers and, when presented with two opposing views, will ask, "Which one is correct?" They often have trouble accepting the professor's response that there is no fully agreed upon answer to that question. Movement from early dualism begins when students see that different authorities give different answers to the same questions.

In the early part of the next stage, *multiplicity,* people believe that the world of knowledge is divided into that which is known and that which is not known. As they come to experience more and more unanswered questions, they recognize diversity of opinions as legitimate. Because they lack the ability to discriminate between opinions as a function of context and particular circumstance, they are unable to make sound judgements as to which is better. Since there are so many legitimate ways to look at an issue, there is little concern for substantiating the one held. Students at this level frequently equate quality with the quantity of work done or the effort expended. Thus a ten-page paper should not receive an "A" while a fifteen-page paper earns a "C."

In the latter part of multiplicity, learners become more independent, self-directed, and self-reflective; peers become credible sources of information; and the teacher is seen less as the final authority and more as a resource. Learners are able to examine events in their lives and to engage in "self-processing."

The move to *relativism* occurs as the locus of control shifts from external to internal, and the self assumes legitimacy in the learning process and in defining reality. While not egocentric, learners experience the self as at the center, dealing with a variety of issues, challenges, and problems. They recognize that while everything is relative it is not equally valid. Persons at this stage are able to consider the thinking of others, experience empathy, and thus understand them more fully.

The last stage is *commitment*. Individuals at this stage are characterized by an ability to deal with paradox, to make decisions in the absence of clear or complete information, and to tolerate ambiguity. They know that commitments do not actually settle things or make them easier, and may generate additional options and present new and difficult questions. Commitments often mean leaving behind parts of the self that are familiar and comfortable.

In the latter part of this stage, persons carry out multiple roles, accept meaningful decision-making opportunities, and engage in reflection about their activities and their lives and the meaning contained therein. They are willing to take on risks to their self-esteem in an effort to reach their full potential. Their ability to think contextually gradually expands to more areas, and they experience themselves as "in process."

While Perry's original work was done with traditional-age students, few of us have difficulty recognizing ourselves and our adult students in each of the categories. Even those who typically function at higher levels may revert to earlier ways of thinking as they enter an unfamiliar environment, and others may return to stages that worked for them in prior experiences with school. Perry suggests that intellectual growth in the adult years is possible if the proper stimulation is present in an appropriate environment.

The challenge comes in designing learning activities and environments that capitalize on learners' present stage and assist them in moving to greater levels of complexity. Students move from one position to the next as a result of confrontation with social and intellectual challenges they encounter or in a planned instructional program. However, faculty members may not be ready or able to teach with the epistemic flexibility characteristic of contextual relativism. How faculty members' level of development affects the design of courses and teaching strategies is important and suggests that professional development programs that address this topic should be included in a metropolitan university's response to adult students.

Both life cycle theory and developmental stage theory seem to stress a major point for metropolitan universities interested in serving adult learners: that individuals recycle through earlier stages and ways of thinking when they encounter new, unfamiliar, or stressful situations. Growth and development do not occur in a linear, hierarchical pattern but rather in an upward spiral fashion, with retracing and relearning taking place as persons find themselves at odds with where they want to be.

Experiential Learning Theory

The work of David Kolb provides an understandable, usable framework for looking at and teaching and learning with adult students and designing activities that enable them to move to greater complexity in their thinking and behavior. He describes learning as a four-step process in which learners have immediate *concrete experience,* involving themselves fully in it, and then reflecting on the experience from different perspectives. From these *reflective observations,* learners engage in *abstract conceptualization* where they develop generalizations that help them integrate their observations into sound theories or principles. Finally, learners use these generalizations as guides to further action, or *active experimentation,* and try out what they have learned in new more complex situations. They then have further concrete experiences, and the cycle begins again, but this time the learner operates at a more complex level.

These four learning modes serve as a guide in the design of learning activities, providing an excellent way to utilize the experiences adults bring to the classroom.

1. Prior experiences may be recalled, or activities may be designed that involve the learner in new experiences either physically or emotionally.

2. Structured small group discussions, reflective papers, or journals provide opportunities to encourage students to reflect on their experiences by making connections with others' perspectives.

3. New information presented through print or lectures engages learners in abstract conceptualization and provides the bases from which to develop hypotheses and principles.

4. Trying out or applying these principles or theories in problem-solving situations completes the cycle with active experimentation.

While experiential learning theory holds great promise for professors working with adult students, it is also beneficial for students themselves. Most adult students have never had the opportunity to discuss or think about how they learn. Learning about their learning can be empowering for them as they come to understand not only their roles as learners in a metropolitan university setting but in their daily lives as well. They are thus encouraged to become life-long learners, to trust their own experience, to link knowing and doing, and to recognize that learning is the process by which growth and development occur.

The Response of Metropolitan Universities to Adult Students

How can the theoretical perspectives on life cycle, developmental theory, and experiential learning inform the metropolitan university's response to adult students? How can this knowledge be brought to bear on individual development as well as contribute to the collective well-being? Their purpose, their policies, and their practices must change if metropolitan universities are to engage and educate adults for civic and economic leadership in the twenty-first century. There must be a commitment to changing the institution and adapting it to adult learners rather than trying to change adults and force them into institutional structures designed for traditional-age students.

Development programs that focus on life cycle, adult development theory, and experiential learning theory can help faculty and administrators to see themselves as adult learners and thus be more empathic in their understanding of their students as adult learners. Faculty members who are self-aware and deliberate about their own growth and development are more apt to be concerned about the growth and development of their students.

Parker Palmer in his book, *To Know as We Are Known*, suggests three characteristics of the institution that seem to respond to the theoretical perspectives presented and that are especially critical if adult students are to learn and derive maximum value from metropolitan universities. The characteristics are: openness, boundaries, and hospitality.

The first, *openness,* speaks to the accessibility of the institution not only in admissions requirements and processes but in flexibility in scheduling. Provisions made for students in remedial and developmental studies, in recognition for prior learning and awarding credit where appropriate and in honoring work and life experiences in class, help to convey an atmosphere of openness. Accessibility of materials, not only in terms of physical availability, but also in terms of psychological accessibility in the sense that they are meaningful against the backdrop of experience the learners bring, is also essential to an open environment. It also speaks to acceptance of the students and a willingness to assist them in overcoming barriers such as fears that may be the result of previously unsuccessful or unpleasant encounters with formal education or fear of the unknown. A classroom that frees learners from excessive anxiety is necessary if learners are to experience achievement they find personally significant.

Openness also allows learners to be honest about their motivation for attending the university. Many may enter school for instrumental reasons. They seek technical skills and the credentialing that college matriculation brings. On a deeper level, however, they bring with them both the capacity and a need to obtain some perspective on compelling questions of life, a more developmental motivation. Openness allows for the recognition of these questions as legitimate in the context of the life cycle and creates sufficient space for them to be addressed as well. An environment in which these instrumental and developmental motivations are complementary rather than dichotomous gives learners the space and support to maximize engagement with that environment.

While openness is essential for adult learning, Palmer suggests learning space needs *boundaries* that give it structure, shape, and a delineation of expectations. Adult learners, often fitting school work into already crowded lives, cannot afford to be surprised by last-minute changes in schedules and requirements. They need to know the rules because their time and resources are valuable. The institution has an obligation to insure timely and effective communication regarding registration and deadlines. Professors should be clear in conveying such information as changes in class location, times of meetings and work expectations.

The curriculum, the course syllabus, and the teacher all play a role in determining the form of the educational experience, along with the counselors and advisors who help adult students set boundaries as they make realistic career and educational plans. Adult students, however, ought to have a role in managing their own learning, thereby encountering choice and experiencing autonomy. In becoming partners in their educational programs, they gain a better understanding of the higher education enterprise and a greater stake in its success.

A third characteristic, *hospitality,* relates to the climate set by the institution, the creation of an arena in which students have a sense of being welcome and at ease. Hospitality implies a sense of caring for learners as opposed to impatience at what may appear to be ineptitude. In the recognition of experiences the learners bring, there is respect for their developmental stage and concern for the central tasks of their lives. It insures a response to a need on the part of adult learners to matter, to believe they are the object of someone's attention and that they are appreciated and cared about. Giving careful attention to all interactions with adult students helps them to see themselves as important and integral to the institution's purpose and function and may help keep them engaged in learning. Such an approach ensures a safe environment in which there is time for reflection, which is essential if the often painful process of learning is to occur. Orientation courses that not only introduce the institution to the learner but address human development as an explicit part of the content help adult students to see themselves as having a legitimate place in the academy.

These three characteristics provide a framework with which to evaluate an institution's effectiveness. How well do our universities measure up in providing an environment that makes our adult learners feel welcome? How successful are we at recognizing and utilizing the experiences they bring? Are we willing to change our role from that of authoritarian to partner with the learner in jointly defining the content and nature of learning? Are faculty and staff development programs in place that promote the centrality of the adult learner? These questions, while not exhaustive, should be addressed if we are serious about serving adults.

SUGGESTED READINGS

Claxton, Charles, and Patricia H. Murrell. *Learning Styles: Implications for Educational Practices.* ASHE-ERIC Higher Education Report No. 4, 1987.

"Cognitive and Ethical Growth: The Making of Meaning." In *The Modern American College,* edited by A. W. Chickering and Associates. San Francisco: Jossey-Bass, 1981.

"Community, Conflict, and Ways of Knowing." *Change Magazine* (September/October 1987): 20–25.

Cross, Patricia K. *Adults as Learners: Increasing Participation and Facilitating Learning.* San Francisco: Jossey-Bass, 1981.

Kolb, David. *Experiential Learning: Experience as the Source of Learning and Development.* New Jersey: Prentice-Hall, 1984.

Palmer, Parker J. *To Know as We Are Known: A Spirituality of Education.* San Francisco: Harper and Row, 1983.

Perry, William, Jr. *Intellectual and Ethical Development in the College Years.* New York: Holt, Rinehart, and Winston, 1970.

Schlossberg, Nancy K., Ann Q. Lynch, and Arthur W. Chickering. *Improving Higher Education Environments for Adults: Responsive Programs and Services from Entry to Departure.* San Francisco: Jossey-Bass, 1989.

Student Services at Metropolitan Universities

Ann S. Coles

A recent study by the author of student services at a number of metropolitan colleges and universities indicated that the services most needed by urban commuter students are available on all campuses but are substantially underutilized. The resulting unmet needs constitute a major problem.

Some of the causes for underutilization of student services are inherent in the pattern of attendance as well as the background of the commuting students in metropolitan institutions. Students typically spend only a few hours a day on campus and have little free time in which to seek out student services. It is difficult to identify those who need assistance and to get them to make use of what is available. Most first generation urban students either have had little, if any, prior exposure to counseling and other support services or have had negative experiences with high school staff and "resource rooms." Many have stereotypic notions that counseling is for the mentally unbalanced and compensatory education for slow learners. Some may also be hesitant to use such services because they fear exposing their problems and perhaps having them noted in their records.

The reality of these barriers often leads to assumption that underutilization of student services is inevitable for urban commuting students, and that metropolitan institutions cannot improve the situation. However, the study indicates that both the organizational patterns and the methodology of student personnel services delivery as they now exist in most institutions impede utilization of services. Both organizational patterns and delivery can and should be adapted to improve the utilization of services by urban students.

Organizational Patterns of Student Personnel Services

Four factors emerge as barriers to the utilization of student services: a compartmentalized arrangement; a *laissez-faire* management style; an emphasis on organizational efficiency; and lack of systematic evaluation of the effectiveness of such services in meeting student needs.

Compartmentalized Services

The compartmentalized arrangement of student personnel services, under which most service components perform only a few specialized functions, was found in varying degrees at all the institutions studied. Almost everywhere, academic advising is treated as separate from counseling. Counselors are reluctant to offer academic advice, preferring that students see their academic advisors for this type of help. The researcher also found that financial aid offices are concerned almost exclusively with the management of aid programs. Students with financial problems who need budgeting help must go to the counseling center where they may or may not obtain such assistance.

Such a compartmentalized arrangement of student services is inconsistent in several respects with the needs of urban students. Most student problems do not fit into neat categories. Students with poor academic skills often have self-esteem problems, and students who have severe financial difficulties are apt to be under emotional stress. The academic problems of students may be caused by a combination of poor study skills, family difficulties, and high anxiety about their ability to achieve in college. Multifaceted difficulties cannot be dealt with effectively by a single specialized student services component. They require an integration of several kinds of approaches. Enabling students to overcome academic deficiencies involves building self-confidence in their ability to learn at the same time as they are being taught techniques for improving reading comprehension. Easing financial difficulties requires both direct financial aid and guidance in budgeting limited resources and cutting commuting costs. Reducing anxiety may require not only counseling but also adjustments in college policies practices in order to accommodate special needs of urban students.

In addition, specialized student service components make it necessary for students to go from one office to another in order to obtain the help they need. Students must often make appointments before they can actually secure assistance. Such an arrangement is impractical for urban students, given the limited time they can spend on campus. The compartmentalized arrangement of services also depends on student willingness to utilize referrals for specialized assistance. Students seeking help with financial problems receive money from one source and are directed to another office for budgeting help. Similarly, students being tutored in basic mathematics who have low self-esteem are referred to the counseling center for reasons that probably are unclear to them. There is no assurance that students will follow through on referrals. Indeed, given their unfamiliarity with counseling and other educational support services, as well as their fears of self-disclosure, it is likely that many students will not do so.

A system of specialized student services also encourages student personnel professionals to define their roles narrowly, even though they may have the capability and interest to respond to a variety of student problems. Faculty advisors may be more effective than a counselor in helping some students with personal problems, but may hesitate to get involved with issues not related to academic matters. Likewise, a career counselor may be in a better position to motivate students to improve their academic performance as a means of enhancing job prospects, but may be reluctant to inquire about grades or study habits.

The possibility of an eclectic, noncompartmentalized approach is clearly indicated by the existence on many campuses of offices or centers which respond to the multiple needs of special groups, such as African-American students, handicapped students, and older women returning to higher education. Typically, such units provide comprehensive support services ranging from personal counseling and crisis intervention to developing specialized instructional aids and barrier-free classrooms. The staff in these units combines academic skills specialists, counselors, part-time student aides, and faculty advisors. Study spaces, student lounges, and even special libraries are often contiguous to the staff offices. Such an arrangement eliminates the necessity of students going from place to place to secure help. It also facilitates the development of unified problem-solving strategies that take into account the various obstacles many urban students must overcome in order to achieve their educational goals.

Just as specialized student services components function in isolation from each other, so student services as an entity generally functions separately from academic programs. On the whole, student services staff have little contact with faculty members in their efforts to assist students. There are few instances of student services being integrated into academic programs and, except for the academic advising process, few college staff members' responsibilities encompass both student services and academic functions. The two groups tend to be separate from one another, even in their physical locations.

Since urban students spend most of their time on campus engaged in academic pursuits, integration of student services with academic programs would make assistance to students more readily available than under the present circumstances. Greater integration of student personnel with the academic enterprise also would promote cooperative working relationships between academic and student affairs staff and facilitate a clearer definition of joint responsibilities for helping students achieve their educational goals. Presently, student services personnel and academic staff tend to hold each other responsible for shortcomings and do not work cooperatively toward a common goal of ensuring that students receive the guidance and support they need to be successful.

Laissez-Faire Management

Another organizational factor that impedes utilization of student services by urban students is a *laissez-faire* style of management. The directors of various student services components have considerable autonomy in carrying out their functions. Much of what happens in each service unit depends on the inclination of the person in charge and the talents and experiences of the staff. Relatively little energy is invested in coordinating the efforts of the various components within an overall framework.

The laissez-faire style of organizational management creates several problems. First, there is no mechanism for ensuring that the objectives and operations of the various components are consistent with the overall goals for student services. Also, the lack of overall coordination and the reliance on individual inclination provides little opportunity to establish and maintain common standards. Consequently, appreciable variation exists in the way services are delivered, the treatment of students, and in the criteria for determining success in achieving goals.

The autonomy with which each service component operates also results in duplication of services and a tolerance of such overlap, particularly in the areas of academic advising, personal counseling, and career planning. When students hear that a particular service is available in several places, they become confused. In addition, the numerous offices offering the same service find themselves competing for students rather than coordinating their efforts.

Efficiency

An excessive emphasis on efficient administrative programs rather than on positive changes in student behavior also contributes to underutilization of services. This emphasis limits many of the possibilities for meaningful contacts between student services staff and students and may, in part, explain why the students interviewed in the study gave little feedback about their relationships with student services professionals. Emphasis on smooth administrative functioning often results in institutional policies and practices that lack the flexibility to respond to the diverse needs of urban students. "Efficient" administrative procedures designed to process batches of like people do not allow for flexible scheduling in order to accommodate part-time job requirements or the extensions students need on bills until they receive their financial aid awards. In some cases, these procedures may penalize students for missing deadlines they don't understand.

The strong emphasis on efficient administration also influences student personnel staff perceptions about responsibilities vis-à-vis students. During the study, the author observed that frequently staff performance reflected greater concern with fulfilling administrative requirements than meeting student needs. For example, many staff members believe addressing a student's problem by letter satisfies the responsibility to communicate with that student.

Evaluation

Another organizational factor contributing to underutilization of student services by urban students is the absence of any systematic evaluation of the effectiveness of service programs in achieving established goals. Except in isolated instances, the author found no regular evaluation process in place. Existing accountability is geared toward assessing the efficiency of operations rather than the degree to which student needs are met. Some form of systematic evaluation of student services in relation to student needs is of utmost importance at urban institutions where the composition of the student body has changed significantly in the last twenty years.

Methodology of Student Services Delivery

The Reactive Approach

Underutilization of services by urban students can also be attributed in part to the methodology employed in their delivery, especially the reactive approach to meeting student needs that is taken by most student services components at the institutions studied. The staff too often responds to problems brought to its attention, rather than seeking out potential problems and taking steps to prevent their occurrence. Most staff devote their efforts to working with students who seek help. Even though the staff knows from previous experience the types of problems students are apt to have and the categories of students who will need assistance but are unlikely to seek it, student services personnel still expect students to initiate contact.

Student services professionals have few systematic ways of identifying students who need assistance. Aside from freshman placement tests and grade report summaries, the primary methods used are individual referrals from faculty and others. The student services personnel rarely conduct either formal or informal assessments, such as determining the adequacy of students' resources for meeting college expenses or reviewing off-campus commitments, as a first step in planning a realistic course schedule. There is also little attempt to learn about family situations even though family pressures are thought to be a major source of difficulties for urban students. The study indicated that counselors, financial aid officers, and student activities staff members rarely communicated with each other in order to ascertain which students might benefit from the services offered by other components and how to encourage students to use a variety or combination of services.

A further aspect of the prevalent reactive manner is the lack of follow-up with students who request assistance. Few institutions make it a standard practice to be aggressive in this area. In fact, many staff members frown on such practice, believing it to be the student's responsibility. If students do not respond to suggestions, the staff assumes they don't need or care about securing available services. There are also some staff members who believe that active follow-up is an invasion of students' privacy or a denial of students' rights to conduct their personal affairs as they choose.

Most student services staff members work only with students who appear at their offices; they seldom contact students referred for help from faculty members or others. They also do not check with students directly to determine reasons for excessive absences, unless they are specifically requested to do so. Such follow-up typically consists of a formal letter and nothing more. The only observed instance of system-atic follow-up involved parents inquiring about their children's progress.

The reactive approach is also reflected in the limited involvement of student services staff with compensatory education programs at the institutions studied. Students in compensatory education courses predictably encounter considerable difficulty surviving in college. Yet there are few instances of student services staff collaborating directly with compensatory education instructors to help students overcome their difficulties and achieve educational success. Collaborative efforts might include developing and implementing methods to help students in compensatory courses build self-esteem, increase motivation, and resolve nonacademic problems before they reach crisis proportions.

Inadequate Communication

Inadequate means of communicating with commuting students about available services and how to use them constitute another barrier. The institutions studied rely essentially on four methods for making students aware of services: printed materials; new student orientation programs; faculty and staff who frequently contact students; and outreach programs.

Both students and student services staff expressed frustration with all of these methods. Printed materials, such as college catalogues, brochures, and letters, are the most widely utilized means of communicating with students. Yet students constantly miss deadlines, misunderstand academic requirements, and are often confused about matters explained in these publications. Clearly, print is not an adequate medium to purvey important information to urban students. Prior to coming to college, they have relied for information on television, radio and informal means such as "the grapevine," rather than the written word. Student services staff should foster an institutionalized grapevine through informed peer counselors and tutors.

Many orientation programs for new students include workshops and lectures on various aspects of the college, campus tours, social gatherings, meetings with academic advisors, and course selection. These typical events provide a flood of information that leaves many urban students feeling overwhelmed, confused, and only a little clearer than before about what to expect of college. The thrust of orientation programs is more on relaying information and dealing with administrative matters than facilitating student adjustment to college. There also is a tendency to accentuate positive institutional attributes, as if it were necessary to convince incoming students that they made the right college choice. As a result, most orientation programs fail to prepare urban students for the problems they will encounter once classes begin, such as the bureaucratic hassles of registration or straightening out billing. Little attempt is made to identify student problems that could be dealt with more easily before classes begin than in the middle of a semester. In addition, no effort is made to find out what students expect of college and how these expectations fit the characteristics and goals of the institution they will be attending.

Fortunately, effective orientation programs do exist. The one at Emmanuel in Boston closely resembles the program for students enrolling in the Educational Opportunity Program at the University of California at Los Angeles, which is considered highly successful. Emmanuel's program begins with a campus visit and an individual meeting with the associate academic dean shortly after the student is admitted. Several other individual and group meetings are held during the summer. Students meet with faculty members in their academic interest areas, select courses, correct financial aid problems, and become acquainted with the campus. A final two-day session for all students is held immediately before classes begin; the purpose is to orient students to the nonacademic aspects of the institution and help them establish friendships with other new students. By the first day of classes, most new students have a reasonably clear sense of what they can expect at Emmanuel and have resolved many of the difficulties that students at other institutions must contend with during the first few weeks of school. Orientation continues after classes begin, under the direction of the associate academic dean who serves as the academic advisor for all freshmen.

Lack of Incentives

A third methodological problem with student services organizations at the institutions studied is the limited number of incentives for students to use them. Utilization of student services is almost entirely on a voluntary basis. The only mandatory services are compensatory education courses for those who fall below a certain level on placement tests and academic advising in instances where an advisor's signature must be obtained in order to register for courses. Use of the other student resources is optional. Hence, whether students take advantage of services depends largely on what incentives exist for using them.

Institutional incentives for students to use student services include college credits, money, the opportunity to develop skills related to student interests and goals, social contacts, and the desire to avoid penalties. Given the financial pressures and time constraints under which urban students attend college, academic credit and money seem to be the most attractive. The need for money is the incentive that motivates students to apply for financial aid; it also is a major reason why students are attracted to cooperative education. Similarly, the popularity of a career planning and job placement center at all the institutions studied indicates the importance that urban students attach to jobs and financial security. The fact that workshops on career and life planning, study skills, preventative health care, and other topics carry academic credit at some institutions undoubtedly accounts for why they have high student participation levels. The availability of academic credit for participation in student activities may also account for more commuter involvement in student organizations. In the institutions studied where incentives such as money and academic credit do not exist, utilization of student personnel services is consistently low. Many urban students have difficulty justifying spending scarce time on personal, intellectual, and social development when they are pressured by more immediate survival needs.

Inadequate Resources

All metropolitan colleges and universities operate under major financial constraints, which constitute further barriers to adequate utilization of student services. The situation is often aggravated by the way in which resources are distributed among student service components. In many urban institutions that have some residential facilities, services for commuting students receive less than their fair share. Frequently, for example, the housing services staff make up a greater fraction of the total student service staff than the proportion of residential students in the institution.

In addition, although all students usually pay the same student activities fee, resident students utilize student unions more and participate in student activities to a much greater extent than do commuters. In the case of health services, a similar situation exists. All students pay the same health services fee even though commuters use these services much less than do residents. On the other hand, services that directly target specific needs of urban students are often underfunded. All institutions have compensatory education courses, but it is rare to find a comprehensive academic skills development center staffed with skills diagnosticians and specialists. Tutoring services also are limited because of scarce resources.

Extending Campus Boundaries

For institutional services to be more responsive to the needs of students at metropolitan universities, administrators need to consider the particular circumstances under which students attend college. While urban students place a high emphasis on college education as career preparation, their requests for assistance from student personnel reflect an interest in intellectual, social, and emotional growth, as well. The desire to overcome inadequate academic preparation/ anxiety about whether they will be successful in college and concern for establishing meaningful relationships with faculty and peers are all examples of students' interests in other aspects of development in addition to vocational development.

The environment for urban commuting students extends beyond the traditional campus boundaries. It includes the community in which the students work and live, sleep, and study. What happens to urban students in the community context directly affects their involvement in college and the degree to which they achieve their educational goals. In their communities, students encounter not only rich learning opportunities but also obstacles to the realization of their college aspirations.

In order to help students maximize their options for personal growth, it is essential that student services at metropolitan universities address the needs of students in the context of their total environment. If student services personnel assume that the only place where they can influence the learning experiences of commuting students is within the traditional campus boundaries, then the developmental opportunities for such students are limited. When the total environment in which urban students function is viewed as the context in which learning and growing take place, opportunities for student development are increased one hundredfold. In addition, viewing learning in this larger context eliminates much of the frustration generated for student services staffs by the limited time that urban students spend on the traditional campus, since learning is no longer restricted to this setting. At commuting institutions, much of the students' environment is outside the control of college-staff members. The job of student services professionals at urban institutions, therefore, is not so much to create an environment that encourages student development, as would be the case at a largely residential campus, as it is to help students capitalize on the positive learning opportunities in the larger metropolitan community and overcome obstacles found in that setting.

Extending the campus boundaries of metropolitan colleges and universities to include the environment in which students live and work has several implications for the conceptual framework of student services at these institutions. To seem relevant to urban students and their felt needs for assistance, student services must attempt to integrate students' off-campus experiences with on-campus learning options. In many instances, it is also desirable to recognize the legitimacy of off-campus learning experiences by granting academic credit rewards if off-campus learning with college credit will provide an incentive for urban students to identify and engage in other community-based opportunities for personal development.

Viewing the off-campus lives of urban students as an integral part of their learning experiences parallels in some respects the concern that residential colleges take in the personal lives of their students. This concern is reflected in the intensive staffing of residence halls and extensive programming of on-campus extracurricular activities.

In the case of urban students, the neighborhoods in which they live are their dormitories and student centers, and the community activities in which they participate are their extracurricular interests.

At urban institutions, student services staff also must be sensitive to racial oppression, poverty, and other obstacles in the larger environment that confront many urban students. Student services professionals cannot change the urban environment. They can, however, acknowledge the societal forces that impinge upon the development of urban students. They also can provide formal and informal learning situations in which urban students can acquire the knowledge and skills needed to overcome social obstacles and make progress toward their goals.

Extending campus boundaries to include the urban environment could involve the utilization of community resources to assist students with nonacademic problems. Such problems include family difficulties, inadequate housing, financial crises, legal hassles, lack of transportation, and child care problems, as well as anxieties resulting from the conflicting roles of spouse, breadwinner, single parent, and student. These problems are commonly found within urban student populations, and they often interfere both with students' academic performance and personal development. Universities are not multiservice social welfare agencies and cannot deal directly with all such problems. But student services staff should be familiar with community-based sources of support and expertise to which they can refer students.

While there are significant limitations to the utilization of student services by commuters, it is possible to make improvements that will increase student use. Urban students need the learning opportunities and assistance provided by student services. Restructuring the present organization and modifying service delivery methodologies will make services more responsive to urban student needs. Services for urban students can be further improved by expanding the definition of the metropolitan campus to include the larger community in which students live and work and by utilizing community resources to enhance student learning experiences and assist with student problems.

PART III

FACULTY ROLES AND RESPONSIBILITIES

INTRODUCTION

$\mathbf{F}$ew issues have generated greater attention and concern among campus faculty and administration leaders than the roles and responsibilities of faculty. The growing interest in this issue prompted the American Association of Higher Education (AAHE) to organize and lead a national discussion, now in its third year, to draw attention to the public's perceptions of higher education, political concerns surrounding the costs and performance of universities, changing societal needs and their implications for faculty and administrators.

A primary mission for most institutions of higher education and a major responsibility for university faculty is the promotion of scholarship. Ernest A. Lynton, in his article "Knowledge and Scholarship," suggests a formulation for the common characteristics of all scholarship and a set of common criteria by which it can be assessed. The nature of scholarship itself, however, also has been a subject of growing interest in recent years, thanks largely to the provocative work of Ernest L. Boyer in *Scholarship Reconsidered* (1990). Because of the broader missions of metropolitan universities, there has been a special interest at these institutions in the meaning and measurement of scholarship.

Gordon A. Haaland, Nell R. Wylie and Daniel A. DiBiasio extend the discussion of scholarship in their article in which they argue the need for a better balance among the traditional functions of American universities—teaching, research, and service. To achieve this balance, they propose a greater emphasis on interdisciplinary research, a broader definition of scholarship, a recognition that faculty interests change, and a process of faculty evaluation that takes these changes into account.

G. Edward Schuh, in his article "The Preparation of Future Faculty for Metropolitan Universities," assesses the role and rapidity of change in higher education. Schuh suggests that metropolitan universities have a special responsibility for preparing future faculty members capable of carrying out their more difficult and challenging missions.

Patricia R. Plante's article, "Form and Texture of a Professional Life," asks an important two-part question that goes to the heart of this discussion of faculty roles and responsibilities in a metropolitan university: "What should a contemporary metropolitan university expect of its faculty?" and, "What should a contemporary faculty expect of its metropolitan university?" Plante's response to these questions is broad, philosophical, and at times poetic, touching on the central characteristics of metropolitan universities and the challenges ahead.

The final article in this section is R. Eugene Rice's call for a broader view of scholarship. Focusing on comprehensive as well as metropolitan universities, Rice questions the changing role of scholarship in a pluralistic democracy.

The above articles demonstrate the lively dialogue occurring among universities about faculty roles and responsibilities. These questions and issues are even more poignant as they relate to metropolitan universities because of their broader responsibilities to their communities and surrounding metropolitan regions. To bring about needed changes, however, this discussion must include a broader representation of faculty, department chairs, and administrators than it has to date. This issue is not going away.

KNOWLEDGE AND SCHOLARSHIP

Ernest A. Lynton

The Flow of Knowledge

In his well known book *The Higher Education System,* published by the University of California Press in 1983, Burton Clark states that

> For as long as higher education has been formally organized, it has been a social structure for the control of advanced knowledge and technique. In varying combinations of the efforts to discover, conserve, refine, transmit, and apply it, the manipulation of knowledge is what we find in common in the many specific activities of professors and teachers. (p. 11)

The advancement of knowledge is indeed the central concern of higher education, and it is, as well, the defining activity of the scholarly profession. Scholarship can exist wherever and whenever knowledge is systematically pursued, enhanced, and communicated, be it through research, teaching, or professional service. Why, then, does research dominate the academic value system?

There are historical reasons for this, as Sandra Elman and I suggested in our book, *New Priorities for the University* (1987). After World War II, the federal government provided vast sums for the support of basic research in universities. This had a marked effect on the measures of prestige for both institutions and individuals. But the current primacy of research in the academic value system is also fostered by the persistent misconception of a uni-directional flow of knowledge, from the locus of research to the place of application, from scholar to practitioner, teacher to student, expert to client. Such a linear process is strongly implied, maybe unintentionally, in Clark's formulation, which lists discovery, conservation, refinement, transmission, and application of knowledge as if they were sequential.

A linear view of knowledge flow inevitably creates a hierarchy of values according to which research is the most important, and all other knowledge-based activities are derivative and secondary. Teaching, according to this view, constitutes no more than the transmission of a codified body of knowledge, professional service only its application. Neither is central to the advancement of knowledge. In a background paper announcing the creation by the American Association for Higher Education (AAHE) of the Forum on Faculty Roles and Rewards, Russ Edgerton points out that a linear model shapes "the prevailing views about what 'real' scholarship is all about; views that rest on conceptions of what *kinds* of knowledge are most worth possessing. Within the reigning paradigm of scientific inquiry, knowledge codified in the form of general scientific principles is supreme; the knowing that is entailed in communicating and representing ideas has lesser value. The kind of 'situational knowledge' that distinguishes expert practitioners from ordinary practitioners is hardly recognized at all" (1992). In *The Reflective Practitioner*, Donald Schon describes how the same linear hierarchy dominates—and distorts—so much of professional education, forcing its curriculum into the sequence from basic to applied science, and then only to applications and clinical practice (1983).

But, as Ernest Boyer emphasizes in *Scholarship Reconsidered*, knowledge is not necessarily developed in such a linear manner (1990, p. 15). It is not an inert commodity, created in laboratory, library, or study, to be stored in libraries like the gold in Fort Knox, or dispensed like a patent medicine in classrooms or a consulting office. It is dynamic, constantly made fresh and given new shape by its interaction with immediate issues and concerns. It emerges when a number of disciplines are brought together in the analysis of a complex problem in a scholarly manner. A scholarly textbook or review article not only increases the knowledge of the readers, but in its creation enhances the insight and understanding of the author. And, all scholarly teaching and application constitute learning both for the scholar as well as for the client and student. The learning of the scholar arises out of his or her reflection on the situation-specific aspects of the activity, and on the details of the transformational process by which students, clients, and readers are helped to understand and to utilize knowledge.

The Eco-system of Knowledge

In short, the domain of knowledge has no one-way streets. Knowledge does not move only from the locus of research to the place of application, from scholar to practitioner, teacher to student, expert to client. It is everywhere fed back, constantly enhanced. We need to think of knowledge in an ecological fashion, recognizing the complex, multi-faceted and multiply-connected system by means of which discovery, aggregation, synthesis, dissemination, and application are all interconnected and interacting in a wide variety of ways. In parts of the system, new information is gathered in laboratory and library, by survey and observation. Elsewhere, data are analyzed and interpreted, aggregated and integrated, taught and applied—and those processes themselves yield new information, new understanding, new insights, and hence new knowledge. They relate to one another, they overlap, they are usually not clearly separable. There is no clear demarcation between creation and integration, teaching and application.

Knowledge moves through this system in many directions. There is constant feedback, with new questions as well as new insights generated all along the way, triggering new explorations and new syntheses. Nor is the process linear. The ecological system of knowledge is complex and multi-dimensional, often messy and confusing, with many modes of feedback and many cross connections. And, at every point of this multiply-connected system there is learning and enhanced understanding, resulting in expanded knowledge. The process operates on many different levels and at various scales. Occasionally a path-breaking set of observations or an innovative approach to application or instruction can lead to a quantum jump of understanding, with fundamental implications that reverberate throughout the entire system. More often knowledge is added in small increments or on a local scale, in instances of teaching or application, research or integration bounded by the specific conditions of time and place. Even then there are likely to be some inferences, some generalizations which can ripple through other portions of the knowledge eco-system.

The concept of an eco-system of knowledge is not just a convenient metaphor. It has profound implications for faculty roles because the system of knowledge is the *territory of scholarship*. Wherever knowledge emerges, scholarship can exist. Any intellectual activity in every part of the system that results in true learning, in added understanding, in an increase in knowledge—as distinct from a mere accretion of facts and figures—is scholarship in action. And all of these activities are of great societal importance. As Boyer has stated:

> [T]he time has come to . . . give the familiar and honor-
> able term "scholarship" a broader, more capacious meaning,

one that brings legitimacy to the full scope of academic work
. . . [and includes] the scholarship of *discovery;* the scholarship of *integration;* the scholarship of *application,* and the
scholarship of *teaching."* (op. cit., p. 16)

Viewing scholarship as professional activity in the interconnected and interdependent eco-system of knowledge underscores
that, as Boyer emphasizes, the four kinds of scholarship he lists are
indeed "intellectual functions that are tied inseparably to each other
[and that]. . . dynamically interact, forming an interdependent whole"
(op. cit. p. 25).

All forms of scholarship, if carried out at equal levels of excellence, should thus be viewed as comparable in importance and in
legitimacy.

The converse holds as well: the integration, teaching, and
application of knowledge—and indeed also the creation of
knowledge—should all be held to the same high measures of quality.
Insisting on this is important because just stretching the definition
of scholarship to cover more categories of faculty activity can be
attacked as a dilution of standards. It is essential to demonstrate
that all forms of scholarship pose intellectual challenges of a similar
nature, and that they can be held accountable across the board to
standards of excellence of equal rigor. What appear at first sight to
be quite different activities must be shown to have substantial
commonalties, which make it possible to compare the intellectual
challenge of the effort.

Common Characteristics of Scholarly Work

What are these commonalties? Are there general statements
which can be made about the nature of the scholarly profession, and
about what constitutes quality in scholarly work? Is it possible to
generate a working definition by which scholarship can be recognized in whatever form it occurs?

To date we have had difficulty in applying a consistent definition
and set of standards to the full range of potential scholarly work
because we have tended to look primarily at the concrete *outcomes*
of a professional activity rather than to consider as well the
intellectual *process* by which these came about. We always ask *what*
did you do? Dossiers used in appointments, promotion, and tenure
review usually include items such as publications, text books, course
syllabi, and consulting reports: the outcomes as well as what have
been called the "artifacts" of scholarship. But the dossiers rarely

contain the reasons *why* the individual undertook a course of action in a particular way. Yet in order to appreciate and understand scholarly activity adequately, and to evaluate its quality, one needs to have as much information as possible about what went on in the scholar's mind as he or she approached a task, analyzed it and decided on an approach, observed and reflected on its progress, and drew inferences from its outcomes. The attributes which research, teaching, the integration of knowledge, and its application all have in common emerge very clearly when, instead of focusing only on outcomes, one also explores the *intellectual process* and asks questions about the thinking behind the activity. Outcomes must be viewed within the framework of the reasoning which created them, the *what* in the context of the *why*. *Why* was the activity undertaken? *Why* was it carried out in a particular manner? *Why* was a particular research topic or course outline chosen, and why the specific method? What was the activity trying to accomplish? Why choose the particular strategy to accomplish it? Were there other possible choices?

The individual's approach to a professional activity is what most clearly distinguishes scholarly work. The scholar does not carry out a recurrent task according to a prescribed protocol, applying standard methodologies. Rote and routine are antithetical to scholarship. What unifies the activities of a scholar, be he or she engaged in teaching, research, or professional service, is an approach to each task as a novel situation, a voyage of exploration into the partially unknown. Along this voyage, the scholar defines the new problem, sets a goal, chooses the most appropriate approach, monitors the ongoing process, making corrections as necessary, assesses the outcome, draws appropriate inferences and, where possible, verifies and then shares what he or she has learned. This intellectual process most readily characterizes scholarly work. It is substantially identical for all its forms, be it teaching or application, writing a text or carrying out research. To recognize and to evaluate scholarship, one must be able to accompany the scholar on the voyage.

What then does one look for in order to recognize this scholarly way of thinking, and to assess its quality in an effective and workable way? No unique formulation exists. It is very desirable for individual colleges and universities to work out their own articulation of the scholarly process in order to foster institutional acceptance and sense of ownership. As an example rather than as a blue print, we suggest the following four universal attributes as a way of describing what is common to the process of all scholarly work: *reasoning, reflection, learning, and dissemination.* These attributes are neither sequential nor distinct. They overlap, they intermingle, they are not fully separable. They are individually listed here because, like the fourfold aspects of scholarship suggested in *Scholarship Reconsidered*, each provides a helpful perspective on the nature of scholarship.

(1) Scholarship is a *reasoned process*. Based on her or his subject matter expertise, as well as understanding of the context and of the audience, the scholar makes conscious and deliberate choices of the desired goals, and then selects the optimal method and resources most likely to achieve the outcomes.

(2) Scholarship is a *reflective process*. The scholar, like all good professionals, is in Schon's words "open to the backtalk of the situation," (op. cit, p. 269) reflecting on what is happening throughout the process, recognizing and responding to the unique and unexpected elements of each situation, and as well, analyzing outcomes .

(3) Scholarship is therefore also a *learning process* not only for the audience to which the activity is directed, but also for the scholar who draws generalizable inferences and thus derives new insights which inform future iterations of the process. The new knowledge thus created can be such as to further an academic discipline, and it can also lead to improved methodology of how knowledge can best be taught, applied, or otherwise disseminated.

(4) All scholarship must include an element of *dissemination* through which what is learned by the scholar is shared with others both for verification as well as to enhance general knowledge.

Criteria to Evaluate Scholarship

These characteristics are common to basic and applied research, to direct instruction, to the development of educational materials, and to all forms of professional outreach. They separate that which is in some measure fresh and innovative from that which is routine and repetitive. They suggest a set of criteria by which the quality of scholarly work can be evaluated. The criteria, like the characteristics, can be formulated in a variety of ways, of which the following is an example, neither unique nor necessarily complete:

1. the expertise informing the scholarly process, as demonstrated by the adequacy of preparation as well as by appropriateness of the choices made by the scholar;
2. the originality and degree of innovation manifest in the activity;
3. the difficulty of the task to be accomplished;
4. its scope and importance;
5. the effectiveness and impact of the activity.

The Documentation of Scholarship

The defining characteristics of scholarship and the kinds of criteria used to evaluate it suggest the nature of the necessary documentation of scholarship. The academic world, quite properly, takes seriously only what it can evaluate—and evaluates only what it can document. Hence *all* dimensions of scholarly work must be documented and evaluated to ensure true multidimensional excellence. The similarity of the intellectual process and the ability to apply similar criteria allows a common approach for all dimensions of scholarship.

The necessary documentation falls into two categories. The first must provide the following:

1. descriptions of *what* was done and *how,* including information about the context and the conditions at the time of the work, how it was carried out, and what the outcomes were;

2. explanations of *why* specific goals as well as method and resources were chosen, and resulting conclusions drawn;

3. evaluations of the quality and significance of both the process and product of the work by the individual doing the work, by those intended to benefit from it, and by others qualified to judge it.

Most of the descriptive and explanatory documentation must be provided by the individual. It should of course include the usual "products" and "artifacts" such as published papers, books, reports, course syllabi, and the like. But these items are not sufficient. If each scholarly activity is, in some sense, a voyage of exploration and discovery, it can be fully appreciated and evaluated only if one can follow the scholar on that journey. Hence the dossier must also include a descriptive and reflective essay which describes and explains the following:

1. the specifics of the situation, in terms of the nature of the intended audience, and the context in which the activity took place;

2. the state of pertinent knowledge,

3. the objective of the activity;

4. the choice of method and resources used in carrying out the activity, following its progress, and assessing its outcomes;

5. the results of "reflection-in-action" in terms of unique and unexpected features encountered, adaptations made, inferences drawn, and lessons learned by the scholar,

6. a self-assessment of the perceived outcomes and their implications.

This descriptive and explanatory material must be validated by evaluative documentation for which there exist, broadly speaking, three sources, in addition to the self-assessment contained in the individual's reflective essay:

1. the primary audience that constituted the direct target of the activity: fellow specialists for research, students for teaching, the staff of client organizations for professional service. These individuals can comment on matters such as preparation, presentation, and pertinence,

2. the clients or sponsors of the activity, such as the funding agency of research, departmental colleagues and academic administrators for teaching, or the executives of organizations receiving professional service. They can evaluate the extent to which the work has met intended goals and needs;

3. pertinent experts in the subject matter and/or the methodology of the activity, who are able to evaluate the work in terms of the norms of the pertinent field and who can speak to the significance of the outcomes.

There clearly exists some overlap among these categories. The documentation should include evaluations from these sources, solicited and gathered by those who are charged with the review of the individual's scholarship. It is important that the solicitation be explicit with regard to the information sought, and that it describe the standards by which the work will be assessed.

Distinct Projects as Units of Analysis

The first of the AAHE publications describing the use of portfolios for the documentation of teaching emphasizes that "good teaching [isl highly situational . . . [T]he more complex examples of good teaching would best be revealed by looking at *discrete examples of actual work"* (op. cit., p. 9). That applies as well to other dimensions of faculty scholarship: their quality can be best demonstrated by looking at distinct projects, with goals that can be defined, processes that can be described, and outcomes that can be identified. The criteria by which scholarship can be evaluated are project-oriented and can only be applied to work that has a clear purpose, identifiable method, and demonstrable outcomes. Hence distinct projects provide the primary measure of a scholar's work within the context of the individual's activities over time.

Choosing a distinct project as a unit of analysis also provides a way of distinguishing between ongoing conscientious but repetitive activities, on the one hand, and instances of significantly creative work, on the other. All aspects of faculty work, be it research, teaching, or professional service, of necessity include much of the former which, in spite of its value, does not fully meet the standards of scholarship.

To focus on distinct projects is particularly important with regard to professional service because of a tendency to throw together all the odds and ends that can be grouped under the category of professional service with more substantive projects. To do so can trivialize the entire category of professional outreach and hide its potential intellectual challenge and scholarly nature. One needs to make a much clearer distinction between the minor professional outreach activities in which a faculty member may be engaged, and specific, more substantive projects which can serve as principal units of analysis for faculty evaluation. For example, as part of collaboration between a university and a school system, faculty members often make themselves available to their school-based colleagues for consultation and discussion. Such ongoing interaction is important and should be recognized as part of an individual's workload if it takes a substantial amount of time. But it is not, by itself, the stuff of scholarship. There is no way of documenting and hence of evaluating the intellectual challenge and hence the scholarly nature of such work unless it is an integral part of a joint project leading to identifiable results. The same difficulty exists in other kinds of professional service. Brief consultations or occasional public lectures are in-and-out activities that are difficult to document and evaluate. The documentation of professional service should focus on substantial projects which have a well defined objective and identifiable outcomes, and a process which can be described. That can occur, for example, when one or more faculty members work with their school-based colleagues in substantive projects such as the redesign of the middle school science curriculum, when an economist undertakes an analysis of tax policies for a state government, when a chemical engineer assists in the design of a processing plant, or a management expert designs a new organization for a public or private enterprise. It is only within the framework of such distinct units of analysis that the standards of scholarship can be systematically applied.

Examples of Best Work

Full documentation should be provided only for examples of best work selected by the faculty member. To do so is important for practical reasons, because to provide such information for every piece of research, every course taught, every outreach activity is clearly much too time consuming both for the individual as well as for the reviewers.

An even more significant consequence of a selective dossier is that it shifts the emphasis from quantity to quality. Former President Kennedy of Stanford University has been eloquent in making the case for a selective approach to evaluation. In his 1991 Essay to the Stanford Faculty, he came out very strongly against "the quantitative use of research output as a criterion for appointment and promotion," calling this "a bankrupt idea." Expanding on his complaint about " the overproduction of routine scholarship," he cites "studies demonstrating that in many fields the majority of published papers are never cited." Kennedy states that "[t]he major learned societies. . . base election to membership on the consideration of an author's most important publication, not on his or her total production." He recommends that in order "to reverse the appalling belief that counting and weighing are important parts of evaluation . . . Stanford should limit the number of publications that can be considered in appointment and promotion" (1991).

The belief which he cites is widely held: The 1989 Carnegie Foundation National Survey of Faculty, as reported in the March/April 1991 issue of *Change,* found that even among the most published faculty, defined as those having eleven or more articles printed in journals, approximately one half or more of those surveyed believed that at their institution, "publications used for tenure and promotion are just 'counted,' not qualitatively measured." According to the same survey, a substantial majority of the most published faculty, with numbers ranging from seventy-seven percent of the biological scientists to ninety-two percent of the engineers, thought that at their institution "we need better ways, besides publication, to evaluate the scholarly performance of the faculty."

The Distinctiveness of the Scholarly Profession

Faculty members belong to and practice the scholarly profession, and have much in common with practitioners of all professions. And the more we understand and appreciate, thanks to the work of Schon and others, the complexity, the intellectual challenge, and indeed also the artistry of effective professional practice, the greater the pride we can take in being members of a profession striving to be optimally effective in its practice.

It is, therefore, neither surprising nor inappropriate that much of what has been described as basic attributes of scholarly work pertains, as well, to the proper practice of other professions. Reasoning and reflection characterize the effective practitioner in many fields, and, similarly, are likely to lead to learning.

Yet, at the same time, scholarship is a unique profession, distinguished by its central dedication to the advancement of knowledge. Knowledge is a central and essential element of all professions, but only scholarship is dedicated solely to its advancement. Furthermore, a scholar also has an obligation to share with others the new knowledge which has been created in the course of a scholarly activity. In no other profession does the dissemination of knowledge play as central a role as it does in scholarship. Indeed, an identification of teaching in its broadest sense with scholarship comes closer to being a valid description than the more prevalent identification of research with scholarship. Thus the profession of scholarship occupies a very special role in the range of intellectual activities, just as colleges and universities have a unique mission among the many kinds of knowledge-related societal institutions .

NOTE: Much of this article is based on work carried out by the author for the Carnegie Foundation for the Advancement of Teaching. The author is grateful for the support of the Foundation, and for many illuminating conversations with Dr. Ernest Boyer, President of the Foundation, reflected in the present article.

SUGGESTED READINGS

Boyer, Ernest L. *Scholarship Reconsidered.* Princeton: The Carnegie Foundation for the Advancement of Teaching, 1990.

Braskamp, Larry A., and John C. Ory. *Assessing Faculty Work: Enhancing Individual and Institutional Performance.* San Francisco: Jossey-Bass, 1994.

Diamond, Robert M. A: *Faculty Guide to Serving on Promotion and Tenure Committees.* Bolton, MA, Anker Publishing, forthcoming.

_____, and Bronwyn Adams, eds. *Recognizing Faculty Work: Reward System for the Year 2000.* San Francisco: Jossey-Bass, 1993.

Edgerton, Russell. *Forum on Faculty Roles and Rewards.* Washington, D. C. American Association for Higher Education, 1992.

_____, Patricia Hutchings, and Kathleen Quinlan. *The Teaching Portfolio: Capturing The Scholarship in Teaching.* Washington, D. C. The

American Association for Higher Education, 1991. Cf. also Patricia Hutchings. *Using Cases To Improve College Teaching: A Guide to More Reflective Practice;* and Eric Anderson. *Campus Use of the Teaching Portfolio: 25 Profiles.* Washington, D. C. The American Association for Higher Education, 1993.

Kennedy, Donald. *The Improvement of Teaching, An Essay to the Stanford Community,.* March 3, 1991, Stanford University.

Lynton, Ernest A., and Sandra E. Elman. *New Priorities for the University.* San Francisco: Jossey-Bass, 1987.

Schon, Donald A. *The Reflective Practitioner.* New York: Basic Books, 1983.

Faculty and Scholarship: The Need for Change

Gordon A. Haaland, Nell R. Wylie, and Daniel A. DiBiasio

The university is one of the longest surviving institutions of society, and a central reason for this longevity is its capacity for change. Throughout history, universities have experienced the full continuum of change, on occasion showing a willingness to make slight adjustments, while at other times boldly making major changes. Pressures for both kinds of changes have come from inside and outside the academy. As American universities prepare for the turn of another century, it is timely to consider the changes that are needed to ensure their continued value to society.

The Modern American University

In the last half of the nineteenth century, American universities emerged as an amalgam of the English "Oxbridge" tradition, the German research influence, and the American penchant for utilitarianism. As a result, American universities were the first to exist for the three-fold purpose of teaching, research, and service. Today, the best American universities have achieved worldwide preeminence, and as a subset of all higher education institutions, they are unrivaled for their quality, diversity, and access.

One of the most important features of American universities is academic specialization, a characteristic that found expression in the creation of disciplinary departments and that has given both form and substance to the university ideal. Academic departments quickly became key organizational units within universities; their development provided a locus for disciplinary scholarship and nurtured in faculty a fierce loyalty and devotion to their disciplines.

99

Academic specialization has contributed significantly to the success of the academy, and it will continue to in the future. However, there have been negative consequences associated with specialization as well, including placing an inordinate value on traditional research and narrowing the definition of what constitutes research. These problems have tended to diminish the role of teaching and service.

Others who have examined the current status of higher education notice a similar imbalance. In a recent issue of *Educational Record*, Alexander W. Astin makes a useful distinction between an institution's explicit values and its implicit values. Explicit values find expression in university mission statements and institutional charters, almost all of which attach equal weight to teaching, research, and service. Implicit values, on the other hand, are the motives that actually drive institutional policies. Most people in research universities, he writes, subscribe to their institutions' implicit value system, which includes teaching, research, and service, with research receiving the most emphasis by far.

Astin maintains that several problems arise when there is a significant imbalance between an institution's explicit and implicit values. The implications for faculty are obvious. Research is important, but teaching less so. And disciplinary research is far more critical than interdisciplinary or multidisciplinary research. Ironically, the incredible success of the modern American university has led to devaluing teaching, especially undergraduate teaching, and to imposing a limiting definition of research. Both trends must be reversed in the universities of the future.

Reversing the Trends

Although we believe that all universities would benefit from placing a greater emphasis on teaching and by encouraging more interdisciplinary and multidisciplinary scholarship, certain types of institutions are ideally suited for implementing these changes. Land-grant universities and comprehensive urban universities in particular have a special obligation to serve their states, their regions, and the nation through direct programs, research, and other forms of scholarship and by preparing new generations of students to understand, appreciate, and solve today's problems.

The traditional mission of land-grant universities—teaching, research, and service—gives these institutions a mandate for implementing the changes discussed in this article. Many modern metropolitan universities also have a strong identity with their community, as well as a national focus. By reclaiming teaching as a central activity and expanding the boundaries of scholarship and service, these universities would be acting within the scope of their institutional charters. They would, in effect, be restoring a needed balance to the traditional functions of American universities.

In order to achieve better balance among teaching, research, and service, universities of the twenty-first century must consider a variety of approaches and strategies. We suggest four in particular: organizational change to create greater compatibility with interdisciplinary research, broadening the definition of scholarship, recognizing that faculty careers change over time, and revising the method and practice of faculty evaluation.

Organizational Change

Universities will engage in more interdisciplinary and multidisciplinary research in the future. This assumption rests on the fact that the issues and problems we face as a nation and a world are far more difficult and complex than they have ever been. In addition, the stakes are getting progressively higher. Terms and phenomena such as AIDS, biotechnology, the greenhouse effect, deforestation, and global economics are becoming commonplace. And what they all share in common is a level of complexity that is best understood and addressed through interdisciplinary inquiry.

A good example of interdisciplinary work in the area of medical technology is provided by the magnetic resonance imaging machines now found in most research hospitals. These machines are the direct result of investigations in quantum mechanics and computer science. While these fields developed independently for many years, they finally came together in the 1970s to better serve the needs of medical research.

Universities can do far more to bring disciplines together, and one structural approach designed to accomplish this is the establishment of interdisciplinary centers. While this is not a new idea, it is still one that is not easily realized on many campuses. Campus politics, resistance to change, and other local factors can conspire to make the creation of interdisciplinary centers difficult. Nonetheless, these types of structures will become as important to the universities of the future as disciplinary departments were to institutions in the past.

The University of New Hampshire, for example, established an Institute for the Study of Earth, Oceans, and Space five years ago. It was founded on the basis of scientific study that reveals that the earth functions as a global system—sun, atmosphere, oceans, fresh water, ice cores, and continents all interact to maintain a delicate yet dynamic balance. Faculty research in the institute reflects the fields of study that will be more prominent in coming decades, fields such as space science, biogeochemistry, glaciology, and paleo-meteorology, to name a few. To work effectively on the problems posed by global change, the knowledge and expertise of faculty from a variety of disciplines are required.

Similar examples can be found at other universities. Centers and institutes in humanities, business, social sciences, and health sciences are becoming more common, and they will continue to grow in number and influence.

A residual benefit of establishing interdisciplinary centers is the visibility that they can give to complex issues. These issues become more real to students, and students are more likely to grasp the importance of developing skills that come from interdisciplinary study, i.e., the integration and synthesis of information. These skills will only increase in importance and will serve students who strive to be active participants in our society.

Academic leaders must do more to encourage and reward interdisciplinary scholarship. They should provide needed incentives and resources and work with faculty to expand opportunities for interdisciplinary effort.

Broadening the Definition of Scholarship

The university is an institution committed to scholarship, including learning and discovering new things, integrating ideas in a different and perhaps novel fashion, and exploring old themes in new ways. The scholar communicates this learning and understanding in a variety of ways—by teaching students in the classroom; writing in journals, books and the popular press; and helping others apply what is known in factories, farms, and forests. Such a broad conception of the work of the scholar is necessary because of the many ways in which scholarship is manifest in universities.

Accordingly, we propose that the modern university adopt a single mission-scholarship. Scholarship is both knowledge acquisition and communication. The one cannot exist without the other. Scholarship can include several diverse forms of knowledge acquisition; in their work in progress, R. Eugene Rice and Ernest Boyer are examining a related framework for ways of knowing:

1. Scholarship is understanding. More particularly, scholarship is the understanding of a particular body of knowledge, a basic expectation for all faculty. To be a scholar is to be an expert.

2. Scholarship is the search for new knowledge. Traditional academic research focuses on the new idea and represents what most academics consider scholarship. Although this approach has been highly successful in the modern American university for all disciplines, the exclusive focus on this form of scholarship has led to a degree of trivialization.

3. Scholarship is the integration of knowledge. Almost every field and discipline now has a journal devoted to work on the integration of existing knowledge. In addition, one of the most important forms of scholarly communication among peers involves symposia, workshops, and other meetings dedicated to the integration of information on some phenomenon. With the proliferation of new knowledge, this form of scholarship is becoming ever more important.

4. Scholarship is both product and performance in the visual, performing, and creative arts. Universities provide an environment to permit creative scholars to write, perform, or paint. Their scholarship is meant to test the intellectual future as surely as the results of laboratory experimentation.

5. Scholarship is problem solving. The application of current knowledge to a real-world problem, whether in traditional agriculture, modern business, or technology, is a form of scholarship that enlightens those who use it. As the scholar applies knowledge, new learning often occurs that enhances future applications.

If scholarship is so diverse, what then is teaching? Teaching represents many forms of expressing scholarship and is a necessary part of the activity of the university scholar. The communication of scholarship is central to its existence. If scholarship is not communicated in some form, it has no value. There is no teaching process apart from research, nor from the application of that knowledge. As Robert J. Oppenheimer observed, the role of the scholar is not complete until he or she teaches.

Scholarship is expressed through all forms of teaching, as much as it is through writing. Such teaching may be intended for a fairly limited group of highly focused scholars in a particular area of study; to undergraduate students directly or through an effective textbook; or, even more generally, to a lay public through a magazine article. All these varieties of teaching can be based on very sophisticated scholarship.

Likewise, consulting, which results in the transfer of technology or information, can represent a significant form of intellectual activity based on scholarship. One would not expect modern scholars to transmit old techniques or outdated information, but rather to utilize the most modern understandings of their field, be it organizational culture, control of pests, or the technology of modern materials.

Both teaching and consulting are valid forms of the expression of scholarship. They are each equally valid, and together with scholarship itself, they represent the range of the intellectual activity of the modern university.

How does this discussion of scholarship help us to understand the problems of the modern university? The problem is that universities have come to focus almost exclusively on published work for peers in fairly narrow fields, as if it were the highest form of scholarship. Indeed, sometimes it appears that this is the only definition of scholarship allowable.

This call, then, is for a different approach to assessment, which may include different individual career patterns. Universities must develop a broader definition of scholarship that can contribute to the quality of institutions, while providing the best scholarship and development opportunities.

Faculty Careers

The faculty form the core of the university enterprise. They are the source of energy and stability in university programs and represent a long-term commitment and institutional investment. It is not uncommon for a faculty member to serve in one of our institutions for three or even four decades, and since in the course of a faculty member's career, many new issues can be expected to arise that cannot be predicted at the beginning of it, we must create an environment for our faculty where flexibility is the norm and where scholarship in new areas is as valued and encouraged as continuing scholarship in old ones.

The traditional model of the academic profession is derived from the most successful national research universities, and the fit with most academic careers at other academic institutions is awkward. Faculty careers are conceptualized as generally linear, following a single specialized research area, wherever it leads. However, we know that faculty members often go through a number of different phases in their careers:

1. The enthusiasm of a new faculty member just emerging from graduate school may be tempered through experience, resulting in new perspectives on his or her discipline.

2. Priorities for scholarship may change—at one time for teaching

graduate seminars and pursuing a single line of research, at other times for more direct public service, exploring new scholarly areas, or teaching more undergraduate courses.

3. New discoveries or new perspectives in the discipline may require new scholarship and necessitate changes in service programs and in undergraduate teaching.

To realize the best return on their investment in their faculties by sustaining faculty vitality over the long run, institutions must actively encourage flexibility within academic careers. To achieve the greatest levels of faculty productivity and responsiveness necessary to address the emerging problems of society, it may be necessary to invest university resources in faculty in new ways and to eliminate or alter some university practices that tend to inhibit flexibility in faculty careers.

Faculty learning styles. David A. Kolb has developed a scheme for describing the learning styles of different people, which may help us to understand the changes which occur in faculty careers. Learning style preferences develop as a result of experience, and people in widely different disciplines typically exhibit different preferred modes of thinking and learning. For example, many engineers are individuals who prefer to deal with abstract concepts and apply them to real world problems. On the other hand, people in humanities disciplines often prefer learning opportunities that permit them to reflect and form conclusions based upon individual concrete experiences. According to Kolb, it is a normal part of human development for learning style preferences to change as people mature and for individuals to want to seek different types of intellectual challenges.

A period of specialization emphasizing a particular learning style typically extends through formal education and into the early years of a professional career. Specialization is succeeded in midcareer by a stage of integration in which the individual begins to undertake activities that use ways of knowing other than those characteristic of his or her early professional life. Because faculty come to seek integration and undergo changes in preferred learning styles over time, anticipating that these changes will occur may make it possible to more effectively maintain faculty vitality over an entire career.

Faculty career stages. Certain types of dilemmas are characteristic, even if not universal, of faculty members at various career stages. The following characterizations may apply to faculty at various career stages at the land-grant and comprehensive metropolitan universities:

1. All faculty probably struggle with defining what it means to be professional at their institutions. Because the professional model taken

from the national research universities is not completely satisfactory, lacking as it does a broader conceptualization of scholarship that includes teaching and service, tensions between the expectations of the university and of the profession commonly arise.

2. New untenured faculty may in some ways experience the greatest professional tension between disciplinary and university expectations. Since they are at the pinnacle of their formal professional training, they may also be the most specialized of all the university faculty in terms of preferred learning style. Although very good at their disciplinary specialty, their degree of specialization may make it relatively difficult for them to teach beginning undergraduates, and they may not understand or value the service commitments of the university.

3. Midcareer faculty who seek integration in their professional activities may experience serious institutional resistance. When the opportunity to explore a new line of scholarship is desired for the second sabbatical, for example, departmental colleagues and university standards may require that the individual continue to pursue a line of research that is the same as, or very closely related to, what has been done in the past.

4. Senior faculty, if they have not been previously encouraged to seek new sources of intellectual stimulation, may simply withdraw from earlier professional disciplinary activities without engaging new ones.

There is an alternate professional model or viewpoint for faculty members that is probably more appropriate for those who work at land-grant and comprehensive metropolitan universities. It takes into account the many sources of vitality and satisfaction experienced by successful faculty members at these institutions. It acknowledges that academic careers may be linear, as in traditional research universities, but it also explicitly recognizes that careers may be much more diversified and that faculty members may express their scholarly proclivities in a variety of worthwhile ways. From an administrative viewpoint, the important question is how to encourage the desired diversity of expressions of scholarship while at the same time maintaining high standards of quality in all areas.

Faculty Assessment and Career Growth

If we are going to encourage faculty to grow intellectually in a variety of directions, we need to look critically at the way faculty are evaluated. Current evaluation procedures are almost exclusively the prerogative of the department and discipline, and often are biased by undervaluing information about anything but the quantity and quality of scholarly publication in the discipline. If we are to view scholarship as the core of the university enterprise and if we are to maintain high standards for that scholarship in all of its manifestations, we need to develop evaluation procedures to mirror our expectations. Suggested changes in evaluation procedures are outlined for consideration.

First, we need to adopt a flexible set of criteria against which to evaluate faculty members. Although it may be completely appropriate for some faculty at certain points in their careers to be evaluated against the most rigorous publication standards of their own discipline, at other times it may not be. Faculty who seek to emphasize teaching or service should also be evaluated stringently, but against other appropriate evaluation criteria.

Second, to avoid chaos and encourage planning, individual faculty decisions to move in a particular direction or to emphasize one aspect of scholarship rather than another need to be negotiated and agreed upon in advance with the department and the institution. Individual growth contracts, approved at the departmental and institutional level, have been successful at a few institutions in creating an atmosphere for diversification and deserve to be used more. For some faculty, an agreement to use an interdisciplinary evaluation process may be appropriate. Periodic individual evaluations that have a developmental rather than simply summative objective are appropriate and can be helpful for tenured as well as untenured faculty.

Third, we need to seek institutional ways to make excellence in all aspects of scholarship visible to the university and to the larger public community. For example, annual awards might be given by each college of the university to honor faculty who exemplify excellence in the scholarly areas of research, teaching, and service. Special awards could also be given for significant interdisciplinary work. An annual series of invited public events might also effectively highlight faculty who exemplify the new spirit and mission of the university.

Fourth, presidents, provosts, and deans should take frequent opportunities to articulate and affirm the underlying scholarly mission of the university in all of its manifestations. Tangible evidence of their commitment to this vision of the metropolitan university could take the form of supporting professional development centers for faculty. These centers would serve to encourage excellent teaching and research, as well as various entrepreneurial and service activities. Establishment of various centers for interdisciplinary and applied scholarship would serve to demonstrate the universities' priorities in these areas.

Implicit in the preceding paragraphs is the view that faculty need to be seen as individuals, and treated accordingly. As we move away from the national research university standard for evaluating all faculty at the land-grant and comprehensive metropolitan universities, so ought we also move away from the unrealistic "super-faculty" model, which asserts that all faculty should always be excellent in, and by implication be able to devote unlimited time to, research, service, and teaching.

Not all techniques for promoting sustained faculty vitality and career growth will be effective for all faculty. Insofar as assessment is concerned, the evaluation process ought to be seen as the process of constructing an individual evaluation template for each faculty member and measuring his or her accomplishments against it. While some techniques for assisting faculty might be most appropriate for certain groups, such as mentoring for junior faculty or curricular and teaching workshops for midcareer and senior professors, it is important not to stereotype even these groups.

We need to develop and keep a long-term perspective on the professional lives of our faculty members. While affirming that scholarship is the glue that holds the university together, we need to encourage faculty members to diversify and grow intellectually in their own ways, share their experiences with one another, and recognize that everyone experiences changes in intellectual interests and motivation over time. To enhance all of the scholarly functions of the university and to respond effectively to the challenges that the twenty-first century will surely bring, we must find institutional ways to permit faculty more flexibility in their careers, to assist in sustaining their professional vitality, and to ensure that they are not locked into the same narrow pattern of scholarship for their entire professional lives.

SUGGESTED READINGS

Astin, Alexander. "Moral Messages of the University." *Educational Record* (Spring 1989).

Bowen, H. R., and J. H. Schuster. *American Professors: A National Resource Imperiled.* New York: Oxford University Press, 1986.

Kolb, D. A. *Experiential Learning: Experience as the Source of Learning and Development.* Englewood Cliffs, NJ: Prentice Hall, 1984.

Rice, R. E. *Faculty Lives: Vitality and Change.* St. Paul: Northwest Area Foundation, 1985.

Seldin P. *Changing Practices in Faculty Evaluation.* San Francisco: Jossey-Bass, 1984.

_____. "Faculty Growth Contracts." In *Improving Teaching Styles* by Kenneth E. Eble. San Francisco: Jossey-Bass, 1980.

Shulman, L. "Toward a Pedagogy of Substance." *AAHE Bulletin* (June 1989).

Wylie, N. "Enhancing Faculty Vitality and Commitment to Careers." In *Academic Effectiveness: Transforming Colleges and Universities for the 1990's,* edited by M. D. Waggoner, R. L. Francis, and M. W. Peterson. Ann Arbor: University of Michigan, 1986: 37-42.

FORM AND TEXTURE OF A PROFESSIONAL LIFE

Patricia R. Plante

Something in all of us thrills to the drama of the death knell. Students continue to feel as if they were engaging in a subversive act by discussing Nietzsche's death of God; professors continue to feel as if they were flirting with the avant-garde by lecturing on Roland Barthes' death of the novel, and administrators, politicians, and pundits of varied hues now cultivate an apocalyptic tone when speaking of the death of the traditional professorate as proclaimed, for example, by a Charles Sykes in *Profscam: Professors and the Demise of Higher Education.*

However, what inspires many to keep talking and writing long after the impact of the notion of finality should have faded is that "death" in these cases is followed by a transmigration of souls; "death" does not really end the story for God, the novel, or the professor. God is spotted working through Mother Teresa; critics await the fiction of Saul Bellow, and ever more students of all ages attend classes taught by faculty in over three thousand institutions of higher learning across the country. In the case of the professor, at least, "death" in this context is a synonym for change.

Change as a threatening element in our lives has become a staple of pop psychology, and acceptance of change, a virtue widely prescribed as the medicine of choice for emotional malaise. However, the gradual transformation of the professor from shepherd of souls and dedicated, though severe, *pater familias* to sophisticated intellectual and worldly individualist has precipitated a rock slide of criticism of far greater magnitude than that occasioned by a common ho-hum fear of change. Upon occasion, legislators, alumni, administrators, journalists, each bear witness to the transformation in such impassioned rhetoric that

110

one would think the bounds of nature themselves had been violated. It is as if they had watched their favorite espalier walk away from the wall to which it had been carefully tied and begin to freely wave its branches in the breeze. The metaphor is apt, for faculty in all American colleges and universities now know their worth and have indeed declared their own forms.

In part, the outsized anger that follows this declaration of independence has two sources. One, the change is both recent and truly profound. Older alumni still speak of professors as secular monks whose central pleasures were limited to the successes, even modest, of their students; older administrators still describe a past where these same secular monks bowed before the authority of abbot-presidents; older legislators and trustees still remember dedicated faculty with a monk-like disdain for worldly goods. And anyone of a certain age can recall the self-image burnished, perhaps in self-defense, by the professors themselves: the impracticality, the absent mindedness, the aloofness from political and larger community concerns, the chilly reviews of all things American as opposed to European, the slightly anarchical choices in matters of dress, automobiles, and home furnishings.

Unquestionably, most if not all contemporary faculty members are leagues away from their older, monkish selves and have the past three decades polished to a brilliant sheen a more professional, more sophisticated image. Their lives are no longer circumscribed by campus walls; their ambitions soar above that of spurring others to great heights; their acceptance of authority is very nearly limited to that of persuasion, and, to paraphrase the poet Richard Wilbur, their loves, both spiritual and worldly, call them joyfully to the things of this world. They are no more impractical or absent minded than bankers or physicians or lawyers, and they are detached only in the special way associated with protecting their teaching and their research from influences that might taint one or the other or both. That they can tell the difference between fair remuneration and abusive remuneration and that they can appreciate the difference between a Hyundai and a Honda has caused serious distress to those who believe strongly in the beauty of monastic living—for others.

The second source of anger derives, quite touchingly, from the sentimental attachment of so many to the romanticized image of their former selves striding across one quad or another toward Lecture Hall 207 where Professor X or Y, in baggy tweeds and rumpled hair, and floating above everything but the text in hand to which he was obsessively attached, inspired them to read Keats or Spinoza for the first time. Even Americans who have no such memory to decorate have imagined the scene as it might be played with their children seated in the front of the class. As cynical a middle-aged narrator as the one encountered in John Barth's *The Floating Opera,* who claims never to expect very much from himself or from his fellow animals, has this to say about his former professors at the Hopkins:

> It was the men, the professors, the fine, independent minds of Johns Hopkins—the maturity, the absence of restrictions, the very air of Homewood, that nourished the strong seeds of reason in our ruined bodies; the disinterested wisdom that refused even to see our ridiculous persons in the lecture halls; that talked, as it were, to itself, and seemed scarcely to care when some of us began to listen, to listen intently, fiercely, passionately. (New York: Avon Books, 1956, pp. 137-38)

Such nostalgic revisitings are what daydreams are made of, and few can shake a daydreamer's shoulder with impunity. However, "Where are the snows of yesteryear?" is not the question that will move a contemporary metropolitan university forward or create and support a professional faculty willing and equipped to do so. Furthermore, it may be worth noting that while the professorate in such universities, indeed in all universities, has changed significantly since, say, the end of World War II, so have the colleges and universities in which they work, the students whom they teach, the administrators with whom they plan, the communities in which they live, and the publishers for whom they write. That being the case, and focusing in this instance on metropolitan universities, the two-part question that might justifiably interrupt all daydreams of the way we were is the following: What should a contemporary metropolitan university expect of its faculty? What should a contemporary faculty expect of its metropolitan university?

Senior administrators, members of search committees, and members of tenure committees in metropolitan universities should seek and retain faculty who are passionately committed to learning and to teaching. Faculty who apply for initial appointments and who present themselves for tenured positions should seek metropolitan universities that are passionately committed to creating and maintaining conditions that encourage and support learning and teaching of the highest order. While many might be tempted to dismiss these statements as the traditional genuflecting before the altar of higher education, all experienced academicians know that in some instances both faculty and institutions have allowed routine to veil their distin-

guished mission. In such cases a dutiful calendrical repetition has replaced passion, and those in question cease to see very clearly or to
care very deeply about discovering the new, preserving the old, and
sharing both.

One of the threats in the professional life of a faculty member is
identical to one of the threats in life itself, namely, everydayness. Scholarship and teaching demand intellectual intensity, and they demand
it year after year after year. They demand it in sickness and in health,
before students and colleagues who are responsive and nonresponsive,
when worries besiege the mind with distractions, in times of success
and in times of failure. While all faculty are energized by a deep interest in a particular discipline, a neophyte scholar/teacher is further
sustained by novelty and the natural exuberance of youth. However,
as one academic term follows another, both novelty and youth go the
way of all novelty and youth, and the faculty member is left occupying
a very large house with interest alone. It is at that moment, whenever
it is reached, that intellectual intensity holds and gains strength or
dissolves and begins to be replaced by mechanical responses.

Colleges and universities are amazingly resilient institutions that
can for years survive mechanical faculty, for good machines do have a
number of characteristics that are valuable, even if efficiency is not
the queen of virtues. Here is one of Max Frisch's fictional characters
praising the qualities of the robot as described in *Homo Faber:*

> Above all, however, the machine has no feelings, it feels no
> fear and no hope, which only disturb, it has no wishes with
> regard to the result, it operates according to the pure logic of
> probability. For this reason I assert that the robot perceives
> more accurately than man, it knows more about the future,
> for it calculates it, it neither speculates nor dreams, but is
> controlled by its own findings (the feedback) and cannot make
> mistakes; the robot has no need of intuition. . . . (New York:
> Harvest/ Harcourt Brace Jovanovich, 1959, p. 76)

However, any university peopled by robots will discover over time
that while faculty meet their classes and students attend them, its
spirit has died. Orientation programs point nowhere; commencements
begin nothing. It will discover that while it feels no fear, it feels no
hope, and that while dreams are no substitute for logic, logic is no
substitute for dreams. The faculty of a metropolitan university, perhaps
more than any other faculty, must guard against the diminution of
intellectual intensity in and out of the classroom, for it is to their public

urban institutions that turn in great numbers the poor, the minorities, the disenfranchised, the newly arrived immigrants—all those who truly need to be pulled back from leading lives of quiet desperation.

Central, therefore, to the challenges of a metropolitan university is the wisdom of attracting and selecting faculty who, throughout their professional careers, can give a novel, a theory, a rendition, a performance, a solution "more life than life has"—to use Toni Morrison's fine phrase. Central to the challenges of a metropolitan university faculty is the stamina to sustain an intellectual vigor that refuses to be ravaged not only by time, but, upon occasion, by political chicanery, by administrative indifference, and by student apathy. A monkish Mr. Chipps, however nostalgically endearing, will not do. The times and the broad mission of a metropolitan university, with its rainbow curricula, heterogeneous population, and demanding complex communities, call for faculty who are both worldly and idealistic, who are both sophisticated and caring, who are both aware of their own worth and the worth of their students.

It follows, therefore, that a metropolitan university faculty and the administrators who support them will neither patronize their students nor accept with equanimity someone patronizing them. Effective resistance to patronizing in either case depends in part on an understanding of the hierarchical nature of the academy.

A few years back, the avant-garde composer Philip Glass had his opera, *Einstein at the Beach,* produced at the New York Metropolitan Opera House at Lincoln Center. Overheard in the lobby during intermission, as reported by the *New Yorker,* were the remarks of one bejewelled matron to another who had just expressed approval of the first act: "But, surely, darling, you saw the premiere performance in Avignon last summer."

Academics, for a set of complex sociological reasons, now work in that kind of Metropolitan lobby world, a world as intellectually hierarchical as a British club is socially hierarchical, a world wherein the technique of staying ahead of others—however one defines "ahead"—has become a source of both jubilation and anxiety. It may be grand to have seen the New York production, but it is grander still to have seen it earlier in Avignon.

Edward Shils, professor of sociology and social thought at the University of Chicago, in a perceptive, fifty-year backward glance at the university world, tells us that this passion for distinguishing an academic aristocracy from a haute bourgeoisie from a petite bourgeoisie is a fairly recent phenomenon. One that, quite ironically, has grown in the same household as the passion against what is perceived to be elitism. In recalling his student days at the University of Pennsylvania, he writes: "We never thought about Harvard or Columbia or Princeton. Nor did we feel inferior to them. . . . Each university was sui generis" *(The American Scholar,* Spring, 1982, pp.164–65). And in referring to his early days as an instructor at the University of Chicago, which was somewhat more selfconscious than others about its place in the sun, he nevertheless points out that: "There was a vague sense of the hierarchy of universities, but it was not acutely felt. A person who had a doctorate from Chicago did not think that he was exiled from the Elysian Fields if he took a post at Vanderbilt or Utah. The hypersensitivity to rank, which is characteristic of the "antielitist" decades in which we are now living, had not yet appeared" (Ibid).

Neither ignorance nor denial of the academic culture's class conscious mind-set will do. In defining and ordering the form and texture of their professional lives, metropolitan university faculty—and the institutions to which they are committed—must, therefore, dismantle at least three traps designed specifically to ensnare academic climbers and/or those prone to seek in apathy refuge from hierarchical systems.

1. Serious scholarship is the exclusive province of research university faculty. The desertion of scholarship or the limitation of it to the preparation of classes should be a matter of grave concern to all those who care about the long-term growth of metropolitan universities. To care so little about the advancement of one's discipline as to abandon it to the sole care of others is to come dangerously close to leading an intellectually parasitic life and most certainly to arousing doubts as to the size of the flame carried into classrooms. All faculty who submitted to the rigors of a doctoral program were at one time presumably alive with the wonders of their field. To become so disengaged from that field as to cease to contribute to it is to give evidence of a detachment that may at worst point to anomie and at best to a serious diminution of interest. For scholarship, broadly defined to include not only frontier research, but synthesizing of discoveries and explication of texts, not only sustains the intellectual vigor of the scholar him/herself, but makes possible as nothing else can a sense of solidarity and common cause with colleagues everywhere. A scholar who masters and then synthesizes, explicates, collates, traces, and applies frontier research is a scholar who collaborates with the most creative, the most imaginative, and the most perceptive world-class researchers. Such collaboration is of immense worth, for many balls would be lost in the sun were it not for the trained eye of a commentator who directs our gaze to their trajectories.

Furthermore, in most if not all cases this sense of being *au courant,* of being poised to receive what might happen next generates an intellectual excitement in classrooms that many students identify as inspirational and influential. For in such classrooms students not only master the subject at hand but appropriate an understanding of what gifts the spurring of intellectual curiosity can bring to man/woman's eternal search for a life with meaning.

Anyone of a certain age can point to an individual who boasts defensively of never having written a line "because he/she came here to teach." And, in fact, a very few of the "quick" *seem* to have remained both knowledgeable and spirited. However, exceptions in this instance, as in so many others, prove the rule and do not contradict it—one who remains passionately interested in a discipline contributes to it. And metropolitan universities will succeed as centers of learning for everyone to the extent that their faculty remain passionately interested and intellectually committed.

Metropolitan university faculty are called upon to direct this interest and this commitment toward meeting external as well as internal needs. Hence, metropolitan university faculty roam far beyond any single campus and develop concerns that include but also extend far beyond the strictly local ones. While such a faculty care deeply about the welfare and growth in quality of their own institution, they care equally deeply about state and national and international environmental conditions that either advance or hamper the advancement of knowledge everywhere and that either ease or curtail the dissemination of information and insights. They eschew the intellectually restrictive and provincial, for their students come from varied cultures carrying gifts of assorted premises. They greet change and discovery with confidence because they have cultivated a robust life of the mind that welcomes unexpected perspectives, and their students fill the classrooms with multicolored views.

2. The nature of scholarship pursued by faculty in metropolitan universities is less worthy than that pursued by faculty in research universities. The fundamental importance of "pure" research, that which extends the frontiers of a discipline, is not seriously disputed by the knowledgeable anywhere, and faculty at metropolitan universities as well as faculty at research universities engage in it with beneficial results to us all. However, when the concept of research is broadened to include the application of new knowledge, the synthesizing of new information, and the creative interpretation of texts, hierarchical notions are let loose upon the land.

This phenomenon might well be dismissed as yet another amusing characteristic of the academic culture if it were not for two damaging consequences. One, many metropolitan university faculty, whose talent and temperament favor a broad definition of scholarship, feel compelled by word and deed and manner to apologize and to seek forgiveness, at times on their own campuses and nearly always in the world of academe beyond, for engaging in activities that can make a significant difference in the biography of an idea or an institution or a community. And this felt need to explain to themselves and others over and over again why they decided to assault Everest by its northern as opposed to its southern route can affect adversely the progress of their climb by diverting energies that should remain well concentrated. Two, these tell-tale signs of insecurity given by the practitioners themselves can, ironically, strengthen the opinion of those who dismiss anything short of "pure" research as inappropriate for those capable of producing vintage works. In turn, that reaffirmation of academe's great chain of being weakens the resolve of faculty whose gifts would allow them to make worthwhile contributions to a field of study, but whose interest can only be sustained by the approbation and collaboration of colleagues. Such faculty are frequently those marked for defeat by time.

Metropolitan university faculty and administrators are perhaps the only professionals in higher education in a position to bestow intellectual prestige and significant rewards upon scholarship that is not so narrowly defined as to exclude everything but the addition of truly new knowledge. For the mission and identity of research universities are all too well defined and too well established to don characteristics that might render them unrecognizable, and those of colleges of liberal arts and community colleges place such institutions *hors de combat*. What is sorely needed is the conviction that solutions to regional community problems; insights into the formulations of public policies; contributions to the artistic life of the city that the university calls home; directions for the reform of public school curricula; gathering and dissemination of important data regarding the challenges of health care, waste disposal, and environmental pollution are, along with innumerable other areas of concern and importance, worthy of the intellectual attention of a faculty well trained to share its considerable expertise. What is additionally needed is the confidence to proclaim the conviction.

A metropolitan university campus that reaches consensus on a definition of extended scholarship/research and that finds the means to reward its faculty for engaging in it must attend to other important related matters. It must, for example, stop counting and start reading. The number of papers published and the number of papers delivered at professional conferences are not where the mind's eye should rest. The quality of those works should be the focus of attention and evaluation. Search committees and tenure and promotion committees should examine a colleague's scholarship with care and judge it with courage. Is the book or the article or the government report alive? Imaginative?

Does it point to future promise? Or is the book or the article or the report humdrum? Pedestrian? Does it give evidence of being the product of one merely fulfilling a duty?

As a way of underscoring the sincerity of its convictions in favoring quality over quantity, a metropolitan university might consider establishing the following policy. "For the purpose of evaluating colleagues, no search or review committee or senior administrator will examine more than four works by assistant professors, more than six works by associate professors, and more than eight works by professors. The works submitted for appraisal will be of the candidates' choosing and will be accompanied by a short essay describing the significance and purpose of each submission." The very act of choosing and defending would in itself reveal certain qualities of mind and point to certain characteristics of imagination.

Deans, academic vice-presidents, and presidents of metropolitan universities, who play a large role in determining and applying any reward system also owe it to their faculty to read their publications, attend their concerts and theater productions, view their exhibits, and promote their expertise. While certain twigs off the branches of technical and highly specialized studies may be beyond the reach of many administrators, it does not follow that a broadly educated dean or president whose own field is, say anthropology, cannot come to some broad judgments regarding the worth of a book describing weaknesses in public policies regarding health care for the poor, or one tracing the influence of African art on the paintings and sculptures of Picasso. At the very least, an educated administrator knows whether the book is gracefully or awkwardly written, whether it reveals an interesting and witty voice or a dull and tedious one, whether it carries a reader to conclusions persuasively or weakly. To deny this knowledge is to fall into unbecoming timidity if not inappropriate humility.

A metropolitan university must also give time and solitude their due. Faculty will begin to trust those who have converted from counting to reading, not only when the quality of their scholarship begins to be discussed seriously, but when certain other additional conditions obtain. Two of these relate to the respect a metropolitan university accords time and solitude. It will, for example, discourage abbreviated probationary periods before a faculty member comes up for tenure, not only because it wants time for careful evaluation, but because it wants to afford the faculty member in question time for careful scholarship and time for visions and revisions of creative projects. It will, as another example, review works in progress and take these as seriously as works that have reached completion, whether yet published, performed, exhibited, or presented. For what the metropolitan university wants above all else is for its faculty to remain interested in and committed to their disciplines and to the knowledge and insights they can bring to students and colleagues everywhere. So the first question asked in evaluations is not "What is the date on the last publication or performance?" The first question asked is "What is the quality of the scholarship now being pursued and how steady is the chase?"

A contemporary metropolitan faculty's need for time is perhaps exceeded only by its need for solitude. Montaigne's advice was to prepare a little back shop all our own wherein we might establish solitude. The counsel is wise, for journeys to the land of intellectual insights are essentially solitary adventures; group tours rarely produce prize slides or diaries. Indeed, the biographical account of all lasting contributions to any discipline points to a scholar's ability to retreat deep within him/herself and to return bearing the individual voice, the individual view. The unconvinced might attempt to imagine *Waiting for Godot* written as a group exercise or Mendelssohn's "Quartet in F minor" composed by a class in chamber music.

Many metropolitan universities are hurly-burly, crowded, noisy, slightly anarchical places where the newly arrived faculty often speak of feeling overwhelmed and where the older faculty often indulge in a remembrance of things past when campus life seemed becomingly leisurely and spacious. The isolating walls, both real and imaginary, have come down: business entrepreneurs walk the halls of Old Main, engineers from local high-technology firms inspect the laboratories, state development officers search the offices for consultants, superintendents of schools and directors of hospitals establish cooperative ventures with schools of education and nursing, and students of all ages, backgrounds, and levels of talent rightfully expect guidance and nurturing. And however vibrant academe in a metropolitan setting has become, all faculty, by temperament and vocation inclined to favor meditation and contemplation, give signs that this splendid world is occasionally too much with them.

Hence, metropolitan university administrators who understand and respect the intense and demanding nature of the work of faculty will take seriously their need for solitude and will whenever and wherever possible seek ways and means of nourishing it. For example, it will provide single, well-appointed offices; it will assign teaching schedules that allow blocks of time devoted to study; it will support generous sabbatical leaves; it will call only meetings and assemblies that have an important purpose and are well prepared; it will encourage faculty to share their expertise with the larger community and to do so generously, but never at the cost of excluding from their professional life a solitude that is essential to its continued vitality. For a faculty that spends all of their time repeating what they already know, will eventually know little.

3. *Metropolitan university faculty should structure and teach courses that are of immediate economic usefulness even to the neglect of those that are of long-term intellectual importance.* A faculty, much in the manner of all professionals, can succeed in preserving their *elan vital* and then direct it toward unworthy ends. A danger as grave as the two cited above lurks on metropolitan university campuses. And since this danger is infrequently, if ever, recognized by even the severest critics of the professoriat and but occasionally acknowledged by many universities themselves, faculty and administrators alike may not be shielding campuses against its potentially hurricane-wind force. This danger lurks behind euphemisms that would have faculty who teach all but the top-tier pupils believe that equal access is to be equated with equal opportunity—that curricula designed to meet immediate economic needs are as valuable as those designed to meet the long-term needs of both the students themselves and the nation they will inherit.

In short, this third trap forgoes a belief in knowledge as spiritual power for everyone and substitutes a creed that justifies establishing curricula especially structured for the poor and the unaware. In the 1990s, one of the major responsibilities of metropolitan university faculty everywhere will be to protect themselves and their students from being pulled into that trap. For those who live by economics will perish by economics.

Faculty who have remained enthusiastic and dedicated, faculty who have looked a hierarchical culture in the eye and not blinked, faculty who now spend long hours structuring courses of study in metropolitan universities must not have taken apart traps one and two only to fall into the maw of trap three. They must guard against being lulled by the *cliché du jour* into concluding that all obligations have been met when a curriculum prepares the poor and the newly arrived immigrants, the intellectually naive, and all those yearning for rebeginnings to enter the economic mainstream and to help the nation's economy remain competitive.

Let no one misinterpret this *cri de coeur* as sounding a retreat to days when aristocrats let their fingernails grow to prove that they never engaged in manual labor. Of course, universities must prepare and prepare well agronomists and chemists and nurses and accountants.

Of course, universities must place these disciplines within their historical contexts, examine their contemporary ethical dilemmas, and charge them with fervor for quality and values. Educating students for the practice of law, the marketing of software, the building of bridges, and the designing of urban centers is both appropriate and worthy of the mission perspective of any university. The conviction that strobe lights this third trap, however, is as simple as it may be controversial: a zest for work succeeds a zest for life. And a better means of achieving a zest for life than long intense treks with linguists and philosophers and artists through the forests, meadows, and caverns of the human spirit—one has yet to invent.

Hence, a valuable curriculum allows all students to share the exclusively human joys that derive not only from analysis but from creativity and perspective. Why should the moments of heightened consciousness occasioned by truly seeing (because someone taught you to see) the windows of Sainte Chapelle be the exclusive domain of those who attend liberal arts colleges or enroll in the better research universities? Why should the turn of a phrase, the structure of an argument, the allusions to the past, or the music of a poem make only those of a privileged background feel intensely alive? Metropolitan university faculty must find ways to empower their students to discover satisfying patterns not only at the end of syllogisms, but also at the end of rainbows.

In all discussions centering on matters as complex as the form and texture of the professional life of a metropolitan university faculty, there are, of course, no formulas. There can, however, be principles. Three that seem worthy of deliberation are: (1) long-term vitality in teaching is inextricably linked to long-term vitality in scholarship; (2) scholarship broadly defined so as to include synthesis and dissemination of the new and explication of both the old and the new is of serious import and worthy of support and reward; and (3) teaching for short-term economic returns should neither displace nor outrank teaching for long-term intellectual growth.

According to Fowlie, the French philologist, Ernest Renan, believed that "good and evil, pleasure and pain, the beautiful and the ugly, reason and madness, have as many indiscernible shadings as those we see on the neck of a dove" (Fowlie, p. 254). Metropolitan university faculty across the nation are happily dedicated to an examination and explication of these innumerable shadings, and the conviction that this probing and interpreting will lead to further examinations and explications is the very source of both their joy and their devotion. No work can boast of a more elegant colophon.

SUGGESTED READINGS

Fowlie, Wallace. "Remembering Renan." *American Scholar* (Spring 1989).
Lynton, Ernest A., and Sandra Elman. *New Priorities for the University.* San Francisco: Jossey-Bass, 1987.
Plante, Patricia R. "Educational Authenticity." *Change* 8 (January-February 1986).
Rorty, Richard. *Contingency, Irony, and Solidarity.* Cambridge: Cambridge University Press, 1989.
Storr, Anthony. *Solitude: A Return to the Self.* New York: Ballantine Books, 1988.

THE PREPARATION OF FUTURE FACULTY FOR METROPOLITAN UNIVERSITIES

G. Edward Schuh

Eighty percent of the population of the United States now resides in metropolitan centers. This share is similarly high in other developed countries. And many developing countries are well on the way to concentrating their populations in urban centers.

Numerous U.S. cities have witnessed major transformations of their physical structures and facilities over recent decades. The clutter of old buildings and transportation systems has been cleared out, and new highway systems and beautiful buildings rise on the wastelands of the past. However, the social problems of our metropolitan centers persist and, if anything, are becoming more serious. Families continue to break down at an alarming rate. An ever larger share of our children are born into single-parent families. Chemical abuse is widespread. Poor people are confined to parts of the city where there are no jobs. Our nation wastes a large share of the potential of its human capital because it has not found ways to solve its social problems or to invest in its human resources at socially optimal levels.

Those who in the past looked to metropolitan or urban universities to solve the problems of our urban centers have been disappointed with their failure to do so. Some observers make disparaging comparisons with our land-grant universities, which are given credit for having transformed rural America and for having given this nation what has been judged to be the most productive agriculture in the world.

This unfavorable comparison is misplaced. The land grant universities *were* successful in modernizing the *production* side of agriculture. They did a great deal less, however, to deal with the social problems of rural America. To their good fortune, an important share of these social problems was dumped into our metropolitan centers.

These problems merged with, and aggravated, the social problems that arose there in conjunction with the enormous transformation of our economy after World War II.

The problems of our universities are far more deeply rooted than their inability to address the problems of urban America alone would suggest. Despite their ability to produce new knowledge at an astonishing rate, they have not yet found ways to organize themselves, and thereby apply that knowledge effectively to the solution of the social dislocations and problems that arise as the fruits of their research efforts transform the economy and society. Moreover, they are failing, even, to transfer the technical knowledge they generate to the private sector. Thus, the nation that spends the highest share of its GNP on R & D, and that has earned a dominant share of Nobel prizes in science in recent years, finds itself lagging in its ability to compete internationally, not only with modern industrial giants, such as Japan and Germany, but also with newly industrializing countries, such as Hong Kong, Singapore, South Korea, Taiwan, and, to a lesser extent, Brazil and Mexico. Similarly, the growth rate of the U.S. lags behind that of other countries, and its urban problems grow like a cancer.

These failures of U.S. universities are rooted, in part, in the education and development of their faculty. Of equal importance, however, is that the failures are rooted in how the faculty are managed in their academic endeavors. This article discusses both sets of issues.

Metropolitan universities vary a great deal in their organization and in what they take to be their mission or missions. An important premise of this article, however, is that such universities have a special obligation both to the population of their region and to the welfare of the nation as a whole. Other important premises are:

1. scholarship and the pursuit of knowledge must be the primary mission of modern universities; and

2. such universities must pay attention to the dissemination and application of the new knowledge they generate. Furthermore, they must contribute to the economic and cultural development of the area they serve if they are to gain (or regain) the public support they need to carry out their primary missions.

The Need for Change

U.S. universities, more than those in almost any other part of the world, have been characterized by two important features: (1) education for the masses; and (2) the application of knowledge to the solution of problems in society. These features are a consequence of the creation of the land-grant colleges and universities, a uniquely American innovation that has been widely emulated both by other countries and by other educational institutions within the United States. The land-grant universities were created as a reaction to the elitism of eastern liberal arts colleges and to their lack of relevance to the emerging problems of a rapidly industrializing society. The establishment of the land grants effectively put higher education at the service of economic development and the further evolution of society.

This important institutional innovation has served U.S. society quite well, and for a time, helped the nation to be both the scientific and technological leader of the world. The general spread of the tripartite mission of resident instruction, research, and outreach or extension among U.S. universities is evidence of the vitality of the basic idea. This also is true of the continued strength of the idea of mass education, as evidenced by the proliferation of publicly supported higher education institutions in the form of additional (non-land-grant) state colleges and universities, as well as community colleges dedicated almost exclusively to resident instruction.

Higher education in the United States, however, has been under stress for some time. Among the manifestations of this are the following:

1. The nation is losing its international competitive edge.

2. The U.S. is no longer the scientific leader in many fields.

3. Employers complain about the inability of graduates to apply their knowledge effectively to current problems.

4. Serious social and economic problems are unresolved.

5. And universities face recurring budget problems and are underfunded relative to the demands placed on them. Moreover, as one looks to the future, the challenges U.S. universities face promise to become even greater.

It is little wonder our universities are undergoing such severe stress. The environment in which they operate has undergone significant change, and the demands on them have grown enormously. Understanding these changes and the increasing demands they represent is the key to revitalizing institutions of higher education and to preparing them to deal with the problems expected to emerge as the twenty-first century approaches.

The first important development has been the veritable explosion in knowledge created by past investments in science and technology in this country, and increasingly in other countries. This knowledge explosion, in turn, has several consequences. For example, advances in science have moved the frontier of knowledge further and further away from the application of knowledge to the problems of society. Academic disciplines have become increasingly specialized, and new knowledge on the frontiers of science is becoming more abstract. This enlarges the communication problems among scientists and professionals in the various fields. The explosion in knowledge also alters the character of education needed, both for those who intend to be scientists and for those who will use that knowledge eventually to address problems of society. Basic disciplinary work and the application of knowledge have become further divorced and separated. In fact, the large research universities in this nation have become increasingly like the German model, emphasizing knowledge for its own sake.

Another consequence is that economic growth and development are becoming still more rooted in human capital than in physical capital. This stock of human resources includes the genetic endowment of the society, knowledge, investments in new technology and in education and training, in the health of the population and its nutritional status, and in its institutional arrangements.

The design, creation, and management of institutional arrangements is to social scientists what new technology is to the biological and physical scientists. Institutional arrangements are the various means by which individuals in society relate to each other. They range from informal and formal rules of behavior, to policies implemented by government, to organizations and entities such as universities, the family, and social security. Sound institutional arrangements contribute to economic growth in the same way as new technology. Equally as important, they strongly influence how the benefits of economic growth are shared in society.

The value of the stock of human capital in a society like the United States today simply dwarfs the value of its stock of physical capital. Moreover, increases in the net domestic output of goods and services results increasingly from investments in science and technology and in other forms of reproducible human capital.

Two important implications follow from this proposition. The first is that in the future, the growth and development of the U.S. economy will be determined increasingly by its investments in the full range of human capital from the *generation* of new knowledge on the frontiers of science, to the *application* of that knowledge, to the training and education of its populace in the latest knowledge as it emerges, to investments in the health *and* nutrition status of its population, and to the design and development of new institutional arrangements for an ever-changing society. Investments in physical capital still will be important, but this capital will be valued more for the knowledge imbedded in it than for the physical capital per se. This is despite the fact that the total rate of investment still will influence aggregate growth rates. The second implication is that this nation's ability to compete in the international economy also will be determined more and more by these same investments in human capital.

The second development in the U.S. economy consists of large and significant demographic changes that already are under way and that can be expected to continue in the future. These changes, too, have a number of important dimensions. The first is the gradual extension of life expectancy and the aging of the population. An important implication of this development is the need for lifetime learning and the institutional means to provide education for that purpose. This becomes especially important in light of the knowledge explosion, which makes old knowledge obsolete.

A further change in U.S. demographics is the emergence of an increasingly ethnically diverse population. Asians and Hispanics make up an ever larger portion of our population. Together with the blacks and Native Americans in our society, important segments of these population groups tend to be educationally disadvantaged. If the nation is to take full advantage of its population stock, and at the same time provide for a more equitable distribution of income, ways will have to be found to provide these population groups with the skills and knowledge to participate in a modern market economy and in the political processes that select our leaders and establish our policies and institutional framework.

In addition, our society has become increasingly urban. We were essentially an agrarian society at the time the land-grant universities were established, despite a rapidly emerging industrial sector. Today, we have become essentially an urban society, with the service sector increasingly the predominant part of the economy. The institutional arrangements that enabled universities to contribute so much to the modernization of agriculture and the development of an industrial colossus have faltered in addressing the problems of urban America and in the modernization of the service sector.

These circumstances present what may be one of the most serious challenges modern universities face. As noted above, the seriousness of this problem is rooted, in part, in the failure of society in the past to address the human capital problems of the rural sector. As migrants from rural areas collected in the urban centers, residents left for the suburbs. The result has been city cores with mostly underdeveloped stocks of human capital. Moreover, modern universities, even those located in such urban centers and mandated to address the problems of the urban core, have failed to devise policies and institutional arrangements to solve these problems.

The Role of the University

Modern universities contribute to society through what now has become a classic triplet of missions: (1) resident instruction; (2) research; and (3) outreach or extension. The first two of these are clear-cut; the third is diverse and characterized by considerable ambiguity. Generically, however, the third refers to the application of knowledge to the solution of problems society faces, to the design of new policies and institutional arrangements, and to the extension of the services of the university to the broader population and society—beyond those of the resident student body.

Operationally, these three missions contribute to the development of society in three important ways:

1. through the development and dissemination of new knowledge and new technology;
2. through the design of new institutional arrangements and the more effective management of the public sector; and
3. through the development of the arts and values for a modern society.

Modern universities tend to pride themselves on, and measure themselves by, their contribution to the development of new knowledge. If they are to contribute effectively to the further evolution of society, however, they need to give more attention to assisting in the conversion of knowledge into technology and to the dissemination of that technology more widely in society. In addition, they need to give more attention to institutional design and innovation, to the management of the public sector, and to the promulgation of the arts and modern values.

New technology is the engine of economic growth in a modern society. It is reflected in new products, which provide new or improved consumer services or contribute more efficiently to production processes. It is reflected also in new production processes, which increase the output from conventional inputs of labor and capital. Such new technology must be disseminated broadly in society if economic growth is to be broadly based. If the new technology is generated with public funds, universities and others have a responsibility to see that it is available widely—to the poor and disadvantaged, as well as to the more well-to-do, and to the small firm and the large.

The failure of modern universities to give adequate attention to the design of new institutional arrangements is an important reason why economic growth is faltering in this country and why such serious social problems have emerged. We witness the breakdown of the family, yet no new institutional arrangement arises to provide the services once provided by the family. We have a health *recovery* system, but not a *complete* health system that would include preventive medicine. Similarly, we experience a society which is increasingly based on knowledge, yet we fail to develop new institutional arrangements to assure that all members of society have access to that knowledge. Finally, a truly international economy and society emerges before us, but we fail to develop the institutional arrangements which would enable us to find our way politically and economically in that new society.

In addressing the important social problems of equity or access, Amartya Sen enjoins us to take individual freedom as a social commitment. Such a social ethic is more widely based than political freedom, and includes economic freedom and the alleviation of poverty constraints as well. In Sen's view, a social commitment to individual freedom must involve attaching importance to enhancing the capabilities that different people actually have; the choice of social arrangements must be influenced by their ability to promote human capabilities. The universities, thus, have a major role to play in promoting individual freedom.

The promotion of the arts and the development and promulgation of values for a modern society are a growing challenge to metropolitan universities. Rapid advances in knowledge pose major ethical and moral challenges. We see this most obviously in the case of medicine, where advances in knowledge give rise to choices and options not available before. The side effects of new technology similarly open new alternatives, while in some cases creating new problems. More generally, important ethical and moral choices between present and future generations are emerging, reflected most obviously in the global environmental problems that are receiving increased attention.

Despite the emergence of these serious moral issues, universities have failed to address them in an effective way. Yet the church and religion, the means by which we addressed such dilemmas in the past, are becoming less and less important in our society—and some would say less relevant to these issues.

At a somewhat different level, advances in knowledge and technology make new concepts possible in the arts, and open up new opportunities and new technologies for artistic expression. They also open whole new dimensions to be exploited by the theater and the literary arts. The rapid growth in knowledge of the universe and its beginning is an important example. The failure to exploit these new opportunities is to sacrifice our potential for personal growth and development and, in turn, the potential for growth and development of society. Modern universities have a responsibility to further such goals, and to broaden access to the arts in society.

The Preparation of Future Faculty

If metropolitan universities are to address and solve the many problems they face, they need to develop the capacity to teach a student body that is increasingly diverse in terms of age, race, gender, and ethnic background. In addition, they need to educate their students to work and to exercise their civic duties in a world that is international in scope. This means that they must understand the cultures of other lands, the institutional arrangements in those lands, and the international economy that stitches nation-states together. Finally, they need to educate their students to address the moral and ethical choices they face in a modern society.

At a different level, these universities need to develop the capacity to do more applied research, to deliver more technical assistance to both the private and public sectors, and to provide more policy analysis and institutional design. The particular capacities they require to deliver these services will depend on their location and the particular problems their metropolitan areas face.

Providing the appropriate teaching skills and the capacity to deliver the necessary services to the local community is, in part, an issue of resource allocation and choice among university administrators. It is also, in part, an issue of incentives. Faculty require financial and status rewards for excellence in applied research, for delivering technical assistance, and for undertaking policy research. It is also an issue of developing a sense of institutional mission, and the willingness and ability of administrators to mobilize and allocate faculty and resources to address the problems of society.

An important issue is how to prepare the faculty for these new teaching missions and for delivering on the outreach or extension missions. A frequent suggestion is that more faculty need to have multidisciplinary training if they are to address the complex problems of society. That suggestion is misguided in my view. It confuses the need to have diverse technical skills to solve a particular problem with the issue of the form in which these diverse skills are to be delivered. Given the complexity of the problems modern society faces, faculty ought to be educated with the most advanced knowledge available. This requires specialization. Similarly, it fails to recognize that the universities must continue to make advances on the frontier of knowledge at the same time they address societal problems.

What is needed are institutional arrangements that can deliver multiple disciplinary capacities. The leadership for such institutes or centers need to be academic entrepreneurs, who can identify and conceptualize problems and who can meld together the various talents needed to solve those problems. Unfortunately, universities tend to undervalue academic entrepreneurship.

Individual faculty might develop additional disciplinary capabilities by adding further schooling to that end, either while they are acquiring their original disciplinary strength, or later in their career. Such capability should be *in addition* to the original strength, however, not at the expense of depth in the original field. The difficulty in not attaining strength in the primary field is that the individual would not be able to communicate with those on the cutting edge in their respective fields.

Another challenge is to have faculty who can teach in a culturally diverse way, who can solve applied problems, and who can extend their knowledge to those in both the private and public sectors through technical assistance or through "external" courses. Not all of these abilities have to be in the same person, nor does each faculty member have to engage in all of these activities. Some understanding of the broad issues of society would be helpful, however, so faculty understand how what they do fits into the larger scheme of things and into the larger mission of the university.

Ideally, future faculty would have a strong liberal arts background. Whether this would be a full, four-year program, or whether a two-year program would be sufficient, would depend on the particular field. For those going into engineering and the biological and physical sciences, two years of liberal arts would probably be sufficient, especially if the liberal arts were related to the major. Two years of specialization following this liberal arts education might not be enough, however, and in those cases, a five-year degree would be necessary. Given the increase in life expectancy, the addition of another year to one's formal education would not seem out of line.

Education should, in general, become increasingly specialized as one goes through one's academic career. For those interested in policy issues, however, or in eventually working more generally with the larger problems of society in their academic careers, a professional degree after the basic undergraduate degree might be appropriate. An M.B.A., a degree in law, or a degree in public policy would be appropriate, depending on the interests of the individual. This would, then, be followed by the Ph.D. degree in the chosen field of specialization.

Broadening the Ph.D. degree itself is another way of widening the skills of potential faculty members interested in these broader issues of society. This could be done by adding a minor in the pertinent field, or fields, to the regular disciplinary requirements of the Ph.D. Just as in the case of the earlier discussion, such minors should be *in addition to* the regular degree requirements, not at the expense of them. This would appear to be a more efficient way of providing the needed breadth for those who want it, than to redesign the Ph.D. degree itself.

An alternative way of approaching this problem is to recognize the importance of lifetime learning for faculty members, in the same way we do for the general population. In that sense, one might imagine future faculty members starting with an undergraduate liberal arts program, possibly in the form of a five-year program, and then going directly into their specialization. They would, then, spend the first part of their academic career specializing in research in their chosen field. For those who want to continue with a research career, the first sabbatical would be dedicated to upgrading their skills in their chosen field. For others, who find themselves more interested in the broader societal issues or who find their vocational interests more on the side of applied work, the sabbatical might be better directed either to more education in one of the professional fields, or to a year of specialized training in fields that would better equip them with knowledge of the institutional arrangements in society.

Whichever approach is chosen, and this choice obviously would be that of the individual, we must recognize that preparing faculty for the mission of a modern university requires a great deal more investment in their own human capital than is being made currently by many, if not most, faculty. To remedy this problem, sabbaticals need to be *required* of all faculty. The advantage researchers have in academic careers is that in doing their research they continue to add to their stock of knowledge. Those interested in nonresearch fields within academia must find some way to continue to invest in their own human capital in a parallel way.

A major issue universities face today is how to further upgrade the skills of their existing faculties. One way to begin this process is to start now to enforce the requirement of obligatory sabbaticals. These sabbaticals can be used for the same purposes as above. Special attention should be given, however, to further education which gives faculty a better understanding of diversity issues, which gives them stronger insights into the problems of society on which their basic skills bear, and which gives them a better understanding of the international economy and society.

If sabbaticals become obligatory, an important issue will be how to ensure that they actually are used to good purpose. Assuring this should be a natural responsibility of the academic leadership. Sabbatical leaves typically need to be approved by the dean. It will be the responsibility of the person occupying that position, or of somebody designated by the dean, to work out mutually satisfying arrangements.

Requiring that sabbaticals be taken may become easier in the future. The end of obligatory retirement at sixty-five or seventy probably will cause most universities to require some form of periodic evaluation that goes much beyond those now in place. This will be added incentive for faculty to undertake additional investments in their skill levels. It also may provide them with the incentive to broaden their skills at later stages of their careers, so their skills will be relevant to the multiple missions of the university. To do so later in their careers is natural, since not only do their own interests broaden, but also faculty become wiser in the needs of society.

Upgrading the skills of existing faculty in the above ways is expensive. Because a larger share of their faculty will be on leave at any given time, universities will need to have a larger faculty to deliver a given level of services. Moreover, programs will suffer discontinuities in some cases. In addition, it is increasingly difficult for faculty to receive financial support for sabbaticals as they move through their careers because their salaries are so high. It may be that in the future, universities will need to provide a larger share of, or full financial support for, sabbaticals.

This problem of costs, however, has to be approached as an investment which will have a high payoff over the longer term to both the university itself and to society. Sustaining and developing the skills of their faculties is critical to universities being on the cutting edge and contributing more effectively to society. After all, universities are uniquely based on knowledge and function in an environment in which that knowledge is always changing. Just as factories always must renovate and renew their machinery, equipment, and physical plant, so do universities need to continually renovate and renew the knowledge base of their faculty. To make this feasible, universities may require establishment of a depreciation fund for their human capital, in the same way a private firm has a depreciation fund for its physical capital. To establish such a fund as a regular part of a university's budget would make explicit the extent to which the knowledge and skills of its faculty are one of its primary resources.

Another important issue is the extent to which suggestions made above require faculty to spend more time obtaining their original education and investing in the development of their knowledge base later in their careers. The costs of this additional time will be made up by increases in life expectancy, and by an increase in productivity. This increase in productivity should elicit an increase in real salaries.

Concluding Comments

Revitalizing our universities is critical to revitalizing our economy and society and to sustaining our place in the international society and economy. This revitalization requires that we develop faculty with the skills needed to fulfill the broader missions that modern universities require, and to cope with the rapidly expanding body of knowledge. This necessitates lifetime learning on the part of the faculty, and the continuous investment by both the faculty and society in the upgrading of their skills. These will not be wasted investments. They are critical to the future health of our society.

SUGGESTED READINGS

Lynton, Ernest A., and Sandra E. Elman. *New Priorities for the University*. San Francisco and London: Jossey-Bass, 1988.
Schuh, G. Edward. "Revitalizing the Land Grant Universities." Minneapolis: Strategic Management Research Center, Carlson School of Management, University of Minnesota, 1984.
Schuh, G. Edward, and Vernon W. Ruttan. "The Research and Service Missions of the University." In *Higher Education and the Development of the U.S. Economy*, edited by William E. Becker and Darrell R. Lewis. Norwell, MA: Kluwer Academic Publishers, 1991.
Sen, Amartya. "Individual Freedom as a Social Commitment." *The New York Review of Books*, 37 (June 14, 1990): 49–54.

THE NEW AMERICAN SCHOLAR: SCHOLARSHIP AND THE PURPOSES OF THE UNIVERSITY

R. Eugene Rice

In 1837, Ralph Waldo Emerson presented to the "president and gentlemen" of Harvard's Phi Beta Kappa Society his famous address, "The American Scholar." In that provocative statement described by Oliver Wendell Holmes as America's "intellectual Declaration of Independence," Emerson articulated a vision of the role of the scholar in the new democracy. He called for the rejection of a past that was alien and debilitating and for the adoption of a new approach to scholarship and the role of the scholar in society—a role that would be vital and self-confident, in his words, "blood warm."

Emerson's address was not so much an assertion of intellectual nationalism as a statement of his own struggle with the problem of vocation, with the nature and meaning of scholarly work in a changing society. It is this same issue—what it means to be a scholar in an evolving democracy—that confronts faculty in American higher education today.

Just as Emerson's American scholar was struggling to break away from the dominance of "the learning of other lands," from patterns of deference that engendered self-doubt and the depreciation of new, adaptive roles, so the majority of faculty in today's colleges and universities are wrestling with a conception of scholarship that is much too narrow and singularly inappropriate for the rich diversity—the educational mosaic—that has become the hallmark of American higher education.

Higher education in the United States emerged from its time of rapid expansion following the Second World War with two primary strengths, characteristics that have become the envy of the world:

1. a research capability in almost every academic specialization, second to none, and

2. a richly textured diversity in its educational system that opened opportunities for advanced learning to most of the nation's people.

These primary strengths have been praised widely and emulated where possible.

The expansion of specialized research and the focus on the role of the scholar as researcher was triumphantly celebrated. Academic hierarchy took on new meaning and prestige ranking grew in importance. So significant was this change that, in 1968, Christopher Jenks and David Riesman could claim, in good faith, that an "academic revolution" had occurred.

There was not just one academic revolution, however; there were two. And the second was every bit as significant and, certainly, as dramatic. An already diverse system of higher education exploded with growth, innovation, and responsiveness; there were major changes in size, complexity, and mission. Regrettably, these two revolutions, as admirable as they were, encompassed serious contradictions. In *The Higher Education System,* Burton Clark writes about the "paradox of hierarchy and diversity" endemic to the system of American higher education. The two strengths pulled in opposite directions, and the enormous incongruity between the two produced serious role strain for faculty and organizational fissures that cut across our institutions. And at the heart of the tension is the meaning of scholarship and the role of the faculty member as scholar.

What has evolved is a hierarchical conception of scholarly excellence that is tied to the advancement of research and defined in zero-sum terms. This restricted one-dimensional view places research in competition with other important scholarly responsibilities and leads to their devaluation. Faculty find themselves divided within, set against one another, and profoundly disheartened when confronted with the disparity between the mission driving the institutions of which they are a part and their own professional self-understanding.

What is needed is a broader conception of scholarship: one that is congruent with the rich diversity of American higher education, one that is more appropriate, more authentic, and more adaptive for both our institutions and the day-to-day working lives of faculty.

Scholarship and the Comprehensives

It is the comprehensive universities that have struggled most with the established definition of scholarship and the hierarchy that reinforces it. Sixty percent of the public universities are in this category, and almost all were created or designated as universities during the postwar period. Many private institutions have moved recently into this general classification as they have grown and changed. These are the institutions that serve the great majority of students and where the sharing and transfer of knowledge through teaching and practice must be honored. The recent emergence of these institutions and— ironically—their success in terms of growth and prestige, have blurred their mandate and sent confusing signals to faculty; there is no clear indication of what is valued. Faculty morale is often low and the protective appeal of collective bargaining most popular. It is here, also, that a broader definition of scholarship promises to make the biggest difference.

The comprehensive university, as in no other institutional setting in higher education, opens opportunities for faculty to work on a wide range of scholarly activities, building on their individual strengths and realizing their own special contribution to a broad-based institutional mission. The comprehensive university could be the sector in higher education where the opportunities for scholarly accomplishments are greatest and the morale is highest, not lowest.

Frank Wong aptly summarized the current plight of comprehensive institutions at a recent conference on that topic at the University of the Pacific. In a speech entitled "The Ugly Duckling of Higher Education," Wong, vice-president for academics at the University of Redlands, said:

> There was no definitive model of the comprehensive university. And somehow, the models that existed, those that faculty intuitively turn to, were a poor fit for the assemblage of activities and dynamics that are found at the comprehensive university. Because that specie of institution is so poorly defined and ill understood, those of us at such universities need to create their meaning and interpret their significance.

Central to this quest for meaning and significance is the conception of scholarship and the faculty activities that are valued and rewarded.

Toward a Broader View

This is a particularly propitious time for the reevaluation of what is meant by scholarship. The structural diversity of higher education has created a press for change, and the recent research on the American professoriate and the undergraduate experience have demonstrated the need. In The Carnegie Foundation's report, *College*, Ernest Boyer drew national attention to the widespread confusion about the role of faculty and the narrow conception of scholarship dominating the profession. He writes:

> Scholarship is not an esoteric appendage—it is at the heart of what the profession is all about. All faculty, throughout their careers, should themselves, remain students. As scholars they must continue to learn and be seriously and continuously engaged in the expanding intellectual world. This is essential to the vitality and vigor of the undergraduate college.

Ernest Lynton and Sandra Elman, in their recent call for *New Priorities for the University,* press the argument further, urging that special attention must be given to the scholar's role in, and the university's responsibility for, the application and the utilization of knowledge. It is now time to reframe our thinking about scholarship, challenge the faculty evaluation procedures and reward systems that are presently in place, and replace the current vertical arrangement that devalues the work of the majority of this nation's faculty with a broader view.

To move beyond the current impasse, we need to be willing to take a fresh approach and think in new ways about what it means to be a scholar in the contemporary context. The language and polarities that are used to frame the present discussion need to be set aside. The old teaching-versus-research debate is especially tiring—minds are closed, not opened.

Different Ways of Knowing

If we build on the recent inquiry into the structure of knowledge and alternative approaches to learning, a different configuration, a more constructive way of framing the discussion, emerges. A review of the literature on the various dimensions of learning reveals two fundamental polarities.

The Concrete-Abstract Polarity. The first polarity deals with how knowledge is perceived. At one pole is the abstract, analytical approach usually associated with traditional academic research. This learning orientation strives for objectivity, requires high levels of specialization, and takes pride in its claim to being "value-free." At the other end of this first continuum is an orientation that begins with concrete experience and what is learned from contexts, relationships, and valuing communities. This is a very different approach to knowing, one that builds on connection and relationship, where values reveal, rather than mask, what is worth knowing. Recent literary studies that attempt to understand literature in terms of time and place would be found here. Ethnic studies and women's studies, in their struggle for legitimacy, have helped us recognize the power of context, relationships, and community in our approach to knowing and learning. Certainly, knowledge comprehended through objective reasoning and analytical theory-building must be acknowledged and honored, but knowledge apprehended through connections grounded in human community— relational knowing—also must be seen as legitimate.

The Reflective-Active Polarity. The second basic dimension of learning has to do with how knowledge is processed. Do we learn best through detached reflection and observation or through active engagement? The liberal arts tend to be more reflective, with an emphasis on learning for its own sake. In contrast, so many of the more recent developments in American colleges and universities and, particularly, the comprehensive institutions, have moved toward the more active pole—toward active engagement with the world, making a difference. The new programs in business, computer sciences, and communicators are found here. The emphasis is on learning that is instrumental, a means to a more practical end. Again, we want the approaches to learning represented at both poles of the continuum to be recognized and honored. Certainly, knowledge rooted in scholarly reflection and observation has its place, but so does knowledge generated out of active practice.

David A. Kolb and others have taken these two basic dimensions of learning—how knowledge is perceived (concrete-abstract) and how it is processed (reflective-active)—and constructed a learning model that is particularly helpful in our effort to define scholarship more broadly. Just as learning can be characterized as a multidimensional process involving different styles and approaches to learning, so our broader conception of scholarship can be depicted as an interrelated whole with distinctive components and different approaches to knowing (see Figure 1).

The Forms of Scholarship

Enlarging our understanding of scholarship became a central concern of The Carnegie Foundation for the Advancement of Teaching during the two-year period between 1988 and 1990. Drawing heavily

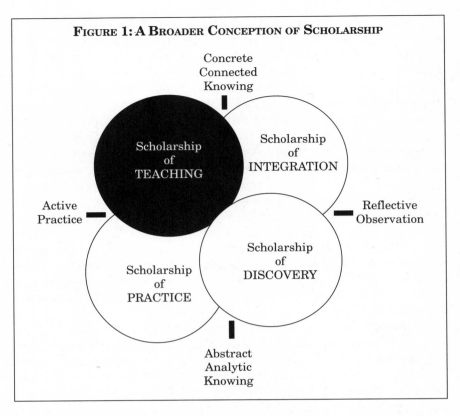

FIGURE 1: A BROADER CONCEPTION OF SCHOLARSHIP

on the previous work of Ernest Boyer, Ernest Lynton, Lee Shulman, and others, four forms of scholarship were identified.

The scholarship of discovery. The first element in this broader conception of scholarship—still a key element—is the discovery of knowledge. On this facet, everyone agrees. And, in no way do we want to be perceived as detracting from the significance of specialized research. If that were the result of this effort, we would have been seriously misunderstood. The place of pure research, the pursuit of knowledge for its own sake, needs to be assiduously defended, particularly in a society primarily committed to the pragmatic and too often concerned more with whether something works over the short term than with whether it is of lasting value.

In 1919, in his famous address on "Science as a Vocation," Max Weber acknowledged that the Western world had entered into a phase of specialization previously unknown and that in his words:

Only by strict specialization can the scientific worker become fully conscious, for once and perhaps never again in his lifetime, that he has achieved something that will endure. A really definitive and good accomplishment is today always a specialized accomplishment.

The contention of this noted German scholar is persuasive. There is no disputing that, if scholarship is to be sustained in our day, the specialized advancement of knowledge is required. In fact, we should urgently insist that scholarship have as one of its anchor points the discovery of new knowledge—what has traditionally been known as original research.

The scholarship of integration. The extension of the frontiers of knowledge is, however, not enough. The second element in scholarship is the integration of knowledge, an undertaking as critical to the understanding of our world as the discovery of knowledge that is new. In fact, the extension of specialization itself requires new forms of integration. Without the continual effort at reintegration, we have fragmentation. It was also Weber who warned of the possibility of a modern world tilled with "specialists without spirit, and sensualists without heart."

The integration of knowledge requires a divergent approach to knowing—a different kind of scholarship—one that reaches across disciplinary boundaries, and pulls disparate views and information together in creative ways. Scholars are needed with a capacity to synthesize, to look for new relationships between the parts and the whole, to relate the past and future to the present, and to ferret out patterns of meaning that cannot be seen through traditional disciplinary lenses.

It is through integrative inquiry that ethical questions will be raised in a natural and systematic way. We will not have to suffer through the ethics spasms that now grip higher education about every decade, triggered either by a Watergate or a scandal on Wall Street. This is not a call for the "gentlemen scholar" of an earlier time, or the dilettante who dabbles here and there, but broadly educated men and women who are serious about making the kinds of scholarly connections so much needed in our time.

Clifford Geertz, the anthropologist, writes about shifts in the world of scholarship as fundamental changes in "the way we think about the way we think." The older disciplinary boundaries are being challenged on every hand; knowledge constantly spills over and the strength of our disciplines is often more political than intellectual.

The scholarship of practice. The third form of scholarship is the most distinctively American. The great land-grant institutions were established during the nineteenth century precisely for the purpose of applying knowledge to the enormous agricultural and technical problems confronting society. These schools and their utilitarian missions matched the mood and needs of an emerging nation. In the academic profession today, however, there is a disturbing gap between what is valued as scholarship and the pragmatic needs of the larger world.

This ironic development in American higher education has multiple roots, but one important strand can be traced back to the emergence of professional education and, specifically, to the impact of the Flexner Report on medical education (incidentally, one of the first of the Carnegie-commissioned studies). The major effect of the Flexner Report was to move medical education into the research university and greatly increase its scientific component. The other professions followed medicine's lead. Practical competence became professional when grounded in systematic, preferably scientific knowledge. The application of knowledge took on value—rigor and prestige—when derived from original research. In the most pragmatic society in the world, scholarship was conceptualized as independent of, and prior to, practice.

Professional schools now are beginning to challenge this hierarchical conception of scholarship that makes the application of knowledge derivative, and consequently, second-best. Donald Schön's work on "the reflective practitioner" calls for a reassessment of the relationship between scholarship and practice—a new "epistemology of practice." His work is especially influential in the field of architecture, where the relationship with the research university and its established definition of scholarship has been one of perpetual tension.

Even in medicine, the connection between basic research and practice is being realigned. Harvard Medical School has instituted a New Pathways Program that attempts to build clinical practice into medical education from the very beginning. Ernest Lynton, Sandra Elman, and others are raising a whole range of important questions about the relationship between scholarship and professional service. Should not the application of knowledge to the problems of society be acknowledged as a scholarly endeavor of the first order?

The scholarship of teaching. This brings us to the fourth dimension of scholarship—the relationship of teaching and scholarship. This is the most difficult form of scholarship to discuss, because we do not have the appropriate language. In the working lives of individual faculty, scholarship and teaching often are seen as antithetical—competing for one's time and attention. This is a reflection of the way in which we conceptualize both tasks. We want to challenge this understanding and argue that quality teaching requires substantive scholarship that builds on, but is distinct from, original research, and that this scholarly effort needs to be recognized and rewarded. This is a special kind of scholarship that has for too long been implicit, unacknowledged, and virtually unnamed. Some are now willing to talk about "a missing paradigm."

This fourth dimension of scholarship has an integrity of its own, but is deeply embedded in the other three forms—discovery, integration, and practice. In addition, the scholarship of teaching has at least three distinct elements: first, the *synoptic capacity,* the ability to draw the strands of a field together in a way that provides both coherence and meaning, to place what is known in context and open the way for connection to be made between the knower and the known; second, what Lee Shulman calls *"pedagogical content knowledge,"* the capacity to represent a subject in ways that transcend the split between intellectual substance and teaching process, usually having to do with the metaphors, analogies, and experiments used; and third, *what we know about learning,* scholarly inquiry into how students "make meaning"—to use William Perry's phrase—out of what the teacher says and does.

While we want to treat the four forms of scholarship as individually distinctive, we also want them to be understood as interrelated and often overlapping—an interdependent whole, with each distinctive form encompassing each of the other three. For example, scholarship that is primarily integrative also can lead to important discoveries and provide the intellectual undergirding for the best sort of undergraduate teaching.

The view of scholarship being proposed here is more inclusive, reaching out to encompass a wider array of scholarly activities than does the present conception. While being more inclusive, however, this enlarged view has its own boundaries; the four aspects of scholarship are discrete types, but form a conceptual whole that is every bit as important as the parts.

Implied here are assumptions about the kind of scholarship appropriate for the academy—colleges and universities. For instance, teaching that is not grounded in the most recent research in the field and is oblivious to the interconnections with other disciplines is not appropriate for a college or university setting. Instruction of this sort might better be found in the corporate classroom or the military. On the other hand, it is important that narrow, specialized research take place in a broader scholarly context—a university—where critical questions are raised and scholars are made mindful by students and colleagues that academic freedom carries with it special responsibilities. The recent debate over genetic engineering underscores the point. As Alfred North Whitehead, in his essay on "Universities and Their

Function," observes:

> At no time have universities been restricted to pure abstract learning. . . . The justification for a university is that it preserves the connection between knowledge and the zest for life, by uniting the young and the old in the imaginative consideration of learning.

We know that what is being proposed challenges a hierarchical arrangement of monumental proportions—a status system that is firmly fixed in the consciousness of the present faculty and the academy's organizational policies and practices. What is being called for is a broader, more open field, where these different forms of scholarship can interact, inform, and enrich one another, and faculty can follow their interests, build on their strengths, and be rewarded for what they spend most of their scholarly energy doing. All faculty ought to be scholars in this broader sense, deepening their preferred approaches to knowing but constantly pressing, and being pressed by peers, to enlarge their scholarly capacities and encompass other—often contrary—ways of knowing.

Faculty Scholarship and Institutional Mission

Institutionally, we have a crisis of purpose in our colleges and universities. Our comprehensive institutions, particularly, are trying to be what they are not, and falling short of what they could be.

Awareness that the dominant notion of scholarship is inappropriate and counterproductive for the majority of our faculty, as well as our institutions, is widespread. The concern runs deep, yet when individual faculty are rewarded and "emerging" institutions launch drives toward higher standards of academic excellence, the older, narrow definition of scholarship as research is reasserted and given priority. As sociologist Everett Ladd points out: "When a particular norm is ascendant within a group and institutionalized in various ways, it is very hard for a member of a group to deny its claim, even if intellectually he is fully convinced of its serious deficiency." In the recent period of retrenchment, when promotions were being denied and positions eliminated, the older, narrower standard frequently was invoked to rationalize very difficult and often arbitrary judgments. In institutions in distress, it was, on occasion, used as an anesthesia in the management of pain.

What is especially needed is greater congruence between individual faculty scholarship and institutional mission. It is this congruence that gives special meaning to academic work, sustains morale, cultivates commitment, and makes possible a more direct relationship between performance, evaluation, and reward.

An enlarged conception of scholarship would address a number of critical problems currently plaguing both individual faculty and colleges and universities across the several sectors of higher education. It would free us to celebrate individual strengths—the rich variety of scholarly talents represented in the faculty—and make it possible for colleges and universities not committed primarily to specialized research (the majority), to feel pride in their distinctive scholarly missions.

Scholarship and Democratic Community

The audacious title of this paper is taken, obviously, from Emerson's famous address, "The American Scholar." That 1837 speech called for a new approach to scholarship and the role of the scholar, one not borrowed from "the learning of other lands," but self-confident and fully engaged with the realities of a vibrant, developing democracy.

One hundred and twenty-six years later—scarcely a block from where Emerson spoke—Clark Kerr addressed the future of the American university and identified four challenges that would transform higher education in this country. He told his Harvard audience:

> The university is being called upon to educate previously unimagined numbers of students; to respond to the expanding claims of national service; to merge its activities with industry as never before; to adapt to, and rechannel, new intellectual currents.

Kerr then predicted that only when this transformation had taken place would we have "a truly American university, an institution unique in world history, an institution not looking to other models but serving, itself, as a model for universities in other parts of the globe."

American higher education stands now on the threshold of that transformation. Over the past thirty years, colleges and universities have taken on the diverse challenges articulated by Kerr, and much has been accomplished. Other nations—Asian, European, African— are looking our way for a model, a decentralized but coherent model, meeting diverse societal needs and responding to the call for both equity and excellence. Looming especially large in our immediate future are the challenges posed by the immense demographic changes in our society. The rich racial, ethnic, and cultural diversity marking America from its beginning has taken on new significance as the minorities in our cities, and even states, such as California, become majorities.

Diversity, which American higher education sees as one of its primary strengths, has taken on new meaning.

What it means to be a scholar in American colleges and universities must be seen within this larger frame. Not only do our institutions have diverse missions—commitments to serving a wide range of scholarly needs within regions, states, and nation—but there is the special commitment to the education of an increasingly diverse population, to the intellectual preparation of the educated citizenry necessary for making a genuinely democratic society possible. Scholarship, in this context, takes on broader meaning.

We believe that an enlarged view would nurture inclusion, draw together rather than separate, and embrace students and their learning, as well as faculty and their research. This understanding of scholarly activity also would acknowledge and build on the relational nature of knowledge, as well as more abstract, objective ways of knowing. The narrower view no longer suffices. For colleges and universities to contribute fully to the vibrant pluralistic democracy this nation is becoming, a vision of the distinctively new American scholar is needed.

SUGGESTED READINGS

Kolb, David A. *Experiential Learning.* Englewood Cliffs, NJ: Prentice-Hall, 1984.

Lynton, Ernest A., and Sandra E. Elman. *New Priorities for the University.* San Francisco: Jossey-Bass, 1987.

Rice, R. Eugene. "The Academic Profession in Transition: Toward a New Social Fiction." *Teaching Sociology* 14, no. 132 (January 1986): 24–34.

Schön, Donald A. *The Reflective Practitioner.* New York: Basic Books, 1983.

Shulman, Lee. "Knowledge and Teaching: Foundation of the New Reform." *Harvard Educational Review* 57, no. 1 (1987): 1–22.

PART IV

PARTNERSHIPS IN THE EDUCATION COMMUNITY

INTRODUCTION

Partnerships for education could never be more timely. Public elementary and secondary schools as well as higher education are undergoing significant change, and it makes sense for them to change simultaneously. By working together as partners to align expectations for students, set standards for accountability, develop new instructional strategies, redesign teacher training and development, better results can be achieved in terms of student success. It is no longer acceptable to argue that the two education cultures are incompatible or that only the public schools are in need of reform. Too much hangs on working together, and metropolitan universities can play an important role.

The following articles illustrate the ways in which metropolitan universities are making connections with other institutions to improve the quality of the education enterprise.

In his article, "Making School-University Partnerships Work," Kenneth Sirotnik argues that effective partnerships must be based on two principles: mutual understanding and respect. He goes on to describe the numerous areas in which higher education and K–12 can work together.

In addition, as illustrated by Freeman A. Hrabowski and James J. Linksz in "Metropolitan University and the Community College: A New Symbiosis," there is virtually no end to the opportunities for collaboration between the university and the community college. Metropolitan universities are ideally suited to serve as catalysts for a consortia including all sectors of education. Such models are emerging in many locations across the country. The "K–16" reform agenda, sponsored by the American Association of Higher Education, is a good example of a new vision for education that will look to metropolitan universities for leadership in its implementation.

Of course, resources are always an issue. The key to attracting external support, according to David C. Sweet, is to communicate to elected officials and legislative bodies the willingness and special capacities of urban and metropolitan universities to serve the state. In his article "Ohio's Urban University Program," Sweet describes the development of a model of universities serving the community that receives state and even federal support.

Ernest Boyer's article, "How Do We Talk About Higher Education's Relationship to Schools," argues that the problems facing American society and its children can only be solved by close cooperation and collaboration of our nation's institutions, especially schools and universities. In Boyer's view, "those of us in higher education have both an educational and moral obligation to support the schools, and most especially the teachers, who are struggling every day to educate effectively a new generation."

MAKING SCHOOL-UNIVERSITY PARTNERSHIPS WORK

Kenneth A. Sirotnik

One of the most difficult hurdles in making school-university partnerships work is helping people to realize that it is not just a bag of tricks, a list of "how-to-do-its." Rather, it is an amalgam of principles and concepts, beliefs and values, conditions and processes, people and programs, and hard work—work that is not neatly packaged for implementation elsewhere, but that originates and develops and improves in context. This work can be informed by the experience of others—hence, the purpose of this essay.

In the introduction to a book on school-university partnerships, John Goodlad and I noted that the concept of schools and universities joining together in partnerships—particularly the type of partnership we envision—is a rather deviant idea. We concluded the book with the statement that school-university partnerships is an idea whose time has come. It has been about three years since those statements were written. It has been over ten years since I began working closely with school-university partnerships. Two years ago, as part of the Study of the Education of Educators, I visited twenty-nine universities and colleges in eight states around the nation and focused on the schools, colleges, or departments of education in these institutions of higher education. As I reflect on all these experiences, I am convinced more than ever that both of our statements about school university partnership are true: it is a deviant idea and it is an idea whose time has come.

Some Context

There has been a veritable flood of collaborative language lately on the educational landscape: coalitions, consortiums, cooperatives, collaboratives, partnerships, networks. . . . When people use these terms to describe some form of interorganizational arrangement, are they describing the same thing? Not at all. At least in theory, only the term network can be reasonably well-distinguished from the others. A network is an informal communication system among entities that think they have something in common. Sharing information, planning forums, conducting seminars and conferences, and exchanging newsletters tend to characterize such efforts.

Collaboratives, consortiums, cooperatives, coalitions, and partnerships, on the other hand, have been invoked at will to describe a range of interrelationships, from the most superficial to the most complex. These can range from symbolic, on-paper arrangements, to one-sided service agreements (like consultants have with schools), to patronage arrangements (like a business adopting a school). These associations can be quite useful if done well for clear purposes.

The kind of school-university partnership being discussed in this essay is on the more complex end of the continuum, and there are many reasons why it is a deviant idea. It is based on the concept of common ground—that is, common dilemmas, concerns, issues, values, and commitments. It is based on real cooperation and equitable decision making by equal partners. For example, a school-university partnership involving one university (through its college of education) and ten school districts has eleven equal partners and a decision-making structure that reflects that kind of parity.

But it is more than common ground and equal partnership. It is being able to meet self-interests as well. In many ways, schools and school districts, on the one hand, and universities and colleges of education, on the other, are worlds apart as organizations and organizational cultures. Yet there would seem to be some obvious connections between grades K–12 and grades 13 and beyond. Certainly there is a connection in terms of students. And certainly there is a connection in terms of teacher education. Improving schools and the preparation of educators, for example, would seem to be territory of both common ground and self-interest.

However, with territory comes territoriality. The antidote to turf battles is collaboration—another deviant idea. I am thinking here about collaboration as a process: people working with one another. I am not thinking about the other meaning of collaboration usually found in the dictionary: consorting with the enemy (although at times, one gets to feeling that way). Rather, it is the first meaning—people working *with,* not *on* one another. It is not one party coming in with answers to another party's problems. It is people coming together, realizing that they are dealing with tough issues, and working toward mutually satisfying solutions. Can such deviant ideas work?

Deviant Ideas Can Work

Progress sometimes comes in the form of establishing and sustaining forums for dialogue. Many people and groups are not ordinarily accustomed to having extended and significant conversations with one another, e.g., teachers with one another, university professors with one another, university professors with classroom teachers. Collegial isolation is just as rampant in universities as it is in the public schools. It is remarkable how hungry people are—school principals and other administrators, for example—for intellectual conversation, sharing of ideas and experiences, and discovering how much they have in common.

More importantly, however, school-university partnerships have made significant progress in other ways—steady, collaborative work between educators in both universities and schools working on common problems and improving programs in both places. Many examples exist; I will share only two from my recent experiences. In the Puget Sound Educational Consortium—a partnership among thirteen organizations: twelve school districts in the greater Puget Sound area and the College of Education at the University of Washington. These examples are particularly significant, as they deal with perhaps the most common of common ground possible between schools and colleges of education— the education of educators.

Middle school education has become a topic of increasing concern in the state of Washington. Many of Washington's junior high schools have been changed (at least in name and grade structures) to middle schools. Teacher certification in the state of Washington is either K through eighth grade generalist, or fourth through twelfth grade subject-specific. And there is talk about eliminating the sixth through eighth grade on the generalist certificate. Clearly, given the nature of the true, middle school concept—interdisciplinary teams and blocks of instructional time (versus the period-by-period, subject-by subject junior high approach)—eliminating generalist credentialing at middle school levels threatens the middle school concept. However, some signs favor a specific credentialing process for middle school teachers, as there is in a number of other states.

Now all this has fairly serious implications for schools and educator preparation programs, especially if people care about the middle school idea, as many do in the state of Washington. How does one mobilize a timely, proactive response to a situation of this kind? In my view, given the complexity of the problem and the multiple actors and institutions involved, the work that is going on now probably would never have even begun without the Puget Sound Educational Consortium already in place.

Using a modest grant from a private foundation, several university faculty and research assistants, a principal and teacher from each of four selected middle schools, a teacher union representative, and a representative from the state department of education are now engaged in an ongoing effort to design the ideal features of middle schools that also would serve as professional development centers (i.e., pre- and in-service training sites). And in the process, of course, the ideal features of a preparation program for middle school educators are emerging as well. This was put together in a matter of weeks, not years. And it involves *educators* working *with* one another—educators from the university and educators from the schools—working on significant educational issues, and benefiting their own interests, to be sure, but also benefiting the educational interests of adolescent youths.

Another example concerns the education of school administrators specifically, our programs for the initial certification of school principals. With the help of two small grants from the Danforth Foundation, the area of Educational Leadership and Policy Studies in the College of Education at the University of Washington has been able to design and conduct what we consider to be an innovative program for developing the leadership capabilities of selected classroom teachers.

Our regular program is a good, traditional program. But we were not satisfied. Neither were some of the superintendents and principals in our school-university partnership. We wanted to find ways to meet a number of quality criteria that go unmet in many educational administration programs:

1. selecting teachers with strong leadership potential;
2. selecting highly qualified mentor principals;
3. releasing teachers at least half-time, Monday through Friday, for real internship experiences;
4. building stronger connections between theory and practice;
5. integrating the program's curriculum and creating something more than the usual lock-step sequence of one course after another;
6. overcoming the usual fragmentation in professional socialization and collegial relationships among students who typically enter and finish their programs at different times; and
7. developing strong ethical imperatives among students regarding implications of serious attention to the education of all children in a pluralistic and democratic society.

Even more deviant, we did not want just to package an innovative program and then try to sell it to the school people. Rather, we wanted to work with educators in the schools to design, from the ground up, an innovative program that would overcome the usual problems in traditional programs. We wanted a program that the university could endorse; yet, true to the theory and spirit of equitable collaboration, program decisions would have to be made by a group having more school than university representation.

How do you even begin such a process? How do you work up interest on the part of faculty and get the support of the dean? How do you get key superintendents and other administrators from the surrounding community involved? How do you identify teachers who show great promise for leadership? How do you get into the schools to identify good mentor principals? How do you put together a decision-making body to design, monitor, and evaluate the whole process and reflect the interests of all involved?

Even *with* a school-university partnership, these are not trivial issues. But without a school-university partnership, any one of these issues, particularly the last one, could be enough to kill off the whole idea. Fortunately, through the Puget Sound Educational Consortium, we were able to secure the required commitments from both the College of Education and the participating districts in a matter of weeks. A Program Design Committee was formed consisting of eight faculty members from the university and thirteen educators from the schools—principals, central office administrators, and a superintendent. This committee has made or approved all program decisions and dealt in a timely and efficient manner with all the issues I have noted above, and more. I do not believe we could have developed this innovative program without the collaborative scaffolding already in place in our school-university partnership.

I could go on with more examples from this partnership and others around the nation. Nonetheless, let me simply summarize by saying: *school-university partnerships can work.*

Some Lessons Learned

But it is hard work! Especially if one wants to work with the kind of partnership concepts that I have outlined here. Each school-university partnership effort will be unique and will need to incorporate learning from participants' mistakes. Nonetheless, some generic lessons are worth consideration.

Lesson 1: Dealing with Cultural Clash. School systems and universities are not cut from the same cultural cloth. The norms, roles, and expectations of educators in each of these educational realms could not be more different, e.g., the regimen of time and space in the schools vs. the relative freedom of these precious commodities in the university setting; an ethic of inquiry in the university vs. an ethic of action and meeting immediate needs in the schools; a merit system with promotion and tenure in the university vs. an egalitarian work ethic in the schools; and so forth.

I do not want to overstereotype the cultural differences. That kind of stereotyping already is done far too much and is part of what usually has to be overcome in working on relationships between universities and schools.

My point, simply, is that these two cultures are quite different, and it is hard to fit them together in productive, long-term, useful ways. However, it is hard work that we must be doing, especially if we feel any moral obligations as educators to be improving schools as well as the education of educators for those schools. Being knowledgeable, sensitive, empathic, and communicative regarding these differences and potential conflicts in organizational cultures are first steps toward heading off (or at least minimizing) the "clash."

Lesson 2: Dealing with Schools of Education. Although there are significant problems on both sides of the partnership "fence," my experience suggests that the university side, usually the school (college or department) of education, is the more intractable. And although the problem of "ed school" commitment and involvement is a complex one, the primary culprit is a misguided reward system that is an outgrowth of misplaced values, status deprivation, and identity crisis.

What is a professional unit in a university about—at least primarily about—if it is not about the profession and connections with the field? A school of agriculture would be in deep trouble if it were not for its connections with the field. Schools of education will have a particularly tough time defending their existence if the education of educators, and solid connections with the field, are not at least somewhere close to the heart of their institutional mission and rewarded appropriately. The publish or perish mentality is counterproductive in a professional school. Scholarship, of course, is crucial to a quality instructional program, and it is therefore an essential component of the promotion and tenure system; but scholarship can be appropriately interpreted in many ways. Service and teaching are essential for professional units; and service must include substantial work with educational constituencies in the field. The reward system, therefore, must be receptive to the work involved in the kind of partnerships envisioned between universities and the local schools.

Lesson 3: Sustaining Leadership and Commitment. One of the more consistent and enduring findings in the research on complex organizations has to do with the importance of leadership at the top, and the ability to clearly, authentically, and consistently communicate mission, vision, a sense of what the organization can and must be about. This appears to be essential to maintaining school-university partnerships of the type I have been describing. University presidents and deans, school superintendents, executive directors—these leaders need to be visible and clearly supportive of the partnership concept and effort.

Lesson 4: Providing Adequate Resources. Much of leadership is symbolic. But symbols, ceremony, and celebration will not go far unless they are backed up by resources. In the Puget Sound Educational Consortium, for example, each district contributes $24,500 per year, plus ten cents times their average daily attendance. The university contributes in-kind resources (staff, faculty, space, support services, etc.) in addition to a dollar amount to bring its total contribution in line with the districts' fees. These resources produce a budget big enough to hire a full-time executive director and a small staff and include funds to support study groups and modest efforts to secure grants and contracts.

Lesson 5: Modeling Authentic Collaboration. An ethic of collaboration and collaborative inquiry and action, more than anything else, characterizes (or ought to characterize) the processes that go on in a school-university partnership. What it means to collaborate needs to be modeled every step of the way. Since building partnerships is mostly a two-steps-forward/ one-step-backward kind of activity, inappropriate, unilateral decisions can destroy the process. Telling people they are involved in genuine participative management and decision making, and then not paying attention to what they do or say, has severe consequences. University faculty hopping into the schools with answers to other people's problems usually does not work out too well in collaborative partnerships. Unless participants make deliberate efforts to work in new and collaborative ways with one another, the partnership most likely will be headed for divorce.

Lesson 6: Living with Goal-Free Planning, Action, and Evaluation. I have used the term "goal-free" to get attention and make a point. And it is the point, not the terminology, that is important. Certainly, we have goals, aims, purposes—human action is never without them. Everything I have been discussing so far has been based on implicit and explicit aims and purposes. Yet, these kinds of broad goals do not necessarily lead to the kind of specific, objective-based or outcome-based models of activity that seem to capture the imagination of so many who need to proceed in very linear and rational modes of operation. Often, in fact, it is precisely as *a result* of activity that we become clearer about what we are doing and why we are doing it. Consequently, the world of human activity in and between educational organizations does not lend itself well to concrete, sequential models of planning and evaluation.

The subtitle of this lesson is "living with ambiguity," and our mentor is the organizational theorist, James March. For March, ambiguity is not a dirty word. Not only does he tolerate it, he embraces it. Closure *is* a dirty word. Rarely is it ever achieved. In fact, if it is achieved, it is a good sign that either the issues are trivial or people are jumping to conclusions too quickly. March advocates being "playful" in organizations. By this he does not mean being irresponsible, but rather he means getting going on things, taking action, taking educated risks—in other words, getting to work and involved in activity without having to hyperrationalize every effort to change and improve the organization.

Lesson 7: Avoiding the Quick-Fix Syndrome. The "quick-fix" syndrome and its kissing cousin, the "let's get something up on the scoreboard" syndrome, are extremely hazardous to the health of school-university partnerships, especially early in their formative stages. As a society, we seem to be growing less and less tolerant of study and inquiry, of reflecting on what we do and how we might do it better.

In school-university partnerships, and especially among the superintendents and deans, there often is a perceived press to get something up on the scoreboard so that various publics believe something actually is going on. This can be a difficult problem, particularly in the early phases—say, the first three years of a school-university partnership. Yet, if it is a serious partnership effort, a lot is going on: structures are being built, lines of communication are being established, working relationships and collaborative processes are being nurtured, and some activities are being explored by pockets of work groups here and there. Unfortunately, structures and processes do not happen overnight, and they cannot be hung on the evaluative hooks the public has grown accustomed to for education and schooling—standardized test score averages, for example.

Lesson 8: Winning the Process/Substance Debate. This leads naturally to the ubiquitous process/substance debate, which, in the current era of the fast-food vernacular, often culminates in the ringing indictment of "Where's the beef?" The debate apparently revolves around this question: What work is of most value—making things happen or the happening of things? "The beef" is usually a referent for something noticeably different going on in the classroom (school or university) plus the student outcomes to "prove" it.

The only way to win this debate is to render it a nonissue; it is, indeed, a false dichotomy to be put up alongside a number of other classic problematical dualities (qualitative/quantitative; theory/practice; talk/action; etc.). There is great substance in process and great process in substance. Developing new ways for educators to communicate with one another and engage in work to solve problems of common concern is highly substantive. Developing and evaluating new programs (e.g., for the education of educators) demands much attention to process. The "beef," ultimately, is in concerted, sustained, and evaluated action.

Lesson 9: Avoiding Over- and Understructuring. Organizing and governance structures are important for developing and sustaining school-university partnerships, but they take different forms depending upon local contexts. The Puget Sound Educational Consortium is highly structured, with a formal governing board (twelve superintendents and the Dean of the College of Education—thirteen equal decision makers), an executive director, two intermediate coordinating committees, and a number of task forces, work groups, and so forth. On the east coast, however, the Southern Maine Partnership is organized very informally. Decisions seem to be made at the levels they need to, anyway, and teachers, principals, central office staff, and faculty are involved in activities in a more grass-roots way.

Both of these partnerships appear to be working well. But watch out for both over- and understructuring; either may interfere with the work most important to partnership efforts. Ultimately, the crucial points of coordination are at the levels where real work is taking place, with the rest of the coordination and structure being in place to *support* that work.

Lesson 10: Translating Leadership as Empowerment and Shared Responsibility. The partnership ethic must be enculturated at all individual and organizational levels. The power to lead cannot reside in just one or several charismatic figures. The more leadership is spread around, the better off the partnership will be.

This should not be seen as contradictory to Lesson 3 and the importance of leadership at the top, of communicating and sustaining vision and mission, and of backing it all up with resources. Power, however, is not a finite concept. The more it is shared, the more there seems to be. And with power comes responsibility; responsible leadership entails creating the opportunities for responsible leadership in others. A viable, school-university partnership cannot depend on the presence or absence of one or several human beings. Certainly, being an "idea champion" is important for leadership, but charisma is not the foundation of partnership.

These deviant and timely efforts—school-university partnerships—will survive and function to the extent that deliberate efforts are made to ingrain the culture of partnership into the woodwork of the participating institutions. Such efforts must promote and sustain the norms, roles, and expectations of partnership in people and organizations as they go about their work and as they develop ways to do their work even better.

SUGGESTED READINGS

Gross, Theodore L. *Partners in Education: How Colleges Can Work with Schools to Improve Teaching and Learning.* San Francisco: Jossey-Bass, 1989.

Jones, Byrd L., and Robert W. Maloy. *Partnerships for Improving Schools.* Westport, CN: Greenwood Press, 1988.

Sirotnik, Kenneth A., and John I. Goodlad, eds. *School-University Partnerships in Action: Concepts, Cases, and Concerns.* New York: Teachers College Press, 1988.

Soder, Roger, and Kenneth A. Sirotnik. "Beyond Reinventing the Past: The Politics of Teacher Education." In John I. Goodlad, Roger Soder, and Kenneth A. Sirotnik, eds. *Places Where Teachers Are Taught.* San Francisco: Jossey-Bass, 1990.

Wilson, Carol, Richard Clark, and Paul Heckman. *Breaking New Ground: Reflections on the School-University Partnerships in the National Network for Educational Renewal.* Seattle: Center for Educational Renewal, College of Education, University of Washington, 1989.

The Metropolitan University and the Community College: A New Symbiosis

Freeman A. Hrabowski and James J. Linksz

Beyond Articulation to Collaboration

Metropolitan universities are no strangers to their two-year counterparts—the community colleges that have emerged as major players in higher education, particularly in urban areas. That is not surprising, because the two categories of institutions have much in common. Both are deeply committed to improving the social and economic future of the areas they serve, while at the same time fostering the intellectual growth of their students.

Over the past decades, the community colleges have become for many the bridge between secondary education and the baccalaureate degree. The process of articulation, therefore, has long been a crucial element in the ability of a community college student to transfer to a four-year institution. Transfer continues to this day as a measurement applied by society to determine the success of a community college. The ease with which students transfer and the lack of credits lost in transfer figure prominently in analyses of transfer success, as does the award of the associate degree. Recently, the American Association of Community and Junior Colleges (AACJC) has increased its focus on the transfer function and has reiterated its commitment to this activity in its long-range planning documents as well as in its research work.

But concentration on the process of articulation is not enough. Rather, it is collaboration among two-year and four-year institutions that ought to be the goal. *Articulation* suggests the mechanics of transfer, with emphasis on the extent to which students take the necessary prerequisites for junior-level college work. *Collaboration,* on the other hand, assumes that there is a process by which students can successfully complete community college courses that are acceptable to the four-year institution, and that the two institutions are working together to complement each other's mission for the benefit of the students and the community. Beyond discussions about courses, the institutions are sharing information about students, about teaching, and about resources available to each other. Even more important is that they are themselves working toward common educational, social, and economic goals within the community. Above all, there is mutual respect for the work of each institution.

In recent years, some community colleges and metropolitan universities have begun to move in the direction of real collaboration, and the prospects for the future are encouraging. In 1987, the AACJC published a report on the Urban Community College/Transfer Opportunities Program (UCC/TOP), which had been established several years before with a grant from the Ford Foundation in order to understand and improve transfer opportunities for students, especially minorities. An overview of the report, "Transfer—Making it Work," was published in the winter 1988 issue of *Change.* It included a list of recommendations for improving transfer and establishing productive collaborations between two and four-year colleges: These recommendations are similar to those made by one of the present authors in 1971, when he characterized effective collaborative interinstitutional relationship as having three principal dimensions: information, communication, and interaction.

The dimension of information includes whether there is strong communication between institutions, both formal and informal, and whether there exist collaborative public relations, publications, and recruitment information pieces. The communication dimension depends on whether counterparts talk with one another, beginning with the chief officers and extending to other administrators and faculty, and whether there are written articulation policy statements. Questions regarding the interaction dimension focus on actual involvement of individuals and groups at both institutions, whether there are cooperatively planned activities and events, and whether there is actual evidence of strong program articulation.

The National Scene

A number of interesting events that pertain to transfer and interinstitutional interaction are occurring at the national level and therefore are particularly noteworthy in this discussion. Throughout the country we have seen new calls for accountability and assessment of learning. This has translated into examinations sometimes given as a prerequisite for junior-level courses, and a variety of other projects aimed at providing quality control indicators for a public increasingly concerned about the quality and consistency of higher education. As part of such efforts, increasing attention is given to the successful transfer of community college students to universities. For metropolitan institutions, this has also meant special scrutiny of the success with which minority students make their transitions.

The development of the National Center for Academic Achievement and Transfer within the American Council on Education is the most visible initiative in this area. This project is funded by the Ford Foundation and is a multiyear, multimillion-dollar effort that attempts to understand and act on issues related to academic achievement and transfer, particularly for low-income and minority populations in the nation's major urban areas. While the project focuses on cities and minorities, the context in which the research and development projects are taking place is generally applicable to the broader issues.

Another related activity is taking place at the University of California, Los Angeles. There, the Ford Foundation has also funded the Transfer Assembly Project, which will attempt to provide a research base for tracking transfer students.

Student transfer issues are particularly important at this time of diminishing financial resources, when increasing public scrutiny is accompanied by calls for accountability. A case in point is the current activity surrounding the reauthorization of federal financial aid legislation. Most institutions would prefer to avoid the impression, however untrue, that students have to repeat courses they have already taken at another institution. Any additional burden on the student financial aid system, delayed entry into the job market, or increases of the federal loan indebtedness of students are not popular issues among the general public or elected officials.

New Forms of Institutional Connections

The increased emphasis on transfer has brought about some interesting institutional connections that transcend the usual models wherein students complete all of an associate-level program before transferring to the baccalaureate degree-granting institution.

The so-called 2+2+2 programs are one collaborative model that is just now beginning to appear in metropolitan regions. These programs provide both mid-point achievement levels and a seamless curriculum that spans high school, the community college, and the university. They address especially the needs of high school students who otherwise might not continue their education. This effort is of particular interest to metropolitan universities, which are trying to find effective ways of helping schools to decrease the number of dropouts among the inner city population. The vast majority of high school students within a metropolitan area need to have their aspirations raised, and they need to be nurtured toward advanced education. Some community colleges, such as Boston's Bunker Hill, are working with schools to develop modified apprenticeship programs that are more work-based than the 2+2+2 programs. A number of educators argue that otherwise unmotivated students tend to do well in such programs because of the close connection between academic work and practical applications.

Two examples of innovative collaborative efforts to bring about new types of interinstitutional connection are the summer project between Vassar College in Poughkeepsie, New York, and LaGuardia Community College, and a similar January term program linking Western Maryland College, in Westminster, Maryland, and Catonsville Community College in Baltimore County. Both of these projects represent new ways of looking at articulation and transfer. In both instances, less emphasis is on defining courses that transfer and more is placed on increasing student awareness of institutions they might otherwise not think of as options to consider as they continue their education. Community college students need more information about the variety of opportunities available to them as university students, including scholarships, majors, career opportunities, and campus life.

Although these projects target nontraditional students, both hold lessons for the general student population. The key to the success of these projects, of course, relies on the commitment, at the executive and administrative level, to the notion that both institutions profit. But the essential, other ingredient is the involvement of faculty and staff in their day-to-day working with the students. Once the four-year college faculty see for themselves, in their own classrooms, the abilities of these transferring students, they become more likely to be open to transfer efforts. Even more important, successful projects lead to increased trust between institutions.

There is another major trend that affects transfer relationships between two- and four-year colleges: the increasing number of students who wish to transfer from career or technical types of programs. The original model of community and technical college programming provided separate tracks: one for those students who, from the very beginning of their collegiate careers, were planning transfer to a four-year college or university; the other, for those who were oriented toward direct job entry. Today, however, more and more students who complete technical programs in a community college recognize that they must continue their education. In the traditional model, this would have meant added years to take transfer-type courses before a student could move on. More recently, educators and, for that matter, the nation have discovered that adult learning does not follow a linear path, and that discovery is leading to the development of a number of innovative programs for this population.

The development of bachelor of technology programs is just one manifestation of this new understanding. Such programs usually enable community college technology students to transfer directly into the upper division of a four-year institution. In some cases, the upper division emphasis is placed primarily on the liberal arts and sciences; in others, the principal focus is on the further development of the technical skills area, coupled with added general education. These programs owe much of their genesis to the allied health professions, particularly nursing, which early on recognized the need for continuing professional development of its members. Across the nation, nursing educators began to create a number of BS/RN programs, in which associate degree nurses can continue to the bachelor of science degree in nursing without losing time for having been in a direct career track earlier in their educational development.

Upper-division colleges and universities are also assisting in broadening the prospects for students in community college career programs. Buttressed by a new awareness that collaboration can be mutually beneficial, collaborative models are beginning to emerge even within traditional university settings. The University of Maryland School of Medicine, for example, has recently created the Department of Research and Laboratory Technologies, which will concentrate on recruiting community college students who will come from both general science programs and career programs in laboratory or chemical/ biological technologies.

Numerous other collaborative projects are being carried out by consortia of colleges or pairs of individual institutions. These efforts are significant. They have found a way to respect the autonomy of individual institutions and their missions; and, simultaneously, they focus on the special needs of today's students. The projects focus on student success and progress through the educational system, and they avoid spurious qualitative distinctions between community colleges and four-year institutions. All of them are contributing to a national climate in which productive conversations can and should occur. The end result of such conversations among those various segments of higher education will certainly improve the transfer situation for students.

Maryland: Transfer in Transition

The state of Maryland is an excellent example of existing and emerging trends in transfer and interinstitutional relationships. A state-mandated transfer policy has existed for many years, but until recently it was subjected to benign neglect. It has now been revised and updated to reflect the needs of students more adequately. In addition, what has taken place is a major reorganization of what had been a strong and very independent mix of state colleges, universities, and community colleges. Now all higher education institutions are responding to a newly established Maryland Higher Education Commission (MHEC) and its cabinet-level secretary. MHEC is responsible for the state's colleges, universities, and two-year colleges. Today, all of these institutions are enjoined to be more specific about their mission and to be accountable in the accomplishment of that mission.

As one of its first tasks, MHEC convened a group of two- and four-year administrators to review and update the state's articulation policy. In turn, this led to the establishment of a Student Transfer Advisory Committee to monitor transfers throughout the state. MHEC asked this committee to consider whether a common course numbering system statewide or a common core of courses should be mandated to meet the general education requirements at all of the colleges in the state. The committee will continue to work on a variety of such issues surrounding articulation and curriculum.

The University of Maryland System has long had a director of articulation who stimulated formal contacts between the two-year and four-year institutions. Recently, that role has become considerably more critical, because the state has developed a computerized course matching system that is able to relate every course offered by the eleven campuses of the university with all of the related courses offered by the seventeen community colleges. This system, ARTSYS, will also be used as a basis for electronic transmission of student transcripts. ARTSYS will be accessible via personal computers at every community college in the state and, therefore, will allow the student to select more carefully the courses that would meet the requirements of individual institutions.

University / Community College Relationship: A Working Model

Not surprisingly, especially close collaboration has developed between the University of Maryland Baltimore County (UMBC) and Catonsville Community College (CCC). The two institutions are neighbors, located within two miles of one another, and both were founded during the 1960s. Of course, they are very different. UMBC is a doctoral degree-granting research university and member of the University of Maryland System; it enrolls almost 11,000 graduate and undergraduate students, about twenty percent of whom are residential; and of its 600-member faculty, approximately 380 are full time. CCC enrolls 13,000 credit-seeking students on its main and one satellite campus; about seventy-five percent are part time, none are residential, and 250 of its 1,000 member faculty are full time.

Yet within the past five years, new presidents arrived at both institutions, and through their combined energies, collaborative initiatives on over a dozen fronts have begun to take shape. Many of those efforts seem almost to assume the seamlessness of articulation and transfer among the two institutions.

UMBC and CCC are located in the southwestern segment of Baltimore County, not far from Baltimore's inner city and its majority black population. Both institutions have been collaborating on minority outreach projects, and today work together with the Upward Bound project, based at UMBC and CCC. In the summer, African-American teenagers attending both institutions live on the UMBC campus, tutors are trained at UMBC through the Learning Resources Center, and students receive remedial education from UMBC and CCC personnel. This involves collaboration between the two tutorial centers year-round.

The two institutions co-host joint on-campus visits for Baltimore County school students who are unlikely to be college bound in the absence of effective outreach. Last year, for example, students from five middle schools were brought to both campuses for tours and learning experiences. UMBC and CCC also cosponsor awareness workshops for parents to give them information about the transition from high school to college—from finances to admissions processes to attitudinal aspects.

UMBC students take lower-division courses for credit at CCC during the summer and often during the main school year because a particular course is not offered, is full, or conflicts with another scheduled course. And as entrance standards at UMBC have become more stringent and the admissions process has become more selective, some students who otherwise might have become lost in a research university are referred to CCC, where they can benefit from the strong teaching environment that it offers.

The two institutions collaborate in a number of ways to ensure student success in the transfer process. UMBC makes available to CCC the academic progress of the transfer students, department by department, in order that professors can know how their students are progressing. And CCC makes available lists of its students who intend to transfer, so that UMBC can begin to work with them well in advance of their entry to the upper divisions.

As early as 1987, the two institutions signed a Reciprocal Borrowing Agreement and both have on-line access to each other's automated library catalog. CCC can search UMBC's microcomputer database of state documents. By 1990, the two campuses had linked into BITNET and were exploring Internet, through which UMBC and CCC faculty have the ability to sign in remotely to a distant computer over the network.

Both institutions are collaborating with Yokohama Academy in Japan. Japanese students live in UMBC residential facilities and are part of the residential life program at UMBC. They study at CCC but have the opportunity of taking some course work at UMBC. The program began in the summer of 1990, and it is assumed that students who are successful at CCC will complete their baccalaureate degree either at UMBC or other American four-year institutions.

Another shared endeavor that has attracted great attention in the media is the Maryland State games, a summer statewide Olympics-type competition that attracts athletes from around the state. Housed at UMBC and in other facilities close by, the athletes use the expansive facilities of both UMBC and CCC for a number of athletic events and draw upon expert management and support personnel available from both institutions.

Discussions are ongoing about other areas of collaboration, including campus security, mutual parking arrangements, shared use of heavy equipment, the roles of the two institutions in relation to a research park being built on the UMBC campus, and the possibility of renovation and shared use of buildings close to the two campuses. Events and lectures are becoming, increasingly, of interest to both campuses. This summer, for example, both institutions sponsored for their faculties and staffs the seminar by Uri Treisman, professor of mathematics at Berkeley, who spoke about minority achievement in mathematics and science.

Some arrangements that have been explored by the two organizations do not work. UMBC's Student Health Services, which is fully accredited by the American College Health Association, operates through a team of nurse practitioners. It attempted to provide women's health services to CCC students. Although the proposal posed no logistical problems, the contractual arrangement did not conform to the accreditation requirements for the UMBC program, and, consequently, the shared initiative was disbanded. Also, the UMBC shuttle bus service was to have been extended into the CCC campus proper. This arrangement has been superseded by the metropolitan-area bus service, which serves both campuses, door-to-door.

Questions for Self-Assessment

Throughout the five-year period of increased collaboration between UMBC and CCC, administrators in both institutions found it useful to assess the strength of the relationship by asking themselves a number of questions:

1. What are our attitudes about the other institution?
2. Do we understand the mission of the other collaborating institution and the roles that it plays in higher education and in the regions that it serves?
3. Do we appreciate the strengths of the other institution?
4. Have we some idea of the resources of each institution?
5. Are we aware of how the two institutions are currently working with one another?
6. Are we aware of some of the problems students experience when they transfer from the two-year to the four-year institution?
7. Do we know how students are advised and counseled before they transfer? And does the two-year institution know through receipt of academic records and other less formal communication how the transfer students are performing in their new surroundings?
8. Do faculty at both institutions have the opportunity to discuss curriculum issues—for example, course content, course sequencing, and student expectations?
9. Do those involved in the transfer process know each other through personal conversation?
10. Is there a system for referrals that provides a team approach regarding the student's education?
11. Do faculty and staff have an idea of how each can complement one another? And do they talk about potential linkages such as the exchange of facilities or other resources?
12. Do the two institutions have any special insights as to how the other is contributing to the support of economic development in the region or furthering service within the community?

Articulation becomes collaboration when most of these questions can be answered in the affirmative. And collaboration is imperative because the trend is clear. Metropolitan universities are accepting more and more community college students. For example, in 1985–1986

UMBC led 861 transfer students. By 1991–1992, that number had grown to 1,366 transfer students. It is also clear that more students are selecting community colleges with the intention of transferring to the four-year institutions for a variety of reasons, including finances and strength of academic programs.

It is imperative, therefore, that the process of collaboration become interwoven into the fabric of both types of institutions, that its importance be fully understood and supported at all levels, and that transfer and articulation receive a priority status in the day-to-day operations and long-range planning of the two. And as we suggest from these examples drawn from the national level, from state initiatives begun in Maryland, and from the university and community college level, personal contact and personal awareness are the key ingredients to making the symbiosis an effective one.

SUGGESTED READINGS

Donovan, Richard A., Barbara Schaies-Peleg, Bruce Forer, eds. *Transfer: Making It Work*. Washington, D.C.: American Association of Community and Junior Colleges, 1987.

Kintzer, Frederick C., ed. *Improving Articulation and Transfer Relationships*. New Directions for Community Colleges 39 (1982).

———————————, and James L. Wattenbarger. *The Articulation / Transfer Phenomenon: Patterns and Directions*. Washington, D.C.: American Association of Community and Junior Colleges, 1985.

Linksz, James J. A *Plan for Improving Articulation in Occupational Education Between Public Secondary Schools and Community Colleges in Maryland*. New York: Columbia University, 1971.

Networks, Ed. *New Initiatives for Transfer Students*. New York: Urban Community College Transfer Opportunities Program, Ford Foundation, 1984.

Pincus, Fred L., and Elayne Archer. *Bridges to Opportunity: Are Community Colleges Meeting the Transfer Needs of Minority Students?* New York: Academy for Educational Development/College Entrance Examination Board, 1989.

Wechsler, Harold. *The Transfer Challenge: Removing Barriers, Maintaining Commitment*. Washington, D.C.: Association of American Colleges, 1989.

Ohio's Urban University Program
Past, Present, and Future

David C. Sweet

An examination of the mission and funding of the urban or metropolitan university suggests that these institutions need to model their funding after land-grant colleges and the cooperative extension services in order to link them to the community with research and outreach. At this time, the urban university has no matching federal or local monies, which will cause the urban universities and the land-grant colleges to either compete, collaborate, or contract. In addition to developing a new funding model, the Urban University Program in Ohio (UUP) has been able to have an impact on the urban community.

In the last generation, the urban university has made many attempts at making its research valuable to the community. In the 1970s, after two decades of frustration with university-city interactions, William Pendleton, lead program officer for the Ford Foundation in this effort, and Peter L. Szanton, who headed the New York City Project of the Rand Corporation, evaluated the successes and failures of existing research and service programs. Working independently, they developed a number of principles necessary to achieve success. Many of these principles concern the relationship between the university and the community. The key to a successful relationship is for the university to be responsive to the needs of the community and to communicate with local officials in an understandable fashion. Once the urban university becomes vital to the community, it has taken the first step in building its constituency.

Creating the Ohio Urban University Program

In 1977, Cleveland State University established the College of Urban Affairs as the focus of the university's commitment to linkage of university resources with the community. A department of urban studies was set up to serve as the administrative unit for the college's academic programs (including a proposed Ph.D. in urban studies) and the Urban Center was organized as the administrative unit for the college's research and outreach programs and to link with other collegial units at CSU and at Ohio's other urban universities: the University of Akron, the University of Cincinnati, Kent State University, The Ohio State University, the University of Toledo, Wright State University, and Youngstown State University.

In 1979, Cleveland State University made a proposal to the Ohio Board of Regents for an Urban University Demonstration Program, which anticipated federal legislation then pending to create the Urban Grant University Program (Title XI). The proposal had three other objectives: to increase the focus of Ohio's higher education institutions on the state's major urban problems; to refine and expand the special research/education capabilities of the state's urban universities; and to establish a prototype urban center to serve as a model for state and national efforts.

The program, initially funded at $1 million for 1980–81, has generated a strong commitment from state and local leaders and has received continued and increasing support from the state legislature, which earmarked $6.9 million for 1990–91. The participating universities have been able to expand or "leverage" the state funds on approximately a one-to-one ratio, with other state money providing the basic support needed to develop effective city/university ties, and to attract additional financial support from city governments, private foundations, state and federal agencies, and private industry.

The eight-university consortium consisting of those universities located in Ohio's urban areas (as defined by the federal Urban Grant University Act) established in 1979 by the Ohio Board of Regents is known as the Regents' Advisory Committee on Urban University Programs. Representatives appointed by the president of each institution meet quarterly to plan, exchange ideas, and share information on successful projects and approaches. A unique foundation of mutual support and assistance has been established that expands the resource base available for urban problem-solving efforts and enhances the overall effectiveness of the UUP. Faculty members from all eight universities contribute and share research in such areas as housing and neighborhood development. The UUP model of exchange and sharing of teaching, research, and service between eight universities is in contrast to the agricultural model, which is focused at one university.

During its first decade, the Urban University Program has maintained its original objectives of organizing an Urban Center at Cleveland State University and providing funds to the other seven urban universities to develop research and technical assistance activities on their campuses. Other components have been added to increase research and service capabilities and to keep the program's focus current. By doing this, the UUP has been able to help serve the needs of the community and become an important resource for local government, as evidenced by the increase in appropriations in the last ten years.

The $6.9 million appropriation by the Ohio General Assembly to the Urban University Program for the 1990–91 biennium was allocated as follows: $3.5M to Cleveland State University's Maxine Goodman Levin College of Urban Affairs for The Urban Center; $730,000 to the Northeast Ohio Inter-Institutional Urban Research Program; $1.9M for the Urban Linkage Program of basic support grants, divided equally among the other seven universities in the program; $366,000 to three Urban Design Centers; and $484,000 for the Urban Research and Technical Assistance Grant Program.

Funding has increased as the resources of the UUP have been linked to the state's urban communities successfully. Part of this success is a result of the four components of the UUP: the College of Urban Affairs and its Urban Center at CSU, the Urban Linkage Program, the Northeast Ohio Inter-lnstitutional Program, and the Urban Research and Technical Assistance Grant Program. Continued success depends on not only how responsive these components can be to the urban community, but also how available and well-received they are.

The Urban Center

The prototypical Urban Center at Cleveland State was designed to incorporate "the principles for success" recommended by Szanton and Pendleton in their evaluation of the Ford Foundation and HUD projects. Those principles included a committed client, one or more specified problems or issues, university advisors with genuine and relevant expertise, communication between the university advisor and city client, and high quality, full-time staff.

The Urban Center, with a full-time director to oversee all of the administrative functions, complies with these principles by requiring that all programs and projects undertaken fall into four major areas: education, research, technical assistance, and database development. The focal points of these include neighborhood revitalization, housing research, public sector training, public works management, regional economic development, and urban technical assistance.

The educational component consists of degree-granting programs with degrees offered in Urban Studies (B.A., M.S., and Ph.D.), Public Administration (M.A.), and Urban Planning, Design, and Development (M.A.). Students in these programs are given the option of completing internships with a local governmental agency, participating in small seminar groups, or becoming directly involved in research and community projects.

In addition to the degree programs, education also includes workshops, seminars, and training institutes for local officials to help them keep abreast of changes in rules, regulations, and funding programs. Other areas of concern are dictated by local officials. In 1990, the Urban Center helped develop and deliver a two-day goal-setting retreat for Cleveland city council members.

One program that combines the educational component with the need for linkage between the university and the city is a joint partnership begun in 1982 between CSU's Colleges of Law and Urban Affairs and the Cleveland Public Schools. This program teaches urban youngsters how to understand their community and how to cope with many of the problems of life in the American city. Toward this end, an innovative approach to urban secondary education was begun at the Martin Luther King/Law and Public Service Magnet High School (MLK/LPS). Students attending MLK/LPS participate in an interdisciplinary program that emphasizes the development of basic skills and their application in addressing community issues and problems. The community itself becomes a laboratory in which students examine and participate in processes of decision making and group dynamics, gathering and managing information to that end. This experiential education is further emphasized by making the "hands-on" experience of various community projects and internships available as a major part of the curriculum.

The research aspect of the Urban Center is a major strength that the university can bring to the community. Recent research includes studying the economic impact of the savings and loan bailout on the recession, the auto industry, and the linkages between the steel industry and northeast Ohio's economy. This type of research is as important to the city dweller as the latest agricultural research is to the American farmer.

The Urban Center provides technical assistance to local officials to help assure the implementation of a solution. One example is CSU's Center for Neighborhood Development, which provides technical assistance to neighborhood organizations and to weatherization and energy conservation programs that help low-income residents.

Development of the urban database has proven to be a valuable component of the Urban Center. With the urban database in place, local officials are better able to address the changing needs of their urban communities. The Urban Center tracks local housing patterns and changes in Cuyahoga County—including all property sales, all mortgage filings, a twenty-five-year history of home sales, property tax and ownership status, and the physical characteristics of all county real estate. Students also benefit from these large data sets, which help to develop their analytical skills.

The Urban Linkage Program

The University of Akron (UA), the University of Cincinnati (UC), Kent State University (KSU), The Ohio State University (OSU), the University of Toledo (UT), Wright State University (WSU), and Youngstown State University (YSU) participate in the Urban Linkage Program, originally intended to develop an area of special strength at each university. In a September 1986 evaluation of the UUP, an external review panel stated that special strength "is perhaps not the right way to characterize what has happened at the participating universities . . . each university had a differing university/city relationship consistent with its institutional history and goals and the character of the surrounding community."

At five of the universities (UA, KSU, UT, WSU, and YSU), funding supports both urban research and technical assistance provided through established centers. Examples of the research and assistance offered include the University of Toledo helping Toledo review and rework the city's 1988 Downtown Master Plan, and Wright State University's Center for Urban and Public Affairs helping design CHALLENGE 95, an integrated set of strategies to position Ohio's Miami Valley to compete as a well organized unit in the global marketplace. The two remaining universities, the University of Cincinnati and The Ohio State University, use their funding solely to support faculty research projects selected by university committee. A subject of discussion within the Advisory Committee is the establishment of a matching pool to leverage additional university funding and to further institutionalize the progress of the UUP on participating campuses over the past decade.

The Northeast Ohio Inter-Institutional Urban Research Program

Four state universities in the Northeast Ohio region—the University of Akron, Cleveland State University, Kent State University, and Youngstown State University—established a consortium to encourage cooperative research and public service work on issues of importance to the region and of mutual interest. Wherever possible, projects involve the participation of faculty, staff, and students from more than one of the four campuses. Also, a high level of networking between faculty and researchers of the universities allows government officials to find solutions to urban problems more quickly.

Funding from the Inter-Institutional Program provides annual fellowship support for doctoral students in the Urban Studies Ph.D. program at University of Akron and Cleveland State University and also supports housing research at all four campuses, a regional migration study, and research on solid waste management and recycling. Students work on projects funded by the urban centers on each campus.

The Urban Research and Technical Assistance Grant Program

A large percentage of the budget for the Urban Research and Technical Assistance Grant Program funds competitive urban research and technical assistance grants, selected for funding by national panels of expert academicians and practitioners. Recently, the competition focused on problems that urban futurists advised would impact the future of Ohio—housing, education, and regional cooperation. A new initiative (begun during the 1988–89 biennium) is the Minority Urban Research Grant competition that supports black American untenured faculty at the eight campuses.

In 1984 and 1985, a portion of the budget was allocated to support three urban design centers housed at the University of Cincinnati, Kent State University, and The Ohio State University where students and faculty are available to provide assistance in community planning and development.

In response to a recommendation by the 1986 review panel for the Urban University Program, the UUP also funds dissemination efforts. These include producing and publishing an informational brochure, a semiannual newsletter, and a biennial report; funding public service announcements; and presenting a radio program on housing research.

Of particular importance are the cooperative projects recently funded by the UUP as components of the Urban Research and Technical Assistance Grant Program, which consists of research on all eight campuses in the areas of housing and regional cooperation. Ten thousand dollars was set aside to launch the efforts of networks in these areas. Although minimal, the funds supported the Ohio Housing Research Network, led by Cleveland State University. Several research reports have been produced, including "Suburbanization of Ohio Metropolitan Areas, 1980–2000." Researchers from all eight urban university campuses participated in an October conference, "Housing

Ohioans: Issues and Opportunities in the 1990s." Key to OHRN's accomplishments is the coordination between the urban campuses to provide a common methodology and format that enables local policy makers to learn from one another's experiences and statewide planners to work from a multiregional perspective. The network has been so successful that the Advisory Committee recently supported a proposal for additional funding to continue its work.

Faculty, staff, and students from five UUP universities—Akron, Cleveland State, Kent State, Youngstown State, and Wright State— have formed the Northeast Ohio Urban University Consortium on Municipal Solid Waste under the direction of the University of Akron and Youngstown State University. The consortium will assist northeast Ohio communities in responding to HB 592, which requires counties to establish single or joint solid waste management districts, and will formulate plans to meet state goals of reduction and recycling.

The Regents' Advisory Committee also expressed its concern for the future of public service employment in Ohio by budgeting $80,000 for the work of the Ohio Commission on Public Service. The new commission, staffed by the Levin College at Cleveland State University, was created by a joint resolution of the Ohio Legislature to assess the current status of public service on the state and local levels and to recommend constructive changes. The Ohio Commission is modeled after the national Volcker Commission, which focused on the federal government.

The Ohio Urban University Program has also made possible the improvement of quality education at all eight universities, particularly in urban-related fields; has had a valuable impact on the state's major urban communities and many smaller urban centers (as attested to by the number of city officials and staff who turn to the program for assistance); and has opened the university forum to public officials, enabling sensitive issues to be examined with a constructive result. The UUP has also provided opportunities for students to apply the knowledge learned in the classroom toward research on actual urban situations and toward providing technical assistance to their communities. In addition, the program has enhanced community awareness of the role and commitment of urban universities.

Facing the Future—The Ohio Urban University Program and Urban Extension

Urban affairs colleges, departments, and centers, as well as agricultural cooperative extension programs, face new challenges in the 1990s as federal, state, and local governments attempt to balance budgets and eliminate costly programs. Urban universities and cooperative extension must prove themselves to their constituencies or face massive budget cuts or extinction. The keys to providing for the future include:

1. institutionalizing the programs in the participating universities;
2. having institutional commitment by matching future growth in UUP support;
3. broadening the participation by the faculty and staff at each university;
4. collaborating with faculty from other institutions on specific issues; and
5. expanding resources by increasing state support by requiring an institutional match as well as using the state support to leverage federal and local support.

Those of us involved in leadership, teaching, research, and service must recognize the need to evolve and to communicate our message to an urban constituency. Over the last two years, Ohio's UUP has begun a process to identify and to suggest approaches to urban problems. Drawing on the expertise of urban futurists, we have begun to focus on housing, regional cooperation, and education as critical issues for Ohio and the nation. We have begun reaping the benefits of funding cross-disciplinary research, creating networks of researchers across the state, and investing in database development.

In recommending continuation of the current components of the program, the Urban University Program Advisory Board has recommended new initiatives for the next biennium. We are proposing the establishment of a demonstration project to link community colleges with Urban University Program members to develop education and public service programs. We are proposing a minority Ph.D. initiative to support fellowships that will increase the supply of minority faculty with interests in urban-related teaching, research, and service. We must communicate our design to elected officials and legislative bodies at all levels, showing them how to mine the special capacities of the urban universities on their behalf. With the Higher Education Act up for authorization and the possibility of a renewed and funded Title XI, we have an opportunity to focus on the national arena. This requires a strategy for increasing the awareness of our research and accomplishments and positioning ourselves to influence federal policy.

To build a constituency, we must be accountable to the public. We must continue to use expert academicians and practitioners to assist us in selecting the best urban research and technical assistance proposals for funding, but we must also emphasize follow-up as seriously as selection and share more information. We must make our research relevant to the practitioners with whom we work and collaborate with them on implementing solutions. We must continue to build partnerships, both public and private, and among universities.

The criteria established ten years ago by Szanton and Pendleton— good leadership, hard funding, a specific problem, relevant experience, a committed client, and effective communication—are still relevant for the Urban University Program and urban extension today. But over the last decade our urban areas have changed and are faced with new problems. Our constituency is urban, suburban, and metropolitan. Our urban universities must strengthen their relationships, pool our talents, and make our message known. We must focus our efforts on the present and the future to fully utilize the important resources available at our urban universities to help find solutions to these changing urban problems.

NOTE: The author wishes to express appreciation to many who have contributed suggestions, specifically to Mary Keller, who assisted in the preparation of this paper.

SUGGESTED READINGS

"The Ohio Urban University Program: A Decade of Accomplishment." The Fifth Biennial Report to the Ohio Board of Regents on the Urban University Program, July 1990.

"Ohio's Urban University Program: Poised for Growth in the Face of Challenges." County Information and Data Service, County Commissioners Association of Ohio, Summer, 1991.

"Ohio's Urban University Program: Tenth Anniversary Colloquium Collection." Cleveland State University, 1991.

"Ohio Urban University Program: Working for Ohio's Future—The First Decade." Cleveland State University, July 1991.

How Do We Talk About Higher Education's Relationship to the Schools?

Ernest L. Boyer

What is higher education's responsibility to the nation's schools? How can the nation's colleges and universities contribute most effectively to the renewal of precollegiate education? Perhaps the best place to begin is January 20, 1990, when President George Bush announced six ambitious education goals soon to become the "reform agenda" for the nation. Every goal the President announced was provocative and consequential, but I found the first goal most authentic and compelling. As the number one objective, the President declared that by the year 2000 every child in America will come to school "ready to learn."

This is an audacious, hugely optimistic proposition, but dreams can be fulfilled only if they've been defined. If "school readiness," in fact, becomes a top priority for the nation, I'm convinced that all the goals will, in large measure, be fulfilled.

The harsh truth is that, in America today, nearly one out of every four children under six is officially "poor." They are undernourished, disadvantaged, struggling. If we continue to neglect poor children, both the quality of education and the future of the nation will be imperiled.

We know, for example, that brain cells develop before birth, and yet one-fifth of all pregnant women in this country receive belated prenatal care—or none at all. We know that malnourished babies are two to three times as likely to be blind, deaf, or intellectually deficient, and yet nearly half a million children are undernourished. We know that children who suffer from iron deficiency may develop poor coordination skills, and yet one tenth of all the nation's babies have deficiencies during their first two years of life. Winston Churchill said a community has no greater commitment than putting milk into babies. If all children are to come to school "ready to learn," we must nourish every child, since good health and good education are inextricably connected.

Beyond a healthy start, school readiness calls for good preschool education to help every disadvantaged child overcome not just poor nutrition but also learning deprivation. It is a national disgrace that a quarter century after the federal Head Start program was authorized by Congress to help three- and four-year-olds get special help, less than half the eligible are being served.

If we want all children to come to school ready to learn, this surely means full funding of Head Start, which President Clinton's administration has pledged to do. I recognize that not every Head Start program is successful, but the evidence is overwhelming that early intervention is highly beneficial, especially for disadvantaged children. And if some programs are not working very well, let's fix them, not close them down and deny access to those who need it most.

In addition to a healthy start and quality preschool, school readiness requires that we help all children become empowered in the use of words. Lewis Thomas wrote that childhood is for language. It's in the first years of life that children are verbally empowered. This is the time when the symbol system exponentially expands. It's absolutely ludicrous to expect a child to be "ready to learn" if he or she grows up in an environment that is linguistically impoverished.

A recent report from Cambridge, England, says that children by the eighteenth month are able to decode sounds and have the phoneme structure well established. We also know that, when children are born, the middle ear bones—the hammer, the anvil, and the stirrup—are the only bones that are fully formed. Babies are, in fact, auditorily monitoring voices and other sounds *in utero,* so they begin to hear long before they speak. The miraculous capacity of children to learn languages begins before birth and is well established during the first months and years of life. If children grow up in an environment where they do not have their questions answered and where they are not immersed in language, they will be unlikely to compensate for the deficiency later on.

Good language means successful learning. We should encourage parents to turn off the TV, listen to their children, tell them stories, and read to them at least thirty minutes every day. We also need day care centers that are "language rich," and community libraries that have story hours.

But what does all of this have to do with higher education? I'm suggesting that higher education's first responsibility is to understand that "ready to learn" is the nation's most essential education goal. For all children, this means good nutrition, quality preschool, and good parenting. It also means that those in higher education must become active partners in the process. Last year, for example, at Texas Woman's University, I visited a residence hall that had been converted into apartments for single mothers and their children. While the mothers worked and attended classes at the college, the youngsters were cared for in a day care center run by college students. And the Nursing School at the university had a medical clinic for mothers and babies at a nearby housing project.

In a recent Carnegie Foundation report called *Ready to Learn,* we suggest that both two- and four-year colleges take the lead in training preschool teachers. It's a disgrace that we are trusting our youngest children to those who are often poorly educated and who are paid far too little. We know that children need continuity of care, but the turnover rate in many of these centers is sometimes forty percent each year. Preschool teaching is an undervalued profession that must be given status and recognition in the culture, and some colleges are already developing a response to this critical need.

Dutchess Community College in New York grants an associate degree in early childhood education. About half of those who graduate teach at child care centers, and the rest transfer to four-year programs. Miami-Dade Community College has a sixty-two-credit child-care degree program, and the college also has established a "satellite" public school on its campus to help preschools make the transition to elementary education. The Bank Street College of Graduate Education in New York offers graduate programs in early childhood education, with an infancy program and a day care program. Bank Street also has a Child Family Center, which serves children six months to four years of age and is a demonstration site for teacher training in infant care.

Simply stated, higher education has an obligation, not only to be aware of the essentials of the early years, but to direct its resources and educational efforts toward more research on early childhood education and toward the preparation of those who will be teaching preschoolers. In our *Ready to Learn* report we say that every community should organize a Ready-to-Learn Council to coordinate services to preschoolers, and a college or university is an ideal institution to help form such a council.

If we wish to have quality schools, we must understand that education begins before formal schooling, before birth itself.

But there's another side to the equation. While children must be well prepared for school, it's also true that schools must be ready for the children. Several years ago, I proposed that we reorganize the first years of formal education into a single unit called the Basic School.

The Basic School would combine kindergarten to grade four. It would give top priority to language, and every student from the very first would be reading, writing, engaging in conversation, listening to stories, in what the foreign language people like to call the "saturation method."

Class size is crucial. In the Basic School there would be no class with more than fifteen students. Frankly, I find it ludicrous to hear school critics say class size doesn't matter, especially in the early years when children urgently need one-on-one attention. I've never taught kindergarten or first grade, but I have grandchildren and find taking them to McDonald's a complicated task—keeping track of all the orders, mustard on the floor, tracking down gloves and boots. And none of this relates to mastering the ABCs or cramming for the SATs. When we were preparing our report *Ready to Learn*, we surveyed seven thousand kindergarten teachers from coast to coast, and we asked them about their kindergarten class size. Teachers reported twenty-seven students per class, and in one state the average class size is over forty.

I've spent forty years in higher education. College education is consequential, and I love to teach undergraduates. But I'm convinced that the early years of formal education are the most important. And if this country would give as much status to the first grade teacher as we give to full professors, that one act alone would revitalize the nation's schools. School-college partnerships should, I believe, focus on primary education, which I'm convinced will be a priority of the 1990s. Too often the focus is on the social pathologies of high school students, but the weaknesses we see there are due to a failure to keep addressing the problems children have in the early years.

We need to create more "Summer Institutes" for elementary school teachers. We need college student volunteers to serve as mentors to these teachers, and to serve in after-school and Saturday reading and recreation programs to keep young students engaged in learning instead of drifting. Martin Luther King, Jr., said that everyone can be great because everyone can serve, and creating a public love of children and a commitment to serve them is the most urgent challenge this nation must confront. Higher education can, I'm convinced, help lead the way.

Of course, the upper grades are crucial, too. When we prepared our report *High School* in 1983, as I went from urban school to urban school, I became convinced that we had not just a school problem but a youth problem. I was struck by the climate of anonymity in many schools and distressed that students seemed disconnected and unrelated to the larger world. I became convinced that many students dropped out because no one noticed that they had in fact dropped in. I would try to reduce the size of every large high school to perhaps no more than four or five hundred students.

The two conditions that overwhelm the public schools most are a climate of anonymity and a sense of irrelevance. If we could make educational programs more relevant and reduce students' sense of anonymity, we would re-engage the young people who do not feel that they belong.

This brings us then to a third responsibility of higher education. Beyond looking at the preschool conditions of children and helping communities strengthen children's readiness to learn, and beyond giving strength to the teachers, those in higher education must help improve the *accountability* in our school system.

In his 1993 State of the Union message, the President declared that by the year 2000 all students would be tested at the fourth-, eighth- and twelfth-grade levels in all the basic subjects to see if they are academically proficient. There is danger in this goal, and many academics argue that it should be opposed. Educators should not resist such evaluation. School accountability will, I believe, be the central issue of the 1990s, and if educators do not help shape the process of assessment, others surely will do it for us. There is a great concern about where this testing objective may take us, and unless we have leadership from higher education, we may continue to ask our students to recall isolated facts, to fill in the bubbles, to put check marks on the paper, and in the process, end up measuring what matters least.

Howard Gardner, psychologist at Harvard, reminds us that children have not only verbal intelligence but also intuitive, social, spacial, and aesthetic intelligences. And yet the tests we use today at both the school and college level often screen out the intelligences of children that are most consequential in their real lives. James Agee has written that with every child who is born, under no matter what circumstances, the potential of the human race is born again, but too often schools declare children failures before discovering who they are or what they might become.

Many years ago my wife, Kay, and I were told by school officials that one of our children was a "special student," because of his performance on a single test and because, as another teacher put it, "he's a dreamer." Craig did dream, of course. He dreamed about the stars and about places far away. He dreamed about how he could go out and play. But we were absolutely convinced that he was gifted and that somehow his talents just didn't match the routine of the classroom or of the system. Let the record show that for ten years this so-called "special student" has lived successfully in a Mayan village. He knows the language, he understands the culture, he runs Mayan schools, he builds bridges across wide chasms, he has a beautiful Mayan family. And he has survived living in conditions that would have totally defeated the psychometricians who concluded years ago he couldn't learn.

Recently, I reflected on why the testers were so wrong, and it suddenly occurred to me that the answer was quite simple. The problem was that they didn't have the right instruments to measure his potential. They didn't have a test on how to survive in a Mayan village. They didn't have a test on how to build a bridge. They didn't have an examination on how to understand the beauty of another culture. The problem was not with the child, but with the test instrument that dealt crudely and with rough judgment about the potential of a life.

I support a carefully crafted program of national assessment, but I also am convinced that we have a very long way to go to devise the appropriate instruments. Once again, higher education has a special role to play. As a national strategy, I propose a three-year moratorium on national assessment. During that period, university scholars should join with master teachers in the schools—in a kind of peacetime Manhattan Project—to design for the twenty-first century a new assessment process that promotes learning rather than restricts it.

In a companion move, colleges and universities must think more carefully about how to evaluate the outcome of collegiate education which would, of course, give guidance to the schools.

This leads to a fourth responsibility for higher education. The push for better testing inevitably will bring us back to the central issue of what we teach. Colleges and universities have a responsibility to develop with the schools a curriculum with more integration and coherence.

Today almost all colleges have a requirement in general education. But all too often this so-called "distribution requirement" is a grab bag of isolated courses. Students complete their required credits, but what they fall to gain is a more coherent view of knowledge and a more integrated, more authentic view of life. And what's even more disturbing is the way colleges impose the old Carnegie units on the schools, requiring students to complete credits in history and mathematics and science and English without asking what's behind the label.

The Carnegie Foundation created the Carnegie unit eighty years ago. High school students were applying to college from places colleges didn't know existed, much less what kind of program they offered. The Carnegie unit was meant to set standards, and it worked in its own way, but it fails now because it focuses on seat time rather than substance. It is time to bury the old Carnegie unit.

The truth is that the old academic boxes do not fit the new intellectual questions. Some of the most exciting work going on in the academy today is, in the "hyphenated disciplines"—in bio-engineering and psycho-linguistics and the like in what Michael Polanyi calls the "overlapping academic neighborhoods." Anthropologist Clifford Geertz, at the Institute for Advanced Study, in his fascinating book called *Blurred Genres,* says that "these shifts in the disciplines represent a fundamental reconfiguration of knowledge. Something is happening," Geertz says, "to the way we think about the way we think."

During the next century, we will see a fundamental reshaping of the typology of knowledge as profound as that which occurred in the nineteenth century when philosophy was submerged by science. And wouldn't it be tragic if a *nineteenth*-century curriculum design were imposed on schools at the very time scholars were redefining the structure of knowledge for the *twenty-first* century?

Frank Press, retiring president of the National Academy of Sciences, has said that scientists are in some respects like artists, and he illustrated his point by stating that the magnificent double helix which broke the genetic code was not only rational, but beautiful as well. This brought to mind watching the launchings at Cape Kennedy when in the final seconds of the countdown, the cameras would zoom in on the faces of the scientists and engineers. As the rocket lifted successfully into orbit, the scientists didn't say, "Well, our formulas worked again." They said, almost in unison, "Beautiful!" They chose an *aesthetic* term to describe a *technologic*al achievement. It suggests that the scientific quest is not only a response to intellectual curiosity, but a response to a deeper need for aesthetic relationships. When physicist Victor Weisskopf was asked, "What gives you hope in troubled times?" he replied, "Mozart and quantum mechanics." Yet, in the academic world, too often the scientist and the artist live in separate spheres.

Collaboration between colleges and the schools should recurringly ask: What do we want our children to learn and be able to do after sixteen years of formal education? Wouldn't it be exciting, as we move toward the next century, if we would start to rethink the nature of the new knowledge that relates not to the last century but to the coming century? How can we organize knowledge in a way that seems to make it relevant and powerful for students in the days ahead? Wouldn't it be exciting if both kindergarten teachers and college professors could view knowledge using understandable categories that would have integration and would spiral upward in common discourse? Wouldn't it be exciting not only to build connections *across* the disciplines but to build them vertically as well, from preschool through college?

Over fifty years ago, Mark Van Doren wrote: "The connectedness of things is what the educator contemplates to the limit of his capacity." Van Doren concluded by saying that the student who can begin early in life to see things as connected has begun the life of learning. And this, it seems to me, is what school and college collaboration is all about—*connections*.

This brings me to a final observation. To achieve school excellence in the coming decade, we simply must give more dignity and more status to the teacher. Today, we hear endlessly about how the schools have failed, and surely education must improve. But the longer it goes, the more I am convinced that it's not the school that's failed, it's the partnership that's failed. And I'm beginning to suspect that the family is a more imperiled institution than the school. I might go further and suggest that perhaps the schools are working better than any other institution in our society, except perhaps higher education.

The reason that schools are imperiled is that they're confronting the pathologies of the disintegrating institutions surrounding them. Institutions that historically have supported the family and the school and children are less reliable today. I think the health care system is in greater distress than public education, surely in terms of equity if not excellence. I think the savings and loan industry is more troubled than the schools. I think the judicial system and the penal system are near collapse. And I don't say this to be flippant, but I'm not sure what SAT score to give to Congress. I'm really saying that it seems odd that we have made the schools the preoccupation of our frustrations, when I believe the schools are in fact struggling to try to hold us together and prevent a cultural breakdown.

Several years ago at The Carnegie Foundation we surveyed twenty-two thousand teachers and eighty-seven percent reported that lack of parental support is a problem at their school. Eighty-nine percent say that the existence of "abused" or "neglected" children is a problem. And sixty-seven percent report "poor health" among their students. One teacher put it this way: "I'm sick and tired," she said, "of seeing my bright-eyed first grade kids fade into the shadows of apathy and become deeply troubled by age ten."

We also surveyed five thousand fifth- and eighth-graders, and thirty-six percent said they go home in the afternoon to an empty house. Sixty percent said they wish they could spend more time with their parents. Thirty percent said their family never sits down together to eat a meal. Another two-thirds said they wished they had more things to do.

My wife recently heard a conversation between two of our granddaughters—one lives in Princeton, the other was visiting from Belize. The Mayan granddaughter was asking her Princeton cousin what she planned to do this summer. The answer was, "Just hang out." To which the Mayan granddaughter said, "You plan to what?"

"Just hang out." "Is that work?" "No, it's hanging out." "What is hanging out?" It was a fascinating exchange. We live in a culture where young people are disconnected from the larger world, and today's teachers are engaged daily with this youth culture. They are being asked to do what families and communities and churches have not been able to accomplish. If they fail anywhere along the line we condemn them for not meeting our high-minded expectations, yet I'm convinced that most school critics could not survive one week in the classrooms they condemn. Excellence in education means excellence in teaching, and higher education has an absolutely critical role to play in reestablishing the centrality of teaching in our society.

During a visit to Trinity University in San Antonio, I was introduced to a group of future teachers, among the brightest and the best. As it turned out, the University had offered a full tuition scholarship to all San Antonio high school students in the top ten percent of their graduating class if they agreed to teach for at least three years in the city's public schools. The students I met were fellows in this program.

Every college and university should have a future teachers' program, beginning the recruitment while students are still in junior high and focusing especially on minority students. In addition, higher education must train teachers who are well educated and well taught in classrooms where there is active, not passive, learning, where students learn to cooperate rather than compete. In-service education is also a key responsibility of higher education.

In 1980, Bart Giamatti, then president of Yale, asked me to visit the Yale-New Haven Institute. This program, which serves city schools, is controlled by New Haven teachers, who each year select the participants, shape the schedule, and decide the curriculum to be studied. The participants are empowered to direct and control the Institute, and the Board of Directors is comprised of teachers. The university, on the other hand, offers distinguished, tenured professors every summer and names each professor a "Yale Fellow," and as an ultimate status symbol, gives each teacher a parking sticker.

I'm suggesting that every college and university should enrich the lives of teachers in surrounding schools by making them partners in the process.

Finally, higher education should give to teachers special rewards of recognition, helping to create in this country a climate, as in Japan, in which "teacher" is a title of great honor. Higher education must honor its own teachers. It's impossible to give dignity and status to school teachers if we do not have a reward system in higher education that honors outstanding faculty.

Several years ago, the State University of New York at Fredonia asked all incoming freshmen to name the most outstanding teacher they had had from kindergarten to grade twelve. The college president then sent a letter to each of those teachers thanking them for their contribution to education. If every college and university sent such thank you's, literally millions of teachers would, each year, be recognized and renewed. As a further step, I'd like to see outstanding teachers speak occasionally at the conventions of higher education, reminding academics that they are in fact partners in the process.

And while speaking of teacher recognition, I also respectfully suggest that President Clinton invite the Teachers of the Year to a dinner in the East Room of the White House. After all, we have state dinners for visiting heads of state from nations overseas, why not pay honor to the heroes from the nation's classrooms here at home?

Education is a seamless web, and colleges and universities have a responsibility to give priority to early education, improve the evaluation of all students, create a curriculum with coherence, recognize the centrality of teaching, and reaffirm the essentialness of public education.

After ten years of school reform, the nation still is very much at risk. We are dividing ourselves between the rich and the poor, the advantaged and the disadvantaged. I am not suggesting that we take public education off the hook. I'm suggesting that the nation's public schools are struggling under inordinately difficult conditions, and those of us in higher education have both an educational and moral obligation to support the schools and most especially the teachers, who are struggling every single day to educate effectively a new generation. We simply must reaffirm the essentialness of public education and avoid being divided by ideological debates that would undermine the common school for the common good.

Marian Wright Edelman sent me a copy of a prayer, and with a little edit of my own, it seems a good way to conclude.

Dear Lord we pray for children
    who spend all their allowances before Tuesday,
    who throw tantrums in the grocery store,
    who pick at their food,
    who squirm in church and temple,
    and who scream into the phone.
And we also pray for children
    whose nightmares come in the light of day,
    who rarely see a doctor,

who never see a dentist,
who aren't spoiled by anybody,
and who go to bed hungry,
and cry themselves to sleep.
We pray for children
who like to be tickled,
who sneak Popsicles before dinner,
and who can never find their shoes.
And we also pray for children
who can't run down the street in a new pair of sneakers,
who never get dessert,
who don't have any rooms to clean up,
and whose pictures aren't on anybody's dresser.
We pray for children who want to be carried
and we pray for those who must be carried.
We pray for those we never give up on
and also for those who never get a second chance.
We pray for those we smother with love,
and we pray especially for those who will grab the hand
of anybody
kind enough to hold it.

This sort of prayer must motivate our work. And if I had one message to convey, I would say that school and college educators should urgently work together not only to define excellence in education, but, above all, to create a better world for children.

NOTE: These remarks are based on a presentation to a meeting of the K-16 Initiative of the American Association for Higher Education, held in Washington, D.C., on June 29, 1993.

PART V

COMMUNITY-UNIVERSITY RELATIONSHIPS

INTRODUCTION

$\mathbf{P}$otential for involvement by metropolitan universities with the community is virtually limitless. Metropolitan universities can foster regional cooperation, improve a community's or region's cultural life, health care, education, economic status, and even the relationships among its various parts. One should not underestimate the benefits that the university receives through its interaction with its diverse community. The interaction creates a stimulating environment for teaching, research, and service.

Wright State University illustrates the important role that a metropolitan university can play in fostering regional cooperation. As Mary Ellen Mazey points out in her article, "The Role of a Metropolitan University in Facilitating Regional Cooperation," universities possess the intellectual resources and the reputation for neutrality that allow them to serve as a catalyst for change on a broad scale. The article gives a detailed account of the process of developing a strategic plan for the Miami Valley region, and the challenges inherent in any community-oriented planning process. Chief among them is the struggle to adjudicate among competing interests for the future of the region. To establish a direction-setting agenda for a region is both an enormous responsibility and opportunity for any institution, as illustrated in Mazey's article.

In "Diverse Communities" and "Scope and Limitations of Community Interactions," the authors describe with a wide angle lens the scope of involvement that is possible for metropolitan universities and their communities. But, they also point out the limits to how a university can deploy its resources.

Metropolitan universities interact with their neighbors as employers and consumers, as fellow members of the business community, with the local school systems, with city and county governments, professional communities, other area colleges and universities, participate in cultural activities, are involved in health care issues, work with local and state governments, the minority community, etc.

193

But, what characterizes the nature of the interaction between the metropolitan university and its environment? Charles P. Ruch and Eugene P. Trani argue that the interaction should be mutually reinforcing, guided by institutional choice and strategy on the part of both parties, and viewed to be one of value and importance. Both the university and community should welcome and encourage the activity. Of course, there are limits to any such activities. Ruch and Trani believe that the boundaries of those limits can be expanded, but universities will need to make changes in areas such as faculty roles and rewards, support services and leadership.

The potential for a new kind of university—a metropolitan university—to generate new and imaginative ideas to address major social issues effecting our nation is the subject matter of "Winds of Change: The University in Search of Itself." Jerome M. Ziegler sees five overarching challenges affecting our nation which are issues for all metropolitan regions: the struggle between individualism and community, the persistent problem of race, the conflict between economic development and environmental protection, the changing nature of both work and family, and problems inherent in the central city and its decay. All the authors in this section share the conviction that the special kinds of talents and abilities that characterize faculty, students and staff at metropolitan universities give cause for optimism in addressing these difficult problems.

THE ROLE OF A METROPOLITAN UNIVERSITY IN FACILITATING REGIONAL COOPERATION

Mary Ellen Mazey

In the second half of the twentieth century, the United States has experienced significant population losses in its central cities along with subsequent population gains and development in the suburbs and exurbs. During this period, particularly since the 1960s, a number of metropolitan universities have developed within our central cities and also on the periphery of America's urban areas. These metropolitan universities have a unique role to play in developing a regional perspective that encompasses a focus on central city issues within a framework of the population, economic, and demographic changes that have occurred throughout metropolitan areas including the suburbs and exurbs.

One such institution is Wright State University, located in the Dayton-Springfield, Ohio, Metropolitan Statistical Area, an area also known as the Miami Valley region. Universities such as Wright State increasingly find that they are being called upon not only to serve the students' educational needs in their region, but also to become proactive leaders in the economic well-being of their metropolitan area. This latter function is exemplified by the facilitative-leadership role Wright State University has played in a regional strategic planning process titled CHALLENGE 95 and is the focus of this article.

As the Miami Valley and other metropolitan areas/regions move into the 1990s, the tempo of social, economic, and political change will be unprecedented. Planning can no longer be left to public officials and the typical governmental planning process, which tends to be limited in geographical scope, reactive, short-range, staff-oriented, and dominated by single issues. Actions from such planning are typically hierarchical in nature and lack community support. In addition, such

195

planning efforts tend to be without a regional, state, national, and international strategic perspective.

Metropolitan areas are on the threshold of an opportune time to build public-private partnerships to resolve their problems and plan for the future. The decade of the 1970s, in which the federal government financially supported local projects, is gone and will not return in the foreseeable future. In all likelihood, the decade of the 1990s will continue the trend of public-private partnerships born in the 1980s. These partnerships are a "bottoms-up" approach to planning and demand a comprehensive approach from individuals and organizations that represent a cross section of a metropolitan region. Although the overriding focus of such efforts is economic development, the social and political elements that impinge on economic development plans force a comprehensive perspective. This perspective includes the human needs of the regions as well as an approach to restructuring the political environment and targeting the region's economic development efforts for the global marketplace.

Metropolitan universities such as Wright State University (WSU) have a unique role to play in building the partnerships to create a regional perspective. The metropolitan university can serve as a catalyst to initiate change on a broad geographic basis within the university's service area. As an institution of higher education, the metropolitan university, with its status and prestige, can institute a new way of thinking about the regional concept through the development of a strategic planning process. In addition, the university is a neutral entity and does not carry the baggage of existing regional organizations such as regional planning agencies or a regional chamber of commerce. Furthermore, the university possesses a logistical infrastructure to facilitate such a process and the substantive expertise to provide technical assistance to a comprehensive strategic regional planning effort. If an existing regional entity were to undertake such a comprehensive grassroots planning effort, it could be seen as a means to enhance its own well-being. Whereas the university, without power and authority, but with prestige and leverage, has the power to broker the influential community leaders and other citizens into working together to build a regional plan and a spirit of regional cooperation in both the private and public sectors.

Development of a Regional Strategic Plan

In 1987, the Dayton Area Chamber of Commerce contracted with two WSU economics professors to analyze the region's economy. The two main threats to the economic development of the Miami Valley were identified as "turfism," i.e., promoting the self-interests of one political entity over another, and lack of leadership. In response to these threats, the CHALLENGE 95 regional strategic planning process was created to promote regional cooperation and establish regional leadership.

The CHALLENGE 95 process was initiated by the private sector, the Dayton Area Chamber of Commerce, soliciting the assistance of the public sector and initiating a contract with the Center for Urban and Public Affairs (CUPA) at Wright State University. The Center for Urban and Public Affairs, an outreach unit for WSU, focuses upon applied research, training, technical assistance, and data base development primarily in the Dayton-Springfield Metropolitan Area. However, as part of the Ohio Board of Regents Urban University Program, CUPA works with other urban centers and members of the urban university program to foster an urban policy agenda in the state of Ohio.

In CHALLENGE 95, the center faculty and staff were not the planners, but rather the facilitators of a process that produced a regional strategic plan. The year-long process involved over ten thousand hours of citizen participation that included over five hundred individuals serving on the CHALLENGE 95 steering committee and nine task forces. In addition, the public forums held throughout the region at two different stages of the process allowed input from a broad cross section of the region's population. By allowing the process to develop over a year with broad-scale participation, political agendas and barriers were dismantled, and the building of mutual trust was established. This latter product of the process was essential in a region composed of approximately one million inhabitants plus 171 general purpose governments, thirty-two chambers of commerce, and fifty-five school districts. If a metropolitan region like the Miami Valley region is to continue to be competitive in a global economy, its strategic plan has to unite the citizens as one interdependent entity that is able to compete as a whole with other regions. The region cannot continue to prosper with over a hundred different localities focusing upon their conflicts with each other.

Because a strategic planning process had never been initiated on regional basis in the Miami Valley, CHALLENGE 95 instantly became highly visible. With such a broad cross section of the region's citizens involved in task forces and the steering committee, Wright State University established a leadership role on a regional basis for the first time in its history. This is particularly noteworthy in a metropolitan region well-endowed with higher education institutions. This latter strength of the region comes with the added problem of inter-institutional turfism among the public and private colleges and universities and with well-respected community colleges. Therefore, it was of utmost importance that WSU be a neutral facilitative leader throughout the CHALLENGE 95 process in order that the buy-in and ownership would come from the region's citizens and those directly involved in the regional strategic planning process. In addition, WSU had to ensure representation on the task forces and steering committee of *all* institutions of higher education in the region. Again, it was paramount to the success of the process and its ultimate end product that CHALLENGE 95 not be seen as a WSU initiative, but rather an effort of the region's citizens.

In maintaining a neutral, facilitative role, the faculty and staff within the Center for Urban and Public Affairs at WSU were able to orchestrate the process with minimum center staff but with maximum utilization of university personnel outside of CUPA's administrative realm in addition to resources outside the university. For example, the Dayton Area Chamber of Commerce produced a video explaining the process, published two newsletters and a newspaper insert detailing the work of the task forces, and supplied the technical expertise for all press releases and public service announcements. In addition, numerous entities, internal to the university, provided logistical support and substantive expertise throughout the process.

The CHALLENGE 95 Process and Plan

When the project began, the overall objective of the CHALLENGE 95 process had an economic focus oriented toward the development of an action program to provide rewarding jobs and satisfying lives for the current and future residents of the metropolitan region. The CHALLENGE 95 process offered the region an opportunity to identify where it wanted to be in 1995 and, consequently, where resources should be invested to realize this vision. The 1995 date was chosen because the target offered sufficient time to enable the public and current leaders to implement the goals of the process.

Since the university played a leadership facilitative role in the CHALLENGE 95 process, it was important to design the process to be widely participatory in order that the final plan could not be faulted as an academic one compiled by university faculty and staff. Instead, the plan was to represent a synthesis of ideas and agendas of those who participated in the process. The approach was to create ownership among a broad cross section of the region's citizens. In order to foster this approach, the county commissions, city councils, chambers of commerce, religious community, health community, education community, labor unions, industry, the media (newspapers and television), and civic groups were all requested to designate appointees to the steering committee chaired by Paige Mulhollan, the president of Wright State University. The steering committee in turn appointed an equally broad cross section of the region's population to nine task forces formed to address strategic issues delineated during an initial two-day retreat.

At this retreat, the steering committee divided into small groups in order to address a series of questions focused upon what the region would be in 1995 without regional planning, what it could be with regional planning, and what could be done to make the difference with a strategic planning effort. This facilitative process produced nine issue areas for the task forces:

1. economic development
2. education
3. environment
4. infrastructure
5. human needs/human relations
6. regional cooperation
7. resource enhancement
8. technology and innovation
9. transportation

Subsequent to the steering committee retreat and within a six-month period, each task force met eight times to pursue the following questions from a regional perspective:

1. Where is the region today?
2. How did we get here?
3. Where are current factors and momentum taking us?
4. What's working—what are our strengths? What do we have going for us?
5. What's broken—what are our weaknesses and problems?
6. What are the region's opportunities on which we should capitalize?
7. What must the region address before 1995?
8. What are the key issues that must be addressed?
9. What should an overall objective statement (vision) say?
10. How does the vision relate to the scope, background, and key issues?
11. What are our strategic goals? These goals should be strategic

in character and represent what needs to be accomplished or begun between now and 1995. They address the key issues and move us toward our vision statement.

12. What are the strategies or mechanisms for accomplishing the goals? Prioritize the goals and develop the action plans for accomplishing the goals. The criteria used for prioritizing the goals include what is critical, doable, and regional.

The synthesis of the material compiled from the dialogue of eight three-hour meetings, plus a public forum held in three different locations within the region for each task force, provided the information and material for the task force reports. The reports were a consensus of the material generated in response to the questions each task force addressed.

The task force on regional cooperation provides a typical example of the process. The group was composed of elected officials, appointed officials, not-for-profit administrators, and representatives from the private sector, and chaired by a major private sector representative. During the course of their meetings, the CHALLENGE 95 Regional Cooperation Task Force members analyzed current, successful regional efforts in order to understand the positive aspects of these efforts. CUPA staff compiled for the task force an inventory of existing regional efforts. These efforts included emergency services such as the 911 hotline, general government consolidation of services, health services, utilities, education, and private sector efforts. By using this base knowledge and working through a total of twenty-seven hours of task force meetings, the regional cooperation task force initiated two efforts that moved the region toward tangible, positive results.

First, the regional cooperation task force empowered the county level of governments with taking the lead in the regional cooperative efforts. Therefore, a Memorandum of Understanding was signed by the county commissioners from each of the participating CHALLENGE 95 counties proclaiming an agreement to cooperate when it mutually benefits two or more parties. This memorandum was signed as the CHALLENGE 95 strategic plan was being formulated and before the elected officials were totally aware of the plan's final recommendations.

Secondly, as an implementation mechanism for the strategic plan, the regional cooperation task force recommended that the CHALLENGE 95 Leadership Network be created. The task force saw the network as a citizens' umbrella organization composed of representatives from the county commissions, cities and villages, townships, and chambers of commerce. Additionally, in order to ensure that all constituencies be adequately represented on the network, this specified group of elected and appointed officials would select members from the not-for-profit sector, from the special districts, and from the public-at-large. The task force explicitly stated that the network's composition of representatives was to be balanced by race, sex, geography, and public-private sector interests. The regional cooperation task force believed that by convening these leaders, the region would establish a leadership forum to build consensus and create a regional perspective. In addition, the task force charged the network to continue to build and advocate regional solutions to regional problems and encourage innovation and change within existing entities.

After six months of task force meetings, final reports of each task force covering the nine strategic issues (including regional cooperation just described) were released to the public and forwarded to the steering committee. The task force recommendations were a product of the process with a focus on regional consensus building. Although 1995 was set as the target date for implementation of the CHALLENGE 95 plan, a number of the task force reports formulated long-range goals important to the region beyond 1995. These long-range goals represent a potential agenda of critical *regional* actions and directions.

In the early stages of the task force meetings, and again after the task forces had issued their final reports, public forums were held in multiple locations throughout the Miami Valley. The earliest forums were oriented toward the substantive issues of the task forces, and in retrospect this was a mistake. Although the philosophy of public input is essential to a strategic planning process, most citizens within the region who attend public forums cannot provide meaningful input on regional substantive issues. Therefore, the major purpose of the forums became public education, and they served as a public relations effort to explain the process, the importance of a regional perspective, and the importance of regional cooperation and coordination. However, the second set of public forums elicited respectable dialogue between the public participants and CHALLENGE 95 leadership. The impressive response was the product of 500,000 newspaper inserts consisting of summaries of the task force reports. These inserts were distributed through all regional newspapers prior to the forums held in each county involved in the strategic planning process.

The final CHALLENGE 95 strategic plan set priorities based upon the recommendations of the nine task force reports. The steering committee analyzed the task force reports and the recommendations based upon the following criteria: regional in scope, measurable, doable (accomplished or initiated within the next four or five years), and critical to the region. Based upon these criteria, the final plan identified and worked to emphasize regional strengths and opportunities. In so doing, the plan itself set twelve priority issues that the region should address immediately. In addition, the plan proposed the creation of the CHALLENGE 95 Leadership Network as a body to monitor and implement the CHALLENGE 95 regional agenda. The CHALLENGE 95 Leadership Network, along with its subject area committees (similar to the original CHALLENGE 95 task forces), composes a regional, voluntary citizens organization intended to help the existing, local organizations work as a unit and provide personnel and funds where possible. In this way, duplication of efforts and the cost of an expensive continuous bureaucracy is avoided.

The CHALLENGE 95 plan is comprehensive in scope and is focused on strategies to realize the full potential of the region. It promulgates the vision for the Miami Valley to become a national leader in:

1. "applying science and technology in innovative ways to enhance strengths in the aviation/aerospace and information systems industries and to continue the revitalization of the region's traditional manufacturing base." In all three of these sectors, the region has economic strengths and potential opportunities.

2. "extending educational excellence through regional cooperation." The citizens of the region realize that no educational institution in the region by itself can establish an international reputation, but by combining educational strengths, particularly in the arena of public and private higher education, the group and, therefore, the region does have the potential to be a center of excellence.

3. "preserving and enhancing the region's environmental assets through regional cooperation." The aquifer system, one of the region's strengths, knows no political boundaries, but unless the environment is protected, it cannot be promoted as a regional asset.

4. "championing the CHALLENGE 95 Leadership Network." This model of regional leadership champions regional approaches to regional success and emphasizes a continuous involvement of the region's citizens in planning and implementation.

Finally, the twelve priority issues delineated in the plan involve specific action items that implement the vision statement. They range from training of graduate level scientists and engineers; to supporting of technology initiatives; to providing support to "Parity 2000," a strategic plan of the city of Dayton's African-American community as a means of improving its economic, educational, and social conditions.

The purpose of the strategic plan was to identify and set direction toward regional strengths and opportunities, and the final report fulfilled that purpose with comprehensive recommendations. Prior to the release of the plan, some of the priorities delineated in the plan had already been initiated, but none had been initiated on a regional geographic scale prior to the regional strategic planning effort.

Role of the University

The primary role of Wright State University's Center for Urban and Public Affairs in the CHALLENGE 95 process and plan was one of facilitation. Although the Dayton Area Chamber of Commerce contracted with the center for $200,000 to create the plan, WSU President Mulhollan committed an equal in-kind contribution to the effort. In so doing, he demonstrated the university's commitment to a regional agenda and ensured the university's independence of any one particular entity in formulating and facilitating the plan. The latter point is extremely important, because the university's neutrality was an asset throughout the process. As a neutral entity, the university was able to minimize the political turf battles that could have destroyed the process. The university faculty and staff continually had to emphasize that the threats and competition were not within the region but rather with other regions. The importance of planning regionally in order to act globally was a major focus throughout the strategic planning process.

Because of the breadth and comprehensiveness of the plan, the university's wealth of expertise and resources was necessary to facilitate the process. Students were indispensable in orchestrating the effort, and they were provided with hands-on experience about the region and its citizens as the plan unfolded. Paramount to the effort was the support within the university by not only the president, but also vice president for Academic Affairs Charles Hathaway, dean of the College of Liberal Arts Perry Moore, under which CUPA is administratively housed, and the university's planning director Robert Fenning, who maintained intense involvement as a facilitator of the task forces and composer of task force reports. In addition, the assistance of numerous university support units, such as printing and duplicating plus university and community events, was essential to the logistical implementation of the process. Logistics are an integral part of the process because if done and done well, the logistics create a positive attitude on the part of the participants.

As a result of the university initiating such a massive and highly visible effort of the region's citizens and facilitating the entire process of over 125 meetings, forums, retreats, and focus groups in fourteen months, its reputation was constantly being scrutinized. In the end, the test of Wright State University's stated metropolitan mission was its ability to assimilate an internal team effort of university administrators, faculty, staff, and students and make our regional weakness, the lack of regional cooperation, into a regional strength: the CHALLENGE 95 regional strategic plan.

Since Wright State University has defined itself as a metropolitan university with a metropolitan mission, it was only appropriate that the regional university provide the leadership for such a plan and develop the partnerships to commence the plan's implementation. However, throughout the process, community leaders were suspicious of the university's role and were constantly questioning the university's purpose or agenda. This is to be expected when the process creates a plan for a region and, therefore, is working at a scale that is larger than any entity represented in the plan's creation. In fulfilling a metropolitan mission, a university must be willing to undertake such risk-taking ventures and never waiver from a neutral position in facilitating such a process and, ultimately, a plan.

At the conclusion of the process, the question becomes: how can a university extricate itself from the plan, but yet monitor its implementation? Such a plan provides such high visibility to the university that the region now sees the university as a key to not only creating the plan, but also to implementing it. As a metropolitan university and independent entity, WSU has the ability to set its own strategic directions based upon the CHALLENGE 95 regional strategic planning process. The university must decide where its strengths lie in addressing the opportunities that have arisen from the plan's strategic priorities. The university will find that the majority of the strategic issues that need to be addressed over the next five years will require public-private sector partnerships, financial partnerships, and inter-institutional partnerships. The challenge for Wright State University is to place itself in a leadership role to build these partnerships on a regional basis.

At the present time, the Center for Urban and Public Affairs is playing a brokering role to implement the major recommendation of the CHALLENGE 95 plan—the creation of the CHALLENGE 95 Leadership Network. Since it was never the intention of the plan to create a new bureaucracy to provide staff support for the network, the Center for Urban and Public Affairs can solicit in-kind contributions from other regional entities, and in turn provide an in-kind contribution to monitor the implementation of the plan's recommendations. The center, through the work of tenured faculty, has the ability to foster change with new partnerships without constantly weighing the political circumstances. Perhaps the tenure of faculty gives the assurance and independence necessary to broker partnerships that otherwise would be too risky to venture.

SUGGESTED READINGS

Hathaway, C. E., P. E. Mulhollan, and K. A. White. "Metropolitan Universities: Models for the Twenty-first Century." *Metropolitan Universities,* Vol. 1, No. 1 (Spring 1990): 9–20.

Kemp, R. L. "Metro Areas in the 21st Century." *National Civic Review,* Vol. 79, No. 2 (March–April 1990): 152–57.

Pearlman, D. H. "Diverse Communities: Diverse Involvements." *Metropolitan Universities*, Vol. 1, No. 1 (Spring 1990): 89–100.

Vogel, R. K. and B. E. Swanson. "Setting Agendas for Community Change: The Community Goal-Setting Strategy." *Journal of Urban Affairs*, Vol. 10, No. 1 (March 1988): 41–61.

DIVERSE COMMUNITIES: DIVERSE INVOLVEMENTS

Daniel H. Perlman

One characteristic of a metropolitan university that distinguishes it from other institutions of higher learning is its extensive involvement with and its impact on the metropolitan community it serves. A metropolitan university may be located on a campus in the downtown area of the city, as is Roosevelt University in Chicago, or it may be slightly outside the business district on its own separate campus, as are the University of Massachusetts at Boston and the University of Illinois at Chicago. It may be bordered by an affluent residential community, such as Beacon Hill in Boston or Georgetown in Washington, or an impoverished one; it may be proximate to commercial or industrial neighbors. Metropolitan universities are either independent or are intimately connected with the larger metropolitan community.

Extensive involvement with the community is often initiated by the metropolitan university, and some is initiated by others who seek to have it serve a specific purpose with which they are involved, such as improved schools, neighborhood stabilization, or economic growth. Most community involvement is cordial, cooperative, and collaborative as the university and the community work together to advance parallel and mutually beneficial interests. Community interaction can involve negotiated agreements or litigation where competing interests are at stake. Far from being an ivory tower removed or detached from the surrounding world, the metropolitan university is an enterprise embedded in the community and linked to its environment by a complex web of relationships, expectations, mutual needs, and opportunities for benefit. The extent and intensity of these involvements distinguish the urban or metropolitan university from other categories of American higher education.

206

Ways in Which Metropolitan Universities Interact with Their Communities

A metropolitan university's involvements with and its service to its many communities derive from the various aspects of the university. Primarily it is an institution of higher education that provides instruction in many disciplines. A metropolitan university serves undergraduate, graduate, and professional students of all ages, levels, and backgrounds, reflecting the variety of the wider community. It assists in the development and application of new knowledge and in technology transfer, providing continuing education to many constituencies and advice to businesses small and large, to government agencies, and to community groups. Metropolitan universities also serve as cultural centers, providing concerts, plays, lectures, readings, and films that are open to the public, often free or with nominal charge. They frequently provide consulting services of various kinds: for example, aiding the public school system and reaching out to primary and secondary school students; stimulating volunteer service by students, faculty, staff, and alumni; and serving as a neutral convener or coordinator for bringing together interested parties who have no history of working together.

A metropolitan university constitutes a substantial physical and economic presence with substantial economic impact: as a large and relatively stable, progressive, and environmentally clean employer; as a consumer of goods and services including large scale expenditures for construction, renovation, and equipment; and through secondary spending by students, faculty, staff, as well as parents and other visitors. A metropolitan university may also be a partner in local real estate development and in the commercial application of new knowledge. Each of these multiple aspects or dimensions of a metropolitan university affects its interaction with the constituencies of its region. In turn, in each aspect of their many-faceted relationships, metropolitan universities must take into account the ethnic and racial diversity of their regions.

Most metropolitan areas in this country, as well as many such conurbations abroad, contain several distinct communities of color as well as a number of white ethnic groups. Each of these groups is likely to have its own leadership, community activities, and social service organizations. In order to be successful as academic institutions and as neighbors, employers, and consumers, metropolitan universities need to be sensitive to different and at times competing priorities and needs of these multiple constituencies. They should reflect the diversity of the metropolitan area in their faculty and staff, as well as in their student body, and they should reach out to the diverse groups in many different ways.

By inviting the leaders of the various ethnic and racial minority communities to visit the campus and speak to student groups, by encouraging the parents and families of current and prospective minority students to visit the campus and share in the celebration of special holidays and festivals, by meeting with minority business groups and hiring their members, by becoming personally visible in the minority communities, and by showing that cultural diversity is not only tolerated but actively encouraged and cherished, presidents of metropolitan universities can promote a climate that will enhance the effectiveness of their institutions both in their academic roles as well as in their function as neighbor, employer, and consumer.

Metropolitan Universities and Their Neighbors

Most metropolitan universities are located in areas adjacent or contiguous to non-university neighbors. Prior to the 1950s the urban university's relations with its neighbors tended to be characterized either by mutual disinterest or tolerance. If the university desired to acquire and develop an additional piece of property or city block, the surrounding community was not organized to express objections or concerns, and tenants were resigned to such treatment, as the history of Suffolk University demonstrates.

When Gleason Archer, the founding president of Suffolk University, in 1920 bought a parcel of land in Boston, behind the State House in what was then "the West End," on which he planned to build a new building for his law school, no one expressed concern when he evicted the nineteen families then living on the site. He voluntarily but grudgingly offered modest assistance in helping some of the families relocate in order to gain earlier access to the property and accelerate the demolition schedule but didn't consider them as having any rights in the situation.

By the mid-1950s, a protracted period of neighborhood neglect extending through the depression and war years, together with the demographic shift due to immigration from the rural south to the inner cities of the north, led to the conclusion that many urban neighborhoods had become blighted and that cities could be saved by excising such decay before it spread. Congress passed urban renewal legislation that was used by cities, by universities, and by developers to level large parcels of shabby housing. Occupants were relocated either to fortress-like public housing units or dispersed to outlying suburbs.

By the 1960s, tenants and home owners began to organize to oppose urban renewal and university expansion. Often students sided with local residents in town-gown confrontations with the community. For the first time, urban and campus planners encountered organized opposition to university expansion and relocation, and Suffolk University felt this shift too. In 1968 Archer's successor, Judge John Fenton, the fifth president of Suffolk University, assumed that he could ignore community concern over his plans to develop and occupy a building proximate to the university's other buildings. To his surprise, he was blocked in court by the local residents.

Thus, as a reaction to the unconstrained dislocation of people during the 1950s and the empowerment of neighborhood groups, the "Robert Moses era" of campus planning came to an end. Some universities learned the lesson more slowly and painfully than others: it is imperative for metropolitan universities to establish cordial relations with their neighbors and to negotiate a mutually agreeable *modus vivendi*. In some settings, so high a level of suspicion, animosity, and antagonism had developed that a decade or more was necessary to restore a climate in which the parties could begin to work together effectively to resolve lingering disputes and develop an agenda of mutual interests and common goals. Indeed, it took two decades to the month after Suffolk University acquired a lot and building on Cambridge Street in Boston, where it had expected to construct without delay a multistory academic building, for a settlement agreement with abutters and other litigants to be signed, paving the way for a project of more modest scale and vastly greater sensitivity to the surrounding architecture and to neighborhood concerns.

Metropolitan universities have come to appreciate that they cannot take neighborhood relations for granted or attend to them only when the institution desires to expand or has a public relations crisis. Community leaders and neighbors are a constituency that cannot be neglected. Most of the larger metropolitan universities have offices of community relations, often headed by a vice president, to maintain dialogue, handle extensive negotiations between the university and the community, and seek to have university's neighbors experience the university in positive ways, as a provider of cultural activities, jobs, public safety, and other benefits. At smaller metropolitan universities the president is apt to be directly involved in community relations on a weekly and sometimes daily basis, attending community events and social functions and inviting community leaders to the campus for public lectures and theatrical programs.

If the university is on a campus created by demolishing homes in the community, it may take a generation before good relations are restored. If a metropolitan university is insensitive to the impact that the comings and goings of students, delivery trucks, and service vehicles have on the neighborhood or if the university allows subcontractors working on campus construction or renovation to operate noisy equipment during evening hours, convenient perhaps to the contractor but grossly inconvenient to the residents, the university risks a permanent state of crisis and tension between itself and its neighbors.

The circumstances are considerably different, of course, if the university's neighbors are commercial or industrial or if it is walled off from its neighbors by highways and other urban obstacles. If the university is in a particularly deteriorated area or adjacent to an industrial zone, it may want to initiate economic development activities in conjunction with other stakeholders to revitalize and upgrade its neighborhood. These activities may take the form of investment in local real estate or shopping centers, the creation of a research park, or improvements in the urban streetscape.

For example, in 1976 Suffolk University, working with the City of Boston, local residents, the State House, and a local architect sensitive to the issues of urban design, used funds made available to the city under a HUD block grant to transform Temple Street, a narrow, early nineteenth-century street fronting several of Suffolk University's buildings, from a congested parking strip for legislators' cars into an attractive and award-winning, brick lined pedestrian walkway with trees, flowers, and a pocket park, enjoyed by area residents as well as by students and legislators strolling to classes and offices. Temple Street residents and the university together maintain the plantings and appearance of the street, which is featured in many of the university's publications. In 1989 Suffolk University took steps to initiate a Main Street Project (a program of the National Trust for Historic Preservation for the rehabilitation of urban shopping strips) together with local merchants and residents, a city councilor, and merchants from other successful Main Street projects, as a means of improving Cambridge Street, a rundown commercial artery bordering the Beacon Hill historic district and Suffolk University.

Whatever the specific circumstances, relations with the contiguous community are of paramount importance for a metropolitan university. They are a significant part of its activities; they require high-level and highly trained personnel and adequate resources and they must be factored by the university into virtually every development decision.

Metropolitan Universities as Employers and Consumers

Metropolitan universities with substantial budgets are major economic enterprises. It is not uncommon for an urban or metropolitan university to be among the larger and more progressive employers in the city. Although untenured faculty, as well as individuals in support positions and those dependent on "soft money" may occasionally feel the impact of enrollment shortfalls (in the independent sector) or reduced appropriations (in the public sector), university employment is on the whole relatively stable. Universities can often compensate for their inability to compete in direct salaries with private industry or law firms for professional and support personnel by providing such indirect benefits as academic environment, tuition benefits, and ready access to courses, concerts, films, and lectures that make the universities attractive places to work. Moreover, many metropolitan universities have been on the forefront of such issues as child care, personal leave for family health needs, staff development, and the recruitment of minorities.

Metropolitan universities also contribute significantly to the local economy through their direct purchases of goods and services, through secondary spending by their staff and students, and through auxiliary and spinoff enterprises.

Relations with the Metropolitan Business Community

The local business community is a significant constituency for a metropolitan university. It hires the university's graduates; provides students with part-time employment, internships, and placements for cooperative education programs; and is a source of participants in instruction designed for individuals with full-time jobs, such as MBA programs and offerings in continuing education. The private sector can benefit a metropolitan university in many other ways. It can provide helpful advice in program development, enter into contractual agreements for specialized training programs for its employees, and be a source of adjunct faculty and guest lecturers. It can, as well, provide direct support of funds and equipment.

The advantages flow in the opposite direction as well. The business community has much to gain from a vigorous metropolitan university of high quality. Such an institution is a source of highly skilled employees who will be increasingly in demand. It can contribute much to the maintenance of employees' competence through a variety of advanced courses and specialized in-service programs. Furthermore, metropolitan universities can be an important source of state-of-the-art expertise in a great variety of fields. Its meetings and conferences, as well as its library and data bases, are readily accessible to members of local business. The university's faculty as well as its advanced students can provide technical assistance, policy analysis, and technology transfer that can help new industrial ventures to gain a foothold and existing enterprises to keep up to date. Strong metropolitan universities often are magnets that attract commerce and industry to their region, because of these potential benefits they can provide. It should also be mentioned that in many metropolitan areas, the local universities and the business community are partners in school reform and in urban revitalization.

Indeed, metropolitan universities can have so many points of interaction with local businesses that a special effort is needed to keep track of these contracts in a systematic fashion. When a senior university administrator visits a corporate executive, that administrator would be embarrassed not to be aware of existing relationships. Therefore, Suffolk University developed a monthly coordinating meeting at which the various university officers who have extensive contacts with the business community share information. Regular participants in these meetings include the dean of the School of Management, the director of management training programs, development, and alumni office staff, and the directors of career services and cooperative education, among others.

To foster mutually beneficial interaction, the presidents of metropolitan universities should become acquainted with other major business leaders in a variety of ways, including participation in activities of the Chamber of Commerce and similar groups. They should, as well, invite members of the business community onto their campuses to better acquaint them with the role, scope, and capabilities of their institutions; to explore potential areas in which cooperation would bring advantages to both sides; and to discuss issues of mutual concern.

Relations with the Local School Systems

Another "community" with which a metropolitan university interacts, often in conjunction with the business community, is the public school system. Historically, few colleges and universities made a strong effort to relate to the public schools in their community, other than to place student teachers. In metropolitan university areas this has now begun to change. Metropolitan universities have recognized their stake in the improvement of urban schools. The schools are the source of students going on to college, a fact so obvious that it would hardly need stating, had it not been overlooked for so long. If the urban schools are not assisted in their efforts to improve, metropolitan universities will be drawn ever more heavily into remedial work and will fail to receive a major segment of urban students who might have benefitted from a college education but instead became drop-out casualties. Much more devastating than the effect on the colleges is the effect on those whose learning is stifled by the multiple troubles besetting urban education in most of the nation's large cities.

Boston serves as an example of what is beginning to happen in school-university-business collaboration in various cities and is a model for other cities where there are educators and business leaders forging new alliances for their mutual advantage. In 1974, as part of a court-initiated settlement of a desegregation suit, the public schools in Boston were each paired with one or more of the local universities and colleges. The pairings were supported with state funds, but came to be supported as well by foundation and other grants raised by the universities for this purpose. The collaborative programs made possible by these pairings provide assistance to teachers and school staff, special instruction and tutoring of students, aid to the central administration, and even programs for parents. The twenty-three Boston-area colleges and universities participating in these pairings form the Boston Higher Education Partnership, which now has its own executive director. Each university appoints a coordinator to manage the relationship between the participating university faculty and the schools. The university presidents, the coordinators, and the director of the Partnership meet regularly with the superintendent of schools and other school personnel to discuss priorities, plan new programs, and air concerns.

In 1984, a formal agreement was signed between the colleges and the schools calling for an increased commitment by the colleges to helping the schools and their college-bound graduates, as well as attention to improving the retention rates of students, both in the schools and in the colleges. Since then, over $35 million has been invested by the participating Boston-area universities and colleges in the form of scholarships for graduates of the Boston Public Schools, non-state funds raised for collaborative programs, and other direct aid. Retention of Boston high school graduates attending universities in the partnership had also improved, although not by as much as had been desired.

Complementing the agreement between the universities and the schools is an agreement between the business community and the schools. Many of the major businesses are also paired with a local school and provide direct assistance of various kinds, as well as instructional equipment. An endowment of approximately $13 million has been contributed by the business community to provide "last-dollar scholarships" for Boston high school graduates going on to college, counselors in the high schools to help students complete the various college application and financial aid forms and meet the necessary deadlines, and grants to teachers for supplemental instructional funds not available in the regular school budget.

Faculty members at Suffolk University have provided for its high school partner supplemental instruction for physics students in computer technology. The school gets to keep the computers assembled by the students during the semester. Faculty members also offer instruction in political science and international affairs. Under the federal Literacy Corps program, a dozen Suffolk University students are tutoring elementary school students in basic reading skills in a multi-racial inner city school in which many children of new immigrant families are learning English before their parents do. Suffolk University is also working with a group of school parents and teachers and provides scholarships for the graduates of the Boston public schools and local community colleges.

The set of agreements among the business community, higher education institutions, and schools is known as The Boston Compact. Higher education leaders and business leaders work directly with the superintendent of schools and the mayor as a steering committee for the compact. This joint effort has already had a significant impact on the quality of the educational opportunity available to Boston Public School students and graduates. It has encouraged, fostered, and facilitated collaboration and beneficial contact among the universities, the schools, and the business community.

Relations with City and County Governments

Many metropolitan universities have developed close ties and productive working relations with local governmental bodies and agencies. The universities undertake sponsored research for these agencies; they provide policy analysis and other forms of expertise, conduct training programs for their employees, and collaborate with them in various ways. Local government agencies are also sources of funding as well as sources of necessary approvals needed by metropolitan universities for their development. It is important for the president of a metropolitan university to be on good terms with local government leaders and agency heads. In the case of certain municipally sponsored metropolitan universities, such as Washburn University in Topeka, the mayor serves as an ex-officio member of the governing board.

Some cities, particularly those without a large industrial base, have pressed the colleges and universities within their borders for annual payments in lieu of taxes. Boston has been particularly aggressive in such requests, particularly targeting the tax-exempt independent universities and hospitals. Boston zoning is hostile to higher education, requiring that every change in a college or university's use of property it owns must be granted a specific variance by the Zoning Board of Appeal. The zoning appeal process provides an opportunity for the city and neighborhood groups to make requests of the institution that are often tantamount to demands. Typically, zoning appeals are granted only when the institution agrees to participate in the city's "PILOT" (payments in lieu of taxes) program. Recent regulations require that approval of construction projects in excess of 100,000 square feet be contingent on "linkage" payments to the city, to be used for neighborhood development. Most of the colleges and universities in Boston have thus been required to make agreements with the city either for direct payments in lieu of taxes based on enrollment or indirect payments that include scholarships for the graduates of the Boston public high schools and city employees. At least one metropolitan institution, Emerson College, has made plans to move out of Boston, in part to avoid pressure of this sort.

Relations with Professional Communities

A metropolitan university interacts with the many professional groups present in every urban area—lawyers and legal aids, health professionals, accountants, and others—to provide initial and continuing education, and interacts with professional artists and arts groups to provide a place for the performance, exhibition, and teaching of the arts. Representatives of these groups often serve on departmental or school advisory committees, speak to classes, counsel students or serve as mentors, judge student competitions, help recruit students, sponsor scholarships, and hire graduates. Close links with the professional communities are another hallmark of metropolitan universities.

Relations with Other Area Colleges and Universities

In a listing of the groups and organizations with which the president and other officers of a metropolitan university are involved, mention should be made of the other colleges and universities in the urban area. Many cities have developed formal mechanisms for collaboration among the colleges and universities in the area. In addition, there are often regular meetings of subgroups of these colleges and universities. The public college presidents and those of the independent universities and colleges generally each have regular meetings to plan and coordinate government relations and to participate in common or jointly sponsored activities. These activities may include cross-registering courses, serving on the board of an educational television station, or protecting civil rights, literacy, volunteerism, or drug awareness. Although competition among colleges continues in many ways, collaboration has come to be the more dominant mode of interaction in many settings and is the stance most commonly taken by the university presidents towards one another.

Limitations and Cost of a University's Involvement

Although metropolitan universities are characterized by their interest in and involvement with their communities and although they are eager to be of service as centers of knowledge and culture and helpful in other ways too, there are limits on the abilities, resources, and responsiveness of metropolitan universities. Moreover, a university as an enduring institution may have a long-range time perspective, and its faculty as scholars of their disciplines may have a detachment that will give them a viewpoint or perspective different from others.

Tensions between any of the metropolitan constituencies and the university often arise because of unrealistic or unreasonable demands on the institution to remedy the community's economic and social problems. During the 1960s, encouraged or emboldened by government or foundation funding, some universities undertook educational, social-welfare, or applied research projects that promised more than could be delivered, heightening community expectations beyond what could be achieved and causing a frustration, cynicism, or anger. Caution, candor, and circumspection must be exercised in this respect.

A metropolitan university's involvement with the community, however desirable, and whether self-initiated or imposed, is not without cost. There are staff costs, for full-time community relations specialists and for the part-time involvement of many others in the university, not least the president; there are such additional financial costs as payments-in-lieu-of-taxes, scholarships for the graduates of local schools, and the operation of day care centers or other facilities, including the library, which may be accessible or available to non-university neighbors and the wider community. Suffolk University, for example, has maintained a policy of keeping its libraries open and accessible to residents of the neighboring Beacon Hill community, local businesses, alumni, and the students of other universities in the Boston area—except during the period immediately before and during final exams.

There are also public relations costs that are incurred from time to time, especially if there are misunderstandings, unfulfilled or unrealistic expectations, clashes of competing interests and "offers that can't be refused." All of these things are part of the complexity of administering a contemporary metropolitan university.

Metropolitan Universities Are Where the Action Is

The difficulty and cost that result from multiple tasks and the many interactions of metropolitan universities should not be minimized. But it is important, as well, to realize that these institutions are at the cutting edge of American higher education. Their overall impact, in terms of the number and diversity of students served and their ability to positively affect the wider community, is unsurpassed by other sectors of higher education. Because of the multiple opportunities they have to serve, metropolitan universities are gaining increased attention, influence, prominence, and recognition, and they are having an expanded and beneficial impact.

It is the extensive community involvement of metropolitan universities and the creative energies they liberate that makes them such exciting and interesting places for their students, the faculty who teach in them, and those who administer them.

SUGGESTED READINGS

Ross, Bernard H. *University-City Relations: From Coexistence to Cooperation.* ERIC Higher Education Research Report No. 3. Washington, American Association for Higher Education, 1973.

"Town and Gown." *Current Issues in Catholic Higher Education.* Vol. 6, no. 2 (Winter, 1986).

Winds of Change: The University in Search of Itself

Jerome M. Ziegler

This article looks at the outreach mission of universities in metropolitan areas from the viewpoint of how these institutions might influence the large social issues affecting our nation. These newer institutions of higher education, which are calling themselves metropolitan universities, may well have a special opportunity to place outreach, or extension as it is known in the land-grant universities, as a mission equally central to the university's purpose as are teaching and research. Several salient characteristics of the academy are described whose influence can determine how the university responds to these larger issues. And possible lines of interaction between the institution and its surrounding territory are suggested. There are innumerable local and regional issues in which metropolitan universities might wish to interest themselves, but this article addresses broader issues facing American society first. Not addressing them makes progress on all the others problematic. If it is justifiable to use the term *American culture* without being accused of hubris, then the quality of our culture and the success of our society will be judged by how we resolve these broader issues in the decade ahead. We ought not enter the next century in the state of social disrepair in which we find ourselves in 1990. The response of our universities to these issues will be an important indicator of how serious our society is to improve itself.

One hundred and thirty-seven years ago John Henry Cardinal Newman published "Discourses on University Education," which together with a later volume entitled "Lectures and Essays on University Subjects," is known to us as "The Idea of a University," one of the most prescient and inclusive statements about the nature and purpose of a higher liberal education. The opening lines of the preface state: "The view taken of a university is the following: that it is a place of *teaching* universal *knowledge* (Newman's italics). This implies that its object is, on the one hand, intellectual, not moral and on the other, that it is the *diffusion and extension* of knowledge rather than its advancement."

Newman's emphasis upon teaching universal knowledge may be taken as one of the foundation stones for a curriculum of liberal arts disciplines and the pursuit of theory which has so informed American higher education in the latter part of the nineteenth and throughout the twentieth centuries. The Morrill Act of 1862, which created a new kind of college with a then new and fresh view of teaching the "agricultural and mechanic arts" to a group of students different than those traditionally attending institutions of higher education, was a remarkable development; and the creation of the land-grant colleges, now grown into the large research universities with which we are all familiar, was one of the truly seminal innovations in the history of higher education in this country. But even in those institutions, as in the liberal arts colleges preceding them, the pursuit of liberal learning was always a basic and necessary part of the educational programs offered to students. For all the development of professional schools and the proliferation of courses about the world outside the campus, and for all the continuous debate about the decline of the liberal arts in favor of vocational/professional courses in our colleges and universities, the disciplines of the liberal arts still form the basis of a great deal of what students attempt to learn, whatever course of study they are pursuing. So, *pace,* Cardinal Newman, your influence is still strong.

Newman's other phrase about the "diffusion and extension of knowledge" was particularly prescient about the mission, as it became enlarged from teaching and research, of the great American universities of the twentieth century, especially the land-grant universities. Recall the famous remark of President Charles Van Hise of the University of Wisconsin in 1906: "The boundaries of the campus should be coterminous with the boundaries of the state." Upon that view, happily subscribed to by many others, including the Congress of the United States with the passage of the Smith-Lever Act in 1914, was built the extension movement which has served agriculture and the farming communities of our country so well, latterly many urban and suburban regions as agricultural extension evolved into cooperative extension after World War II. Indeed, the success of the extension model impelled many in higher education situated in urban areas to seek its replication in "urban extension." Much of the conversation in the past quarter-century about the role of urban universities in connection with their "surround" has been framed by the hope that federal and state money would become available for an urban extension program. Many downtown, university evening colleges used the forum of the American Adult Education Association in the 1950s and 1960s to lobby for federal support for their institutions' programs. They were reaching a new kind of audience, adults who could only study part-time in the evenings, and they reached them with new kinds of offerings, many non-credit as well as credit, and taught them with a faculty who understood the needs and aspirations of part-time adult students from the city and its suburbs.

Now we have the conceptualization, really the reconceptualization, of the urban university into the "metropolitan" university. The question now arises: What should be the proper role, place and function of such an institution with respect to the geographical area of which it is a part? If the term "metropolitan" is useful in describing a set of characteristics and functions attending a certain set of universities, all well and good. In the course of time, if there be truthfulness and distinctiveness to what these institutions are doing, then the term will persevere; if not, not. The important issue is whether this category of relatively new universities can do something different, useful, necessary, indispensable for the different communities which comprise metropolitan areas or regions.

Characterizing the Metropolitan Area

It may be useful to characterize a metro area because it can include several different kinds of populations, very different land use and large contrasts between industrial and agricultural sectors—all of which, in turn, give rise to different kinds of needs and problems and which will require different kinds of treatment by the metropolitan university. As readers will know, "metropolitan area" was a term first used in the 1940 census to describe what had clearly become a rapidly developing geographical entity, and 140 such areas were so designated. Twenty years later in the 1960 census, the term "Standard Metropolitan Statistical Area" was introduced to describe and categorize various kinds of numerical relationships pertaining to the people and communities of the SMSA. The SMSA had to have at least one central city of 50,000 with surrounding suburbs, again with certain characteristics of density, transportation networks and the like. Today, the census lists SMSAs which abut one another, and in many parts of the country a metropolitan region will have more than one SMSA.

In describing a typical metropolitan area, let us say that it has a central city of 350,000, immediately surrounded by a ring of inner suburbs, followed by a second ring of outer suburbs or "exurbs," followed by unincorporated, often agricultural land. Some of the unincorporated spaces may be directly adjacent to the central city, may lie between or among the inner suburbs, and similarly with the outer suburbs. Dotted across the unincorporated land, there may be smaller cities, towns, and villages—in short a pastiche of populations and communities. The largest city will often have an old central business district, an inner city, low income, residential area with a non-white population, and a mix of working class, middle income, and wealthier wards or sectors. In many such cities, particularly in the Northeast, Middle Atlantic, and Middle West regions of the country, the wards or sectors will have distinct ethnic communities. But as the post-World War II migration from the central city to the suburbs continues for a variety of reasons, including an increase in economic level, white flight, and a desire in the younger generations for a more "American" status, the suburbs become less ethnic in their composition than the older city wards. These sectors of the city are now a mix of left-behind, older, poorer, European ethnic family members (grandparents, aunts, uncles, cousins who do not wish to move from their familiar neighborhoods) and the recently arrived immigrants from all over the world—Southeast Asia refugees, people from the sub-continent of India and Pakistan, from Africa, and larger numbers of Latinos from Central and South America. This extraordinary mix of populations presents the city with a new-old set of problems arising out of language barriers, ethnic and racial tensions, and economic aspirations and competition. In the Elmhurst community in the borough of Queens in New York City, the first-graders come to school from thirty-nine different language backgrounds. Would you like to be their teacher?

Within the metro area, a number of smaller cities will have developed, and indeed we now see many urban counties with blurred boundaries among their cities, towns and villages. Often enough, these smaller cities and towns are competing fiercely with one another for local industrial development, (some examples include the numerous communities of Nassau and Suffolk Counties on Long Island, Cook County surrounding Chicago, Cayuhoga County for the Cleveland area, Fulton County of Atlanta, and Los Angeles County). But at the same time a number of these smaller communities are beginning to cooperate in providing services in the interests of efficiency and economy.

The reason for rehearsing this rather well-known typology is to make a simple but important point; if a metropolitan university wishes to be of concrete service to its metro area, its faculty and administration must know how to analyze carefully the different geographical elements, subdivisions, and populations. It is an obvious point, but long experience with cooperative extension programs of land-grant universities tells me that those working on outreach, including faculty, often fail to make such an analysis and fail, therefore, in their understanding of a community's culture. With that kind of failure comes trouble for the university's program, and the recouping or resolution takes more time than an earlier effort to understand.

The analysis of community needs and aspirations is surely complicated. While it may be true that most of us have similar needs, hopes and aspirations, these take different effect in different environments and local cultures. So how does an urban university, now turned "metropolitan," deal usefully with a rural farm and non-farm population at the same time that it interacts with wealthy exurbs, ethnic city wards and people of color? Do size and complexity of a metropolitan area make any difference? Is the metropolitan area old or recent? Does the nature of the local or regional economy affect the university's relation to its area? What is the agricultural-industrial-services mix? What is the nature of local community leadership? These questions must be examined by a metropolitan university wishing to create an effective outreach system.

The University Transformed

In thinking about how metropolitan universities ought to relate to the metropolitan areas in which they are situated, about what ought to be their educational mission and about the reciprocal impact of the metro area on these institutions, I refer again to Cardinal Newman's idea of a university as a seat of teaching the universal knowledge, and of the diffusion of that knowledge. In the almost century and half since Newman wrote, an educated person's view of what constitutes knowledge has expanded beyond imagining. So, too, with the ways in which the university chooses to diffuse knowledge to its constituency.

Let us think for a moment of who and what is included in the constituency of any major contemporary university: undergraduate and graduate students on the main campus; evening school students taking courses for credit towards a degree or for a professional certificate or further professional training or simply for pleasure; a similar range of students at other than main campus locations which may include central city, suburban or exurban sites; the organization of a powerful array of courses, conferences, workshops, meetings, through the evening division or university college; general extension, cooperative extension and industrial extension to all corners of the state or region, or even upon occasion half-way across the nation, for various professional groups, citizen organizations and the like; the interaction of university faculty and other personnel with federal, state and local government through the provision of special courses for advanced training and through the myriad of funding agencies which are involved in the financial support of university and faculty research; the special relationships of a university's professional schools and colleges with the organizations and associations and business firms of that profession; the assiduous courting of the university's alumni as well as philanthropic foundations for obvious reasons, and finally in more recent years, the reaching out of the university to hitherto unserved or scarcely served groups and individuals, chiefly minority, often low income and not regarded as a university's "natural" constituency. Placing this constituency grid against a map of the metropolitan area reveals just how complex the university's interactions with its many communities is likely to be.

Clearly not every major university engages in all the activities in this list. But what this catalogue describes is the range of involvement by a modern university with the wider society. This modern university was characterized by Clark Kerr as the "multiversity," a term he chose in the Godkin Lectures at Harvard in 1963 (so long ago as that!). Is it not this concept of multiversity which most of us now accept and believe to be correct? That is, it is the *right* concept, it describes not only what is but what ought to be in the relation of the institution to its "surround." In short, there is a kind of moral quality, a required involvement of the university with the larger society, and with its immediate local community and with the several diverse communities of its region. I hasten to add that not everyone in higher education subscribes to this view. There are significant numbers of university faculty and administrators who hold that teaching and research are the sole missions of a proper university. Nevertheless, for the land-grant colleges and universities and for the leading private institutions of the country, and for many of the newer publicly supported regional institutions, many of which would be termed metropolitan universities by Hathaway, Mulhollan and White's definition (see pp. 5–16) it is the requirement of outreach that, added to the missions of teaching and research, has changed the university. I would argue that outreach and extension have truly transformed the university, and it is not only different but better because the mission of applying research to communities, populations and issues outside the campus improves both teaching and research inside the campus.

Many would argue that the public university has no choice. It must interact with and serve a wider population beyond those who are able to matriculate on campus. It is President Van Hise's vision come alive. But even in those institutions which have made their commitment to extension in its broadest terms, and which place extension equal with teaching and research, there remains a tension, probably on every campus, that must be dealt with if the university transformed is to be successful in each of its missions. If not dealt with, the conflict can turn into the delegitimizing of the one by the other, with difficult consequences for morale and nasty fights over funding allocations.

The Tension Between Liberal Arts and Outreach

If a metropolitan university is to be engaged with its many surrounding communities in new vigorous style, that is with continuous commitment of university resources, there is a further issue that must be addressed. It is the dispute about mission or missions between the faculties of the liberal arts and sciences with their views about the centrality of research and graduate education in their disciplines, and those in the professional schools and the extension divisions who are concerned with professional training, and education, and "outreach." This is no "straw man" issue. It goes to the heart of what the university is and may become. Is the faculty of the liberal arts central to the university? Yes, resoundingly yes. Is it the only unit central to the university? No, not any longer; indeed, not since the end of the Second World War and the advent of Dr. Kerr's multiversity.

The liberal arts are central to the university because by their study students are exposed to some of the greatest works of the human mind and because the disciplines into which we have divided knowledge over the centuries are the basis for studying everything and anything. At the same time, enough of us in the academy also realize that the world is not divided into the disciplines of the arts and sciences and that many of the issues and problems which human beings and social systems confront cannot be approached, let alone managed or resolved, except by going beyond disciplines. Many in the academy have been struggling to discover the right integration of knowledge from more than one discipline, to understand how theory combined with experience might offer better answers and solutions to the problems we face. But going beyond discipline is not a comfortable journey for some of our faculty colleagues and unfortunately many of them are found in the traditional liberal arts units of the universities. Thus we find conflicts among faculties: on the one side, those who hold to the primacy of the disciplines and to rather traditional research and who do not look with much favor on "outreach"; on the other, those in the more professionally oriented units usually with closer interaction with the professions and the world of work. This is not always a clear-cut division; there are enough exceptions to render the comment above inapplicable to this or that institution. But a more traditional view of university mission is an obstacle which must be overcome if the metropolitan university is to achieve the purpose of broadened and deepened interaction with the communities of its geographic area. And despite its newness on the academic scene, the metropolitan university will have some faculty who wish only to be super traditional in order to establish their own legitimacy and status equal to that of the older institutions. So there will be this tension, and it must be addressed, and if not resolved, at least handled directly by those with authority to speak for university administration. The equivalence of missions must be forcefully affirmed together with the proper allocation of resources.

National Issues Affecting All Metro Regions

Having argued that university personnel must analyze their own local, metropolitan and regional communities carefully in order to understand how their institution can be effective beyond the borders of the campus, there are a number of overarching issues facing American society which seriously affect what a metropolitan university, or any university, can do as it creates programs and services for its own area. These issues are of national dimension and scope but clearly they exist in every metropolitan area and thus must also be dealt with at that level. The university cannot escape from them merely by saying a national solution is required. A national solution may be attempted by federal legislation and allocation of funds, but national solutions take effect in regions, states and localities. Furthermore, national issues become national when they are experienced in a sufficient number of towns, cities and counties. The metropolitan university has to be involved in some way because it is part of a community and is itself subject to these influences and conditions.

First, and perhaps foremost, is the tension between individualism and building community. Not a new issue: it is the conflict between equality and the individual's right to life, liberty and the pursuit of happiness in the Declaration of Independence and the construction of a united society of laws under the Constitution. Tocqueville in *Democracy in America,* first published in 1823, commented on this opposition of individualism to community:

> Although private interest directs the greater part of human actions in the United States, as well as elsewhere, it does not regulate them all. I must say that I have often seem Americans make great and real sacrifices to the public welfare; and I have noticed a hundred instances in which

they hardly ever failed to lend faithful support to one another.
The free institutions which the inhabitants of the United
States possess, and the political rights of which they make
so much use, remind every citizen, and in a thousand ways,
that he lives in society. *(Democracy In America,* volume 2,
page 112, Vintage Books 1945)

But Tocqueville also noticed the effect of succeeding waves of
immigration from Europe and the force which the ideas of equality
and freedom had on new arrivals. Every man was every other man's
equal; each could pursue his star and would. A democratic society
fostered and protected individualism, in contrast to the despotisms of
Europe.

This tension continues today with a rhythm of its own. There are
periods when individualism and the pursuit of material goods take
precedence over public policy. Many would argue that we have been in
such a period during the 1980s, and that we are still in it: thus the
debate over taxes to provide the resources necessary for social programs.
Social programs include not only those public and private efforts aimed
at solving a certain class of social problems—housing the homeless,
improving the education of poor children, providing health insurance
to some thirty million American citizens without it, creating sufficient
treatment centers for substance abusers, overcoming welfare
dependency, and the like—but also all activities whose purpose is to
make us a better society by solving a difficult or important problem. So
I include a very wide array of items: the repair of roads and bridges,
getting rid of ground water contaminants, strengthening bio-medical
research, finding new methods of fueling automobiles, improving
nutrition, deepening basic research in the nation's educational
institutions and industrial laboratories—and on, and on.

How do we make the public understand the need for public policy?
By political leadership, certainly; but pointedly for readers of this
collection, by having institutions of higher education accept that
education for public responsibility is a necessary and continuous task.
This requires rethinking the undergraduate curriculum in order to
include civic literacy as a crucial component, no matter what subject a
student may pursue. It also requires creating new kinds of outreach
programs which, whatever their specific learning objective, includes
sensitizing the clientele to the idea of community and to the need for
public policy. The new metropolitan university is in a good position to
engage this task, for it should have fewer old patterns of thought and
action as constraints to fresh thinking about both of these endeavors.

And it may be, despite the earlier remark about faculty traditionalism, that these newer universities will have more faculty who are seriously interested in creating curricula for civic literacy, producing graduates of their institutions who understand the need for public policy, and working with officials and adults off-campus whose energies are directed at solving society's problems.

The second major social issue which universities must examine as they think about all their programs of study is the persistent problem of race in America. Doubtless, it is closely connected to the first issue, for undeniably race prejudice has roots in economic competition among individuals and groups along with the current fissures and angers among and across ethnic cultures. Although the issue of race penetrates every corner and segment of the American society, in a curious way it is not really discussed. Epithets in a working class bar, stereotypes in the country club dining room, even studies by social scientists in the academy do not serve to get at the deep and persistent attitudes and actions of racial bias throughout our land. Race and politics, race and education, race and housing, race and communities, race and the economy and the changing nature of work are matters which go to the heart of so many difficulties in our society.

Is there a special opportunity for all institutions of higher education to do something about this issue? Is there an obligation? In particular, can metropolitan universities offer fresh approaches, new activities, new programs? Can they use their burgeoning leadership role to bring better thought and better answers? Will they themselves become stronger models of multi-racial hiring? Will they have larger multi-racial student bodies? Will their curricula attend to the issue of race in such a way that their graduates and all others who are reached by the metropolitan university's programs have a different, better, sounder way of thinking and acting about race? Can metro universities contribute to a more peaceful multi-racial society through new outreach efforts?

The purpose of education is to impart knowledge, to help students think clearly about all manner of subjects, to raise questions about difficult issues, to go from what is known to the unknown by scientific experiment, to examine values and deeply held beliefs—in short to expand and enhance the mind so that better trained human intelligence will constantly seek human betterment. The issue of racial prejudice hinders this quest. So any institution of higher education, worthy of the name in my view, must address this issue. To the question, Is there an obligation? the answer is yes.

Metropolitan universities are in a unique position to attend to the issue of race. Their very newness, relatively speaking, should allow a fresh perspective and a more vigorous commitment on how to handle the many thorny aspects of race relations within their own institutions and in the communities they serve. For example, in the development of undergraduate and graduate curricula, one could imagine a faculty group energized by the opportunity to teach all their students about the distinctive nature and history of race in our country, thereby giving students a quite different lens through which to view this issue. One could imagine a metropolitan university reaching for the goal of a truly integrated campus, students, faculty, staff, with different expectations given form by different recruiting policies, different student living arrangements, different administrative practices. In its outreach mission, a metropolitan university, by very specific intention, addresses its programs to issues that involve or include race as a critical factor. It could invite the participation of persons of color in educational programs of special pertinence to them. More importantly, it could design and organize those programs so as to reach for the objective of an integrated society by new forms of collaboration with citizen organizations, other educational institutions and local government. By these efforts metropolitan universities could offer an interesting challenge and alternative to established extension education.

Third, the conflict between economic development and environmental protection has now penetrated the consciousness of many citizens. We are confronted by environmental degradation which only a short time ago was dismissed as the concern of kooks. But our national penchant for persistent and continuous economic progress runs headlong into this more recently understood goal of perceiving our natural environment. More than a goal of policy, protecting and preserving our natural environment is now seen as a necessity; yet many communities are still following older patterns of thought and action which, it is believed, will bring economic improvement while the environment cost is dismissed or lightly regarded. Every daily newspaper is full of stories about this conflict. What should metropolitan universities do about it, or, if they cannot do anything, how should they take account of it?

One way of looking at this problem is to examine the role of technology. It seems clear enough that the American people will not give up economic development. The "rising tide that lifts all boats" is an ingrained concept in our country; and the movement of individuals, families and whole groups from poverty to middle income to wealth has been a part of the social fabric of our nation since its beginning. American social and political institutions have been designed to encourage this basic human aspiration. No politician and no policy contravening economic growth stands a chance: less is less and more is more is a trademark for all politicians. But experts tell us that the nation, indeed the planet, is in danger.

Cutting into this dilemma is the vector of technology. New processes for making things, new sources of energy and ways of transporting people and goods, new methods of growing and using food and disposing of waste, new possibilities for conservation of natural resources of all kinds—these will be the effects of scientific and technological innovation. Universities are directly involved in the basic and applied research that will produce the new technology. All universities can teach about this dilemma, all can help their students understand the conflict between economic growth and environmental degradation, understand what is at stake, and how to balance the demands of society with responsive public policy. Because a metro university can reach to its regional communities, multiple business and industrial groups, many different kinds of citizen organizations and associations, and officials of local government, this issue of the economy and the environment could become a major educational program. It is also the kind of issue that could be treated by coalitions and combinations of institutions. There is an opportunity for innovative education here. Will the metropolitan universities take it?

Fourth is the double issue of the changing nature of both work and the family. Each could be considered separately but I consider them together because the nature of family structure today is greatly influenced by the economy. The change from an economy based on the manufacturing and extractive industries to one of services and information has been massive and sudden. Our society has not yet caught up with it. Although some of its effects are clear, such as the effect on male breadwinners, this transformation is not well understood. We are only beginning to fathom what new educational and social policies and programs the country needs in order to train the workforce for the next century, and how work and the lack thereof affects family structure. Professor William Julius Wilson's work in Chicago provides us with important insight about the connection between jobs and job training, and black men and their families. Many scholars have been studying these and similar matters relating work and family; and many policy proposals have been suggested dealing with some aspect of work and family, the latest of which, child care and parental leave, was debated by Congress quite recently. These are not questions which have been neglected. But the changing nature of work and changing family structure have not usually been considered together in university extension programs.

Other than providing resources for scholars to study the phenomena, what can or should universities do about these immensely complicated interactions of family and work? It is not easy to say. The changing nature of the economy is no doubt very much influenced by what occurs in university laboratories and through the experiments and writings of university scientists and scholars. Scientific knowledge, inventions, and new technological processes based on new theory certainly change the economy. University extension programs provide opportunities for local government officials and citizen organizations dealing with family issues, as well as for those concerned with local economic growth, to consider these questions. But how to create a curriculum and an outreach program that take account of the interconnections between work and family has, so far, eluded most of us. It remains an unexplored opportunity.

Finally, a metropolitan university must look to its central city and the culture and problems of that city. For it is the city, writ large, that remains the dominant influence in our society. No matter the development of suburbs and satellite cities and towns, of urban counties; no matter the movement of populations out of central cities; we are an urban society and the core meaning of urban is city. The metropolitan university must be encouraged to assist in the solution of the problems faced by our cities. Many of these problems are part and parcel of the issues discussed earlier. Many will be narrower or more technical. Many, perhaps, will not be affected by what the university can offer. And almost all urban issues are by definition complex and will only be solved or ameliorated by a combination of forces and factors more powerful than a university.

Still, a university is not without power. It has special kinds of resources—its faculty and its students. Their energies, if concentrated on the right issues, and consistently supported by university administration, can make a difference in the life of cities, of metropolitan areas and of our country. So it is that a university calling itself "metropolitan" may be thought of as having an obligation and a special opportunity to interact with the diverse communities of its area, and to structure itself so that its resources will be employed in new ways. The metropolitan university, because it is a new institution, may be able to imagine new relationships with other institutions and bodies in its region; it may be able to bring new experience and ideas from outside the university onto its campus with immense benefit to its programs of study. William Blake once said: "What is now proved was once imagined." Let the metropolitan university greatly exercise its imagination and it may become the university of the next century.

SCOPE AND LIMITATIONS OF COMMUNITY INTERACTIONS

Charles P. Ruch and Eugene P. Trani

Metropolitan universities derive a significant element of uniqueness from the breadth and character of their interactions with their communities. While many universities reside in urban or metropolitan areas, not all universities consciously and as a matter of mission and strategy, seek to build mutually beneficial relationships with many of the diverse elements characteristic of their service area. It is the interactive nature of these activities that defines their scope and contributes to their inherent limitations.

Metropolitan universities are not simply in the city but of the city, and the importance of activities with their surrounding environment is central to the life of the institution. These universities have as their mission the land-grant tradition of institutional research and public service conducted within the growing metropolitan centers of the country. Furthermore, public service is expanded to include the broadest of interactions with the community interactions that are naturally reinforcing to both institution and city.

As an institution of the city, the metropolitan university, by design and conscious action, seeks to draw upon the rich tapestry and fabric of the community in strengthening its programs of instruction, research, and public service. Conversely, the institution plans and delivers programs and activities that contribute to the improvement of the urban environment in which it resides. Through its many interactions with the community, the metropolitan university seeks to contribute to and ultimately improve the quality of life in the metropolitan area while enhancing its primary mission of knowledge generation and dissemination.

Three characteristics identify the particular nature of the interactions between the metropolitan university and its environment.

First, the interaction is mutually reinforcing. In all of the aspects, both the institution and the environment are richer for the participation. Some institutions tend to see their role as only to enrich the environment, ever maintaining an invisible wall that keeps their cloisters tightly knit, yet opening the doors to the community to participate within those cloistered walls. Other institutions seek to move beyond the cloistered walls as they move their activities into the greater community. It is the task of the metropolitan university to build relationships and activities that are mutually beneficial to both partners. As ties between the university and the community strengthen, the results of these interactions encourage cooperation on new projects.

Second, the interaction is guided by institutional choice and strategy. A metropolitan university is rich in its resources and possibilities. Conversely, the environment is a pool of unlimited diversity and opportunity. In developing mutually reinforcing relations, choice on the part of the institution as well as the needs of the community must prevail.

A third characteristic undergirding the university-community interactions is one of value and import. The university values and prizes the interactions, rewarding participants and building such interactions into the ongoing life of the institution. On the other hand, the community is reinforced and rewarded through its participation with the university. It welcomes and encourages university participation.

Making Mutual Interactions Happen

Interactions of mutual interdependence do not just occur. Potential activities require the assessment for mutuality, appropriateness, and quality. Examples drawn from experiences at two metropolitan universities—Virginia Commonwealth University (VCU) and the University of Missouri-Kansas City (UMKC)—illuminate these dimensions. The most successful interactions are characterized by mutually reinforcing qualities, carefully selected and valued by the university. While it can be argued that these interactions enrich both the metropolitan university and the community, and are consistent with the institution's mission and role and beneficial to the core mission of the university, they do not occur spontaneously. Careful institutional actions are also necessary. These include:

1. *Strong Leadership.* In each of the examples cited in this article, strong institutional leadership was necessary to initiate, develop, and sustain the interaction. Institutional leaders need to be visible and involved in community affairs.

2. *Clear Goal Statements.* Interactive community relationships need to be articulated in clear goal statements. Both university and

community members need lucid statements of the importance and value of productive university community interactions.

3. *Supportive Institutional Policies.* Institutional policies frequently inhibit strong university-community relationships. Academic requirements, promotion and tenure guidelines, salary and workload policies are but a few of the institutional policies that need to be reviewed to support community-university relations.

Teaching and Research

Mutually beneficial relationships between the university and the community, directed at the core mission functions of teaching and research, are legion. To be most effective, such interactions need to be not only mutually advantageous, but also carefully selected, and integrated into the fabric of the institution. Examples of experiential education, alternative program design, adjunct faculty and cooperative research illustrate the point.

Cooperative education, first designed to support engineering programs, is an ideal program for a metropolitan university. Both VCU and UMKC have programs of growing size and importance. At VCU, students extend their classroom into the world of work by serving as members of a corporate team for one or more semesters. Consequently, the curriculum is expanded and enriched. An additional benefit of cooperative education is that it offers students an opportunity to earn money to defray college expenses. Participating corporations contribute to the education of talented students, and at the same time identify prospective workers.

Expanding the curriculum into the community is not limited to a formal co-op program. Internships, practica, and other opportunities are found for every discipline and academic major. At VCU, for example, students in history, political science and English find internship experiences with state and local government to be particularly helpful. Students in the sciences take advantage of fieldwork opportunities in local corporations as well as state and local government. Students from the arts find work in museums and galleries. Projects and field trips within individual courses help to expand the curriculum into the community.

The boundaries between the classroom and the community can be made permeable, and the extent to which the flow of ideas and people is accelerated is to the mutual benefit of both. However, the full impact on the curriculum will not be met by including only community activities. Inductive pedagogy, case methodology, and cooperative learning strategies will need to be introduced into the classroom. Only by restructuring the instructional process so classroom content is tied with community experience will the full potential of these boundary-spanning strategies be achieved.

An additional hallmark of metropolitan universities has been the willingness to deliver instruction in the community and the work place. VCU offers an executive MBA program at a corporate location, a program for health administrators through closed-circuit television in regional hospitals, and courses for teacher certification in area schools. Courses taught in shopping malls and corporate executive centers are additional examples of the metropolitan university moving its instruction from the campus into the community.

An example of intra-institutional cooperation that benefits the community is the UMKC-UMC (University of Missouri-Columbia) engineering program. Engineering programs tend to be housed at the land-grant institution in a rural location, while city populations and corporations are frequently in need of affordable, convenient engineering programs. UMKC solved this problem by bringing UMC engineering faculty to the UMKC campus. The faculty work in Kansas City but earn tenure and promotion through the engineering departments at UMC, 120 miles east of Kansas City. UMKC provides the physical facilities as well as the basic general education and science curriculum; UMC engineering faculty the professional engineering course work. The needs of the land-grant university, metropolitan university, and the community are all served through this model arrangement. This concept might prove to be particularly effective in getting programs offered in urban settings without duplicating such degrees. It also builds good will between land-grant and urban campuses.

Staffing is another area where metropolitan universities enjoy unusual opportunities. Adjunct and part-time faculties can be drawn from the local area work force, thus contributing directly to the maintenance of the community economy. At VCU, practicing professionals bring up-to-date life experiences each semester from the community into the classroom. Judicious use of adjunct faculty in selected courses leaves the overall curriculum with the dimensions of the real and the possible, a necessary counterpoint to the theoretical and the imagined.

Knowledge generation is central to the mission of the university. The opportunities for faculty and students to identify real world problems, to draw community and professional members into the research teams, and to develop solutions to critical issues of academic and community interest are important opportunities for metropolitan universities. Research activities, mutually developed and pursued, provide yet another opportunity for the curriculum of the metropolitan university to be enhanced through community interactions.

If the academic life of the institution is so enriched through its interactions with the community, why are such arrangements so difficult to sustain? The answer lies in several of the characteristics of mutually interactive relationships. Unless carefully designed, the community perceives internships and practica experiences only as academic exercises. If students do not develop usable skills on campus, on-the-job difficulties develop. If adjunct faculty cannot enter the academy and learn to integrate their real-life experiences with theory, their instruction becomes dysfunctional. In each case choices must be made. Faculty and administrators need to ensure that off-campus programs are of the same quality and dimension as campus programs. Faculty and students alike need to be rewarded for their activities. Institutional policies need to be examined to support the off-campus instruction. Credit needs to be awarded for co-op and practica experiences, and reasonable salaries need to be paid to adjunct faculty. In short, each element of the university needs to be examined to ensure that it is consistent with the desired goal of productive community interaction. This examination must start with a clear and consistent mandate from institutional leadership.

Cultural Life of the City

Universities have always been central to the cultural life of the city. However, it is the metropolitan university where these activities have been developed in an interactive way to the mutual benefit of both. In Kansas City, for example, the UMKC houses the Missouri Repertory Theater, Incorporated. This repertory company, now twenty years old, has its own board, annually guarantees the funding of the Missouri Repertory Theater, and has even raised an endowment for it. The theater employs an artistic director, the university employs the chairperson of the theater department, and, jointly, these individuals coordinate the academic and professional programs.

In both Richmond and Kansas City there are joint appointments between the university and the city's symphony. In Kansas City, the first and second chairs of the symphony are faculty members of the Conservatory of Music at UMKC. In Richmond, the director of the Richmond Symphony holds an appointment at VCU. With community support, VCU sponsors the Terrace Concert Series in Richmond. This program provides an opportunity for musicians performing in the Terrace Concert at the Kennedy Center in Washington to appear in Richmond.

In both cities, the university operates an art gallery. Both galleries have clear niches within the overall art community. A joint appointment for the UMKC museum curator with a city museum is a useful strategy. In Richmond, the VCU sculpture department frequently displays its work at festivals and is joined by the painting and printmaking department in providing artistic work for display throughout the city. The VCU fashion show, produced by the fashion department, provides an opportunity to demonstrate their accomplishments within the fashion industry in the city.

Another shining example of an exchange beneficial to both university and community is VCU's free university. Staffed primarily with emeriti faculty, this program annually provides fifteen hundred senior citizens an opportunity to participate in lectures, discussion groups, and short courses on a variety of topics.

Extended university-artistic relations are not without problems and limitations. Differences in style and emphasis within the artistic and cultural community can lead to unnecessary misunderstandings. Dual institutional involvement exacerbates the potential for competition. Community expectations may clash with academic and artistic expression. Consequent pressures for perceived or actual censorship may emerge and will need to be repelled. Only with clear policy direction and implementation is it possible to move these relationships from competition to cooperation. Careful discussion and constant communication is necessary to ensure the continuing interactive nature of these relationships. A necessary prerequisite for success is the direct involvement of senior university leadership when establishing and maintaining these activities.

Health Care

Health care is an area where university and community interaction is essential to the benefit of both. VCU, through its Medical College of Virginia campus, and UMKC, through its Health Sciences Center, provide not only training of health care professionals, but direct and indirect health care service to the community at large. Central to both is the teaching hospital, the Medical College of Virginia Hospital in Richmond, and Truman Medical Center in Kansas City. Both are tertiary care centers and serve large indigent populations. The academic health center serves as the locus for the training of health care professionals, the conduct of basic and clinical research and delivery of direct patient care.

At UMKC, integrating and coordinating leadership responsibilities between the School of Medicine and the city/county hospital administration assures key strategic policy development and the delivery of first-rate medical care. For example, the executive director of the Truman Medical Center, the city/county hospital, also serves as dean of UMKC's medical school. The further involvement of health care and researchers ensures that the health care is on the cutting edge of medical practice.

Beyond direct service activities, the major academic health care centers are reaching out to disseminate knowledge to the larger medical and lay communities, often in rural settings. For example, at VCU the Massey Cancer Center conducts a rural cancer project linking the researchers and practitioners at the health science center with cancer patients and their physicians in outlying rural counties. While initial patient diagnosis and treatment, coupled with in-service training of practitioners, is done in the city at the cancer center, the goal is to make sure the patient returns to the local community where first-rate care from a local health care team is provided. This care is augmented and supported by the cancer center through telecommunications and on-site health consultations. Similarly, the Virginia Center for Aging and the Gerontology Education Program deliver outpatient education programs to the larger health care community, who in turn can turn to the unit for additional help and support.

The greatest challenge to the university health center and its relations to the community is the increasingly competitive health care environment. Balancing additional costs, patient acuity, training requirements, and care to indigent populations places the academic health science center at a competitive disadvantage with the community private hospitals. Conversely, through collaborative relationships and activities the competitive nature of the health care environment may be lessened. Only through such an approach can the health care across the metropolitan area be improved.

Community / Economic Development

As the call to strengthen competitiveness in the American economy has gone out, universities have responded with a variety of strategies to strengthen community and economic development. In many ways metropolitan universities have been at the forefront of developing these strategies. Two of the more frequent strategies have been the creation of a small business center, and the participation with area businesses and corporations in development of incubator centers, technology transfer projects, and/or research parks. At both VCU and UMKC, small business centers provide an opportunity for the prospective entrepreneur to receive technical assistance and support from business faculty and students. The VCU center provides help in developing a business plan, organizing a small business, taxes and legal advice, marketing strategies, and other business concerns. Faculty have an opportunity for hands-on experience confronting many of the issues faced as a new business is created. To the extent that students are included in the consulting activities, the curriculum and educational opportunities are strengthened. When developed in cooperation with the chamber of commerce and other civic organizations, as in Richmond, the Small Business Center provides strong support for the development of small businesses in the metropolitan area.

Similarly, the development of incubator projects and research parks are viable strategies for cooperative relationships between the metropolitan university and the business community. In Richmond, the Richmond Technology and Enterprise Center (RTEC), and in Kansas City, UMKC, are working to develop an area research park. RTEC is a business incubator facility and provides small business with temporary support space and technical advice for the transfer of biotechnical discoveries from the medical center into a commercial enterprise. Once developed, the new company moves into the community. The research park strategy at UMKC has already resulted in a five-year contract between the university and United Telecommunications. United Telecommunications funds faculty members for research on basic and applied research consistent with United Telecommunication interests. The long-term goal is a center, close to UMKC, where several businesses can be housed, drawing on the expertise of other UMKC faculty.

At both settings the future of incubators and research parks reflects the complexity and uncertainty of this strategy. New companies are difficult to sustain. Venture capital is not always readily available. Technology transfer, critical to both the metropolitan university and its community, is a complex, resource-intensive undertaking.

Economic development and technological transfer are areas where the business community and the university interface most directly. However, their short-term interests are not always compatible. The business community is looking for a return on investment, and a marketing and competitive edge that drives the private sector. University research faculty are more inclined toward matters of intellectual inquiry and development. Nor are faculty efforts in patent and copyright activities always rewarded within the academic promotion and tenure system. Consequently, the economic and commercial application of their activities may not be of high importance. Furthermore, state and institutional policies relating to patent and copyright ownership, conflict of interest between university and private sector activities, and priority of interests suggest that planning and delivery need to be carefully monitored.

K–12 Educational Improvement

The involvement of the metropolitan university in the improvement of kindergarten through twelfth-grade education is an area of mutual benefit. There are a number of examples of how metropolitan universities can play a major role in this improvement.

In Kansas City, an exchange program between senior administrators in the School of Education and the Kansas City school district led to the development of a "community service fellowship" program where faculty (while on university payroll) went into the community to tackle city educational problems. The university developed a Mathematics and Physics Institute where students from Kansas City area schools come to campus to receive programs of advanced mathematics and physics instruction not available in area schools. This institute is funded by four school districts using gifted and talented funds from the state.

In Richmond, the Capital Writing Project has allowed faculty from English and English education to work with almost all of the K–12 teachers in the area to improve writing skills and teaching of writing. Similarly, the mathematics department working with math educators developed the Richmond area Teachers' Professional Network, allowing mathematics teachers at all levels to work together to improve K–Collegiate mathematics instruction. The centerpiece of this activity has been a teacher-in-residence program where teachers from area schools spend the academic year on campus teaching in the mathematics department. A similar program occurs in the School of Education with teacher exchanges. Project BEST is an example of a university/school partnership, which encourages middle school students to continue further studies in mathematics and encourages retention of VCU students. VCU students serve as counselors and mentors for the middle school students, and in turn VCU faculty administrators serve as mentors for the VCU students.

The Richmond Community High School is an example of mutual interaction at its best. Now over ten years old, this Richmond City school is run by a community advisory board which includes VCU faculty. Talented, economically disadvantaged students are enrolled in an enriched academic curriculum supported by resident teachers, visiting faculty (frequently emeriti faculty), and university faculty. Students may enroll in VCU courses (for high school or advanced placement credit), and use VCU libraries, laboratories and computers.

The continued improvement of urban education depends on the mobilization of all community resources, including those of the metropolitan university. Building bridges through joint meetings with area superintendents and university leadership, presidents and provosts, serves as a way to coordinate the activities. Recognizing faculty contributions to area schools through the normal tenure and promotion process is critical to building these interactions. But central to the success of such enterprises is the creation of an atmosphere of mutual respect and collegiality. This can only be achieved through successful long-term exchanges of personnel and successful joint projects.

Support to Local and State Government

The metropolitan university has a strong stake in improving the civic life of the city and state. The university can provide a set of resources which, if properly marshalled, can improve the quality of state and local government. Examples include exchange of governmental officials and university faculty. The commonwealth governmental exchange program at VCU allows VCU faculty to take key roles in state government. Currently, the director of training in the Virginia Office of Personnel Training, the Virginia Commissioner of Mental Health and Mental Retardation, and staff to members of the finance committee of the general assembly are VCU faculty. Similar arrangements have allowed senior scientists in Kansas City to work on water control problems, and education faculty to assume school administration responsibility. The Center on Public Affairs at VCU conducts research and training activities designed to inform on public policy matters. Recently the state's Transportation Commission turned to the center for its staff work, as did the Attorney General's office for help on the development of drug abuse and awareness programs. VCU's Survey Research Laboratory periodically conducts the Commonwealth Poll, an opportunity to tap public opinion on key state issues.

It is clear that the metropolitan university can be an important participant in strengthening state and local government. Limitations in developing these activities are equally obvious. The university clearly needs to remain neutral in matters of partisan politics. This is not always easy, but it is the position the university must take. However, the university does have an obligation to provide the most accurate information that might inform public policy. This, too, is an area where those within the academy will differ. Much contract work requires interdisciplinary coordination and may frequently exacerbate matters of vested interest among faculty members. The university needs to be sensitive to these forces and respond accordingly. Finally, the movement of faculty into bureaucratic life or that of agency heads into the academy is not without its problems.

Employer / Landlord / Investor

Metropolitan universities are major employers and owners or occupiers of significant property within the metropolitan area. Their impact on the overall community cannot be underestimated. The necessity of managing these corporate affairs with the understanding of the overall community is integral to the continued development and esteem of the university. Yet it may be in this area more than any that the "town-gown" relationships become strained.

Metropolitan universities are major employers. Their employment levels directly affect the overall economy. The indirect economic effects through student purchasing and other activities are significant. As public entities, their tax-deferred status is of some sensitivity to the community. The sound business practices of competitive bidding and prompt payment of institutional accounts are matters of considerable import in building community support.

However, it is in the area of land use and land use planning that metropolitan universities may have major difficulties. A major accomplishment, for example, is a joint parking deck on the VCU campus. The deck, constructed with university, state and city funds, provides parking not only for a portion of VCU's commuter students, but for public events because of its location next to the City Auditorium. In similar fashion, the university is discussing with the city the possibility of managing a run-down park adjacent to the campus. The university proposes that the city transfer the responsibility of the park's maintenance and security to the university, which in turn would enhance both its usefulness and attractiveness for the community. On the other hand, the university seeks to expand and is in the process of trying to negotiate a land-use plan and acquire new property.

Particularly sensitive is a metropolitan university's interest in acquiring low-income housing property or moving into areas of perceived residential communities. Similarly, a university may have a variety of historically sensitive properties on its campus which it seeks to maintain, although at additional expense. There is simply no avoiding the conflict in relationships as the university tries to plan for its future as a constructive neighbor. Like most land-use debates, core community values frequently stand at the center point: economic development versus environmental protection, cost versus aesthetics, public versus private, academic versus commercial.

Minority Communities—A Special Opportunity

Metropolitan universities have a special opportunity to build mutually reinforcing relationships with their minority communities. More than other sectors of higher education, metropolitan universities have a responsibility to make a significant contribution to improving the educational opportunities for minority and low income citizens from surrounding communities. Most of the examples of university-community interactions reported above involve and benefit the minority communities in both Richmond and Kansas City. But the metropolitan universities must also undertake activities specifically targeted to providing increased educational access and employment to members of the minority communities. The metropolitan university plays a major role in making higher education accessible and available to the broadest cross section of the community. Programs designed to attract and assist minority youth with academic promise, such as VCU's academic support program, furnish a vehicle to extend higher education to an ever-widening population. Delivering courses at times and places convenient to the working, part-time student provide yet another mode of increasing educational access. Strong community college-metropolitan university transfer arrangements provide another strategy to extend educational opportunity to all members of the community.

As an employer, the metropolitan university is the first place significant numbers of the minority communities become employed. Throughout the institutional work force, occasions to hire and strengthen all employees, including minority members, should be pursued. A VCU program to provide free tuition for courses available to all employees permits work-study arrangements to the mutual benefit of the employee and the university. Completion of a college degree creates additional opportunities for the individual. Similar arrangements for graduate students strengthen both the degree program and the graduate.

In meeting these special responsibilities, the metropolitan university will need to be especially responsive and innovative. It will have to conduct programs of developmental education and academic support. Structured mentoring programs, employee training, and flexibility in recruitment and hiring are necessary institutional responses if the metropolitan university is to maximize its opportunities to its minority communities.

A Final Admonition

Significant elements defining the character of metropolitan universities are the breadth and character of their interactions with their communities. The nature of these relationships is defined by their mutuality, appropriateness, and quality. As illustrated earlier, the scope of such activities runs across the gamut of institutional and community life. If developed with imagination, cooperation and energy, the university, as well as the community, will be richer.

Such activities do not occur spontaneously nor easily. Several limitations inherent in current institutional life mitigate against the enhancement of community interactions.

First, there is the matter of faculty role, responsibility, and reward. The traditional professorial role of teaching and research needs to be expanded to include active public service in the local community. The traditional view of scholarship must be broadened to value action research and problem-solving methodologies. A view of teaching that focuses on active learning in an extended classroom needs to be encouraged. Perhaps most necessary is the revision of the traditional reward system to include these as valued activities in the tenure, promotion and salary considerations.

Second, metropolitan universities must become more consumer-oriented. Degree programs need to be planned and scheduled at times, places, and locations convenient to community members. Service units need to schedule hours to accommodate working students. Support services need to be provided to assist community members in making the transformation into university life.

Third, and most important, throughout all its activities, involvement with the community needs to be extolled as an institutional value and characteristic. The power of such symbols as presidential leadership, frequent discussion of successful community projects in local media, and visible community-university advisory councils cannot be underestimated.

Metropolitan universities and their communities have much to offer and gain from each other. They are not always natural partners. Their successful interactions necessitate the university to take a broader view of its mission, role, and activities.

SUGGESTED READINGS

Elman, Sandra, and Sue Smock. *Professional Service and Faculty Rewards: Toward an Integrated Structure*. Washington, D.C.: National Association of State Universities and Land-Grant Colleges, 1985.

Lynton, Ernest, and Sandra Elman. *New Priorities for the University: Meeting Society's Need for Applied Knowledge and Competent Citizens*. San Francisco: Jossey-Bass, 1987.

Seymour, Daniel, ed. *Maximizing Opportunities Through External Relationships*. San Francisco: Jossey-Bass, New Directions for Higher Education, No. 68, 1989.

PART VI

CONTINUING AND DISTANCE EDUCATION

INTRODUCTION

As a new model for higher education, metropolitan universities are rethinking the role and scope of various campus support functions such as continuing education. In "Revisiting Continuing Education at the Metropolitan University," Daniel W. Shannon argues that in order to extend the resources of the university to the community as outreach, it is necessary to redefine the role of this key support function beyond simply instruction. A similar argument can be found in Paul A. Miller's piece, "A View from the Center: The Future of Continuing Education in Metropolitan Universities," where he argues that a much expanded role for continuing education should include identifying new learning formats, services, and related information to serve both community needs and university expectations. Miller's article "advances knowledge utilization for greater emphasis among the functions of the university and urges that it be enhanced in the practice of civic competence, broadly defined." The article also examines the future of education and industrial practice as the restoration of what he calls "primary citizenship."

As Shannon points out, continuing education, "as a function and an organization, must be seen as an integral part of the fabric of the university." Because continuing education is change-driven, client and issue-oriented, multidisciplinary, and constituency-focused, it can play an important role on behalf of the university to engage a diverse community in urban problem solving.

REVISITING CONTINUING EDUCATION AT THE METROPOLITAN UNIVERSITY

Daniel W. Shannon

Continuing education, whether as a provider or facilitator of campus outreach activity, experiences tension in balancing its market orientation with traditional university demands for autonomy and the narrow reflection of the instructional patterns of the campus. As Philip Nowlen pointed out in the Spring 1989 issue of the *Educational Record,* there are "contending frames of reference through which to find meaning and direction [for continuing education]" (p. 46). The scope of continuing education at times is broadened by reading its special competence as extending the resources of the university to the broader community in an outreach mode. This view of continuing education does not limit its role to instruction, but includes other outreach services consistent with a university setting, such as the provision of technical assistance, public information, and even the creation of research parks. More frequently, however, continuing education is viewed only as "instructional outreach," manifested in freestanding credit courses or degree programs for nontraditional students and noncredit seminars, workshops, and conferences related to the academic entitlement of the university. This is the usual pattern at the metropolitan university, where the local, typically urban population accesses university resources through continuing education.

The Value of Continuing Education

Continuing education adds value to the university in creating access through credit and noncredit instruction; continuing education also adds value to the community by raising the level of public and professional discourse. Despite its instructional character, this modality of continuing education is considered to be "service" in the frequently used metaphor of the three-legged stool of research, teaching, and public service. And while, even in this conceptual framework, continuing education plays many roles within the university—missionary, advocate, and guardian of the adult student, programmatic boundary spanner, and convener—it nonetheless characteristically engages in *instruction* for the nontraditional student. Its instructional interests span the disciplines, frequently serving as the venue for multidisciplinary approaches, and meeting demands for new instructional products.

However, a broader framework for continuing education is preferable. Continuing education's greatest potential is in assuming broader responsibilities to engage the university in forms of outreach that are not typically associated with continuing education's instructional responsibilities. Both the university and the community benefit when continuing education is given an expanded function. The notion that continuing education is limited to instructional outreach is no longer adequate for the 1990s and beyond. American universities today are increasingly looked upon as an important resource in bringing improvement to some of society's most intractable problems. This is particularly true in major metropolitan areas of the country, where over seventy percent of the country's population resides. It is a challenge that more metropolitan universities are accepting. As the late Marguerite Ross Barnett remarked in her inaugural address at the University of Houston in 1990, "What will characterize the superb twenty-first-century university will be its ability to manifest and focus areas of unquestioned excellence on the challenging issues of the day." Even prestigious private universities see themselves as a source of creative social problem solving. Outgoing President Derek Bok of Harvard University remarked in his final address to the faculty that Harvard's "mission should clearly include the use of education and research to address great human problems, such as poverty, hunger, crime, and environmental destruction."

Continuing Education and the Community

The metropolitan university, particularly, is being asked to join forces with government, business, and social agencies to ameliorate serious social and economic problems in the metropolitan areas, to help ensure economic vitality; to assist in restructuring education; to enhance the professional skills of teachers and government workers; to improve environmental quality; to contribute to improving the health and safety of the communities' residents; and to increase the level of civility in communities. The litany varies little from community to community.

The metropolitan university today is adopting a more assertive posture in the life and politics of its community. The evidence is in the popular and professional press—and apparent on our campuses. The metropolitan university is building on its traditional research and teaching roles, but creatively adapting to the peculiar needs of the metropolitan area of which it is a part. This adaptive behavior covers a wide range. At one end is the subtle influence the university has by articulating moral order in the conflict of ideas and providing a sanctuary for reflection on theory and practice. At the other end is active engagement with the private sector in creating products and services such as research parks. Manfred Stanley sees the university as a "civic institution," an institution "central to the production or maintenance of goods defined by a large majority of citizens as vital to the material and moral prosperity of the commonwealth" (p. 5).

Ernest Boyer eloquently argues the case for a stronger bond between the university and its community in *Scholarship Reconsidered.* He acknowledges an historical link between campus and contemporary problems, but argues that link must be strengthened. By what instrumentality will this link be forged, assuming the university is committed to making a difference in the life and times of the community? How will multiple connecting points be established to link community and university? While no single entity within the university should be viewed as the sole contributor to this effort, continuing education on most campuses possesses the historical mission of extending the resources of the university into the community. Hence it is the logical starting point for analyzing or initiating linkages to the community. On some campuses this historical continuing-education mission has much meaning for the entire university, acting as a metaphor for the role the university has historically played in enriching the entire community. The Wisconsin Idea comes to mind: "the boundaries of the campus are the boundaries of the state." In this tradition, continuing education plays an important facilitating role in the engagement of the university in the affairs of the state.

Continuing Education as Part of the University

In its usual form, as essentially an instructional outreach, continuing education is limited in its ability to perform the bridging role necessary to position the university as a major contributor to societal problem solving in our metropolitan areas. To bring about this linkage, continuing education must be viewed in a much broader framework, as spanning and connecting to the entire university. Continuing education, both as a function and an organization, must be seen as an integral part of the fabric of the university. It must become a major participant in the business of the university. It must be reconceptualized to perform a larger role on behalf of the university in order to engage the entire university to affect the community in which it resides in a variety of ways and in a positive manner. This will require, in many instances, the reinventions and in others a reinvigoration, of continuing education. On some campuses noninstructional outreach or extension activity is already imbedded in continuing education. In concept the campus at large should assume responsibility for the bridging function, either as contributors to the process or as facilitators of the process. Continuing education, by assuming a larger outreach role, is positioned to provide leadership in this effort. This leadership potential is based on a disposition of continuing education to relate naturally to the external world and on a talent for translating worldly problems into educational approaches.

A reconceptualized continuing education expands upon its usual role as a provider of "instructional outreach" to include the roles of facilitator, convener, or broker of other university resources. Continuing education becomes an integral and active component of the university's central concern with the "knowledge process" by being a principal provider of access to the university's knowledge base by the larger community. It is, however, not a passive conduit for knowledge transmission, but rather an active participant in the process of knowledge dissemination and application. Hence, it is part of the fundamental mission of the university. In an essential sense, continuing education helps to convert knowledge into readily useable forms for immediate application. It is a given that a tension exists between the internal priorities and customs of the university and the pressures applied by external groups or external issues. Possessed bodies of knowledge must be fitted to new applications in unaccustomed ways and reorganized to meet external needs. Communication must be established with the users of that knowledge. Against this background of tension, continuing education plays the role of facilitating the continuous interplay between the knowledge enterprise of the university and those external to the university actively engaged in societal problems.

External demands on the university are many. Universities are being asked to help ensure economic vitality by providing society with new products, services, and new methods of manufacturing. They are expected to engage in technology and knowledge transfer, provide better management skills, and improve the skills and knowledge of workers in an international marketplace. Universities are asked to enhance practitioner skills in traditional fields through updating and to provide training in new areas of specialization where no traditional faculty exists, such as hazardous waste management. Universities are also being asked to create a level of civility in our civic community by training emerging leaders, by enlightening the public on issues of common concern, and by celebrating cultural diversity.

This conceptualization of the role of continuing education in the knowledge process is in contrast to the three-legged stool metaphor of research, teaching, and service, which assigns continuing education the role of service. Continuing education is more central to the knowledge activities of the university than that appellation would imply. The concept of the knowledge process provides a more useful way of describing the fit of continuing education to the fundamental roles of the university.

It allows us more definitional precision in describing the appropriate activities of continuing education within various institutional cultures. In its instructional mode, continuing education contributes to transmitting knowledge. When continuing education is engaged in activities such as policy analysis or program evaluation, it is appropriately participating in another dimension of the knowledge process, knowledge generation. When it facilitates technology transfer or provides technical assistance, it is engaged in knowledge application.

Expectations vary between institutions regarding what is appropriate for continuing education among the several dimensions of the knowledge process. But whatever the mix, and whether viewed as provider or facilitator, continuing education in this conception participates in all the fundamental knowledge-based activities of the university as do the other academic units of the university.

The Expanded Function of Continuing Education

Continuing education can carry out its expanded function because it has five important characteristics: It is change driven, client oriented, issue oriented, multidisciplinary, and constituency oriented.

Continuing education is *change driven* by virtue of its commitment to the ongoing improvement of professional practice, the encouragement of public discourse on foreign and domestic issues, its engagement in cultural enrichment, and its dedication to the expansion of opportunities for all people. All of its activities are in response to or in anticipation of needs and conditions brought about by change.

Continuing education is *client oriented*. Its activities, services, and programs are shaped by the demands of users of its products. The processes employed for program development are generally predicated on market demand, with relatively short timelines and a tight fit between client need and the character of the program. In most instances the budget of continuing education contains a substantial requirement for fee-generated income. This requirement creates the condition for the development of a product that is much closer to the needs of the client than one developed without the market environment.

Continuing education views the world in terms of *problems or issues*, which is the way in which the public bundles its concerns. This means, as well, that continuing education must take a *multidisciplinary approach*. The external community does not structure its concerns in a manner that readily replicates the structure of the university or the organization of its knowledge base. The tendency toward specialization, characteristic of all disciplines, works against the creation of an appropriate fit between issue and university. Disciplines are vertical, problems are horizontal, and society operates in a matrix of these. The closest the university comes to a fit is through centers and institutes. Hence, the interface between societal problems and universities is frequently inadequate and results in unrealistic expectations and frustration. By having a multidisciplinary, issue-centered orientation, continuing education can create a better fit between institution and community. It can mobilize all pertinent resources and approaches within the university. It can draw upon several disciplines and subdisciplines, as well as various departments, centers, schools, and colleges. Hence it can structure responses, regardless of modality of outreach, that have a better chance of ameliorating a condition existing in the community.

The successful engagement of the university in all forms of outreach will depend upon its ability to organize its product principally on the basis of an issue-centered, multidisciplinary approach. It is the only feasible response, but requires, *inter alia,* the coordination of curriculum development, mediation of differing practice approaches, and coordination of faculty resources among the various disciplines and organizations involved. Continuing education provides a neutral venue for this coordination, as well as a positive and experienced environment for creating an interface with clients of the program or activity.

Finally, continuing education must adopt a *constituency orientation.* Continuing education has traditionally been learner-centered, focused on the structure, modality, and outcome of participation in an individual learning experience. While this orientation remains appropriate when structuring such experiences, it is not fully consistent with the broader conceptualization of continuing education as an interface with the knowledge process and with the issue orientation described above. Just as the concerns of the community are bundled into issues, the beneficiaries of university responses to those issues are likely to be grouped into constituencies that are identifiable to the continuing educator. It is the constituency group qua group that will benefit, with potentially subsequent benefit flowing to the individual member. There are collective points of view, issues, and concerns that inhere in the group that may not be shared universally and uniformly by the individual members. Addressing the needs of the group will ameliorate a common problem and improve the situation for the group as a whole.

This constituency orientation, as well, builds a base of university support that is clear and easily accessed and mobilized. By addressing the broad interests of constituency groups in a common pursuit of the interests of the commonweal, the university creates the potential for reciprocal support of its interests through this partnership. A constituency orientation also provides the university with easily identifiable and recruitable partners for problem-solving initiatives. By linking issues and constituencies with an appropriate university response, strategic alliances become feasible and increase the impact of any such activity.

By adopting these characteristics, continuing education positions itself to play a larger role within the institution. Building upon its traditional instructional outreach role, it assumes a broader responsibility for building linkages with the external community. In so doing, it accepts an additional responsibility to engage the resources of the university in forms that are not typically associated with continuing education's instructional responsibilities. For some institutions this expansion will be consistent with the present functions of continuing education or outreach; for others it will require a new approach.

In its expanded mode, continuing education provides a mechanism to integrate the faculty and staff of the university with the larger community in a problem-solving enterprise, whether this be the expansion of the knowledge base, the pursuit of traditional degree and nondegree instruction by nontraditional audiences, or the extension of new forms of knowledge to new constituencies. While the form of the university's contribution to problem solving may vary, the constant is the human resource that the university contributes in faculty and staff expertise to efforts with the community. It is the interaction between university faculty and staff and community participants that gives shape to the joint university-community activity. Thus a principal role of continuing education is the engagement of faculty and staff and the facilitation of an interaction with the community to structure a response.

Continuing Education and University Outreach Activities

How does the university shape its response to external pressures for engagement in social and economic issues confronting the metropolitan area? There exists a variety of forms of university activity that can be used to support the outreach mission and to fashion an institutional response to external needs:

1. applied research;
2. program evaluation and policy analysis;
3. technical assistance;
4. clinical services;
5. development and demonstration of intervention models;
6. student internships and volunteer activities;
7. academic support services;
8. credit instruction;
9. noncredit, informal, or self-directed instruction, including conferences and workshops; and
10. public information.

There is no single mode or model of outreach. A university response to external issues may utilize any one or any mix of the list, which indeed may not be complete. However, each response must rest upon the special competencies and academic strengths of the university, as well as on the appropriateness of the response to the culture of the institution. The match between the institution's strengths, the issue to be addressed, the character of community alliances created, and the modality of the response will drive decision making about (a) the locus of the response within the community, (b) the character or form of the response, and (c) the source or sources of the response from within the university.

While some forms of university outreach activities are immediately recognized as appropriate to application in community problem solving, others are not so readily apparent. For example, we do not usually think of academic support services in the framework of outreach, but the consoling and assessment skills found in academic advising fit well with inner-city initiatives targeting employment and further schooling. Even those activities, such as credit instruction, that are most usually associated with outreach, invite reexamination for innovative ways to link them with community issues. For example, much can be gained by an evaluation of the catalog of summer session courses to determine their fit with issues of current importance to the community. The intention should be to offer courses that would prepare professionals or the public to deal more effectively with current community concerns. Such courses might be grouped with a summative conference, to which both students and the public are invited, to discuss community initiatives or new approaches to issues the courses have addressed.

The array of forms of potential response exists on most metropolitan university campuses today. But usually they are not coordinated or not oriented toward outreach. They are distributed broadly within the institution and are structurally unrelated. To mobilize the proper mix of forms for any targeted initiative is a challenge to which continuing education, viewed in its broad framework, is particularly well suited. This approach organizes knowledge and human resources around problems. To the extent that multiple forms are used, it creates a matrix organization approach to problem-solving interventions. Various segments of the university are simultaneously organized in a coordinated manner to create a targeted initiative, with leadership coordination being provided by continuing education or one of the other participants.

While this approach creates a framework in which to imagine a response by the university to a pressing community issue, it does not provide a filter through which to evaluate which issues the university should address among the pressing concerns expressed to it. In the address mentioned earlier, Bok suggests a simple set of criteria to decide which issues the university should address:

1. "potential to achieve special quality, not readily available in another institutional setting, because of its ready access to the intellectual resources of the university; and

2. should have capacity to benefit the university by contributing in some important way to education or research."

I would add two additional criteria. Issues tackled by the university should:

3. possess the potential for a measurable positive impact on the *community*, responding to the *community's* issue agenda; and

4. fit the special competencies of the university.

Conclusion

These are challenging times for government, businesses, nonprofit organizations and citizens, as well as universities. It is not, however, an unreasonable expectation that our constituencies would regard their metropolitan university to be among the principal resources for assistance in the arduous task of resolving what often seem to be intractable problems, irrespective of where those problems are located in the community. The peculiar mission of the metropolitan university is to relate in significant ways to the urban community and to create relationships that are reciprocally beneficial. Continuing education, in an expanded mode, should more rationally relate the university to its broader community and support more meaningfully the initiatives undertaken with that community.

SUGGESTED READINGS

Bok, Derek. "Worrying About the Future." *Harvard Magazine,* Vol. 53, No. 9
    (May-June 1991): 37–47.
Boyer, Ernest L. *Scholarship Reconsidered: Priorities of the Professorate.* Princeton,
    NJ: Princeton University Press, 1990.
Lynton, Ernest A., and Sandra E. Elman. *New Priorities for the University.* San
    Francisco: Jossey-Bass, 1987.
Nowlen, Philip. "Continuing Education: Two Perspectives.*Educational Record*
    (Spring 1989): 46–47.
Stanley, Manfred. "The American University as a Civic Institution." *The Civic
    Arts Review* (Spring 1989): 4–9.

A VIEW FROM THE CENTER:
THE FUTURE OF CONTINUING EDUCATION IN
METROPOLITAN UNIVERSITIES

Paul A. Miller

The Paradox

Academic institutions hold paradoxical places in American society, none more so than those in metropolitan communities. While free to interpret the past and anticipate the future, they must also respond to current social need and pressure. Such balancing can be difficult. How else can one explain a vibrant university, a vast storehouse of knowledge, that is surrounded by social chaos and human despair! How continuing education may help metropolitan universities to grapple with this paradox in the future is the focus of this article.

University services in metropolitan areas and the strengthening of continuing education have grown apace, especially in the past three decades. Conferences and workshops abound, as do exhibits and lectures, art and musical performances, weekend colleges and media presentations. Catalogs burst with evening courses. Distance learning and other uses of communications technology enable the tailoring of special ventures in further learning. As one outcome, continuing education in academe has won increasing legitimacy.

Despite such gains, however, rampant urbanism on a world scale has come to defy all institutions, colleges and universities among them. Cities everywhere are filled with civic puzzles; urban chaos together with skepticism of institutional efficacy have produced a genuine crisis. Public confusion fuels voter apathy, which is then compounded even further in this country by the realignment of American federalism and a greater pressure on the resources and institutions of local communities. The challenges are as varied as they are difficult to confront. For example, attempts at mediating the risks and benefits of technical initiatives can trigger a whole range of controversies that turn into a peculiarly American epidemic of litigiousness. Moral traditions bouncing between relativism and hedonism, find slippery footing in family, school, church, and other neighborhood institutions. All the while, the gulf between ethnic and racial groups persists or even widens, as does the distance between rich and poor.

Along the way, a growing focus on special client groups has swept across the American community life. Metropolitan communities are made up of intricate webs of private and public agencies. Each agency provides a special service, builds a client base, and defends its claims for resources and acceptance. Agency networks make the city a receiver and contributor in larger systems, but they do not create visions of the whole nor take much account of shared concerns. Indeed, narrowly focused agencies may prosper while the common enterprise weakens. Nor has the university escaped the process of being narrowly client-driven. It is also overtaken by specialized, fragmented, and entrepreneurial pursuits in the name of growth and support.

This overlap of the urban revolution with strong client orientation provokes a decisive consequence: while urban problems grow more general and interdependent, the solutions grow more specialized and disconnected. The material that follows explores how continuing education might work to correct this lack of coherence, open windows on the future, and help the university play a greater role in the development triangle of education, business, and government. The abundant and detailed panoply of programs that characterizes today's continuing education is recognized, but the commentary suggests a more general framework as the field moves toward the future.

Civic Culture and Competence

Metropolitan universities, along with their continuing education divisions, have indicated for some time a renewed concern with the meaning, direction, and method of public service. In response to these signals, the thesis of this article is this: the metropolitan university might well look at the meaning of "public" as civic culture and the meaning of "service" as helping people with the utilization of knowledge. These are orientations that will suggest a paradigmatic shift in emphasis among the functions of universities in metropolitan areas. It is one that brings continuing education, public service, and outreach into better balance with traditional teaching and research.

Tides of credentialed entrants flow from American colleges and universities into the labor market. The emphasis on career preparation is widespread and likely to increase. This development has also legitimized continuing education and will continue to do so in the future. American education is organized for creating individuals with a strong sense of self-worth and personal skills who are determined to advance themselves in pursuit of their own ends. Such individualism would also help them serve as citizens in a free constitutional democracy, as people enabled to achieve their personal preferences and to adjudicate conflicts among competing preferences by resorting to acceptable rules of fairness.

This orientation is now being challenged. Personal preferences, and the strong individualism that underwrites them, run afoul of organized special interests. Adjudication may fail, personal preferences frustrated, with disappointment leading to retreat or even anomie. Thus human connection and interaction may weaken as well as the institutions that foster them. Lately, however, people ask if the common good cannot be better recognized and pursued. They reach out, however dimly, for a consensus on general goals that requires citizens who are able to influence the preferences of others and who are prepared to alter their own. Citizen behavior here must be receptive, flexible, imaginative, speculative, and adventuresome in solving problems. These are the skills of civic competence, broadly conceived, embodied in the acts of a primary citizenship. Both civic competence and primary citizenship have been shortchanged by American education. They need to be restored, for they affect almost every sector, including economics and the entire production system. In this manner, civic competence and knowledge utilization are concepts for thinking about the priorities of metropolitan universities. They give unity to otherwise disparate activities, serving as elements of theory and practice for continuing education toward urban reconstruction.

Two qualifications, however, are in order. Despite the danger of too narrow a response to client demands, countless services of metropolitan universities will continue to focus on specific needs, among them the whole repertory of continuing education itself. Such targeted services cannot be replaced, nor should they be, but with patience and skill, and however ambiguous the process, they should gain from examination, linkage, and a unifying vision. The second caveat is a reminder that continuing education has to reckon with the institution as a whole, understanding that teaching and research provide the substance that supports the projects of importance to the community.

Principia Media

Karl Mannheim, perceptive analyst of social change, once referred to *Principia Media* as those functions capable of special leverage in urban society. Once identified, he believed that the skillful use of these levers would yield constructive change. Using this principle seems especially fitting for metropolitan universities and continuing education. Ortega y Gassett in his *Mission of the University* said: "The university must intervene as the university in current affairs, treating the great themes of the day from its own point of view: cultural, professional, and scientific. . . . the university must stand for serenity in the midst of frenzy, for seriousness of purpose and the grasp of the intellect in the face of frivolity and unashamed stupidity" (p. 91). In light of Mannheim's media and Gassett's themes, the commentary turns now to a pair of guidelines for the future of continuing education in urban universities. They are *education and industrial practice* and the *restoration of primary citizenship.*

Education and Industrial Practice

The rise of continuing education is due in no small part to meeting the needs of industry. There is new recognition by the industrial sector of human resource demands in the workplace. Opportunities are abundant for partnerships of universities with industries, and many are underway. However, the academic institutions too often operate in a reactive mode that stops short of real collaboration with business and industry in defining the purposes and designing the content of training and education. A true partnership of education, business, and government is needed in order to deal with what has haunted industrial civilization from the outset: the separation of the home from the workplace. More attention is now paid to the worker as a social being, one who desires to play stronger roles in family and neighborhood. Human resource investments now gear themselves to a span from prenatal care to learning in the retirement years. New aspirations grow from old ideas: cooperation, participation, quality performance, job security, rotation, flextime, egalitarian values, joint consultation, and teamwork. Sometimes misunderstood by their business associates, continuing educators have never ceased probing the humanistic parameters of their human work. This stands them in good stead as they lead their field into stronger working relationships with business and industry.

Enriching the meaning of work leads not only to greater economic productivity but also to fuller lifestyles. The process goes beyond the human relations school that keeps workers happy but with little care for their total development, and much beyond scientific management that routinizes tasks and isolates the worker from supervision. Side by side with today's pragmatic challenges to productivity and competition is also the trend to decentralize work and reconnect it to family and community life. It finds workers exclaiming: "I want to grow, contribute, and enjoy not one at a time, but at the same time, all the time."

The new agenda requires that business and industry, university, and government join in ways heretofore not accomplished. Continuing educators, long the facilitators between campus and corporation for upgrading the skills of workers, can now interpret and emphasize such understandings as these following.

1. Learning, working, and leisure need to be interwoven throughout a lifetime;

2. Leisure needs to be redesigned for creative use rather than escape from work;

3. Demonstrated competence is properly overtaking paper certification;

4. Flexible patterns of time spent at work, and of education, training, leave time, and pension systems are in need of more emphasis;

5. More knowledge is needed of the structure of job markets and labor mobility, the relation of education to job success, and how best to merge occupational and social aspirations;

6. Ways are needed to determine both the human value and the market value of continuous learning.

An extended and more carefully articulated partnership of industry, government, and the university will recognize that, for whatever the reasons, work itself seems troubled in American society. Taking up the agenda, the partnership will surely mark this uncertainty for early attention. Americans hold work as a fundamental measure of self-esteem. For those who desire work but find it withheld, and for those who are underemployed, the American dream will seem far off indeed. Over the social agenda on work hangs a special failure: the continuing plight of youth trapped in the central cities. How to help these youth get on a pathway to mature adulthood and meaningful careers is such a crisis that until it is better done the partnership of education, business, and government will remain embarrassed. Other issues also deserve more than casual notice: how to resolve the tension between being a good worker and being a good parent; enhancing the retirement years by inviting older people to the campus for further learning and then helping them enter community service. Just as the insurance agent helps people plan for death, more can be done by the educator to help people plan for life.

The Restoration of Primary Citizenship

Perhaps the 1990s will establish a new baseline for urban

reconstruction. The 1960s and its war on poverty gave strong emphasis not only to a stream of urban initiatives but also to models for what metropolitan universities might do. Departments of urban affairs sprang up, and the Ford Foundation supported fruitful experiments in several institutions. While remnants of these initiatives remain, the momentum of the period was not sustained.

But now a fresh and positive urgency is sending signals to the universities and other institutions of metropolitan America. There are fresh stirrings of primary citizenship, that overlap of actions people take in their families and at their workplaces, in other local institutions and associations as distinct from civic allegiance to the state for which this citizenship is the ultimate foundation. Indeed, these stirrings indicate a desire that expert-led and specialized approaches from the top give way to citizen action from the bottom. While social fragmentation and discord may lurk in grassroots enthusiasms, they can also become the chemistry for igniting an urban renaissance and building up a genuine affection for cities, an affection which, on the whole, Americans seem not to possess.

It is important that metropolitan universities hear these stirrings and become major actors in shaping the vision and the goals of their respective areas. Continuing education and its outreach instruments should seize upon those initiatives that are peculiarly suited to the educational mission of the university. Three recommendations follow:

1. to educate people about education, especially as it concerns urban schools;

2. to provide training to enhance the quality of local government and volunteer leadership; and

3. to take steps to heighten science literacy in general and the use of knowledge for problem solving in particular.

Metropolitan Education

Americans in every metropolitan area are asking what their schools can do for them. No reversal of the urban crisis is possible until this question is answered, consensus is built, and the solutions are worked through to completion. Little will happen until the citadels of learning, the universities, become truly serious about the process, which, on the whole, they have yet to do. Theodore Hesburgh, the former President of Notre Dame University, minced no words when he said in 1984: "The general lack of concern on the part of higher education for elementary and secondary education is at the heart of the nationwide educational crisis."

To make matters more difficult, the concern does not stop with the schools. It also includes the behaviors of families and parents, technical support services, and the many aspects of community atmosphere that influence youth. All such factors considered, American youth are failing because society is failing them. Fully a fourth of America's youth risk joining an underclass with little hope of taking up the responsibilities and privileges of an active, positive citizenship. And no group or location in metropolitan communities is exempt from such misadventures of youth as dropping out of school, teenage pregnancy, and substance abuse. Also taking their toll are oppressive poverty, racial discrimination, a work force that many youth are not prepared to enter, and conflicting interests that impede workable policies for families and youth.

Continuing education that is backed by the entire university and directed toward neighborhood and community understanding, commitment, and action, should be among the primary influences of this crusade. While each situation will require unique approaches, such actions as those following might help guide continuing educators along the way:

1. Gather, update, organize, and share research *knowledge* on how youth move to self-confident adulthood; form partnerships to retrieve and share existing information; facilitate applied research; and evaluate and document youth development efforts.

2. Form school and/or community partnerships that devise *strategies* for prevention programs, including placing multiple university projects in common pilot areas

3. Conduct research-based *training* for those who serve school and youth organizations, as well as systems that recruit and train volunteers.

4. Devise with others and evaluate *policy* options that will improve on such complex and related domains as taxation, economic development in neighborhoods, welfare and social security, equal opportunity, and the justice systems.

5. Provide leadership on behalf of the university and other institutions for research-based *advocacy* programs that place the concerns about youth so high on the metropolitan and national agendas that they become the basis of strong and lasting resolve.

Strengthening Local Leadership

Due to a rising cynicism that the public's work is being poorly done, the need to train leaders of metropolitan efforts is now greater than ever. Even more frustrating is the suspicion that yesterday was better than tomorrow will be. Meanwhile, people feel that they are stranded outside the communication networks of politicians, lobbyists, and journalists, a perception aimed mostly at distant governmental domains but now seeping into local communities as well. Ironically, such notions become apparent at a time when new burdens fall on local areas. Fortunately, however, it may be counter-balanced by the stirrings in primary citizenship.

Training issues become, therefore, as numerous as they are varied. To begin with, models that demonstrate the use of knowledge need to be developed and tested. Both elected and volunteer leaders need to meet and understand neighborhood people and their desires, feel at ease with them, and grow skilled with connecting their own efforts to them. More congruence is required among municipal, state, and federal jurisdictions now so numerous at the local level that overlap and conflict are inevitable. Such problems need to be understood, simplified, and better managed. Superior talent must be recruited into local government and other metropolitan posts, and then be kept up to date. Tactics for achieving a consensus on visions and goals must win over those used by special interests. Not to be overlooked are training ventures for the media that support journalists and others who interpret the ups and downs of metropolitan affairs.

Tangent to training are those skills of continuing educators which enable them to convene individuals and groups in or out of the universities. Getting people together can help close the gap between citizen and expert. By means of carefully designed ventures, they can be assisted in inventing and adapting service delivery models, organizing neighborhood action, bringing knowledge to bear on policy formation, and helping establish advocacy campaigns. Continuing educators in metropolitan universities may also improve upon the rather poor "memory system" of American society, which allows projects of merit in one community to remain unidentified, and fails to transfer and review them elsewhere. At a minimum, techniques for such searches can be included in the training effort. Continuing educators might better rally themselves and their universities for such sharing on a national and perhaps international basis.

Science Literacy

The thesis that primary citizenship and civic competence are determinants in the future of complex metropolitan regions requires an emphasis on science and technology. Both are ruling themes of modern society, whether they provide the artifacts of daily living, attract interest in the policies that govern their creation and distribution, or simply give people a delight in their elegance. Science has indeed become the basis of industrial civilization, but it cannot save that civilization. Human values must come into play and insist that personal and social discipline control the exploitation of nature.

Yet only about twenty percent of the American population, what some call the "attentive minority," concern themselves with matters related to science and technology. The interests of the remainder are limited by lack of understanding, the insularity of technical experts, and the confusions rendered by conflicting interpretations of the same evidence. This creates a major need for adult education as a source of social learning, a need that especially fits the metropolitan university.

A Postscript

This article advances knowledge utilization for greater emphasis among the functions of the university and urges that it be enhanced in the practice of civic competence, broadly defined. Furthermore, the article looks at the future of, first, education and industrial practice, and, second, the restoration of primary citizenship. The first moves easily from where most continuing educators find themselves; the second remains elusive and requires more as well as new forms of financial support and administrative organization.

Such directions inevitably make the continuing education division into something that resembles an educational research and development arm of the university. It identifies new learning needs, services, and related information and convenes partners in both the university and the community to address them. Learning modes are engaged and tested in urban realities. Community-wide social learning, and the knowledge it requires, is actually an intervention in community development and serves the entire university as a unifying strategy. Finally, partnerships with industry, schools, and government prompt both the university and its partners to become more accessible to widening consultation.

Continuing education, moving down this track, must keep its own house in order by remaining adaptable to community needs and university expectations. At the university's center, continuing educators will surely need a core unit, requisite budgets, a designated staff, and advisory elements capable of linking it to home base and the community-at-large. Access to physical facilities will enable the representatives of campus and community to feel at home and work effectively together. Surrounding the core unit and throughout the university will be instruments to marshal, combine, and focus intellectual and other resources in a flexible manner on specific programs and tasks: contracts, commitments, joint appointments, and special institutes. These techniques and supports back up nontraditional projects, which, when proved effective, can join the traditional system.

No one doubts that the university must be independent in its service as a benevolent critic of society. But by its own conduct, the university can serve its community as a beacon of public discourse, hope, and aspiration. Moreover, by seizing the potentials of worldwide communications that are now embodied in the connections of television, data banks, computers, and satellites, the university can enliven and promote discourse on the community's common good, ensuring that the community is informed by the full range of intellectual, artistic, and cultural experience. And given the vision, will, and self-confidence, a single university, together with the great number of other urban institutions and organizations, may lead the city itself into becoming a university in outlook and behavior.

SUGGESTED READINGS

Bellah, Robert N., Richard Madsen, William M. Sullivan, Ann Swidler, and Steven M. Tipton. *The Good Society.* New York: Alfred A. Knopf, 1991.
Bennis, Warren G., William C. McInnes, G. M. Sawyer, and Marvin Wachman. "Urban Involvement: Roles for Higher Education." *Educational Record* (Fall 1974): 223–47.
Berger, Peter L. and Richard J. Neuhaus. *To Empower People: The Role of Mediating Structures in Public Policy.* Washington: American Enterprise Institute, 1977.
Boulding, Kenneth E., and Lawrence Senesh, eds. *The Optimum Utilization of Knowledge.* Boulder: Westview Press, 1983.
Lynton, Ernest A., and Sandra E. Elman. *New Priorities for the University: Meeting Society's Needs for Applied Knowledge and Competent Individuals.* San Francisco: Jossey-Bass, 1987.
Ortega y Gassett, José. *Mission of the University.* Princeton: Princeton University Press, 1944.
Ravetz, Jerome R. "Usable Knowledge, Usable Ignorance: Incomplete Science with Policy Implications." *Knowledge: Creation, Diffusion, Utilization* (September 1987): 87–116.
Yankelovich, Daniel. *Coming to Public Judgment: Making Democracy Work in a Complex World.* Syracuse: Syracuse University Press, 1991.

PART VII

PROFESSIONAL EDUCATION AND THE ARTS

INTRODUCTION

Elinor Brantley Schwartz, recent guest editor of *Metropolitan Universities*, assembled an excellent compilation of articles and essays on professional education. She begins her Overview of the issue with the observation, "A university is a university is a university. Unless, of course, it is a metropolitan university." This important distinction has implications for nearly every aspect of higher education including professional education and the arts.

The three articles selected for this section are but a small sample of the essays on these topics to be found in the journal, *Metropolitan Universities*. Readers with interests in these areas are encouraged to review the editions of the journal devoted specifically to professional education, (Volume 3, Number 3, Winter 1992) and the fine and performing arts (Volume 4, Number 4, Winter 1994).

The article by Ronald R. Sloan and Richard T. Wines examines the criticisms of business schools and argues that the thirty-year dominance of the academic model over the professional model offers a basic explanation for these shortcomings. The authors discuss the role of AACSB, the business schools' accrediting agency, in fostering needed change as well as special opportunities created by this reform environment.

Alexander E. Sidorowicz's article, "The Outreach Role of the Fine and Performing Arts," is an excellent interpretation of the special role of the arts in a metropolitan university. Sidorowicz argues that the fine and performing arts in metropolitan universities can "provide outreach programs that positively influence the image and mission of the university as a cultural partner in the community." He discusses how special events, nondegree programs, and collaborative associations with metropolitan arts agencies simultaneously fulfill the mission of the university and the artistic goals of the community.

In his article "Converting the Barbarian," Jan P. Muczyk addresses the challenging role of metropolitan universities in preparing students for the world of work. This challenge is greater than for traditional colleges and flagship universities in that metropolitan univesities are expected to provide all necessary remediation and still produce educated graduates in the same amount of time. The unique policy implications associated with being a metropolitan university are clearly evident in this candid article.

Professional education and the arts constitute a considerable component of the curricula of metropolitan universities. They also constitute special challenges and provide unique opportunities for faculty, administrations, and the communities they serve. In many respects, these programs have led the way in serving the needs and interests of their communities long before the concept of "metropolitan university" took root.

Management Education Reform: Opportunities for Metropolitan Business Schools

Ronald R. Slone and Richard T. Wines

Management education is in the midst of an exciting renewal period. A remark of Dean Lester Thurow of the Sloan School at the Massachusetts Institute of Technology is frequently quoted: "If our business schools are doing so well, why are our American companies doing so badly?" It forcefully captured the rising tide of discontent during the eighties with American management education. During the last years of the previous decade, business schools began to heed the call for change and the management education reform movement shifted from rhetoric to remediation. It may well be that the new energy and creativity devoted to improving all aspects of business schools will qualify this decade as a time of genuine renaissance in the preparation of future business leaders.

The Criticisms of Management Education

The implications for business schools concerning the numerous management education shortcomings discussed in the popular press may be better understood if the criticisms are classified into three groups:

1. Deficiencies in the adaptation to change,
2. Structural deficiencies, and
3. Philosophical deficiencies.

Failures of business schools' traditional disciplines to keep abreast of the growing complexity of the management task include insufficient emphasis on:

1. The global forces influencing business decision making;
2. The management of information and technology as organizational assets;
3. Non-market trends: political, governmental, legal, ethical, and societal forces, including demographic diversity, that are shaping business opportunities and behavior.

Structurally driven failures are the outgrowth of faculty members' principal allegiance to the agendas of their individual disciplines rather than to management challenges embracing several fields. Failure is also due to the relative isolation of business schools from the broader academic community. They include too little attention to:

1. Problem framing in a truly multidisciplinary context;
2. The Total Quality Management (TQM) imperative;
3. Integration of the baccalaureate business and nonbusiness curricular components to achieve a better educated business school graduate.

Business schools' strong philosophical bias in favor of problems and issues amenable to rigorous quantitative treatment have led to neglect of:

1. An appreciation of the relevance of general education for professional effectiveness, particularly the potential contribution of the humanities as useful ways of knowing and thinking;
2. Visionary and creative thinking skills, the ability to see new possibilities and combinations;
3. An emphasis on problem identification as much as on problem solving;
4. People-oriented action skills and attitudes, including speaking and writing,
5. Delegation, influencing and political effectiveness, conflict management, negotiation, team participation, and leadership.

Many of the management education shortcomings identified in recent discussions cut across the several classifications. For example, a strong case can be made that failures to adapt to change are a result of business schools' inability, structurally, to solve problems that do not fall neatly within the so-called "functional silos" such as accounting, finance, marketing, and production. And the strong philosophical preference for analytically based learning creates barriers to thoughtful integration of the business and non business components of the baccalaureate curriculum, particularly of the humanities. In the final analysis, a growing consensus exists among business school leaders that the management education deficiencies, however classified, reflect a more fundamental problem.

The Paradigm Problem

Although *paradigm* has gained currency as a fashionable buzz word, an understanding of the root cause of the above deficiencies is enhanced by the notion of paradigms. A paradigm has been defined as a set of rules and regulations, written or unwritten, that performs two functions: it establishes or defines boundaries; and it tells one how to behave inside the boundaries in order to be successful. Perhaps nowhere is the paradigm concept better illustrated than in the two contending frameworks governing business school values: 1) *the academic school model* and 2) the *professional school model.*

Excellent descriptions of these models have been provided by the former dean of the business school at the University of California at Berkeley, Earl Cheit. His characterization of the academic business school model includes the following boundaries and behaviors:

1. The school regards the field of business as a science;

2. Its approach is essentially discipline driven, with an emphasis on the theoretical subjects pertaining to business;

3. The goal of instruction is, through rigorous intellectual work, to develop the habits of the mind and analytical competence that will be useful to the solution of problems unknown today;

4. The school trains specialists;

5. Overall, the curriculum gives priority to disciplines and techniques;

6. Advanced graduate instruction is oriented toward research;

7. The Ph.D. program is the "flagship" and the faculty most enjoys working with advanced graduate students;

8. The school values the pursuit of knowledge for its own sake;

9. Faculty are rewarded for publication, especially for creative work that demonstrates theoretical treatment of issues;

10. The faculty is productive, and its published scholarship has academic standing and commands respect among peers.

By contrast, a business school in Cheit's professional model has the following characteristic boundaries and behaviors:

1. The school will give primary emphasis to the functional fields of business and to the application of pertinent techniques;
2. Its approach is essentially practice driven;
3. Because management is considered more art than science, the object of instruction is to develop judgment and encourage students to exercise it in dealing with complex, unstructured problems;
4. The curriculum emphasizes general management responsibility, leadership, and decision making;
5. Business strategy and entrepreneurship are important courses;
6. The school's "flagship" program is the M.B.A.;
7. The school maintains many contacts with the business community and engages in joint projects with companies in research and management development;
8. Published research is an element in faculty advancement, but it is not the most important one;
9. The focus of research is on applied problems of current or evolving concern to managers;
10. Publication is mainly in journals of interest to practitioners, not those with prestige in academic disciplines.

Clearly, the academic school model, both in its established boundary and described behaviors within the boundary, allows scant opportunity for efforts that synthesize business theory and practice. However, Cheit is quick to point out that "In practice, every business school employs aspects of both [models] and, consciously or not, develops its own approach in primarily following one of the two models described here." Nevertheless, there is little argument among most observers of the management education scene that the prevailing paradigm for the past thirty years has been the academic model.

The dominance of the academic model during the past three decades may be traced back to the generally dismal state of management education as documented by the two milestone reports, one by Gordon and Howell commissioned by the Ford Foundation, and the second, by Pierson, for the Carnegie Corporation. Both were issued in 1959. On the basis of surveys of existing business schools, both reports concluded that the curriculum was largely devoid of a sound theoretical foundation, faculty were generally weak in their analytical methodology, and students, by and large, were not comparable in ability to their nonbusiness counterparts. Reacting to these findings, business schools for the next thirty years set about the task of achieving academic respectability.

The next major assessment of business schools, the Porter-McKibbin report commissioned by the business schools' accrediting agency, the American Assembly of Collegiate Schools of Business (AACSB) and issued in 1988, demonstrated that the quest had largely succeeded.

Fortunately for management education, the comparatively simpler challenges and slower pace of change confronting business leaders during the sixties and seventies made it possible for business schools to pursue their inward agenda without incurring external constituency concerns. However, the inward posture became increasingly problematic during the eighties as dissatisfaction with the product of business schools mounted. What had seemed to be a successful academic model was found to lead to many shortcomings because of its isolation from management practice. The emphasis on analysis and rigorous problem solving let the scientific methodology drive problem identification. As a result, the problems chosen were increasingly separated from those faced in actual practice.

It is also difficult to imagine that the seemingly universal complaint about business schools' failure to develop students' skills in people management could have prevailed so long if a strong professional school orientation had been maintained during the last three decades. The same can be said for business schools' tardiness in acknowledging the practitioner-led TQM movement, a concept that could also have stimulated earlier attention to business schools' structural defects. Even the concern for a broadly educated business school graduate had its most forceful advocates in external constituencies among those occupying business leadership positions. Recently AACSB has changed its accreditation standards to move the minimum requirement for non-business subjects from forty percent to at least fifty percent of the baccalaureate curriculum.

This step is part of an emerging reform movement for which two events may have served as the principal wake-up calls. One was the warning in the Porter-McKibbin report about a dangerous complacency in most business schools, not a surprising result in the face of many apparent successes, such as continuing enrollment growth and increasing demand for graduates. The second was a change in the way prominently published rankings of the best business schools were conducted. For example, in 1988 *Business Week* changed the basis of its ranking of business schools from the evaluation by business school deans to a survey of the opinions of recent graduates and recruiters. The results, which could not be easily dismissed as ill-informed, were shocking to some schools that had traditionally been at the top of the deans' rankings, and triggered an almost headlong rush to implement corrective measures. Some of these appear to be influenced by two

predictions made by a number of leaders in management education:
1) the M.B.A. credential will become less important and business
schools will go through the classic shake-out of a mature industry;
2) management education will become more of a collaborative effort
with industry.

The newly emerging management education paradigm represents
a rediscovery of the long-neglected professional model in a number of
important respects. However, the new paradigm also reflects two
defining management education realities, which were not nearly so
apparent in the fifties:

1. The dramatically increasing rate of change and growing complexity that characterize the management task are such that no school
can hope to assemble the resources needed for excellence in all preparation areas—schools must concentrate on what they can do best; and

2. These same dimensions of change and complexity suggest that
no school can predict the best preparation formula for future management success. Prudence lies in diversity of approach and energetic
experimentation.

The Role of AACSB in Breaking the Prevailing Paradigm

During the eighties, AACSB leaders began to realize that accreditation had become a significant part of the problem. Accreditation
standards were essentially static and inwardly oriented. Instead of
being responsive to the mounting challenges confronting business leaders, the standards had become the easy and familiar benchmark of
excellence for too many business schools. This insight led to a *de novo*
reconstruction of the AACSB accreditation standards overwhelmingly
adopted by the AACSB membership in April, 1991. They contain a
provision that reflects the new thinking about the requirements for
business education excellence:

> Development, promotion, retention, and renewal of business
> school faculty should reflect both the mission of the school
> and the demanding competitive and technological challenges
> faced by businesses. To gain understanding of these
> challenges, faculty should interact with people in
> organizations on subjects related to the phenomena about
> which they teach, perform research, and publish. Business
> schools need mechanisms through which faculty observe
> business practices in action so they may learn the

applicability and relevance of the ideas and concepts developed through their intellectual activities. Moreover, this improves the content of instructional development and teaching. Faculty whose primary emphasis is theory development can benefit by efforts to integrate theory with practice. (AACSB, Standard FD 3, p. 12)

From this statement it is clear AACSB has thrown down the gauntlet: it is declaring that *quality* business education and an isolationist posture are fundamentally incompatible. Stated alternatively, a business school mission for mediocrity is one which has the effect of distancing faculty from the practitioner world.

The new accreditation standards also include two overarching expectations that echo the defining realities of management education: 1) the requirement to achieve a rigorously developed mission identity that focuses attention on comparative institutional strengths, and 2) the requirement to institutionalize change and continuous improvement. These expectations are expressed as follows in the new standards document:

The school should articulate its mission as a guide to its view of the future, its planned evolution, and its infrastructure and use of resources. The accreditation evaluation process for a school is linked to its mission. Each school of business is faced with choices as a result of a wide range of opportunities and inevitable resource limitations. The development of a mission requires decisions regarding these alternatives, and the mission embodies these choices. . . . To satisfy the Mission and Objectives Standards, *these choices must be documented.* (Emphasis added) (AACSB, Standard M, p. 8)

Just as managers face rising expectations for their performance and the performance of their organizations, programs in management education also should anticipate rising expectations, even within a given mission. . . . The processes used to strengthen curricula, develop faculty, improve instruction, and enhance intellectual activity determine the direction and rate of improvement. Thus, these processes play an important role in accreditation, along with the necessary review of inputs and assessment of outcomes. (AACSB, Preamble, p. 2.)

The revised AACSB accreditation standards establish a new conception of business schools by calling for an emphasis on diverse missions and continuous improvement and adaptation instead of the traditional approach with its common mission orientation and single threshold of quality.

A Metropolitan Business School Action Agenda for the 1990s

Metropolitan universities have advantages that closely parallel the requirements of the new paradigms for management education and the accreditation of business schools. As a result, these institutions, as a class, may well move into a dominant position by the dawn of the new century. However, this will require leadership that can recognize and exploit these opportunities. The following two sets of action initiatives illustrate the steps to be taken by metropolitan business schools in order to leverage their special advantage of proximity to management practice. Each initiative's key premises are identified along with metropolitan school opportunities.

Action Initiatives to Develop Niche Advantages

Each metropolitan school should:

1. Identify its unique core competencies and educational values-added (the mission niche) upon which a reputation will be built that leads to sustainable competitive advantage.

These distinctive core competencies and educational values-added should be focused and limited. They should vividly demonstrate a deliberate rejection of an "all things to all persons" thinking, which is in conflict with the new management education realities. These core competencies and values-added should be selected with a view towards exploiting metropolitan proximity advantages in so far as possible.

2. Examine the potential of strategic alliances with other schools with similar niches and with other campus units.

Leveraging of core strengths is increasingly important in a constrained resource environment, which includes the resource of time, made even more precious because of the imperative for rapid change. As schools generally move toward more clearly defined niches, it will become easier to identify likely partners that can mutually accelerate each other's learning curve. Certain similarities in core strengths among metropolitan schools serve as an excellent starting point. In addition, many beneficial partnership opportunities exist with other campus units which may have learned how to exploit their metropolitan advantages. Benefits of these campus partnerships may include ways to facilitate students' understanding of the relevance of general, nonbusiness education for professional competence and lifelong learning.

3. Fundamentally reconsider current faculty "portfolio" premises and strategies, with a view to achieving rapid implementation of the new management education paradigm and identified mission niche.

No longer can there be only one path to professorial competence. The pace of change and complex realities of management require multiple searching of professorial talent. Schools must seriously consider as regular faculty—not just lecturers—those who can bring to their assignments records of successful business leadership and a reflective capacity, the ability to acquire the knowledge, skills, and attitudes necessary for effective scholarship. The need for such appointments is particularly great in those areas of reform where traditional faculty are at a comparative disadvantage. Metropolitan business schools are likely to have particularly rich resources of such rare individuals in their vicinities.

4. Fundamentally restructure support and reward systems for traditional faculty so as to place increasing emphasis on "knowledge of the intricacies and challenges of business practice" as a criterion for advancement in rank.

This outward focus requires different skills in the interpretation of findings, but it should not be misunderstood as a call for reduced emphasis on scholarly rigor nor be limited to those with an applied research bent. Even an agenda emphasizing theory development can benefit from a mind informed by managerial realities. Decisions will be required, however, on how far the school's posture should go in implementing this initiative. At the least aggressive end of the continuum is the expectation for meaningful exposure to practitioners and their world. At the other boundary is the expectation that scholarly output must meet the test of acceptance by practitioners as well as academic peers.

The success of this redirection of performance expectations will depend on unprecedented external and internal leadership by academic administrators with respect to both support and rewards. Administrators must develop multiple avenues of clinical exposure that address the differing needs of faculty in various career stages. For example, corporate residencies for junior faculty would likely reflect a more handsome operational improvement orientation, whereas senior faculty may function at a more policy development level. Metropolitan schools' proximity to a broad array of clinical opportunities gives added feasibility to this reorientation. Academic administrators must also be prepared to act as mentors in assisting faculty in building their case for knowledge of the intricacies and challenges of business practice. This help certainly should include assistance in the formulation of annual development plans, which lead to up-front agreement on the activities to be engaged in and the bases for judging results. It is important to overcome the faculty member's reasonable fear that an investment in this departure from conventional wisdom may not count after the fact when it comes to promotion and tenure, and may also impair marketability, at least in the near term. This attitude underscores that academic leaders must artfully utilize all the reward systems at their disposal to overcome deeply entrenched disciplinary/marketplace forces.

5. Achieve growing racial and ethnic diversity in both faculty and student ranks, and incorporate diversity issues within the curriculum.

Such diversity mirrors the emerging reality of the workplace. Students will be increasingly well served for long-term career effectiveness when they have experienced real diversity in their learning and problem-solving environment. The initiative to broaden the profile of business school faculty can facilitate racial and ethnic diversity as well. Metropolitan schools often are advantageously positioned to pursue this goal.

6. Achieve a better mix of traditional- and nontraditional-age students who can assume increasingly meaningful roles as managers of their own learning.

Metropolitan schools frequently are distinguished by their nontraditional student population. Their diverse learning environments can also be attractive to talented full-time traditional-age students drawn from a broader geographic region. Together, both groups can learn from each other, particularly in an experiential oriented learning environment that emphasizes the "self-managed work team" philosophy gaining currency in business.

7. Aggressively seek out foreign exchange students and faculty as a means for further enrichment of the school's diverse environment.

Metropolitan schools should exploit their attractiveness to foreign students in order to create a richer cultural diversity deeply embedded within the learning environment. Students as managers of their own earning will find opportunities for firsthand insights gained from fellow students and faculty from other countries.

8. Pursue learning partnerships with technology and information-driven organizations in the area so as to facilitate systematic understanding of visionary and innovative leadership and of the concept of technology and information as strategic organizational assets.

Learning partnerships are mutually beneficial problem-solving arrangements which reflect the distinctive and complementary insights of both partners. On the school side, such partnerships can enhance teaching, research, and service and include students, faculty, and administrators. Continuous strategic renewal and an embedded entrepreneurial mind-set represent performance expectations in an increasing number of organizations. Students and faculty in metropolitan schools may have the opportunity to gain firsthand exposure to organizations working to implement these paradigms for renewal. Often organizations that have operationalized the notion of technology and information as strategic assets are also excellent learning partners in the development of a student's understanding of the influences that global market and nonmarket forces have on decision making.

9. Develop learning partnerships with area firms that serve as exemplars with respect to clearly articulated organizational values and corporate citizenship behavior.

Metropolitan schools can often observe first hand the achievements of organizations that function within a framework of enlightened corporate citizenship, clearly articulated values, and penetrated understanding of nonmarketplace forces. These behaviors can provide tangible insight into the very conceptual foundations and philosophy of the business enterprise. Schools that also create opportunities for students to become involved in community betterment projects demonstrate the adage that preferred behaviors must be modeled, not taught.

10. Explore learning partnerships with area organizations possessing experience in the development and assessment of action skills.

Such organizations often are considerably more advanced than business schools in techniques for identifying and developing individuals with creativity and vision and with skills in communication, delegation, influence, conflict management, team work, and leadership. Because these qualities are increasingly important to employers, such partnerships may have important payoffs for student placement.

11. More fully utilize noncredit management development programs as a way of testing clinically based curricular and pedagogic change in degree programs.

The much higher expectation for applications to management practice held by those enrolled in noncredit continuing education encourage development of more clinically based teaching materials. Such materials can accelerate implementation of a synthesis of academic and practitioner insights within degree programs. Accordingly, when these noncredit offerings emphasize a rigorous clinical orientation, they provide opportunities for the reorientation of more senior faculty to the realities of the practitioner's world. Metropolitan schools often have a competitive edge with regard to both breadth and depth of continuing education markets. This provides many opportunities for customer partnerships in the development of practice-focused learning materials. Successful implementation of such initiatives presupposes the existence of systems that facilitate close integration of the noncredit service activity with the school's degree programs and research activities.

Initiatives to Institutionalize Change

Each metropolitan school should:

1. Develop an overall management plan that ensures all systems and subsystems are a) mutually consistent and b) supportive of the school's distinctive mission identity.

For example, the new faculty "portfolio" thinking should be directed by the chosen mission niche and, in turn, should be supported by appropriate strategies for faculty recruitment, orientation, and development. Metropolitan schools have proximity to business organizations—especially those that have implemented a TQM philosophy—that are more accustomed to thinking operationally in a systems-subsystems context.

2. Institutionalize continuing conversation among faculty, administrators, and key stakeholder groups, especially students, graduates, and employers, concerning all aspects of program and process.

External stakeholder groups, when drawn from the metropolitan vicinity, can, as a practical matter, become full partners in a continuing dialogue about program *and* process improvements. Often such partner organizations have implemented TQM systems that achieve a profound customer focus and involvement in many operational aspects. An important outcome of this thinking is the development of broad ownership in the school's "product." This result also helps overcome the constrained resource environment through greater success in raising contributions of both time and dollars.

3. Emulate business models for achieving "short cycle times."

The typically slow response of business schools to changing external circumstances—some would call it glacial—will become increasingly problematic for management education. Metropolitan schools exist within a venue of firms that live or die by short cycle time performance. Key to response in the academic setting is the rethinking of prevailing school organizational structures. Currently, these are increasingly out of phase with business work patterns that emphasize boundary spanning and parallel processing to achieve rapid new product development. Responsive businesses provide learning partnership opportunities for contributing to a better understanding of cross-functional integration and problem solving.

    4. Measure results systematically.

    Outcomes assessment—qualitative as well as quantitative—of all programs and processes must become a standard operating procedure if change and continuing improvement are to be institutionalized. Such information stimulates "what if" thinking, which encourages further change. Metropolitan schools have access to organizations that are far ahead of academe in functioning on the basis of the adage "In God we trust, all others must bring information."

NOTE: The authors wish to acknowledge the insights of William R. Dill, former president of Babson College, as contained in his working paper entitled: "Management Education: Is Success Breeding Failure?"

SUGGESTED READINGS

American Assembly of Collegiate Schools of Business. *Final Report: The AACSB Accreditation Project.* St. Louis: AACSB, 1991.

Barker, Joel A. *Future Edge: Discovering the New Rules of Success.* New York: Wm. Morrow and Company, Inc., 1992.

Cheit, Earl F. "Business Schools and Their Critics." *California Management Review,* 27/3 (Spring 1985).

The Commission on Admission to Graduate Management Education. "Leadership for a Changing World: The Future Role of Graduate Management Education (condensed version report)." *Selections: The Magazine of the Graduate Management Admission Council* (Spring 1990).

Gordon, R. A., and J. E. Howell. *Higher Education for Business.* New York: Columbia University Press, 1959.

Pierson, F. C. *The Education of American Businessmen.* New York: McGraw-Hill Book Company, 1959.

Porter, Lyman W., and Lawrence E. McKibbin. *Management Education and Development: Drift or Thrust into the 21st Century?* New York: McGraw-Hill Book Company, 1988.

Prahalad, C. K., and Gary Hamel. "The Core Competence of the Corporation." *Harvard Business Review* (May–June 1990).

THE OUTREACH ROLE OF THE FINE AND PERFORMING ARTS

Alexander E. Sidorowicz

The role of departments of fine and performing arts in higher education in the United States is a multi-faceted one, going well beyond the traditional academic services of offering courses for both major programs and the general education curriculum. More than other academic departments on campus, the fine and performing arts, by the nature of their disciplines, can be involved in a large variety of publicly viewed and interactive activities which spring from the curricular offerings.

Production and Presentation

These activities encompass performing arts productions and visual arts exhibitions presented to the campus community and the public-at-large. They can consist of a whole range of events including music and dance performances, theatre and opera productions, visual art exhibitions, and video and film screenings.

A department can act both as producer and presenter in offering these experiences. In the former capacity, the faculty, staff, and students are usually the producers or creators of the performance or exhibition, which is then presented as part of the university's contribution to the cultural events of the region. As presenter, the department or certain agencies in the university contract with off-campus performing or visual artists to appear as part of the university's events.

Both types of these events can be accompanied by support activities such as pre- and post-performance lectures, discussions, workshops, and demonstrations by the performers, choreographers, composers, playwrights, or filmmakers.

A number of promotional and support services need to be coordinated in conjunction with the presentation of events, not the least of which is the management of an effective public information service. This includes regular contact with print media for the placement of calendar of events information, special feature articles and photographs, as well as the preparation of video and audio public service announcements and their distribution to radio and TV stations for special events. Such publicity is crucial to attract an appropriate audience.

It is also necessary to handle those who will be attending arts events in a professional manner, providing them with box office services and ushering service and, perhaps most difficult of all for urban universities, with parking facilities that are convenient to performance, screening, and exhibition spaces.

Non-Degree Educational Programs

In addition to presenting a wide variety of cultural events, departments in the fine and performing arts can also regularly sponsor and sustain non-degree arts education programs for persons of all ages. These can run the gamut of one-time or periodic workshops to ongoing, weekly, sequential instruction based on a multi-year program of study geared to developing specified competency levels. The programs are usually derived from the type of instruction provided for the degree program, are operated on a fee basis outside the typical registration process of the university, employ regular faculty and adjuncts as instructional staff for off-load compensation, and often involve students as instructors or as interns, especially those in arts education and graduate programs.

Included in such programs can be: music preparatory schools that offer individual and group applied instruction in all performance media, ongoing performance ensembles offering venues for performance by its applied students, workshops and master classes for advanced performance students, and performance experiences for older persons; dance programs for children from as young as four through sixteen or seventeen; and visual art programs for people of all ages.

In all of these areas, special one-time, or periodic workshops can be offered, again on a fee basis, to those interested in special topics or skills. This can range from attending two or three lectures detailing information about a certain art exhibit or an upcoming performance, to a one-time presentation on a specific, sometimes corollary topic, such as how to identify and select the best stereo components for home listening.

Collaborations

As a third category of outreach, departments of fine and performing arts in metropolitan areas can form collaborative associations with urban arts agencies. These collaborations can be event-specific ventures, as when a university participates with metropolitan art institutions in sponsoring and exhibiting a variety of exhibits. They can be ongoing relationships, where staff, as performers and faculty in their respective organizations, are shared and jointly appointed. They can be activities which enrich curricular instruction when dance, music, or theater departments regularly work with metropolitan booking agents to secure a master class for their students by touring performers who are performing off-campus.

The University as Patron of the Arts

The scope and mission of such programs within metropolitan universities, especially those located in large urban areas, usually include a great variety of these noted activities. In part, this results from the fact that with few exceptions, our main artistic centers are connected with large population centers. The performers and artists in universities need their audiences, their publics, those who on a regular basis seek live performance and interaction with the arts, either as a spectator or as a student. Additionally, a number of institutions of higher education whose growth and development have been attached to the growth of such population centers, have naturally responded to the cultural growth and needs of this population, and have welcomed the arts and their practitioners as part of both curricular and co-curricular educational offerings.

In fact, taken as a single entity, higher education in the United States is the most supportive patron of the arts and arts education. According to the 1991–92 Higher Education Arts Data Service (HEADS) summary of art, dance, music, and theatre programs, almost $1.6 billion was spent in that year by higher education on supporting the arts and arts education.

In comparison, foundation giving and federal funds for the arts are much less. According to the Foundation Center's 1993 edition of "Foundation Giving," in 1991, private, corporate, and community foundations gave over $680 million to organizations categorized by the Foundation Center as "arts and culture." And in 1991, the National Endowment of the Arts had an annual budget of about $175 million.

Although it can be argued that higher education's support is directed at providing the instruction needed for the degree programs, the resultant product of the curriculum and the scholarly and creative activity of the faculty and staff—many of whom are practicing artists— and students, provide all of the events and activities noted above. In the United States, the university has become for these artists, musicians, dancers, actors, playwrights, and composers the patron that the church was to the arts in centuries past.

The Towson State University Program

The College of Fine Arts and Communication (COFAC), with approximately 2,000 students, is one of six colleges at Towson State University (TSU), which has a total of about 15,000 students. TSU, founded in 1866 with a state normal school heritage, is located just north of the Baltimore City line, in a metropolitan area of 2.3 million people. TSU's mission heavily emphasizes teacher training and its role as a center for the fine and performing arts in the State of Maryland. This role, as a producer and presenter of arts, grew throughout the twentieth century as an outcome of co-curricular and extramural activities supporting the teacher training mission. As the university grew in conjunction with the metropolitan area, these activities developed into curricular offerings and degree programs. In the present day, COFAC has five departments, with a seven million dollar budget, offering degrees in the visual arts, dance, music, speech and mass communication, and theatre.

COFAC has a total of eight performance, exhibition, and screening areas and in an average year sponsors close to 400 events of both the production and presentation type, attracting 50,000 people to these spaces. In addition, COFAC, through its academic departments, sponsors and administers a long-established Music Preparatory School with close to 200 students, a newly formed Community Art Center which offers visual arts experiences and classes for seventy pre- and post-college age students, and a very successful Children's Dance Division, which enrolls over 1,500 students in three semester-long sessions throughout the year.

COFAC maintains two ongoing collaborations with professional arts presenters, one in theater and one in dance. The overall goal of these two is the enrichment of degree programs through the interaction of students and faculty with professional performing artists brought into the Baltimore area by these presenters.

The remainder of this paper will describe specific outreach activities in each of the three categories mentioned earlier: the metropolitan university as arts producer and presenter; as provider of non-degree arts instruction; and as collaborator with metropolitan arts agencies.

The focus will be on important characteristics of the functions that need to be considered in developing or modifying such activities. Obviously, situations differ from institution to institution depending on mission breadth of programs, availability of resources, geographical placement, etc. However, the issues mentioned below are likely to require consideration in most situations.

The University as Arts Producer and Presenter

The most important aspect of this function is coordination: coordination in producing events; coordination in presenting events; and coordination in promoting events. No institution or department would want a large number of people (great promotion) coming to see a poorly produced play, or a badly prepared and lighted exhibit (bad production). A great play or critically acclaimed exhibit (good production) can be spoiled if there is no space to park, or if patrons have to stand in line for thirty minutes to buy a ticket (bad presentation). Conversely, it would be unfortunate if only a few people arrived (bad promotion) to hear an excellent rendition of Beethoven by the university orchestra (good production), or worse yet, to see a nationally noted dance company to whom the institution just paid $8,000 to perform in its 1,000-seat auditorium at ten dollars a ticket, to be handled by the thirty student workers hired as box office and house staff (good presentation).

In addition to the caliber and merit of the arts product, support resources and their coordination are the answer to being successful as producer or presenter. Even with only a few events a semester, resources must be budgeted to support them to avoid the scenarios listed above. This is so critical, that given a typical arts production/presentation/promotion budget at a metropolitan university, one should plan to allocate normally at least twenty-five to thirty percent, and in some instances close to fifty percent, in support. To a great extent, the percentage depends on how difficult it is to promote such events, and how important that promotion and the resultant audience is.

In planning and coordinating promotion of arts events, priority should be given to their relevance in attracting an outside audience and to the artistic merit which the event represents. This must be done at the departmental level in coordination with a university public relations agent. Setting priorities is extremely important both from the point of view of the institutional producers/presenters, taking into consideration how they rank the importance of their events; and from that of the broadcast and print media, who may have their own criteria for ranking arts events.

Many public events result from the students' completion of degree requirements: student music recitals, BFA exhibits, studio theater productions, student film and video screenings, and dance class showings. These events need their audiences and appropriate promotion, but they naturally rank low in priority of promotion efforts of the department, college, or university. Many student producers of arts events take on their own promotional activities in attracting fellow students, faculty, family, and friends. Also helpful for these events are department listings and calendars of events that are distributed and posted on campus.

Departments naturally have events for which they will desire a wider distribution of promotional material. This would include performances in the main stage theater produced, directed, and acted by students and faculty; student dance companies, directed and choreographed by faculty; year-end or semester-end student art exhibits or film/video screenings juried by faculty with awards being given and mentioned; performances by the university orchestra, band, chorale, or recitals by the student winners of a specific department-sponsored competition. These events are not only targeted at the campus community but at the larger metropolitan area. With the exception of some special events of this type, such as the chorale and the orchestra combining under the direction of a guest conductor with guest soloists performing a special composition, normal promotion would entail calendar listings in local and regional print media and inclusion on special semesterly or calendar listings mailed out by the department and/or college.

The university can use faculty performances and exhibitions to showcase the artistic caliber and quality of its faculty and its programs. To these events, a wider public is invited, promotionally taking into consideration the outlets mentioned above along with special print media articles, photos, public service announcements, or special radio interviews on arts-affiliated stations. As described in an article by Joseph Misiewicz (see *Metropolitan Universities*, Winter 1994, Vol. 4, No. 4, pp. 67–74), such promotion can be furthered by collaboration with academic departments of media and communication. Even higher promotion priority might be given to performances by artists-in-residence.

The role of the university as a presenter in a metropolitan area is directly related to the number of non-university agencies who already provide this service. For example, if the university enters into direct competition with the performing artists series of the city chamber music society, little will be gained either in ticket sales or good will. On the other hand, if no such presenter already exists, this can be a professional contribution that the university can make to the city. At the same time, it would bring nationally respected performing artists to the campus to work with faculty and students. In these cases, where because of the fees presenters pay to performers ticket sales are very important, top priority must be given in terms of promotion and scheduling. In terms of promotion, this requires all that mentioned above with a good amount of purchasing paid advertising in local media.

In larger metropolitan areas, working with presenting agencies in the city may be a preferable option to taking on all of the responsibilities of being a presenter. One of the best results of this can be that artists who come into the city regularly visit the university to do master classes and workshops with students. This usually will require a fee payment, but at a much reduced level than if the university were to be the sole sponsor of the artist. When arranging these master classes, the department should work with the arts presenters in the city to contact the artist's agent. Not only will the educational mission be enhanced, the cooperation with arts agencies will be a positive link to the city's cultural scene.

An expected pitfall in all of this is that no matter how judicious a department or public relations officer may be about prioritizing promotional activities for events, there will be those who feel that their event merits the highest promotional profile. This usually results in a number of complaints being lodged with university administration by those who feel slighted. It is extremely important that chairpersons and deans understand and be cognizant of the public relations and promotional efforts going on to support the events so that when these complaints arrive, they can respond to them in an informed manner. What must not happen is that individuals be allowed to refocus the activities of the public relations officer by pressuring that person into changing promotional priorities. Therefore this officer, who in large institutions may report directly to the dean of the college, must receive the support and protection of that office. To do otherwise would encourage all involved in the events to seek changes in priority, for after all, everyone wants a large audience. But with a large number of events, a system of prioritization must be in place.

This is of great importance as well from the point of view of the media responding, or trying to respond, to the public relations activities of the arts units on campus. If there is no organization to the presentation of materials to the media, if there is no prioritization of events, if there is no coordination between the departments in offering their events to the public, there will likely be no space for promotion given by the media. Most of the promotional strategies that have been mentioned so far depend upon the public service attitude and mission of the print and broadcast media that are contacted. They are not going to spend their time organizing and prioritizing materials sent to them. The institution may jeopardize the response it might get to the point that the media will simply ignore what the institution sends out or worse, emphasize the wrong events and overlook the events that are deemed a priority.

For the same reason, the failure to coordinate all promotional releases through a single public relations officer or office can be very harmful. If print and broadcast media receive materials from various sources at the university, their response is likely to be one of ignoring what they receive or giving misguided coverage.

The deans or chairpersons must judge the efficiency and effectiveness of their public relations officers while protecting them from internal pressures. The success of the promotional effort can in many cases be measured by the overall image held by the public of the fine and performing arts, one that is largely shaped over a number of years by print and broadcast media coverage. A means of assessing this image is periodically to put together press release materials, copies of public service announcements, along with annotations on the use of such announcements and clippings of articles and photos in print media. The circulation of these collections can act as evidence to all constituents of the degree of success of the promotion of events. In addition the simple and regular counting of those who attend events provides very important data.

A final but important factor in the presentation and production of events is the box office and other front-of-house (FOH) staff. When the public is invited to the campus the presenters of the event must be ready and able to handle it in an efficient, effective, and courteous manner. This must occur if people are to return to hear and see events in the future. A person who comes once, struggles to find a place to park, roams around a building to find where the event is being held, and spends thirty minutes in line to buy a ticket, will probably not do that a second time, and, worse, will never recommend others attend campus events. An Academy-Award-Winning actor may be giving a performance on campus, but if the critic had to go through the gauntlet described above, at least half the review will be dedicated to complaining about it. Most critics who review campus events are judicious about their criticisms of the performers or artists, but are merciless with their negative comments if the event was not supported correctly.

Proper support for a large offering of public events requires a full-time fine arts facilities manager, with a full or part-time assistant and a large cadre of students trained as box office personnel, ushers, and house managers. Appropriating an adequate portion of production budgets to the support and presentation of the artists is important to the success of the overall event. In addition, many institutions take the opportunity to run internships in arts management and structure degree emphases or even degree programs centered around these support activities.

Central administration cannot expect that department chairs will take responsibility for all of these functions, or use students exclusively to handle them. Ideally, in the program described for COFAC, there should be a manager for each of the departments, whose sole responsibility is the scheduling of events, the directing of promotional materials to a separate public relations officer, and the organizing, training, and assigning of students as ushers, house managers, gallery guards, etc. In support of these would be the fine arts facilities manager as mentioned above, who, with an assistant, would be responsible for appearance of the public areas, all ticket sales, in general the control and direction of those attending by use of FOH staff, access to the facility, security, and parking.

The simultaneous scheduling of two events by different departments can have a catastrophic result on both, not only by competing with each other for media coverage and audiences, but also if parking is in short supply or if limited public areas and box offices are shared in handling those attending. The facilities manager should be able to exercise control of scheduling of all events, act as a coordinator in so doing, and be a liaison to campus police, housekeeping, food services (for receptions), and any other services needed for special events.

By the very nature of campus events with a large resident population, most box office purchases are not reserved, but are bought by "walk-ups," those who buy their ticket just prior to attending the event. It is necessary in these instances to have readily expandable box office services, perhaps starting with one or two ticket selling outlets thirty minutes prior to the performance, and expanding to four or five outlets fifteen to ten minutes before.

Unless well-endowed with extra parking space or with easy access to public mass transportation, fine arts facilities in metropolitan universities must rely on normal commuter space. This directly affects the scheduling of events, since putting an event at the same time a large number of evening classes are scheduled will certainly result in over-filled parking lots. One solution is to run shuttles to satellite parking spaces for arts patrons. Another is to limit commuter parking spaces on performance nights with prior notice and instructions on where else to park, reserving the space for arts patrons, and requiring a small parking fee for this service. A third is to schedule most events on Friday evenings and weekends, avoiding the conflict with classes.

All of this may seem far removed from the academic mission of the university and college. I submit that it is not and that this aspect of outreach is a natural and desirable outcome of fine and performing arts programs in metropolitan universities.

In addition, these events and activities, with all of the proper support noted above, can greatly enhance the cultural image of the university, and define an important role for it in the realm of the fine and performing arts of the metropolitan area. Whereas many land-grant and flagship research institutions use their athletics programs to gain a reputation in the media, metropolitan institutions with fine and performing arts programs can use this medium to build a prestigious image within the urban areas that surround them. For example, the amount of press clippings from Baltimore-area papers about the arts at TSU far outweighs the coverage given the university for any other area, including sports. In many instances, they can become recognized as an important contributor to the arts and culture in the area, and at the same time attract those who support the arts as an enrichment of the entire metropolitan area. But this will not be possible unless it is accompanied by all of the support mentioned above, no matter how fine the artistic product may be.

Non-Degree Educational Programs: The Community Arts Schools

The growth of community arts schools, either sponsored by and through university programs or private agencies, is a direct result of a need, perceived by concerned parents, for the cultural education of their children. These schools existed as a primary provider of such instruction prior to the wholesale inclusion of music and art education into the curriculum of both secondary and elementary school systems. School-based music and art blossomed in the 1950s and provided experiences in these fields for all children, instead, as with the community schools, for those who could afford it. The programs flourished through the sixties and into the seventies. Since then, curriculum changes and budget cutbacks have eliminated many longstanding and very productive art and music programs from the schools. In some instances, for example, public school systems "farmed-out" musical instruction, providing facilities to instructors who received their fees directly from students wanting to continue with music lessons.

The erosion of public school arts programs again created a market for those who can provide quality instruction in the fine and perform-ing arts. If institutions of higher education contemplate entering into this market they must be very clear about their objectives in doing so.

There are several misperceptions about such programs, the main one being that programs for pre-college age students will automatically provide students for the college degree programs. In a conference session on such programs in music, held by the National Association of Schools of Music (NASM) in a recent annual meeting, all of the presenting participants who had long-standing programs agreed unanimously that matriculation of students from the preparatory programs into the degree programs is minimal.

A second major misperception is that such programs can be managed by the staff of the arts unit in the university. Experience indicates the need to hire both administrative and instructional staff specifically for the non-degree programs, and not count on the good will or extra work provided by university staff. The programs must be able to pay for the administrative and instructional staff they use: to do otherwise will automatically damage the degree programs and jeopardize the success of the non-degree effort.

However, this flow of cash cannot become a substitute for university funding of programs. If this happens, the proverbial tail will begin wagging the dog as more and more emphasis is placed on the financial success of the non-degree programs, rather than the initially described goal and mission of these programs: to provide quality arts instruction in an outreach capacity to the metropolitan area.

Adults who are seeking to learn about the arts they may never have experienced, or who may want to pursue a life-enriching activity by participating in dance, music making, or creating art, constitute a new market that is being tapped by these programs. Both the Children's Dance Department (through an adult division) and the Community Art Center (which almost immediately after it began changed its name from the Youth Art Center) are now offering courses for adults of all ages.

As all of these non-degree programs grow, there are discussions and considerations in the profession of developing arts education degree programs with a main emphasis on training individuals who will work in arts education outside the realm of the elementary and secondary schools. At this time many find themselves involved in this capacity as a result of circumstance rather than planning, and without adequate preparation. As curricula in the public schools change, as more and more parents seek arts instruction for their children in well-qualified and accredited community arts schools, and as the cadre of prospective older students grows larger and larger, the focus in preparing those who will be their teachers must necessarily change. It will not be surprising to see combinations of curriculum that will prepare arts educators and arts entrepreneurs as well.

Examples of Collaborative Associations

As Philip Arnoult and Carol Balsh state in their article, "A Collaboration: The Artist's View" (*Metropolitan Universities* 4 (Winter 1994: 57–66), with the declining economic situation, it became clear in the 1980s that associations between arts agencies in metropolitan areas and educational institutions became a matter of ensuring the existence of many non-profit arts organizations. This is evidenced in the 1989–90 annual report of the Foundation for the Extension and Development of American Professional Theater (FEDAPT) entitled, "The WorkPapers: A Special Report—The Quiet Crisis in the Arts." The report on the declining health of American theater is chilling, and the conclusion of seeking collaboration with educational institutions is obvious.

I have been associated with educational institutions in small, medium, and large population centers, and have worked with the arts programs of those institutions to establish associations and collaborations with non-profit producers and presenters in the cities. Following is a brief description of some of these programs.

In Peoria, Illinois, a metropolitan area of about 350,000, Bradley University established official associations with the Peoria Symphony Orchestra and the Peoria Opera Company. With the symphony, the university's music department co-hired the concertmaster as performer and teacher, and both sponsored, in conjunction with the public school system, a string quartet of which he was a member. With the opera company, the university co-sponsored a performance in which qualified students in the program were able to perform with and learn from nationally ranked performers hired by the opera company.

In San Antonio, Texas, a metropolitan area of 1.3 million, the Art and Music Divisions of the University of Texas at San Antonio (UTSA) participated with metropolitan arts agencies in several projects. One, initiated by the university, was centered on the exhibition of Mayan artifacts, involved the governments of Guatemala and the United States, and was exhibited by the National Geographic Society in its Explorers' Hall Museum, the Denver Museum of Natural History, and the Los Angeles County Museum. Along with the San Antonio segment of the tour, UTSA staff put together a consortium of twelve metropolitan arts agencies and the culture and arts department of the city to cooperate in a month-long celebration and exposition of Guatemalan arts and crafts. This was recognized by a city proclamation and received an award by the San Antonio chapter of the Business Committee for the Arts.

In Baltimore, besides the formal association with Theatre Project, the TSU Dance Department and the College of Fine Arts and Communication have a somewhat similar agreement with the non-profit avant-garde dance presenter, Dance on the Edge. Additionally, this past summer, COFAC was asked to work with the Baltimore Development Corporation, an agency of the Baltimore Mayor's Office, in establishing a dance, theatre, and media center in downtown Baltimore as part of the city's bid to revitalize a part of its arts corridor. And recently, COFAC's art department was approached by a nationally recognized ceramics museum to begin to consider how both can work together.

Working with the Community

The outreach projects mentioned here provide just a few examples of how universities, especially those in metropolitan areas, can act as patrons and supporters of the arts in a city and state. Besides having a significant artistic influence, the universities can also help bolster the economic impact of the non-profit arts. In 1988, the State of Maryland, with a population of 4.7 million, had over 650 non-profit arts organizations which attracted over six million visitors, employed 12,000, and contributed over $350 million to the state's economy.

Following a planning conference in October 1993 at the University of New Mexico in Albuquerque entitled "Arts for Universities and Communities: Daring To Do It Together," twenty teams selected from nineteen states planned a national conference held in June, 1994 on the topic of collaborative associations and partnering. Each team was composed of a university representative involved and a representative of the arts agency or public school with whom the collaboration exists. This was the first such national effort, and the first national forum at which the whole issue of collaborative associations was discussed.

I would like to close this article with three observations that I made at the planning conference in Albuquerque.

In the first place, the community members of the conference eventually became frustrated with the academics' urge to abstract issues and their attempt to build models rather than talk about specific partnering examples. The academics were participating in the typical model of shared governance and consultative leadership that is the essence of university life. However, after one session, some community representatives expressed their concern with the process. One of them asked me if that was the way all university administrators talked. I pointed out that this was the way all meetings in a university operated, whether it involved faculty, staff, or administration. There was a look of disbelief.

It drove home, once more, that when we seek to collaborate with agencies outside the university, we must change our method, our mode of operation, and in some instances, the way we make decisions. This is not to say that studied analysis and the construction of theoretical models is improper, but they do have their limits. The community people in the conference wanted to share their ideas directly, not in some distilled, abstract way. They wanted to decide on concrete objectives and actions and move decisively, fully agreeing to take any risks.

Secondly, it is, unfortunately, extremely easy for universities, especially in these days of widespread criticism, to be perceived as being patronizing without even realizing it. One community member in the conference noted that he felt the very term "outreach" was condescending when used by universities, that it implied what universities had to give was inherently better than what could be gotten without them. To avoid this, universities must enter into collaborative associations understanding that the goals for the association must be equally beneficial for both. The community agency must be a full partner in the association and must feel that their contribution is as valid as the university's.

Finally, a community member of the conference made the observation that most of the collaborative efforts of universities were led and organized by administrative staff. And that at times, when faculty were involved, the activities were skewed to focus the result of the activities to benefit the promotion and tenure requirements in the area of service. Faculty needed to be able to reconcile these activities with the manner in which they would be evaluated by the promotion and tenure process: would such activities fit into the service category or into the research area? Could they be listed in a tenure file or a promotion request? Community members of the conference saw this as self-serving, rather than being truly invested in the collaborative association.

Of the twenty university members attending the planning conference, fifteen held some administrative appointment. This fact and my own experiences as noted above, convince me that most collaborative efforts between the fine and performing arts areas of universities and urban arts agencies do originate within the administrative area. Although this may seem to be a natural outcome of faculty, so involved with their own teaching and creative work, having little time to do so, it also highlights the fact that the present system of promotion and tenure evaluation puts little emphasis and gives little reward for service in forming collaborative associations. Until this changes, faculty initiative will most likely not increase.

This makes it very important to bring faculty into the issues and discussions surrounding collaborative efforts early on in the process, if only to obtain consent. If this is not the case, faculty will feel that the resources that are spent and even the time itself is being taken away from support of their goals and directed elsewhere. And in an era of diminishing fiscal resources, this can create damaging misperceptions.

Summary

The outreach capability of the fine and performing arts in metropolitan universities is almost endless, and is defined by the overall university mission and time and resources that can be channeled into such efforts.

The arts can be an extremely effective and positive image builder for the metropolitan university, and can attract the support and largess of benefactors for the entire university as well as the arts programs themselves.

Universities, especially those located in urban areas, can themselves fulfill the important role of patron of the arts: a role that contributes to the cultural fabric and creative capacity of metropolitan areas positively redounding on its image and contributing to its economic welfare both directly, and in making the city an attractive and artistically vibrant place to live and work.

NOTE: I would like to thank Cathy Burroughs and Randall Rutherford, both on the staff of the College of Fine Arts and Communication at Towson State University, for their advice in formulating segments of this article.

SUGGESTED READINGS

McDaniel, Nello and George Thom. "The WorkPapers: A Special Report—The Quiet Crisis in the Arts." New York, Foundation for the Extension and Development of American Professional Theater, 1989/1990. Annual Report, 1991.

Converting the Barbarian:
The Role of a Metropolitan University

Jan P. Muczyk

As our society encounters what appear to be intractable problems, many of them concentrated in metropolitan areas, certain politicians, civic leaders, and members of the media have begun to look to the metropolitan university for solutions. They look to the university out of frustration instead of demanding that institutions that currently have the responsibility for solving these problems do a better job.

Unfortunately, those well-intended individuals lose sight of the weaknesses and the distinctive competencies of a university, including the metropolitan university. American universities all along have been uniquely designed to convert the barbarian, and more recently have been given the mandate of preparing students for the world of work beyond the priesthood, law, and medicine. Research produced in universities can certainly lend insights into solutions of contemporary problems, and some academics can assist implementation of solutions through consultancy. However, in the main, universities are simply ill-equipped to execute the solutions.

The Greeks called those who did not speak Greek "barbarians" because the languages of the foreigners sounded to them like "barbar." Or so the story goes. As the Romans ascended into dominance, they too referred to anyone who was neither Greek nor Roman as a barbarian. Subsequently, the word was associated with anyone not imbued with what we know as the classics—the study of Greece and Rome. Peoples were called barbarians even when it was indisputable that they had mastered many crafts; acquired the rudiments of science; and possessed effective forms of governance, a tradition of music and art, and, in many cases, a written language.

Of course there aren't that many classicists today, and most of us nonclassicists would object to being called barbarians. Classicists were displaced in large numbers by persons with a "liberal arts" education, which continued the emphasis on matters Roman and Greek to be sure, but added the study of history and literature of other cultures, and the fine arts. As stated in the famous Yale Report of 1823, the traditional defense of a classical education—that it provided "the discipline and the furniture of the mind"—was quickly adopted by "liberally" educated persons.

As early as the 1820s, a movement was being born that would attempt to connect the study inside a university with what was taking place in the world outside by supplementing the liberal arts course of study with modern languages, mathematics, and the sciences. This movement was provided the needed energy by the likes of Thomas Henry Huxley. Some would refer to this approach to higher education as the "utilitarian paradigm," but I prefer to consider the expanded curriculum as an updated definition of a liberal education for reasons that follow.

Words constantly evolve, and "barbarian" is no exception. Thus, the word barbarian must be used in a manner that will not insult the majority of educated people who are nonclassicists, and who possess an education at variance with the severe formula of the dyed-in-the-wool liberal arts purists. In order to accomplish our objective, let us briefly look at a few erstwhile but stellar scholars, for their lives may provide us with examples of the essence of a liberal education.

Nicolaus Copernicus entered the Jagiellonian University (also known as the University of Cracow), then famous for its mathematics, philosophy, and astronomy curriculum, where he concentrated on astronomy. He studied the liberal arts at Bologna, medicine at Padua, and law at the University of Ferrara, from which he emerged with the doctorate in canon law. He was elected a canon of the church and diligently executed the duties associated with that office. He also practiced medicine and authored a treatise on monetary reform.

Thomas Jefferson was a statesman, author, architect, inventor, naturalist, and linguist. Moreover, he studied law and wrote on the topic of monetary reform. Vilfredo Pareto was an economist, sociologist, mathematician, engineer, and philosopher. Blaise Pascal was a philosopher, mathematician, physicist, and theologian. These individuals declared as their specialty the study of what was important at the time.

But once a critical mass of curious investigators embarked on the endless road to new intellectual discoveries, the body of knowledge started exploding at an exponential rate. It has been estimated that approximately sevemty percent of all scientists who have ever lived are alive today and publishing furiously. This geometric expansion of the knowledge storehouse has rapidly advanced the extinction of the *Renaissance man* to be replaced just as quickly by the age of *specialized man*.

Having so much more to learn is not the only obstacle to becoming a latter-day Renaissance person. Since the passage of the Morrill Act in 1862, the practice of offering in universities technical and vocational subjects that previously had been taught in other institutions has become so firmly ingrained that the social class dichotomy of "educating the minds" of the elite while "training the hands" of the masses has lost its meaning. Today, for better or for worse, colleges and universities are viewed, especially by first-generation college students and their parents, as instruments for preparing students for the world of work. But producing competent specialists, technicians, and professionals is insufficient.

Clearly, Copernicus, Jefferson, Pareto, and Pascal were not only liberally educated men, they were among the most gifted of their age, and no course of study alone creates genius of that order. However, we can strive to attain what they aspired to, to master what was important in their time. Thus, the definition of a nonbarbarian or a liberally educated person hinges on acquiring at least a basic understanding of what is important in our time. To define liberal education differently would imply that the significant eternal verities were discovered hundreds of years ago, and what has been developed more recently is immaterial. That is hardly a defensible position. The specific contents of a liberal education evolve over time, but always should concern themselves with what is important at the time.

In regard to this objective, the results of a recent nationwide Gallup Poll are most disconcerting. Twenty-five percent of the 696 surveyed college seniors did not know that Columbus landed in the New World before 1500. Only fifty-eight percent of the college seniors knew that the Civil War was fought between 1850 and 1900, and twenty-three percent believed that Karl Marx's phrase "from each according to his ability, to each according to his need" appears in the U.S. Constitution. Sixty percent could not recognize the definition of Reconstruction as the period that followed the Civil War. Fifty-eight percent could not identify Plato as the author of *The Republic*. Fifty-four percent did not know that the Federalist Papers were written to promote ratification of the U.S. Constitution. Forty-four percent did not know that Herman Melville wrote *Moby Dick*, and forty-two percent could not identify the Koran as the sacred text of Islam.

But should anyone be surprised? Students can graduate from seventy-seven percent of the nation's colleges and universities without taking a foreign language, and, to listen to many of them speak, one would think English was a foreign language as well. From forty-one percent of academic institutions they can receive degrees without taking mathematics and from thirty-eight percent without taking history. In the interest of civilization, culture, and freedom—to say nothing about the interest of economic and technological well being—our colleges and universities, especially our metropolitan universities, should convert barbarians as well. After all, our society, like all others, depends for its cohesiveness on common knowledge.

Before I propose a solution, I would like to address a fundamental contradiction. Society expects much more than before from colleges and universities, and there is so much more to learn. Yet we are asking academic institutions to convert barbarians into educated persons who are ideally prepared for the world of work in the same amount of time that colleges and universities previously devoted to the teaching of the classics, simple mathematics, and some rhetoric. The challenge is particularly unattainable as far as the metropolitan universities are concerned, since they accept in large numbers young men and women who are inadequately prepared for college or university work.

I submit that this objective cannot be attained even with well-prepared students, and that the current attempts to restructure curricula are analogous to being in more than one place at the same time. In other words, the result of these futile exercises is an unacceptable trade off. It substitutes one important subject for an equally important one.

For example, in a computerized nuclear age with dazzling medical advancements, substituting physics for chemistry or chemistry for biology solves very little. An educated person should have at the very least one course of each at the college level. Frequently, one physics course might be a person's only opportunity to understand the nuclear age in which he or she lives; a biology course, the only chance to comprehend the disease from which he or she is suffering; one chemistry course the only occasion to fathom the cure.

The strategy of substituting Western Civilization for American history, or Non-Western Civilization for Western Civilization is just as flawed. History on a social level is the functional equivalent of memory at the individual level. How effective can a society with collective amnesia be in a global economy, or with its foreign policy, especially if history repeats itself? And if college and university students are permitted to graduate without art and music appreciation courses, what eventually is to become of our museums and symphonies?

In the absence of a grounding in economics, how is a person to understand how wealth is created and how resources are efficiently allocated? Without a sound grounding in mathematics, a person will have difficulty understanding much of what is important in our time, as well as finding and keeping a challenging job.

I submit another important argument on behalf of a liberal education, as I have defined it. The scientific method as developed by the traditional sciences has been aped by the social sciences, education, and business administration. The reductionist tendencies of this method of knowing produce a molecular view of the world that frequently lacks cohesion. The more molar analytical approaches employed in the arts and humanities might provide a useful counterpoint to the scientific method.

Unlike most of my academic colleagues who have the courage of their convictions but lack the courage of their doubts, I would prefer not to determine single-handedly what is important in our time. Had I attempted, I might have included the study of organizations in the important category, since our lives are dominated by organizations, and run the risk of being condemned by my liberally educated colleagues to perdition. Collectively, however, I believe we can reach a consensus on what is important in our time, if we are not forced to make unacceptable trade offs. The avoidance of such trade offs would require a course of study that would consume all or the better part of four years and produce a generalist.

Yet, we cannot afford to short shrift professional education; for in a global economy where most countries have lower wage levels than in the United States, the sections of our nation that will prosper are those with the best educated work force and the finest infrastructure for research and development. The United States will have to compete in capital-intensive goods and services requiring high-level cognitive skills. Perhaps shifting professional education to the graduate level, the model of law and medical schools, should be given serious consideration. Some American universities have already adopted this model for business administration, although the course of study is not nearly as long. In any case, if a choice at the baccalaureate level must be made between professional courses and courses that produce a liberally educated person, then the benefit of the doubt should go to the latter.

How then do we create a specialist or a professional who is not a barbarian at the same time? First of all, we must recognize that to attain our goals we must provide more time for the requisite course of study. Either we must adopt the law school model or we must configure five-year and even six-year degree programs. Five-year baccalaureate degrees already exist, and were originally intended to ensure curriculum breadth. However, as the result of increasing complexity of technical fields, these five-year degrees too frequently have evolved into opportunities for increasing the number of required technical courses. That is not what I am proposing. The suggested alternatives may require rethinking and restructuring graduate study as we know it today.

Furthermore, public and private financial assistance needs to be increased so that students without financial means would not be excluded from such an important opportunity as a college or university education. Cooperative programs should be inaugurated by more metropolitan universities not only in the interest of ameliorating financial insufficiencies, but also for the other benefits that cooperative programs engender.

One could even make a cogent argument that the U.S. economy would be more competitive if employers assumed a greater responsibility for vocational skill training, thus freeing up the time for universities to do a better job with English, mathematics, and the sciences. After all, a young person entering the work force today will have to retrain at least several times before she or he retires. Hence, what we will need most of all in the work force of the future are quickly retrainable workers, and those are folks who have a sound grounding in the fundamentals.

Demands for our limited national resources are great, and increasing support for higher education will require hard choices. Yet we must decide what sort of society we are to become, and how this is to be accomplished. Clearly, the task of providing a liberal education would be made easier if elementary and high schools taught more, and every effort should be made to bring about this result. If more of the conversion were to take place at the secondary educational level, fewer demands would be placed on metropolitan universities.

I single out the metropolitan university because its first-generation college clientele frequently lacks the opportunity to begin the conversion process on the home front, the way scions of the economically advantaged do. Moreover, U.S. high schools do not contribute to the conversion process nearly as well as do secondary schools in Europe and other parts of the world. Thus, the post World War II metropolitan universities in the United States have to compensate for these deficiencies as well.

Cities, unlike towns and rural areas in which many American colleges and universities are located, contain museums; symphonies; theaters; corporate headquarters; city, county, and state administrations; and media centers. Therefore, metropolitan universities should enrich the educational experience of their students by exploiting the urban environment to a greater extent than currently is the case through field trips, guest lectures, adjunct professors, and co-op arrangements. Exposure to these precious urban assets may prove even more appealing to many students than offering them a football team and could be used as a recruiting strategy.

What I am proposing will not come about by itself. Those of us who subscribe to these ideas must persuade the body politic in the marketplace of ideas that our proposals will create a better society and a stronger safeguard for freedom than the competing ideas and models, including the ones on which we are currently embarked. And there is no better time to begin than now.

Suggested Readings

Huxley, T. H. "A Liberal Education and Where to Find It." In *Science and Education*, edited by Charles Winick. New York: Citadel Press, 1964.

Leatherman, C. "Madison Shuns Journalism Accrediting, Stirring a Curriculum Debate." *The Chronicle of Higher Education* (December 18, 1991): A19.

Turner, J. and P. Bernard. "The Prussian Road to University? German Models and the University of Michigan 1837–c.1895." In *Rackham Reports*, Horace H. Rackham School of Graduate Studies, The University of Michigan, 1981–1989: 6–52.

PART VIII

LEADERSHIP NEEDS AND ISSUES

INTRODUCTION

At no time in history has American higher education been subject to as much public criticism, legislative questioning, and competition for funding from health care, criminal justice and other institutions as in the 1990s. All indications are that these challenges are not a temporary historical blip but rather the initial signs of a long-term, fundamental societal transformation that will lead to major changes in the structure, funding, and delivery of advanced education in the United States and throughout the world.

The call for change is everywhere. Nowhere is this more evident than in the journal, *Metropolitan Universities*. There are legitimate questions being raised by public officials and education insiders, however, regarding the capacity of the higher education community to respond to the mandate for change. One of the bright spots in American higher education has been the efforts of the leadership of this growing number of metropolitan and urban universities to address these challenges head-on by strengthening the linkages between our institutions and the metropolitan regions they serve. Metropolitan universities and metropolitan regions have, in many respects, common agendas, i.e., to improve the quality of life. Strong and effective leadership at all levels of the academy is needed to bring about the institutional changes required of truly metropolitan universities.

Tom McGovern's article, "Navigating the Academic Department into the Twenty-first Century," focuses on the leadership role of the department chairperson. He argues that becoming an effective chairperson requires "orchestrating" institutional mission, personnel resources, and student and societal needs. McGovern recognized that what some have called "leading from the middle" is one of the most challenging responsibilities in today's metropolitan universities.

Dan Johnson's "Leadership Challenges for Metropolitan Universities: Issues and Approaches" points out that while American higher education has been universally admired for decades as "the finest, most

311

productive national system of colleges and universities," its stature is now threatened by an "historic transformation driven by technological, economic, and societal forces" over which it exercises little control. It is within this context that Johnson assesses the major leadership tasks and challenges for metropolitan universities. He also proposes several models and strategies for addressing these challenges and guiding these institutions into the twenty-first century.

NAVIGATING THE ACADEMIC DEPARTMENT INTO THE TWENTY-FIRST CENTURY

Thomas V. McGovern

In a 1994 speech delivered at the Association of American Colleges annual meeting, Ernest Boyer described the "New American College" as:

> . . . an institution that celebrates teaching and selectively supports research, while also taking special pride in its capacity to connect thought to action, theory to practice. This New American College would organize cross-disciplinary institutes around pressing social issues. Undergraduates at the college would participate in field projects, relating ideas to real life. Classrooms would be extended to include health clinics, youth centers, schools, and government offices. Faculty members would build partnerships with practitioners who would, in turn, come to campus as lecturers and student advisers.

My first reaction to this "new college" was its similarity to an ethos already established at metropolitan universities in the post-World War II period. All of the elements that Boyer lists, I encountered as an undergraduate at Fordham University in New York City in the late 1960s, as a faculty member and department chair at Virginia Commonwealth University in Richmond from the late 1970s through the 1980s, and now helping to build a brand new, twenty-first-century campus at Arizona State University West.

The purpose of this article is to reflect on my experiences at these three metropolitan universities (Fordham, VCU, and ASU West) and to suggest issues for a chairperson to consider in navigating the department into the twenty-first century.

My biases should be stated at the outset. First, I believe that being a department chair is the best administrative job in the academy. Leadership can focus on the essential players in higher education—faculty and students—and not on the multiple other audiences which occupy the time of deans, vice presidents, and presidents. Second, my past work has been in departments of psychology and I have written elsewhere about similar issues from that disciplinary perspective (McGovern, 1993). Third, I now chair an interdisciplinary arts and sciences department with full-time, tenure track faculty from astronomy, business and environmental ethics, history and philosophy of science, mathematics, psychology, and philosophy. Our faculty's multicultural heritages include African American, Asian American, Argentinean, Rumanian, and Spanish, along with a native Californian and a New Yorker. All our colleagues in the other arts and sciences programs at ASU West use multiple hyphens to list their academic specializations and they too reflect the gender and ethnic mix of the broader society. Thus, the themes about which I write are topics of daily conversations on our new campus.

My comments will be organized around three intellectual priorities for most chairs—students, faculty, and the undergraduate curriculum. I will not talk about economic issues (either struggling with scarcity or developing fund-raising initiatives), management issues (TQM or all of its alphabetical antecedents), or graduate education. Leadership in these areas is too often a matter of steering between Scylla and Charybdis with little sense of control, much less satisfaction. My premise is that the audience for this article is invested more in reflection and affirmation of their thinking than in reading about someone else's problem-solving techniques for their particular environment.

What do we know about how students learn in college?

Pascarella & Terenzini (1991) synthesized the research on how a college education affects students and the findings are consistent across almost thirty years. They concluded that, by going to college, students: (a) think more critically, complexly, and reflectively; (b) increase their cultural and artistic interests; (c) develop personal identities and healthy self-concepts; (d) extend their intellectual interests, personal autonomy, interpersonal horizons, and overall psychological maturity. Going to college, not simply maturing with age, positively affects students' intellectual, moral, and career development. A major limitation of this past research is its lack of attention to individual differences. The research findings are about overall effects; effects attributable to "non-traditional" student status—age, ethnic minority status, part-time or re-entry enrollment patterns—need to be investigated and understood. Such research is especially needed for metropolitan university students because such characteristics are their "traditional" demographics.

Pascarella and Terenzini (1991) noted also that "similarities in between-college effects would appear to vastly outweigh the differences" (p. 590). The power of college is directly related to how intensely involved students become with their faculty, programs, peers, and with opportunities that arise on campus. In a conclusion applicable to any chairperson's priority list, these authors suggested:

> . . . there is some evidence to suggest that departmental environment, whatever the department, may be more important than the characteristics of the discipline in shaping psychosocial and attitudinal changes among students. The interpersonal climate and value homogeneity and consensus within a department appear to be particularly important. (p. 614)

What is the specific role of the chair in addressing these empirically based student learning issues? First, the chair can organize all data collection and assessment activities so that student descriptors are identifiable (e.g. age, ethnic-minority status, registration patterns, etc.) and can be used to examine the effectiveness of departmental programs for sub-groups as well as for the whole. Second, the chair needs to be attentive to environment-building activities that free faculty to become more involved with their students in their intellectual work. In setting priorities for faculty recruitment and in guiding curriculum development, this translates into focusing faculty expertise and curricular choices rather than covering the panorama of any disciplinary or professional area's specializations. A third aspect of what Pascarella and Terenzini label as "interpersonal climate and value homogeneity" will be covered in a later section of this paper on faculty development. That is, the chair must be able to communicate clear signals to faculty *and* to students about balancing their scholarly pursuits and instructional responsibilities.

How can we foster student learning more effectively?

The research on college effects and the recommendations from several higher education task forces indicate that the quality of student learning is directly related to the quality of students' involvement in their education. Astin's (1985) talent development model was an early catalyst for this perspective. Departmental environments in which (a) clear and high expectations are stated, (b) concerted faculty effort fosters active learning in every course or out-of-class activity, and (c) systematic assessment and feedback are provided—these are places where students and faculty thrive. The capacity to build these environments is not necessarily related to institutional resources or prestige; instead, the capacity is related to shared values in which administrators, faculty, and students recognize and reward quality effort in behalf of undergraduate learning.

Heterogeneity not homogeneity in the student population will be a defining quality of departments into the next century. Heterogeneity includes changing proportions of women and men students in particular majors; uneven preparation in basic skills such as literacy, numeracy, and critical thinking; even wider differences in levels of cognitive development and in twenty-first-century skills such as information literacy and language/global/multicultural knowledge and sensitivities. Common expectations for learning among all the different students who take undergraduate courses will require sensitivity by faculty, expanding their roles as teachers and providers of university and community service. To achieve a common excellence in learning will require particular attention by faculty as scholars, to measure the differential effects of the major for a variety of undergraduate student characteristics. This research and evaluation effort should be synthesized with assessment mandates already expected for departments.

Teaching peoples of color will challenge departments to extend themselves beyond institutional boundaries and levels of education. In college student enrollment demographics reported for 1991, 55.2% of American Indians, 40.2% of Asian Americans, 43.3% of African Americans, and 55.8% of Hispanic Americans in all higher education were enrolled in public, two-year institutions (Almanac: College Enrollment by Racial and Ethnic Group, 1993). If departments are to recruit more people of color into their ranks, as students and as future faculty members, partnerships must be initiated with the public, community colleges. In the latter half of the 1990s, overall college enrollments are projected to increase, but state expenditures for higher education and federally funded financial aid programs will not keep pace with student needs. Community colleges will maintain their role as a safe harbor for students of color with even minor academic or economic constraints.

Again, what are some ways that department chairs can provide leadership on these issues? First, faculty meetings and colloquia can be organized around the topic of "how students learn," what are the "different ways of knowing" (Belenky, Clinchy, Goldberger, & Tarule, 1986), or the power of feminist pedagogies (Weiler, 1991) to motivate broader spectrums of students. Second, the chair must become an articulate and sensitive spokesperson to multiple audiences on and off campus. Intellectual alliances of all types developed with middle schools, high schools, and community colleges can best be initiated by the chair; in metropolitan universities, student "pipelines" originate locally and public school administrators and faculty will respond favorably to sincere efforts at building bridges across the levels of education (right within one's own neighborhood!). Third, bringing selective faculty on these ventures into the community broadens the sensitivity and knowledge of the department and will have direct pay-offs in higher quality advising and faculty's capacity to evaluate non-traditional students' work.

What will stimulate faculty development?

Most faculty, regardless of institutional type, experience periodic feelings of isolation and hope for some sense of academic community. Studies on the professorate attest to a national sense of malaise *and* hope among current faculty, but suggest that differences may be based on institutional settings and academic disciplines as well. Rice's (1991) article on "the new American scholar" is a thought-provoking piece about contemporary faculty values and the sense of community. Rice's title comes from Ralph Waldo Emerson's address to the Phi Beta Kappa Society at Harvard in 1837 in which he articulated an American definition of academic scholarship, distinguishing us from our European ancestry. At the heart of Emerson's and Rice's argument is the almost 200-year-old struggle to define what is a distinctively American university.

Gray, Froh, and Diamond's (1992) findings of different levels of satisfaction reported by faculty in different academic specialties attest to this ongoing struggle. They described the tensions in faculty values at research universities. These tensions result from perceived differences among faculty and administrators about how faculty spend their time and how they should be rewarded, especially in finding an appropriate balance between time spent on research and on undergraduate teaching. They concluded that narrowly defined reward systems on many campuses not only stress research over undergraduate teaching, but emphasize the quantity rather than the quality of research and scholarly work.

These authors received over 23,000 surveys (50% response rate) from faculty, unit heads, deans, and central administrators at thirty-three public and fourteen private universities. The authors' analyses revealed that: (a) there was more variability within each of the three groups (faculty, unit heads, deans) than among them; (b) each level perceived the group above as more biased toward research over teaching than the higher level reported for themselves; (c) older (i.e. longer appointed) faculty and unit heads advocated more emphasis on teaching.

Do these national studies suggest faculty development priorities for the coming decade?

Faculty's intellectual development, often manifested in traditional forms of research activity but always required for effective teaching regardless of institutional setting, is paramount. New definitions of scholarly activity must be discussed at departmental meetings in all settings. The chair, having been promoted as a faculty member in a single culture, must now interpret that culture as one of many academic disciplines and professional specializations, and must moderate departmental values in response to constantly evolving, broader institutional cultures.

Rice's (1991) synthesis of different ways of knowing with the four forms of scholarship (discovery, integration, practice, and teaching) introduced to the public debate by Boyer (1990) is a good starting point for the discussion:

> . . . what is being proposed challenges a hierarchical arrangement of monumental proportions—a status system that is firmly fixed in the consciousness of the present faculty and the academy's organizational policies and practices. What is being called for is a broader, more open field, where these different forms of scholarship can interact, inform, and enrich one another, and faculty can follow their interests, build on their strengths, and be rewarded for what they spend their scholarly energy doing. All faculty ought to be scholars in this broader sense, deepening their preferred approaches to knowing but constantly pressing, and being pressed by peers, to enlarge their scholarly capacities and encompass other—often contrary ways—of knowing. (Rice, 1991; pp. 15–16)

In the coming decade, faculty in metropolitan universities, as in other institutions, will experience continued pressure and role confusion. As enrollments increase, there will be more administrative and external demands to shift institutional missions toward more teaching and community service. Without a concomitant redefinition of the relation between scholarship and teaching, or a redefinition of roles and rewards, faculty will struggle without clear signals about priorities and without a sense of support for their own intellectual development, which renders good teaching all but impossible.

The chair's leadership responsibilities in the area of faculty development are among the most important in a complex job description. First, chairs must foster an intellectual and systematic discussion of these issues at faculty meetings. Second, in the recruitment of new faculty and the annual evaluations of continuing faculty, chairs must have a clear vision for balancing teaching and scholarly pursuits. Moreover, they can effectively respond to differing faculty needs at different stages of academic careers. Must all tenured faculty members contribute the exact same mix of teaching, scholarship, and service activities every year of their career? The chair is in the best position to facilitate not only the discussion of creative alternatives but the fair (albeit difficult) implementation of an agreed upon faculty policy.

Curricular Transformations

The first issue of *Current Directions in Psychological Science,* a journal of the American Psychological Society, appeared in February 1992. The editors' plan was to cover the breadth of scientific psychology as ambitiously as authors of current, introductory psychology textbooks. I was struck by the primary authors' departmental affiliations for the ten articles in this first issue. Three were from departments of psychology. The remaining seven used a variety of interdisciplinary addresses (e.g. Center for the Study of Child and Adolescent Development; Institute for Social Research; Institute of Cognitive and Decision Sciences; Center for Neural Science).

Most discussions of the curriculum begin with faculty arguing about the essential knowledge base of the discipline. The interdisciplinary, yet specialized research interests epitomized by the authors mentioned above will be a challenge for many departments to incorporate into their undergraduate curricula in the coming decade. What is the content of the field which bears the academic department's name? What curriculum covers that field?

Department chairs may be aided by having an historical perspective about the evolution of disciplines and professions when they lead these discussions. After reviewing catalogues for the years 1890, 1900, 1910, and 1920, I was amazed at the similarity between curricular transformations in psychology that took place at the turn of the last century and those that are taking place now. The 1990s department of "psychology" may be similar to the 1890s department of "philosophy" as a broad descriptor of many emerging specialties. "Cognitive and Decision Sciences" parallels the 1890s "Experimental Psychology" as faculty research and undergraduate study become shaped by theoretical perspectives and more sophisticated methodologies. And in the midst of trying to reconcile new definitions of the field and its consequent curriculum, chairs might also remind faculty of the 1884 label I found at the University of Arkansas— Department of Psychology, Ethics, Sociology, and Evidence of Christianity. A 1990s version could make for good conversation!

Faculty discussion about curricular change will continue to be influenced by the breadth versus depth theme that has characterized debate for the entire twentieth century. Faculty proponents of depth will advocate curricular requirements that are linear, sequential, and modeled on those of the sciences. For faculty in research universities, such a position is easy to advocate as the undergraduate equivalent of specialized graduate study. Faculty of like mind, but in institutions without the staff expertise to offer such a specialized course of study leading to a new baccalaureate, will advocate tracks or minors that mirror some of these new content areas. Assessment of student learning outcomes will be easiest in such programs because of the narrow content focus.

Beyond specialization, there is a new focus on synthesis that is being reflected in recent reviews of undergraduate curricula. A three-volume work was sponsored by the Association of American Colleges in collaboration with faculty representatives from ten arts and sciences disciplines, interdisciplinary studies, and women's studies (Project on Liberal Learning, Study-in-Depth, and the Arts and Sciences Major 1991a, 1991b, 1992). Stark and Lowther (1988) reviewed the common ground of arts and sciences outcomes and those of professional school majors as well. This emphasis on "coherence" or "synthesis" from recent groups targets the academic major. These reports should become required reading for department chairs who want to broaden their faculty's discussions beyond the parochial interests of one disciplinary or professional specialization area.

In coming decades, the renewed questioning of curricular objectives stimulated by these national groups, coupled with the transformation of disciplinary fields and their curricula by new knowledge, will prompt new definitions of university "general education" and the "major." The B.A. in Integrative Studies at ASU West is one example of this transformation of the traditional major. It is especially attractive to re-entry, metropolitan university students.

Multidisciplinary, upper division courses with titles such as "Moral Dilemmas" and "Evolution of Ideas" require our students to synthesize disparate forms of knowledge and inquiry. For example, in "Moral Dilemmas" students examine individualistic versus communitarian forms of ethics; problems are analyzed from historical, political, psychological, and philosophical perspectives. In "Evolution of Ideas," faculty and students explore paradigms and paradigm shifts in astronomy, genetics, and the arts. Across these required, major field courses, our faculty focus their teaching on outcomes such as scientific and information literacy, critical thinking, effective communication in multiple media, and multicultural understanding. It has been particularly rewarding to chair a department where student learning, faculty development, and curricular planning has been so integrated from its very inception.

Conclusion

In a 1985 commencement address, Timothy Healy S.J., then President of Georgetown University, reminded faculty and students at Virginia Commonwealth University in Richmond that big cities and universities go together and always have. As a department chair, I find the following passage as inspirational today as I did, dressed in academic regalia, hearing it for the first time. It places daily events in perspective:

> . . . the city never lets its universities escape the most priceless lesson, the correctives of facts and pain. Walk off campus and you meet the "strained, time-ridden faces, distracted from distraction by distraction" that fill any city streets. A walk around any city can douse the ebullience of youth and curb the arrogance of learning. In all our streets we meet the myriad masks of God, but we find also in all of them God's antidote against mistaking the generosity of the young for understanding, or the theoretical skill of the old for fact.

Being a chair in a metropolitan university demands an admixture of ebullience, arrogance, generosity, understanding, theory, and fact. Becoming an effective chair requires orchestrating these qualities into a coherent agenda for student learning, for faculty development, and for curricular transformation.

SUGGESTED READINGS

Astin, Alexander W. *Achieving Educational Excellence*. San Francisco: Jossey-Bass, 1985.

Belenky, Mary F., Blythe McVicker Clinchy, Nancy R. Goldberger, & Jill M. Tarule. *Women's Ways of Knowing: The Development of Self, Voice, and Mind*. New York: Basic Books, 1986.

Boyer, Ernest L. *Scholarship Reconsidered: Priorities of the Professorate*. Princeton, NJ: The Carnegie Foundation for the Advancement of Teaching, 1990.

Gray, Peter J., Robert C. Froh & Robert M. Diamond. *A National Study of Research Universities: On the Balance between Research and Undergraduate Teaching*. Syracuse, NY: Syracuse University Center for Instructional Development, 1992.

McGovern, Thomas V., ed. *Handbook for Enhancing Undergraduate Education in Psychology*. Washington, DC: American Psychological Association, 1993.

Pascarella, Ernest T., & Patrick T. Terenzini. *How College Affects Students*. San Francisco: Jossey-Bass, 1991.

Project on Liberal Learning, Study-in-Depth, and the Arts and Sciences Major. *The Challenge of Connecting Learning*. Volume One. Washington, DC: Association of American Colleges, 1991a.

Project on Liberal Learning, Study-in-Depth, and the Arts and Sciences Major. *Program Review and Educational Quality in the Major: A Faculty Handbook*. Volume Three. Washington, DC: Association of American Colleges, 1992.

Project on Liberal Learning, Study-in-Depth, and the Arts and Sciences Major. *Reports from the Fields*. Volume Two. Washington, DC: Association of American Colleges, 1991b.

Rice, R. Eugene. "The New American Scholar: Scholarship and the Purposes of the University." *Metropolitan Universities* 1 (1991): 7–18.

Stark, Joan S., & Malcolm A. Lowther. *Strengthening the Ties that Bind: Integrating Undergraduate Liberal and Professional Study*. Report of the Professional Preparation Network. Ann Arbor: The University of Michigan, 1988.

Weiler, Kathleen. "Freire and a Feminist Pedagogy of Difference." *Harvard Educational Review*, 61 (1991): 449–474.

Leadership Challenges for Metropolitan Universities: Issues and Approaches

Daniel M. Johnson

Introduction

A decade ago, Richard M. Cyert, President of Carnegie-Mellon University, began the foreward to George Keller's popular and influential book, *Academic Strategy* (1983), with the warning that the next decades will be a time of great change in American higher education. By the 1990s, he warned that there will be fewer high school graduates, greater competition for college candidates, higher education costs, difficulty attracting brilliant young people to university faculties, and fewer federal dollars for research and student support. For higher education, it will a time of "novel threats" but also some "fresh opportunities." In this uncertain future, Keller warned, college and university officers must provide careful, expert management and *"decisive campus leadership. . ."* [pp. vi-vii, emphasis mine].

Even with the numerous forecasts of significant changes that were to take place in the 1980s and early 1990s, few of us were fully prepared for the rapidity of the changes nor the magnitude of the challenges and threats to higher education we have experienced in the past half decade. If anything, the forecasts of the 1980s underestimated our current difficulties. Who in the early 1980s would have predicted the decline in public confidence in universities? What indicators signaled legislative disenchantment with higher education? Why was there no warning that expenditures for prisons and public safety would surpass the investments in higher education? Who was alerting regents, presidents and deans that higher education was becoming a "discretionary" item in many state budgets?

Nevertheless, American higher education, universally admired for decades as the finest, most productive national system of colleges and universities, is in the throes of an historic transformation driven by technological, economic and societal forces over which it presently exercises little control.

The major leadership challenge for higher education for the remainder of the 1990s, though enormously complex, can be simply summarized: Higher education must reestablish public confidence and influence with representatives in state legislatures and Congress. Without public confidence and legislative support, higher education cannot hope to sustain the level of quality and provide the programs which have made it internationally admired.

This paper has two purposes: The first is to describe the major tasks associated with these leadership challenges for metropolitan universities. The second is to assess selected leadership models and strategies for addressing these challenges and guiding these institutions into the twenty-first century.

Leadership Tasks and Challenges

Reestablishing Public Confidence

Multidirectional Communication. To argue that one of the major leadership challenges facing higher education and metropolitan universities is to reestablish public confidence may be seen by some as an oversimplification. While that may be true, it is no exaggeration to say that unless we are able to restore public confidence in higher education soon, we will have even less support and be less able to successfully address the challenges and opportunities facing our universities.

There are several popular explanations for the sudden erosion of public support for higher education: increasing emphasis on research at the expense of instruction, decreasing relevance of higher education to the needs of society, escalating costs, self-serving missions, faculty work patterns, etc. This shift in public expectations has been as rapid as it has been dramatic. As one of my colleagues put it: "It is almost equivalent to pulling the rug out from under these large, complex institutions."

The public needs to be assured that higher education is serving *their* interests. However, for universities to adopt as their mission serving the public interest, faculty and administration leaders must first gain an understanding of the public's perceptions, concerns, and needs. The challenge to university leadership is to develop effective mechanisms by which institutions can gain this knowledge in a continuing, systematic, reliable, and usable manner.

Our traditions, as well as the stereotypic image of the university as the "fountain of knowledge, have led us to believe that the professorate is the dispenser of knowledge while the public, business, media, and policymakers are the recipients. Few doubt that we of the academy have something of value to say about the present community condition. However, we must also listen to what the public and their representatives are saying that has value for informing our agenda. Tom Peters tells corporate leaders that "the listening organization is . . . the one most likely to pick up quickly on changes in its environment." Metropolitan universities, with their special mission to serve their communities, must be "listening organizations."

The challenge for university leadership is to increase *and improve communication* between the academic community and the publics it serves. This communication must be multidirectional, effectively linking the university with public officials and agencies, businesses, and health and social services organizations in a network that fosters the flow of information and encourages interaction and partnerships in addressing important community issues. The *process* of working together is as important as the specific results of university-community interaction in rebuilding public confidence.

The communications gap between universities and their communities is becoming so serious—as evidenced by declining community support—that it warrants concerted, strategic thinking, planning and action on a level that parallels our strategic planning efforts in teaching, research and service. University administrators, faculty, planners and public affairs staff must ask: How and with whom should we be communicating? When and on what topics? How do we know when and if our message is getting out? More importantly, how do we know when our publics' messages are "getting in" i.e., that we have a sympathetic understanding of their expectations of higher education?

If education is power, universities, through lack of communication, have not always effectively "empowered" their publics to work on their behalf. Likewise, we in universities need to take the lead by inviting our communities to inform us about their concerns, problems and needs. Community leaders, state policymakers and other influentials must be able to argue for their college or university with knowledge of the institution's mission and useful data on programs and program opportunities. Effective communication with the community is essential to restoring public confidence in higher education.

As academics we have developed elaborate, sophisticated mechanisms for communicating among ourselves. We have not, however, developed ways to effectively communicate with the community. University characteristics often act as obstacles to effective communication, i.e., the highly specialized language of the academy and our "ivory tower" traditions that value splendid isolation and the solitary scholar. Our tendency is to be inward looking and focused on the development of our disciplines and professions with little regard for the ways they relate to broader societal concerns.

Communicating is mutually empowering. University leaders, working with community leaders, must devise channels of communication that convey needed information between and among institutions of higher education, business, government and other organizations. University-community forums, databases and clearinghouses, service learning and community-based internships, faculty-practioner exchanges, industry-education television networks, and other innovations are only the first steps toward developing effective systems for communicating between campuses and communities.

Clarity of mission and identity. Faculty and administrative leaders have the challenge and responsibility for effectively articulating the institution's mission and goals as well as fostering an identity that reflects these priorities. Too often, universities attempt to be "all things to all people." Our historic tri-fold mission of teaching, research and service invites overly ambitious and ambiguous institutional missions and goals. Consequently, university missions are not always well understood or agreed to by those charged with carrying them out.

This lack of understanding and support of institutional missions is also due to the rapidly changing character of many universities. Faculty members in the early 1960s understood that they were, above all, to teach and teach well. This message was reinforced by workloads of four or five courses each semester. Little time was allocated for research, writing and publication. Those energetic enough to conduct research and publish in addition to teaching and advising were rarely rewarded for their additional efforts.

Many "teaching oriented" institutions were transformed by the need, opportunity, prestige and financial support for a broadened, national research agenda that was in full swing by the mid-1960s. Federal funding and rapid developments in computing technology transformed many university missions from primarily teaching to research-and-teaching, with an ever increasing emphasis on research. Reward structures changed accordingly, leaving little uncertainty about institutional priorities.

By the late-1980s, the growing neglect of teaching in favor of research began to capture the attention of state legislators, the public and education policymakers. About the same time, new challenges were being heard for a broader university service role in the community.

Mayors, city councils, and city managers, desperate for technical assistance and intellectual resources to address the escalating problems for urban America, began turning to their local universities for assistance. For the second time in less than a generation, universities were being called upon to transform their missions to re-emphasize teaching—particularly for undergraduates—and to broaden their scholarship to include applied research and professional service to help address growing community and social problems. (See Boyer, 1990).

The changing goals and missions of many universities, especially those located in large, urban areas, have created confusion among faculty and differences among department chairs, deans, provosts and presidents over institutional priorities. Needless to say, if universities are unsure or confused about their missions and goals, how can communities and policymakers be expected to understand the priorities, much less support them? One of the major leadership challenges for universities—particularly those developing a metropolitan university orientation—is to clarify and communicate the institution's mission and establish reward, policy and organizational structures that reflect this mission. Administration and faculty leadership together must convey to their constiuents a common sense of purpose which includes responsiveness to their concerns.

Deregulation of Higher Education. One of the paradoxes challenging higher education leaders is that universities must not only have a clear sense of purpose and mission (which requires a certain degree of institutional stability), they also must be able to change, adapt and respond to ever new problems, increasing competition, new technologies, diverse populations, and often conflicting expectations. The phenomenal growth of American higher education and the increasing requests for universities to address community concerns have been accompanied by increasing state and federal regulations that significantly limit higher education's ability to be responsive.

Among the strengths of American higher education is the variety of institution types and the modalities for coordinating the flow of resources to these varied institutions. State higher education coordinating boards have sought to balance growth in university programs with the growth in resources, avoid unnecessary duplication, set standards for quality, and ensure accountability (See Gilley, 1991). The chief mechanism for achieving these objectives has been the development of a regulatory environment that, in some states, extends into nearly every facet of public university poliiy and administration. For better or worse, the character of higher education today is, in many respects, the product of the regulatory environment in which it exists.

While the degree of regulation varies from state to state and the debate over the appropriate role of state higher education coordinating boards intensifies, many university leaders and education policymakers are advancing the proposition that the time has come for a fresh look at the goals, objectives and outcomes of regulation in higher education in today's economy. New and growing demands for creative partnerships and consortia with other universities to improve the quality of teaching, research and service functions often go unheeded due to bureaucratic obstacles. State regulatory policies frequently impede efforts to respond to public needs for instructional programs. New technologies for delivering higher education services go unused because of outdated rules and restrictive policies. Program reviews and detailed reports, often duplicated by accrediting bodies, consume valuable resources that detract from instruction and service delivery to communities. Deregulation in other sectors of the economy has stimulated growth, fostered invention and innovation, provided choices to an increasingly sophisticated and demanding public, and improved the quality of many products and services. Careful deregulation in higher education will produce many of the same results. Community leaders do not know that a university's failure to respond to a request for a program or service is often due to restrictive regulations. The image of the un*iversity* is diminished because it is prevented from providing the desired program by state regulations even when the university is able, willing, and desires to be responsive to the request.

The leadership task for public higher education generally and metropolitan universities in particular is to inform and educate legislative bodies and the public about ways our institutions can more efficiently and effectively serve community interests and be more responsive with less regulation. Specific approaches to this effort will vary among states, reflecting the character of regulation, the politics of higher education, the needs of our communities, and our institutions' abilities to respond to these needs in a less regulated environment.

This is a politically complex task and is not likely to be successful while public confidence in higher education is declining. Some argue that there is a direct relationship between the decline of public confidence and the increase in expectations for accountability and regulation. Thus, an important first step toward deregulation of higher education is restoring public confidence that universities are serving the public's interests.

Fiscal Realities and the Metropolitan Mission. The fiscal struggle among institutions of higher education has preoccupied the agendas of nearly every university administrator for the past half decade. Escalating costs, flat or decreasing budgets, increasing competition for students and external funding, strategic reallocations, and program cuts and closures have been the dominant challenges for university leaders.

The fiscal challenges for metropolitan universities with their broader, more complex missions, and community responsibilities have been significantly greater than in other sectors of higher education. Students from more diverse populations, many with special learning requirements, are being served. Faculty members are being called upon to invest increasing amounts of time providing needed expertise and technical assistance for social, health and other community issues. Providing needed and mandated educational and professional services to communities exacts higher costs and frequently yields lower revenues than those services provided by flagship and traditional institutions.

The task for leadership is to effectively communicate this complex message to legislators, members of Congress, foundations and others who provide the resources needed for carrying out this ambitious mission. More difficult, perhaps, is conveying a vision to the university community of the need for new, cost effective models for integrating and delivering instruction, professional services, and applied and basic research. These three basic functions—teaching/advising, research and professional service—are currently perceived, carried out and rewarded as distinct activities. The separateness of these activities is reflected and reinforced through "formula funding" and university accounting systems which provide separate budgets and department accounts against which faculty time is charged for, and thus reifying, these "different" activities.

As the demands on metropolitan universities continue to grow, success at even one function, much less all three, will require new ways of conceptualizing the role of faculty so that teaching/advising, research and professional service are more intrinsically connected. Technology can and will, undoubtedly, play an increased role. Job descriptions, evaluations and compensation for faculty must also reflect this integration. Moreover, these increasing responsibilities will have to be carried out at most universities with equal or fewer faculty members.

The resulting fiscal challenge for metropolitan university leaders is two-fold: convincing external audiences (i.e., public and state legislators) of the need for increased resources to implement the expanding mission and growing public expectations for metropolitan universities, while simultaneously developing new approaches with internal audiences—e.g., faculty, administrators and staff—for integrated, quality enhanced, lower cost outcomes. Even marginal success in meeting these two challenges will provide the resources and flexibility needed for investments in ongoing faculty development, new technologies, and enhanced interaction with university constituents.

Recreating Community. The loss of community and growing atomization of American society are emerging as our nation's greatest concerns. The decline of neighborhoods, erosion of normative standards, loss of trust, growing anomie, and the sense meaninglessness in personal lives have forced the American public and its leaders to recognize the harsh, new realities of our existence. Loss of confidence in our institutions is believed by many to be eroding the foundations of society (Robert Bellah, 1991). Our dazzling technological accomplishments and scientific breakthroughs have not stopped the growing sense of an impending crisis in our major urban regions.

A century ago, a similar sense of crisis prevailed as wave upon wave of immigrants sought to find their place, often displacing those who had preceded them by a few years. William Rainey Harper, President of the University of Chicago, envisioned his university playing a powerful, positive role for its city during this period of intense growth and disruption. He saw this new university as a source of knowledge and service to Chicago and beyond. Influenced by John Dewey's ideas about education and character, Harper fostered a university environment that encouraged professors to be active in community affairs, social welfare and political reform.

Many faculty members, reflecting Harper's (and Dewey's) philosophy, became deeply involved in and developed their intellectual lives around the problems of Chicago. Midway through the first decade of the new century, forces of academic professionalization began to take their toll on university organization and faculty roles. Faculty community involvement gave way to pressures from the disciplines and professions. Within twenty years, the effort to create an integrated, community-oriented, democratic university degenerated into what we have come to call the "multiversity" or "research university" reflecting the *dis*integration occuring in the larger society, with faculty pursuing their own ends, integrated more by bureaucratic procedures than a shared vision of a useful role in the larger community (Bellah, et al; 1991).

In his insightful and challenging keynote address at the 1993 Conference on Metropolitan Universities, Blaine A. Brownell portrayed the role of metropolitan universities in terms that described the early vision of the University of Chicago:

> The most important role of the metropolitan university is to be a facilitator, communicator, convener, and bridge. What other institution—except perhaps government itself—has the capacity to interpret one group to another, serve as a

neutral site and forum where problems can be discussed and resolved, bring the latest knowledge and technologies to bear on the problems of the dispossessed, join the vigor and capacity of business with the compelling needs of the public at large, and—perhaps most importantly, *help restore a sense of civitas, of belonging to one polity and community?* (p. 19. Emphasis mine.)

It is not clear that even metropolitan universities have the capacity to fill these awesome roles. Many who understand the metropolitan university paradigm believe it has the potential but only if this role is understood and accepted by the faculties, publics, state legislators, and education policy makers. This, no less, is a leadership challenge for faculty and administrators of metropolitan universities.

Leadership Approaches for Metropolitan Universities

The issues outlined above illustrate the complex challenges leadership facing higher education generally and metropolitan universities in particular. More difficult than identifying issues, however, is the task of matching these challenges with effective leader-ship models.

Leadership is one of the most exhaustively explored topics in the corporate world. A recent survey of leadership research cited over 7,500 studies (Bass, 1990). The increasing importance of leadership studies also is reflected in its growing acceptance as an object of study in university curricula. Academic programs and schools are devoted to leadership studies.

Leadership studies focused on higher education, however, constitute only a small portion of the existing literature. Far less attention has been devoted to the unique and more demanding leadership issues that confront metropolitan universities. The unique challenges facing metropolitan universities argue persuasively for devoting more attention to finding effective leadership models for administrators and faculty responsible for developing and directing changes in our missions, goals, strategies, and programs.

The following is a brief summary of selected leadership types. The question is which of these leadership types is most effective in addressing the issues facing metropolitan universities.

Leadership Typologies

Strong leader / weak leader models. In Birnbaum's review of the university leadership literature, he concludes that most of the writing is descriptive or prescriptive and tends to explicitly advocate or implicitly accept the notion that leadership—and particularly presidential leadership—is a critical component of institutional functioning and improvement. He also points out that this view is not universally held and that, in fact, there are *two* models that deserve consideration, i.e., the "strong" leader and the "weak" leader models (1992, 7). Birnbaum argues that "any comprehensive consideration of academic leadership must be able to accommodate both the strong leader and the weak leader views, because evidence suggests that while both may be incomplete, both are in some measure correct." Evidence for this position is drawn from Cameron's (1986) study and others that show institutional effectiveness so closely related to the strategies of senior administrators. Thus, those who would argue the efficacy of the strong leader model in higher education can do so with some empirical grounding as well as common sense, i.e., "the actions of leaders have important consequences."

Less understood is the "weak" leader model. This model suggests that many important measures of institutional functioning remain unchanged even when the senior leader is replaced. According to Birnbaum (1989), "institutional fate may not be closely related to who presidents are or what presidents do." Such arguments are consistent with sociological research on bureaucracies in which "institutional cultures," are shown to restrict or predispose members to follow established patterns of behavior. Social and organizational structures place constraints on what is "acceptable" and discourage the unconventional. Accordingly, institutional cultures are more likely to control leaders than leaders are to control their institution's culture.

Similarly, recent management literature asserts that in many new organizations central control will not work. Rather, a form of "weak" leadership is advocated in which employees are encouraged to define tasks they can see and are given the funds and discretion to do them. The role of the managager/leader in this model is to do less defining of tasks and controlling and do more caring for the people. As the literature on "self managed work teams" suggests, the people will manage themselves.

Most people in leadership positions would probably agree that they are frequently unable to do as they would like. The "degrees of freedom" in leadership choices often leave little room for decisions that would significantly alter institutional culture. Instead of asking if leadership matters, perhaps, as Birnbaum suggests, it is better to inquire, "Under what conditions or on what issues or problems can leaders make a difference?"

Instrumental leader / expressive leader models. Early research in group behavior reveals that two different leadership roles commonly emerge within groups and organizations, i.e, instrumental and expressive (Bales, 1955). Instrumental leadership is leadership that emphasizes the completion of tasks, i.e., getting things done. Relationships with such leaders tend to be formal and rely on "status" rather than personal qualities. Concentrating on performance, instrumental leaders are prone to issue directives and to "discipline" those who frustrate progress towards the leader's goals. Instrumental leaders are not particularly concerned about being "liked" but do desire and, if successful, enjoy a distant respect. There is a tendency among such leaders to employ authoritarian-like management methods and techniques, focus on instrumental issues, make decisions on their own, and expect compliance from subordinates.

Expressive leadership, in contrast, emphasizes collective well-being, i.e, providing emotional support and minimizing tension among group members. Such leaders often cultivate informal, personal relationships and work to keep the group or organization united emotionally and morale high. The desire for respect is usually surpassed by a need for personal affection from the organization's members. Management methods are generally more democratic and are aimed at including all group members in the decision-making process. Some leaders may even downplay their position and power, encouraging the group to function on its own if this produces unity and collective well-being.

Team leadership. Team leadership accepts the view that the increasingly complex, rapidly changing world requires diverse perspectives and multiple talents. Individuals are limited in their abilities to comprehend today's large, complex organizations that are trying to survive and prosper in ever more rapidly changing environments. The notion of the solo leader who can assess these complex situations, consider the options, and make all the right decisions is increasingly unrealistic. Although we hold to the myth of solo leaders, and our organizations reinforce the view of the person at the top who is "in charge," the reality is that such leaders rarely succeed, much less survive for any significant period.

Team leadership is, in contrast, a collective action occurring among and through a group of people who think and act together (Bensimon and Neumann, 1993). Leadership viewed as a team effort is, according to Eisenstat and Cohen (1990), more effective than individual leadership for several reasons, including: a team's decisions are more apt to represent a wider range of interests present in organizations; there is a possibility for more creative solutions; and team members will better understand and be more likely to support decisions they helped shape. Team leadership promotes inclusiveness over exclusiveness. The challenge for leadership, however, is how to get people involved as responsible participants, not keep them out of decision-making (Bensimon and Neumann).

The obvious disadvantages of team leadership are that it can be more complex, time-consuming, and require more compromise. These disadvantages may be more than compensated for if the end product of this approach is superior decision-making and stronger, more effective institutional leadership.

Institutional leadership. Most of the leadership literature deals with the leadership of persons—individuals and teams. Far less attention is devoted to, nor do we know much about, organizational or institutional leadership, especially in higher education. What literature there is focuses on businesses and corporations (e.g., Peters, *In Search of Excellence*). While it is not uncommon for us to use phrases such as "X University is one of the leading universities in the nation" and "Y University seeks to be a leader in addressing the social and economic problems in the metropolitan region," more rigorous and systematic attention needs to be devoted to understanding how universities as institutions become leaders in their communities, states, or, for that matter, higher education.

Our notions of institutional leadership as they relate to universities are commonly based on indicators that reflect selected values including number of students, size of endowment, Nobel Prize winning faculty members, scholarly publications or amount of external funding. *U.S. News and World Report* annually publishes a rating of universities based on the perceptions of leaders of peer institutions. These popular indicators of institutional leadership have produced sizeable followings in which many universities take pride at being in the "top 10" or "top 100" of this or that category.

The challenge for higher education, particularly metropolitan universities, is to continue development of a new model of institutional leadership for addressing and solving some of the pressing problems of our communities. During the past two decades, several urban and metropolitan universities have achieved significant success in playing a leadership role in addressing community problems and improving the quality of life, e.g., George Mason University, University of Louisville, University of Memphis, University of Arkansas at Little Rock, Towson State University, Cleveland State University, Portland State University and Wright State University to name a few. We need to know, for example, what factors contribute to their successful institutional leadership within their communities and states. How do they view and communicate their institutional values and missions to students, new and seasoned faculty members, community leaders, and the public? What personnel, workload, recruitment, and compensation policies contribute to this success? More importantly, what forms of internal university leadership contribute to successful external institutional leadership in the community and state in addressing and solving problems?

The answers to these questions are important for the general success of the metropolitan university movement and the particular success of individual institutions working to develop a new role in their communities and regions. Metropolitan universities and their faculty and administrative leaders have the added responsibility as participants in this new model of higher education to document and communicate their experiences—successful and otherwise—as they relate to their institution's leadership performance. The journal *Metropolitan Universities* and the regular Metropolitan Universities conferences are increasingly effective mediums for this exchange.

Fostering Leadership in Metropolitan Universities

To meet the complex challenges facing metropolitan universities will require effective leadership in all its individual, collective and institutional forms. Figure 1 suggests hypothetical relationships between certain leadership approaches and effectiveness in addressing various problems challenging metropolitan universities. For example, certain problems may be more effectively addressed by *strong leaders* who are willing to take risks, experiment with novel approaches, and learn from mistakes and successes. Other issues may be more effectively addressed by *weak leaders,* so called, who are comfortable in allowing their institution's culture to respond without their direct intervention.

Notwithstanding the value of strong, charismatic leaders and tough decision-makers in higher education today, the major leadership challenges and opportunities facing metropolitan universities cannot be successfully addressed through the individual, solo actions of the person "in charge." Communication, interaction, collaboration, shared responsibility, and team *leadership* appear to offer the greatest promise for addressing the multidimensional problems characteristic of those challenging metropolitan universities.

New definitions of institutional success such as those adopted by metropolitan universities (see Declaration of Metropolitan Universities p. viii) will take root and flourish only when there is collective *institutional leadership* supporting the mission and implementing the university's goals and objectives.

FIGURE 1

HYPOTHESIZED LEVELS OF EFFECTIVENESS OF SELECTED LEADERSHIP APPROACHES FOR ADDRESSING PROBLEMS FACING METROPOLITAN UNIVERSITIES*

Leadership Problems	Strong	Weak	Instrumental	Leadership Approaches Expressive	Team	Solo
Communicating						
Internally	M-L	M-L	M-L	H	H	M-L
Externally	H	L	H-M	H-M	H	M
Clarifying Mission	H	L	H	L	H-M	M
Deregulating Higher						
Education	H	L	H	L	H	L
Achieving Fiscal						
Adequacy	H-L	M	H-L	M-L	H	M
Recreating Community	L	M-L	L	H	H	L

*Hypothesized levels of leadership effectiveness: High (H), moderate (M), and low (L).

Note: The hypothesized levels of leadership effectiveness above are only *suggestions* for further exploration. The leadership approaches are obviously not mutually exclusive and presented only as *illustrations* of a much wider range of leadership types.

Adopting appropriate goals and objectives is only part of the process. Equally, if not more important, is gaining broadbased, internal commitments to the expanded role of the metropolitan university. This is particularly important in view of the deeply imbedded traditions of faculty governance, antonomous departments, and independent scholarship. Team leadership involving faculty, staff, administration and students in the development of new missions, goals and objectives will help insure gradual, broad-based acceptance. Gaining commitment to the metropolitan mission, however, requires trusted, reliable, articulate spokespersons who understand and can describe the vision and model. It also requires continuing reinforcement in institutional symbols, personnel policies, faculty workloads, reward structures and budget allocations.

Equally important, but more time consuming, will be changing external images and public expectations of the university. The image of the traditional university common earlier in this century is so deeply imbedded in our national culture that few community leaders and even fewer ordinary citizens know what they can and should expect from contemporary metropolitan universities. Defining the new university for the community, state legislators and national leaders must keep pace with internal redefinitions. The community must be informed of the mission, role and resources of the university as it addresses issues and seeks solutions to problems. Further, the community also must be made aware of the university's significant potential for leadership in addressing these problems. This task cannot fall to the chancellor or president alone. To succeed, this task must involve *every* faculty member and administrator as well as each department, school, and college in the university.

Because of the essential differences among disciplines and organizational units—not to mention individual differences—within the university, each will approach this task differently. Flexibility to develop different approaches to achieve institutional goals and objectives must become part of the institutional culture. Junior faculty as well as seasoned senior professors should be encouraged to challenge conventional wisdom in their pursuit of institutional goals. Experimentation will provide the only solid basis for developing more responsive and effective universities capable of meeting the challenges of the twenty-first century.

Conclusion

Nearly a decade ago, Derek Bok argued that the American university system is the most successful and adaptable system of higher education in the world. His criterion of success is the production and dissemination of knowledge. Bok's positive assessment does not hold, however, if one goes beyond the criterions of "production and dissemination of knowledge" to include the expanded mission of metropolitan universities, i.e., "broadened responsibility to bring these functions to bear on the needs of our metropolitan regions" and "to be responsive to the needs of our metropolitan areas by seeking new ways of using our . . . resources to provide leadership in addressing metropolitan problems."

True, this is a relatively new mission for universities. A decade is needed within which to develop and test the models, mechanisms, and leadership required for success. Others, however, might question whether this is a mission at which metropolitan universities can succeed. For more than a quarter-century, many academics have invested their careers in the proposition that higher education must pursue this new course and that certain strategically located universities with the appropriate mission and resolve can be successful in this expanded role.

If success is possible, charting a course to achieve this complex and challenging objective will require the best leadership in all its individual, collective and institutional forms. To paraphrase the American philosopher, Charles Peirce, it will require not only carrying on the basic traditions of the academy but also constantly amending and expanding them in active participation. Being responsive to the needs of metropolitan areas is a social enterprise that requires a new and expanded vision of the role of higher education that is understood and shared by faculty, central administrators, higher education policymakers, community leaders, legislators and the public.

Universities must begin to *redirect* a portion of their major resources, i.e., faculty interests and expertise, research priorities, and service activities, from discipline-defined issues to community-defined problems. The need for change is urgent. The need for effective leadership in the prevailing academic culture, which seems capable of only gradual change, is essential if higher education is to escape a full-blown crisis. Metropolitan universities have taken an important first step in accepting the need for change and represent a model for much of higher education for the remainder of this century and the decades ahead.

NOTE: I am indebted to my colleagues at the University of North Texas, Drs. Blaine A. Brownell, Suzanne LaBreque, David Hartman, David Williamson, and Ms. Lottie Joy Wright for their helpful comments and suggestions.

Suggested Readings

Bass, B. M. *Bass and Stogdill's Handbook of Leadership: Theory, Research and Managerial Applications*. (3rd ed.) New York: Free Press, 1990.

Bensimon, Estela Mara and Anna Neumann. *Redesigning Collegiate Leadership: Teams and Teamwork in Higher Education*. Baltimore: The Johns Hopkins University Press, 1993.

Birnbaum, Robert. *How Academic Leadership Works*. San Francisco: Jossey-Bass Publishers, 1992.

Boyer, Ernest L. *Scholarship Reconsidered: Priorities of the Professorate*. Princeton: The Carnegie Foundation for the Advancement of Teaching, 1990.

Brownell, Blaine A. "Metropolitan Universities: Past, Present, and Future," *Metropolitan Universities: An International Forum*. Vol. 4, No. 3, pp. 13-22.

DePree, Max. *Leadership is an Art*. New York: Doubleday, 1989.

_____. *Leadership Jazz*. New York: Doubleday, 1992.

Eisenstat, R. A. and S. C. Cohen. *Groups that Work (and Those that Don't): Creating Conditions for Effective Teamwork*. San Francisco: Jossey-Bass, 1990.

Gilley, J. Wade. *Thinking about American Higher Education: The 1990s and Beyond*. New York: American Council on Education and Macmillan Publishing Company, 1991.

Keller, George. *Academic Strategy: The Management Revolution in American Higher Education*. Baltimore: The Johns Hopkins University Press, 1983.

Kouzes, James M., and Barry Z. Posner. *The Leadership Challenge: How To Get Extraordinary Things Done in Organizations*. San Francisco: Jossey-Bass, 1990.

Lynton, Ernest A., and Sandra E. Elman. *New Priorities for the University*. San Francisco: Jossey-Bass Publishers, 1987.

Parsons, T. and R. F. Bales. *Family, Socialization and Interaction Processes*. New York: Free Press, 1955.

Peters, T. J. and R. H. Waterman. *In Search of Excellence*. New York: Harper and Row, 1982.

_____. *Thriving on Chaos: Handbook for a Management Revolution*. New York: Alfred A. Knopf, 1987.

Williamson, John N. *The Leader Manager*. New York: John Wiley and Sons, 1984.

EPILOGUE

EPILOGUE

THE FUTURE OF METROPOLITAN UNIVERSITIES: A CALL FOR RESEARCH

Alfred F. Hurley

The emergence of Metropolitan Universities in the 1990s may prove to be one of the most significant developments in higher education since the establishment of land-grant universities in the late 1800s. Building on a series of land grant acts—the Morrill Act of 1862, the Hatch Act of 1887 and the Smith-Lever Act of 1914—Congress laid the foundation for a system of higher education devoted to research and service that would revolutionize American agricultural productivity and efficiency. In less than a half century, America's land-grant universities enabled a nation emerging from a crippling civil war to become the world's leader in agriculture and food production.

Today, America's major challenges are no longer in agriculture and the nation's rural areas but in its urban and metropolitan regions. The range and depth of urban social economic problems confronting this generation are documented daily in the news media and are major issues of our time. Our nation's metropolitan and urban universities have the potential to provide significant research and service programs in support of public and private efforts to meet these growing challenges.

Recognition of this potential was one of the major motivating forces that led a large and growing group of publicly supported universities, located in or near major metropolitan regions, to modify their missions and focus more of their teaching, research and service programs to be responsive to the needs of their communities. Today, more than fifty of the nation's major public universities have committed themselves to a mission that not only embraces the historical values and principles which define all universities, but also includes a broadened responsibility to bring their intellectual resources to bear on the education needs of the region's citizens and the research and service needs of their metropolitan communities.

Responsiveness to the needs of the communities, however, alters the character of a university in many important respects. One very important difference between traditional universities and metropolitan universities is in the types of students they attract. As the essays in this volume point out so well, metropolitan university students are much more likely to be commuter rather than residential; to be employed full- or part-time; to be married and have families; to take five, six, or seven years to complete a baccalaureate degree; and to come from more diverse social backgrounds. These "non-traditional" students often require more and different support services and facilities than commonly found at traditional universities. Traditional institutional performance and outcome measures such as "four-year graduation rates" do not apply in any meaningful way to metropolitan universities. These and other important differences are not always well understood by national and state higher education policy makers as they seek to develop measures of institutional performance.

Likewise, faculty members serving in metropolitan universities are often expected to perform roles and have responsibilities that their counterparts in traditional universities would find unusual. Teaching in highly diverse environments is often more challenging and requires greater preparation. Funding for research on local issues and problems, commonly requested of metropolitan universities, is frequently more difficult to identify and obtain. Faculty are also more likely to find expectations for public service more demanding than on many traditional university campuses. In many ways, metropolitan universities place more demands on faculty members than traditional institutions.

Responsiveness to and interaction with communities takes on a higher priority in metropolitan universities and, consequently, university administrative and organizational structures sometimes differ from more traditional institutions. Specialized administrative offices, research centers and institutes addressing local problems, and unique academic programs and curricula are common on metropolitan university campuses.

These unique characteristics of metropolitan universities are not well known or understood in the nation's high education community. Because of the growing number of metropolitan universities and the increasing importance of their role nationally and locally, it is essential that we begin to take steps to gain a better understanding of the unique character of these institutions. The need for an empirical assessment of metropolitan and urban universities was discussed at the 1993 national Conference on Metropolitan Universities and was forcefully expressed again at a 1994 meeting of presidents representing these institutions.

Higher education policy makers, university leaders, faculty members, community organizations and foundations, and student groups need accurate, timely, and comparable data from metropolitan/urban universities that include information on students, faculty, programs, organizational structures, and communities served. It is particularly important that all constituents of higher education begin to recognize the broader missions, responsibilities and challenges facing metropolitan universities that differentiate them from flagship and other more traditional institutions of higher education.

As we in the United States are increasingly looking to higher education for assistance in addressing the problems of our cities and metropolitan regions, it is interesting to observe that we are not alone. Similar movements and changes are occurring in England, Canada and Mexico. Representatives from each of these countries, and others, attended the 1993 conference on Metropolitan Universities held at the University of North Texas. There we heard about the increasing importance in these countries of basic and applied research and service focusing on the needs and concerns of the universities' immediate communities. It is increasingly clear that what some have called the "metropolitan university movement" is international in character and that we need to use every opportunity to learn from one another how most effectively and efficiently we can fulfill our "metropolitan mission."

Metropolitan universities need congressional recognition and mandates to do for urban and metropolitan regions what land-grant legislation did for agriculture in rural America earlier in this century.

ABOUT THE AUTHORS

MARGUERITE ROSS BARNETT served as Chancellor of the University of Missouri at Saint Louis and Professor of Political Science. She also served as Vice Chancellor for Academic Affairs of the City University of New York and has taught at the University of Chicago and at Princeton, Howard, and Columbia Universities.

DAVID A. BELL is Vice President for Administrative Affairs and Associate Professor of Medical Humanities at the University of North Texas Health Science Center at Fort Worth. Formerly Executive Assistant to the Chancellor of the University of North Texas, he also served as Director of the Dallas Education Consortium, a K–16 Council. Prior to moving to Texas, he served as Associate Provost for Institutional Planning and Research at the University of South Carolina. Address for correspondence: University of North Texas, Denton, TX 76203.

ERNEST L. BOYER is President of the Carnegie Foundation for the Advancement of Teaching. He has served in many leading positions in higher education, including being Chancellor of the State University of New York and United States Commissioner of Education. Address for correspondence: Carnegie Foundation for the Advancement of Teaching, 5 Ivy Lane, Princeton, NJ 08540.

BLAINE A. BROWNELL is Provost, Vice President for Academic Affairs, and Professor of History at the University of North Texas. The author or co-author of *The Urban Ethos in the South, 1920–1930*, *The Urban Nation*, *1920–1960*, and *Urban America: A History*, he also served for thirteen years as editor of the *Journal of Urban History*. Address for correspondence: University of North Texas, Denton, TX 76203–3707.

347

ANN S. COLES is Vice President of Education Information Services of
The Education Resources Institute and Executive Director of its
Higher Education Information Center in Boston. She has had over
twenty-five years' experience working in programs to enhance access
to higher education for traditionally underrepresented students of
all ages. Address for correspondence: 330 Stuart Street, Suite 500,
Boston, MA 02116-5237.

TODD M. DAVIS is an Associate Professor of Research Methodology
and Higher Education in the Center for Higher Education, College
of Education, at the University of Memphis. His interests include
the utilization of assessment data in institutional change, and equity
and excellence issues in higher education. Address for
correspondence: University of Memphis, Memphis, TN 38152.

DANIEL A. DIBIASIO is interim Vice President for Student Affairs at
the University of New Hampshire where he previously served as
Executive Assistant to the President. He also served as Executive
Officer of the Council of Presidents of the New England Land Grant
Universities and as Assistant Dean of the Graduate School at The
Ohio State University. Address for correspondence: University of New
Hampshire, 102 Thompson Hall, 105 Main St., Durham, NH 03824.

GORDON A. HAALAND is President of Gettysburg College. He
previously served the University of New Hampshire as Chairman of
the Psychology Department, Vice President for Academic Affairs,
and President. In addition, Dr. Haaland was Dean of Arts and
Sciences at the University of Maine. Address for correspondence:
Gettysburg College, President's Office, Box 418, Gettysburg, PA
17325-1486.

CHARLES E. HATHAWAY is Chancellor of the University of Arkansas
at Little Rock. Previously he served as Vice President for Academic
Affairs at Wright State University. Dr. Hathaway also served as Dean
of the College of Sciences and Engineering at the University of Texas
at San Antonio, where he initiated new programs in engineering,
neurobiology, and geology. Address for correspondence: University
of Arkansas at Little Rock, 2801 S. University, Little Rock, AR 72204

FREEMAN A. HRABOWSKI III is President of the University of
Maryland–Baltimore County where he previously served as
Executive Vice President and Vice Provost. He has been instrumental

in radically improving the quality of the student body, and is especially interested in relationships with community colleges. He is nationally recognized for establishing the multimillion dollar Meyerhoff Scholarship Program for talented black students in science and technology. Address for correspondence: University of Maryland–Baltimore County, 5401 Wilkens Ave., Catonsville, MD 21228.

ALFRED F. HURLEY became President of the University of North Texas (UNT), as well as Chancellor of UNT in Denton and the University of North Texas Health Science Center at Fort Worth on February 1, 1982. He first joined the administration of UNT as Vice President for Administrative Affairs in 1980, and in the next year, also became a Professor of History. He currently serves as Vice Chairman of the North Texas Commission and Co-chair of the Coalition of Urban and Metropolitan Universities. Address for correspondence: University of North Texas, Denton, TX 76203.

BARBARA JACOBY serves as the Director of the Office of Commuter Affairs at the University of Maryland at College Park. She is also the Director of the National Clearinghouse for Commuter Programs. Her book, *The Student as Commuter: Developing a Comprehensive Institutional Response*, has just been published as an ASHE–ERIC Higher Education Report. Address for correspondence: University of Maryland, College Park, 1195 Adele H. Stamp Union, College Park, MD 20742.

DANIEL M. JOHNSON is Professor of Sociology and Dean of the School of Community Service at the University of North Texas. Prior to coming to UNT, he served as Director of the Survey Research Laboratory at Virginia Commonwealth University. He is co-author of *Black Migration in America* and *The Middle-Size Cities in Illinois*. Address for correspondence: School of Community Service, University of North Texas, Denton, TX 76203.

JAMES J. LINKSZ is President of Bucks County Community College. Following doctoral studies at Columbia as a Kellogg Fellow, Dr. Linksz has been an administrator and professor in community colleges for more than twenty-five years. He previously served as dean of Rappahannock Community College in Virginia and dean at Catonsville Community College in Maryland. Address for correspondence: Bucks County Community College, Newtown, PA 18940.

ERNEST A. LYNTON is the Executive Editor of *Metropolitan Universities*, Commonwealth Professor of the University of Massachusetts at Boston, and Senior Associate of its New England Resource Center for Higher Education. Address for correspondence: 100 Morrissey Blvd., Boston, MA 02125.

MARY ELLEN MAZEY came to Wright State University in 1979 as an Assistant Professor of Geography. In 1986, she initiated the development of the university's Center for Urban and Public Affairs and served as the Center's Director. In addition, she worked with the university administration in 1988 to create the Department of Urban Affairs, of which she is currently Chair. Address for correspondence: Department of Urban Affairs and Geography, Wright State University, 177 Millett, Dayton, OH 45435.

THOMAS V. MCGOVERN is Professor of Psychology, Chair of the Department of Integrative Studies, and President-Elect of the Academic Senate at Arizona State University West. At Virginia Commonwealth University, he received the University Distinguished Teaching Award and the Riese-Melton Award for the Advancement of Cross-Cultural Relations. Address for correspondence: Arizona State University West, Arts & Science Department, P. O. Box 37100, Phoenix, AZ 85069-7100.

PAUL A. MILLER is President Emeritus of Rochester Institute of Technology. Sociologist, former extension worker, and public servant, he has also served as Professor and Provost of Michigan State University, and Assistant Secretary for Education in the U.S. Department of Health, Education, and Welfare. Address for correspondence: 1909 Walden Court, Columbia, MO 65203.

JAN MUCZYK is Professor of Management, Cleveland State University. Previously, he served Cleveland State University in a variety of administrative positions, including Senior Vice President of Resource Planning and Campus Operations, Executive Assistant to the President, Chair of the Department of Management, and interim Dean of the College of Business Administration. Address for correspondence: Department of Management and Labor Relations, College of Business Administration, Cleveland State University, Cleveland, OH 44115.

PAIGE E. MULHOLLAN served as President of Wright State University from 1985 to 1993. Prior to Wright State he served as Provost and Executive Vice President of Arizona State University and Chief Operations Officer for Arizona State West. Address for correspondence: 72 Spindle Lane, Windmill Harbour, Hilton Head, SC 29926.

PATRICIA H. MURRELL is Director and Professor in the Center for the Study of Higher Education at the University of Memphis. She has worked extensively in the areas of effective teaching, student development, and corporate education. Address for correspondence: University of Memphis, Memphis, TN 38152.

DANIEL H. PERLMAN was President of Suffolk University in Boston until 1989. After leaving Suffolk University, he was Visiting Fellow at the New England Resources Center for Higher Education, University of Massachusetts at Boston and Visiting Scholar, Harvard Graduate School of Education.

DONALD PHARES is Professor of Economics and Public Policy at the University of Missouri–St. Louis where he also served as Vice-Chancellor for Budgeting and Planning. He has published four books and more than seventy articles and reports. Address for correspondence: University of Missouri–St. Louis, 8001 Natural Bridge, 401 Tower, St. Louis, MO 63121.

PATRICIA R. PLANTE is former President of the University of Southern Maine. She served earlier as Vice President for Academic Affairs at Towson State University in Maryland. She has written numerous articles on issues in higher education and two books, both published by ACE/MacMillan: The *Art of Decision Making* in 1987 and *Myths and Realities in Academic Administration* in January 1989.

R. EUGENE RICE is Director of Forum on Faculty Roles and Rewards, American Association of Higher Education. He previously served as Vice-President and Dean of the Faculty of Antioch College. Prior to that, he was Senior Fellow at The Carnegie Foundation for the Advancement of Teaching (Princeton) where he collaborated with Ernest Boyer on a study of the changing role of scholarship in American higher education. His research and teaching focus on the sociology of the professions and higher education. Address for correspondence: American Association of Higher Education, 1 Dupont Circle, Suite 360, Washington, DC 20036-1110.

CHARLES P. RUCH is President of Boise State University. He served previously as Provost and Vice President for Academic Affairs at Virginia Commonwealth University. Dr. Ruch also served as Dean of the School of Education at VCU and was a faculty member and chair at the University of Pittsburg. Address for correspondence: Boise State University, 1910 University Dr., Boise, ID 83725.

G. EDWARD SCHUH is Dean of the Hubert H. Humphrey Institute of Public Affairs, University of Minnesota. He previously was head of the university's Department of Agriculture and Applied Economics and was Professor at Purdue University for twenty years. He has been visiting professor at various universities in Latin America and has held positions in the United States government and with the World Bank. Address for correspondence: Hubert H. Humphrey Institute of Public Affairs, 301 19th Avenue South, Room 300, Minneapolis, MN 55455.

DANIEL W. SHANNON is Dean of Outreach and Continuing Education Extension at the University of Wisconsin–Milwaukee. He is past president of the National University of Continuing Education Association and editor of the *Continuing Higher Education Review*. Address for correspondence: Division of Outreach and Continuing Education Extension, University of Wisconsin–Milwaukee, P. O. Box 413, Milwaukee, WI 53201.

ALEXANDER E. SIDOROWICZ is Dean of the College of Fine Arts and Communication at Towson State University. He has held a number of other positions as an arts administrator at the University of Texas at San Antonio, Bradley University, Ithaca College, and Hiram College. He is an active performer and a composer with over 30 music compositions. Address for correspondence: College of Fine Arts and Communication, Towson State University, Towson, MD 21204-7097.

KENNETH A. SIROTNIK is Professor and Chair of Educational Leadership and Policy Studies, College of Education, University of Washington. His work and publications range widely over many topics, including measurement, statistics, evaluation, computer technology, educational policy, organizational change, and school improvement. Address for correspondence: College of Education, DQ-12, University of Washington, Seattle, WA 98195.

RONALD R. SLONE is President, Strategic Directions. He previously served as Director of Research and Planning at the College of Business, Boise State University, and Director of Accreditation for the American Assembly of Collegiate Schools of Business. He also serves as a consultant to schools on accreditation preparation and strategic planning. Address for correspondence: 330 Fall Dr., Boise, ID 83706.

DAVID C. SWEET serves as Dean of the Levin College of Urban Affairs (CUA) at Cleveland State University and Chair of the Ohio Board of Regents Urban University Program (UUP). The CUA is the focus of the CSU commitment to linking the university's programs to the Cleveland metropolitan area. As Chair of the UUP, Sweet directs a statewide university research and extension program involving faculty and staff from Ohio's eight urban state universities. Modeled after the land-grant university program and funded by the Ohio General Assembly, the UUP is the only one of its kind in the nation. Address for correspondence: Levin College of Urban Affairs, Cleveland State University, Cleveland, OH 44115.

EUGENE P. TRANI assumed the presidency of Virginia Commonwealth University in 1990. Prior to assuming his present position, he served as Vice President for Academic Affairs for the University of Wisconsin System and was Vice Chancellor for Academic Affairs at the University of Missouri–Kansas City. Address for correspondence: Office of the President, Virginia Commonwealth University, 910 West Franklin Street, Richmond, VA 23284-2512.

KAREN A. WHITE is Dean, College of Fine Arts, University of Nebraska–Omaha. She previously served as Special Assistant to the President of Wright State University where she was a 1988–89 Fellow of the American Council on Education. In addition, Dr. White also served as Associate Professor of Music and former Associate Head of the Department of Music at Southeastern Louisiana University. Address for correspondence: University of Nebraska, 60th & Dodge St., Omaha, NE 68182.

Richard T. Wines is Director of Accreditation Candidacy, American Assembly of Collegiate Schools of Business. He oversees operational support for the business administration accreditation program, including staff analysis of self-study reports and development of workshops for applicant schools and accreditation teams. Address for correspondence: AACSB, 600 Emerson Rd., Suite 300, St. Louis, MO 63141-6762.

Neil R. Wylie is Executive Director, University of New Hampshire. He previously served as Executive Officer of the Council of Presidents, New England Land-Grant Universities, as a faculty member, department chair, and Assistant Academic Dean at Cornell College, and as Vice-President of the Great Lakes Colleges Association. Address for correspondence: University of New Hampshire, 11 Brook Way, Durham, NH 03824.

Jerome M. Ziegler is a Professor of Human Service Studies and former Dean in the College of Human Ecology at Cornell University. He teaches urban social planning and political development, ethics and public policy, and the future of cities. Before joining the faculty at Cornell, he was Commissioner of Higher Education of the Commonwealth of Pennsylvania, and Chairman of the Department of Urban Affairs and Policy Analysis at the New School of Social Research. Address for correspondence: New York State College of Human Ecology, Cornell University, Ithaca, NY 14853-4401.

INDEX